Contemporary Issues in Management Development in Africa

Adonis & Abbey Publishers Ltd/University of Ghana Business School
St James House
13 Kensington Square,
London, W8 5HD
United Kingdom

Website: http://www.adonis-abbey.com
E-mail Address: editor@adonis-abbey.com

Nigeria:
Suites C4 & C5 J-Plus Plaza
Asokoro, Abuja, Nigeria
Tel: +234 (0) 7058078841/08052035034

British Library Cataloguing-in-Publication Data
A catalogue record for this book is available from the British Library

ISBN: 978-1-909112-64-3

Contemporary Issues in Management Development in Africa

Edited by

Kofi A. Osei, Joshua Y. Abor, Robert E. Hinson, Richard Boateng, Joseph M. Onumah, Kwasi Dartey-Baah and Albert Ahenkan

Acknowledgements

This reader titled "Contemporary Issues in Management Development in Africa" is put together by the University of Ghana Business School in an attempt to bring out a publication which informs readers about the current management development issues in Africa. The editorial team acknowledges the interest of the Dean of the Business School who initiated this publication project. His interest and commitment have been sustained throughout the period of putting the book together. The publication became possible because of the hard work by the editorial team. The contribution of the editorial team in coordinating all the processes involved in the publication including the call for papers, screening, reviewing and final selection of quality papers is acknowledged. The team sincerely thanks the writers of the chapters as well as the reviewers of the various papers. Their contributions are acknowledged and appreciated. Finally the editorial team is thankful to the publisher - Adonis-Abbey for partnering with the University of Ghana Business School to publish this reader.

Introduction

This reader titled "**Contemporary Issues in Management Development in Africa**" is being published by the University of Ghana Business School (UGBS) in partnership with Adonis & Abbey Publishers. The reader spans the broad areas of management and development and seeks to address a wide variety of issues that are important for Africa's present and future economic and social development and their implications for management. The reader reflects recent and contemporary developments which help throw light on the nature, rationale and impact of management strategies developed in different African countries.

The reader is divided into three main parts namely:

Part 1 – Management Development in Africa – A Historical Review

Part 2 – Contemporary Issues in Management Development in Africa

Part 3 – Policy and Institutional Perspectives of Management Development in Africa.

Chapters among others cover comprehensive discussions on the following:

- Africa's democratic development since independence, the challenges of the public and private sectors and their potential effects on management decision-making;
- The evaluation of developments in Africa's markets, including financial and accounting reforms and their current trends and challenges;
- The major contemporary socio-economic challenges faced by Africa and their implications for future sustainable growth and investment;
- The effect of strategic planning on corporate performance and efficiency

PART I: MANAGEMENT DEVELOPMENT IN AFRICA – A HISTORICAL REVIEW

Before we look at contemporary management development issues in the different African countries, we first give consideration to the historical background since the underlying policies can be understood by first looking at the historical background. Two chapters have been covered under this sub-heading on historical review.

Chapter 1

In chapter one titled "Ghana: a success story and model for Africa?" Abdul-Gafaru Abdulai underscores the rapidly changing image of Africa. A continent which was once held as a 'hopeless continent' has been documented by studies to have made tremendous improvements in the socio-economic development trajectories in a wide range of African countries. The author indicates that one country whose developmental records have increasingly been highlighted within the continent is Ghana, with some experts even suggesting that other African countries should look up to Ghana as a development model. This paper undertakes a critical assessment of Ghana's developmental progress and concludes that, although the country has made impressive developmental gains in the socio-economic and political spheres, it equally faces very crucial developmental challenges ranging from rising socio-economic spatial inequalities, high levels of public sector corruption, and existence of an enduring threat to her democratic stability from potential election-related violence. The paper indicates that failure for the country to address these challenges could overturn Ghana's developmental gains, and transform its so-called success story into a rather hollow triumph.

Chapter 2

Chapter two is titled "Social exclusion, adverse incorporation and spatial poverty traps in Africa". In this chapter, Abdul-Gafaru Abdulai continues the historical analysis by arguing that Post-colonial regimes laid a basis for uneven patterns of development in the regions of Africa, through the simultaneous exclusion of some ethno-regional groups from public investments and the adverse incorporation of those regions into the colonial economy as labour reserves. His findings suggest that the most important question to ask when thinking of the development prospects of lagging ethno-regional groups is not simply whether they are included or excluded from decision-making structures, but more importantly the terms and conditions of their inclusion. In the context where elites from marginalized ethno-regional groups are incorporated into political structures on disadvantageous terms, their inclusion may only help legitimize the very institutions and structures that underpin their poverty.

PART II: CONTEMPORARY ISSUES IN MANAGEMENT DEVELOPMENT IN AFRICA

Part two made up of nine chapters covers current issues in management development in Africa. The chapters evaluate developments in Africa's economic markets including financial and accounting reforms and other current trends and challenges in health, banking, marketing, and small scale enterprises among others.

Chapter 3

In chapter three titled – "Corporate governance, shareholder activism and firm performance in Ghana", Alex Kwame Abasi, Elikplimi Komla Agbloyor, and Joshua Yindenaba Abor, examine the effect of shareholder activism, as a corporate governance mechanism and how it affects firm performance.

The study adopts contemporary value-based performance measures: Economic Value Added (E.V.A) and Market Value Added (M.V.A), to measure firm performance from 2007 to 2013. The results show that shareholder activism actually improves firm performance. The implication of the study is that shareholders should be active investors and monitors of their firms because active monitoring improves shareholder wealth. The results also suggest that an investor conference should be encouraged to improve manager-shareholder relations to mitigate the agency problem.

Chapter 4

Julius Aikins-Hawkson, Michael Graham and Alfred Yawson examine the relation between directors' use of current account, as a means of owner-director remuneration, and operating performance in small owner-managed firms. The study hypothesizes that owner-directors exhibit self-serving opportunism through the use of the directors' current account to reduce their tax burden, which invariably impacts negatively on reported operating performance. The findings have important implications for public policy regarding small firms. Small and medium sized enterprises are important sources of economic growth and are credited with an essential role in creation of employment opportunities in many economies. Thus they are put at the forefront of business policy making.

Chapter 5

In chapter five, Joseph Abor, Kofi Osei and Lord Mensah assess the impact of financial inclusion on financial development in Africa. In their paper titled "Does financial inclusion spur financial development in Africa?" they reveal that higher levels of financial inclusion lead to banking sector financial development.

Chapter 6

Chapter 6 is titled "Strategic banking competition efficiency nexus: A perspective from Africa", and in this chapter, Obi Berko Damoah, Emmanuel Carsamer and Kwasi Adjepong Darkwah, use a sample of 329 banks from 29 Africa countries over a period of eight years (2002 -2009) to test the extent to which competition impacts on the efficiency and soundness of African banks. The key finding of this study is that competition increases efficiency and soundness in banks. The chapter also identifies asset size and GDP growth as a channel through which competition affects a bank's soundness and efficiency. On policy front, the study recommends that the environment of banks in Ghana must not be left to the market forces only, but the regulator must also facilitate the dynamics of the industry with appropriate policies and regulations, in order to ensure a fair level of competition at any point in time. This will prevent some banks from becoming excessively large and thereby creating monopolistic power. On the practical front, it is recommended that the management of banks must not shy away from competition, whether large or small, but develop specific strategies to embrace competition to become efficient and sound

Chapter 7

In this chapter titled "Strategic Planning and Corporate Performance: An Exploratory and Comparative Study of Leading Ghanaian firms", Daniel F. Ofori, Obi Berko O. Damoah and Freda Addu use a sample of 35 firms drawn from the "Ghana Club 100" companies to establish a significant relationship between strategic planning formality and performance. Strategic planning intensity which was also found to significantly depend on the strategic planning expertise and planning performance beliefs of senior management. Furthermore, with the exception of the use of strategic planning tools and techniques, no significant differences were established with regard to strategic planning practices among the local and internationally connected firms.

Chapter 8

Using a dataset from 2007 to 2012 representing the post International Financial Reporting Standards (IFRS) adoption period, Joseph Mensah Onumah, Mohammed Amidu, and Augustine Donkor in their study titled "the effect of internal audit quality on earnings management of listed firms in Ghana" assess the relationship between the internal audit function (IAF) and earnings management (EM). The authors use the discretionary measure of accrual to estimate EM practices in Ghana, and use the IAF measure based on a composite measure generated on ISA 610. Their results show an existence of EM practices in Ghana and a significant negative relationship between IAF quality and EM. IAF quality in Ghana was also found to be moderately high, which could be used to check EM practices among managers. The authors indicate that by extension the results have important policy implications for regulators, particularly in assessing the effectiveness of corporate governance on earnings quality.

Chapter 9

In their study on energy conservation behavior of a sample of 300 respondents from East-Legon and La-Bawulashie in Greater Accra Municipality in Ghana, Ernest Yaw Tweneboah-Koduah and Weetsa Marian Adinku use a 5-point Likert rating scale to measure pre-contemplation, contemplation, preparation, action, maintenance, and termination constructs. To ensure that each population element was represented, the authors employed the stratified sampling technique. The study shows that, only 36% of respondents have reached the termination stage when it comes to their energy conservation behaviour. The study also found that respondents with no monthly income or monthly income less than Ghc100 are more likely to be careless when it comes to actions leading to energy conservation in Ghana. The findings of the study constitute a series of marketing ideas, useful in decision making with social marketing organisations.

Chapter 10

In this chapter titled "Philanthropic and corporate models of hospital governance in Ghana: A comparative study", Patience Aseweh Abor examines the healthcare governance of private hospitals in Ghana. Specifically, she compares the governance structures of not-for-profit (mission-based) hospitals with the private-for-profit hospitals. She hypothesizes that the ownership type of the hospital has implications for the form of governance system adopted by the hospital. The study results indicate that mission-based hospitals have a significantly higher proportion of non-executive directors represented on the board than private hospitals. Private hospitals were seen to have a higher percentage of medical staff on the board than not-for-profit or mission hospitals. However, in terms of board participation of medical staff, the results indicate that both forms of hospital have medical staff represented on their boards. With respect to board leadership structure, the results indicate that less than half of all mission hospitals have the CEO also doubling as the board chair. Also, the results indicate that while the boards of private-for-profit hospitals meet more frequently, the boards of not-for-profit hospitals fall short of the required number of meetings. The author recognizes that the findings of this study have implications for the efficient governance of hospitals in Ghana.

Chapter 11

In chapter 11, Aaron Asibi Abuosi interviews 818 patients and 152 healthcare providers from 17 general hospitals in Ghana to analyse how to improve the quality of healthcare in the Ghanaian hospitals. Reponses from the point of view of patients is that cost of healthcare services is high and needs to be lowered. Patients also felt they needed to be part of the decisions regarding their treatment. Healthcare providers' concern was that there should be prompt reimbursement by NHIS for services provided to their clients. Both patients and healthcare providers expressed concern about inadequacy of resources, and poor interpersonal aspects of care. By interpersonal aspect of care is meant the need for respect, tolerance and decent speech towards patients by hospital staff. The study concludes that efforts must be made to improve financial access to healthcare for the vulnerables. Additionally, innovative strategies must be developed to train more clinical staff, involve patients in their care, and improve upon interpersonal relationships.

PART III: POLICY AND INSTITUTIONAL PERSPECTIVES ON MANAGEMENT DEVELOPMENT IN AFRICA

The chapters under part 3 look at policies and dimensions of the institutional environment surrounding both public and private businesses, including the role of stakeholders and the need for new collaborations in African markets.

Chapter 12

Under chapter 12 titled – "Issues in the Management of Urban Areas in Africa: Towards a Stewardship, Collaborative and Sustainable Framework", Innocent Chirisa, Liaison Mukarwi & Aaron Maphosa, discuss major contemporary issues pertaining to the management of urban areas in Africa. The discussions cover availability, control, utilisation and access of land for urban development, housing markets, infrastructure financing, and transport management viewed from the supply-side of the urban economies. On the other hand, there are forces putting the urban space into a crucible. These include environmental challenges like increasing pollution and the effects of climate change which induce challenges like flooding as well as human-induced challenges like patronage and clientilism, global financial crises, diminishing development aid and increased vandalism of urban assets coupled with increasing mass protestations. These forces increase the complexity of urban management and hence exert a lot of pressure on the urban manager. The question becomes, how the populace and officialdom should be trained so that they can withstand the pressure while steering the urban local government on a path of sustainability. The authors recommend a collaborative and stewardship model for sustainable urban management in African cities.

Chapter 13

In chapter 13, Kwasi Dartey-Baah discusses how leadership affects the efficiency and effectiveness of the decentralization system in Ghana. The paper identifies the leadership challenges confronting the efficiency and effectiveness of the decentralization system in Ghana as: leadership mistrust, poor leadership capacities at the local levels, leadership's over-reliance on economic indicators of development, and finally public mistrust of leadership at the regional and local levels. In view of these, the author recommends a total commitment on the part of the leadership at both the national and local levels in order to ensure that the Ghanaian decentralization system meets the needs of Ghanaians in an efficient and effective manner.

Chapter 14

In chapter 14, Charles Andoh and Daniel Quaye assess the profitability of a private entity going into partnership with a public entity for the construction and management of highways. Using data from the Ghana Highway Authority, the authors demonstrate that public-private partnership financing can work for a number of highways through the right mix of two variables, the concession period and the road toll rate. The findings from the study can assist investors interested in partnering with government in highway financing on the type of highway to choose and its accompanying cost. Furthermore, this study provides the government with better insight when partnering with the private sector in highway financing. The authors believe the study should provide governments both in Ghana and elsewhere in Africa with better insight when partnering with the private sector in highway financing.

Chapter 15

In chapter 15 titled "tax planning practices of small and medium enterprises in Ghana", Cyprian Amankwah, Mohammed Amidu, and S.N.Y Simpson, examine the nature and tax planning practices of small and medium enterprises (SMEs) in Ghana. Using a panel dataset of 122 SMEs, and employing effective tax rate (ETR) as a measure of tax planning, the study results reveal that SMEs in the sample have low ETRs. The paper also shows that manufacturing sectors have, on average, higher ETRs than those in the services sector. This shows that SMEs in the manufacturing sector for the period studied were not very effective in managing their tax burdens, compared to SMEs in the services sector. The study by implication is that SMEs in the manufacturing sector have lower tax savings, while SMEs in the services sector have higher tax savings. The study facilitated a deeper understanding of tax planning of SMEs in Ghana.

Chapter 16

Chapter 16 looks at the audit expectation gap in the public sector of Ghana. The authors, Ibrahim Bedi, Joseph M. Onumah, and Emelia B. Derkyi look at the global economic challenges and how the collapse of giant multinational companies have led to deepening audit expectation gaps (AEG). The study examines AEG in the context of the public sector audit of Ghana, using the framework of Chowdhury (1996). The study's objectives were to establish the existence of AEG, identify its components, examine the perceptions of AEG and identify ways of reducing AEG in the public sector. Using respondents grouped into four (4), namely the general public, Ministries, Departments and Agencies (MDAs), the Public Accounts Committee (PAC) and the Audit Service (AS), the study confirms audit independence, competence, audit scope, audit ethics, audit reporting and audit performance as the six (6) components of AEG. Additionally, the study confirms the existence of AEG in the public sector just like in the private sector. The study realises that AEG in the public sector is more pronounced than in the private sector. The study ranked the audit scope as the lead component of AEG in Ghana's public sector audit. Education through mass communication remains the preferred approach to reduce AEG.

Continuous public education through the mass media and ensuring accurate media reportage of public sector audits is critical for reducing AEG. This requires funding and a holistic approach.

Notes on Contributors

JOSHUA YINDENABA ABOR is a Professor of Finance and the Dean of the University of Ghana Business School

ABDUL-GAFARU ABDULAI is a Senior Lecturer in the Department of Public Administration and Health Services Management of the University of Ghana Business School

ALEX KWAME ABASI - was an MPhil student in the Department of Finance of the University of Ghana Business School at the time of writing

ELIKPLIMI KOMLA AGBLOYOR is a Lecturer in the Department of Finance of the University of Ghana Business School

JULIUS AIKINS-HAWKSON – is a Senior Consultant at the Ghana Institute of Management and Public Administration (GIMPA), Accra, Ghana.

MICHAEL GRAHAM – is a Professor, Business School, University of Stellenbosch, Cape Town. South Africa.

ALFRED YAWSON – is a Professor of Finance at the University of Adelaide Business School, Adelaide, SA, Australia

JOSEPH ABOR - was an MPhil student in the Department of Finance of the University of Ghana Business School at the time of writing

KOFI A. OSEI is an Associate Professor of Finance at the University of Ghana Business School

LORD MENSAH is a Lecturer in the Department of Finance of the University of Ghana Business School

OBI BERKO O. DAMOAH is a Lecturer in the Department of Organisation & Human Resource Management of the University of Ghana Business School

EMMANUEL CARSAMER is a Lecturer in the Department of Economics at the University of Education, Winneba, Ghana

KWASI ADJEPONG DARKWAH – was MPhil student of the Department of Statistics, University of Ghana at the time of writing

DANIEL F. OFORI is an Associate Professor in the Department of Organisation and Human Resource Management of the University of Ghana Business School

FREDA ADDU - was an MPhil student in the Department of Organisation and Human Resource Management of the University of Ghana Business School at the time of writing

JOSEPH MENSAH ONUMAH is a Senior Lecturer in the Department of Accounting of the University of Ghana Business School

MOHAMMED AMIDU is a Senior Lecturer and the Head of Department of Accounting of the University of Ghana Business School

AUGUSTINE DONKOR is an Assistant Lecturer in the Department of Accounting of the University of Ghana Business School

ERNEST YAW TWENEBOAH-KODUAH is a Senior Lecturer in the Department of Marketing and Entrepreneurship of the University of Ghana Business School

WEETSA MARIAN ADINKU - was an MPhil student in the Department of Marketing and Entrepreneurship of the University of Ghana Business School at the time of writing

PATIENCE ASEWEH ABOR is a Senior Lecturer in the Department of Public Administration and Health Services Management of the University of Ghana Business School

AARON ASIBI ABUOSI is a Senior Lecturer in the Department of Public Administration and Health Services Management of the University of Ghana Business School

INNOCENT CHIRISA is an Associate Professor in the Department of Rural and Urban Planning, University of Zimbabwe, Harare

LIAISON MUKARWI is a Graduate Planner and Researcher of the Department of Rural and Urban Planning, University of Zimbabwe, Harare

AARON MAPHOSA is a Graduate Planner and Researcher of the Department of Rural and Urban Planning, University of Zimbabwe, Harare

KWASI DARTEY-BAAH is a Senior Lecturer and the Head of the Department of Organisation and Human Resource Management of the University of Ghana Business School

CHARLES ANDOH is a Senior Lecturer in Risk Management and Insurance in the Department of Finance of the University of Ghana Business School

DANIEL QUAYE is a Senior Lecturer in the Department of Marketing and Entrepreneurship of the University of Ghana Business School

CYPRIAN AMANKWAH - was an MPhil student in the Department of Accounting of the University of Ghana Business School at the time of writing

S. N. Y. SIMPSON - is a Senior Lecturer in the Department of Accounting of the University of Ghana Business School

IBRAHIM BEDI - is a Lecturer in the Department of Accounting of the University of Ghana Business School

EMELIA DERKYI – is the Chief Accountant at the Ministry of Justice and Attorney General's Department

Table of Contents

PART 1
MANAGEMENT DEVELOPMENT IN AFRICA – A HISTORICAL REVIEW

CHAPTER ONE

Ghana: A Success Story and a Model for Africa?

Abdul-Gafaru Abdulai

1. Introduction

In recent years, Africa's image within the international community has been witnessing significant shifts. Within just one decade, *The Economist* characterized the region as progressing from being a 'hopeless continent' to becoming a 'rising star'.[1] Within the context of this broader paradigm shift, Ghana is often held up in a significantly different light: for Western media institutions and international donor organizations such as the World Bank, Ghana is not just seen as a success story, but indeed as a model for Africa. A recent World Bank study described Ghana as 'a model of stability, democracy, and prosperity to 11 low-and–middle-income countries in Africa' (Molini & Paci, 2015:1). Similarly, Ghana is the first country in Steven Radelete's list of 'emerging' African countries, where he draws attention to the country's sustained growth and poverty reduction, improvements in primary-school enrolment and life expectancy, as well as significant achievements in the political arena such as the growing competitiveness of elections, the existence of a vocal press, better protection of basic rights, and stronger governance, among others (Radelete, 2010).

While some elections in Africa have been followed by violent conflicts and other political struggles, Ghana has held

---

[1] For details, see The Economist (2000), The Hopeless Continent, May 13th, 2000; The Economist (2011), The hopeful continent: Africa rising, December 3rd 2011.

six relatively peaceful and successful national elections between 1992 and 2012, including two that resulted in an alternation of power between the country's two dominant political parties, the National Democratic Congress (NDC) and the New Patriotic Party (NPP). Indeed, for the World Bank (2009), given that the NPP lost the December 2008 presidential elections by a razor-thin margin of less than 0.5 percent of the votes and still handed over power peacefully to the then opposition NDC, 'Ghana . . . became an example to the rest of Africa, and the world, on successful democratic practice'. Beyond successful multiparty elections, Ghana's rankings on political rights, civil liberties and press freedom are among the best in Africa, with the 2008 Freedom House indicators of press freedom placing Ghana at the same level as Greece and Israel, and second out of 48 African countries (Abdulai & Crawford, 2010). Indeed, it was precisely due to these democratic credentials that U.S. President Barack Obama chose Ghana – rather than Kenya (his father's homeland), or Nigeria (Africa's economic giant) – for his first visit to Sub-Saharan Africa where he presented his foreign policy vision on Africa. As Obama remarked:

> We think that Ghana can be an extraordinary model for success throughout the continent. Part of the reason that we're travelling to Ghana is because you've got a functioning democracy, a president who's serious about reducing corruption and you've seen significant economic growth.[2]

But to what extent are these accolades accurate? Can, and should, Ghana be held up as a model for Africa? This paper

---

[2] See AFP News of 11 July 2009, 'Politics: Barack and Michelle Obama in Ghana'. Available at: http://ghanarising.blogspot.com/2009/07/africa-why-obama-chose-ghana-question.html. [Accessed 13/02/16].

undertakes a critical review of Ghana's development progress and challenges along four sets of indicators: multiparty elections, building democratic institutions, economic growth and poverty reduction, and control of corruption. The overall evidence suggests that, although Ghana has made impressive gains in the economic and political spheres, there is need for caution in holding it up as a model for Africa. Ghana faces crucial challenges in its development processes, ranging from growing inequality and polarization in household consumption, large and growing spatial disparities in welfare, excessive executive and presidential powers vis-à-vis oversight institutions, high levels of public sector corruption and patronage forms of politics, and more importantly, an enduring threat to the country's democratic stability from potential election-related violence. Failure to address these shortcomings could yet overturn Ghana's developmental gains and transform its so-called success story into a rather hollow triumph.

2. An Assessment of Ghana's Development Landscape: Progress and Challenges?

This section examines Ghana's development progress along four key indicators: free, fair and transparent multiparty elections, building democratic institutions, economic growth and the reduction of poverty and inequality, and the fight against corruption. It highlights the progress made along these dimensions, how progress has been achieved, and then discusses the remaining key challenges that ought to be addressed to help consolidate the country's developmental gains.

2.1 *Successful Multiparty Elections and Its Implications*

Between the mid-1960s and the late-1980s, Ghana vacillated between civilian and military rule. But since 1992, the country has enjoyed a significant amount of political stability as demonstrated by six successful multiparty elections, the last one of which was held in 2012. Several factors account for Ghana's relative political stability, including the development of a democratic culture, transparent electoral processes, and the gradual nurturing of functional democratic institutions, both state and non-state. However, election-related violence continues to pose a potential threat to future political stability, if underlying issues are not addressed.

The embedding of a democratic political culture in Ghana has occurred at the interrelated levels of the political elite and the mass population of society. At the elite level, two significant developments suggest an increased commitment among key political actors to preserving the country's democratic regime. The first was the decision by former Presidents Jerry Rawlings (1993-2000) and John Kufuor (2001-2008) to comply with the two-term limit of presidential tenure imposed by the 1992 constitution. Second, Ghanaian political actors have commonly turned to the appropriate democratic institutions to address their political grievances, leading to the resolution of potentially destabilizing electoral disputes. This was witnessed in the hotly contested December 2008 and 2012 elections, in which aggrieved parties, including defeated presidential parliamentary candidates, resorted to court petitions rather than violence in addressing alleged electoral fraud.

This apparent elite commitment is reinforced, or perhaps informed, by the preference for democratic government as expressed by the mass of Ghanaians. Data from all rounds of

Afrobarometer surveys since 1999 suggest that Ghanaians have increasingly come to the conclusion that democracy is 'always preferable' to other forms of government. In the 2008 Afrobarometer survey, for example, nearly 80 percent of adult Ghanaians indicated that they preferred democracy to military rule, one-party government, or dictatorship, while 86 percent said that they considered elections and the rule of law as the best vehicle for selecting leaders and maintaining law and order (Afrobarometer, 2009)

The strong support for multiparty democracy among Ghanaians is further exemplified by the large voter turnout during national elections, especially since the 1996 elections. Although voter turnout in the 2008 presidential run-off dropped from the historic 85 percent recorded in 2004 to 72.9 percent, it was still considerably higher than the rate of 61.7 percent in the U.S. presidential elections in November 2008. Turnout for the 2012 elections was also high at 80.15 percent.[3] This underscores the significance that ordinary Ghanaians attach to the organization of political life along democratic lines, suggesting a significant entrenchment of democratic culture at the mass level.

Ghana's transparent electoral procedures have also contributed significantly to the country's political stability, and are worth explaining in some detail. Following the much-disputed election in 1992, significant innovations were introduced, including transparent ballot boxes, voter identification cards with picture to prevent multiple voting, as well as an Inter-Party Advisory Committee as a forum for building consensus on contested electoral issues, not only among political parties but also between parties and the

[3] For details on voter turnout in Ghana since 1992, see http://www.idea.int/vt/countryview.cfm?id=81

Electoral Commission. On the day of voting, all contending political parties have polling agents who are required to observe the entire process at each polling station. After votes are counted and collated at each polling station, the party representatives are required to append their signature, confirming their agreement to the accuracy of the results. The official results from each polling station then go to the constituency headquarters, where they are logged onto a sheet before being faxed to the Electoral Commission's (EC) headquarters. Again, all contesting political parties have representatives at the EC who observe the final collation of the results for each constituency, and who are required to certify the figures as they are tallied by EC staff. This highly participatory and transparent process helps to instill trust in the credibility of election results, and thus minimizes the chances of acrimonious electoral disputes and post-election violence.

However, Ghana's electoral process is not perfect, and the highly competitive 2008 and 2012 elections exposed its weaknesses, as well as its strengths. Since the return to multiparty democracy in 1992, no election has ever drawn Ghana so close to widespread political violence as the 2008 and 2012 elections, indicating a threat to future democratic stability. This threat stems largely from the persistent manipulation of electoral processes by party elites in their regional strongholds – the Ashanti region for the NPP and the Volta region for the NDC. In the 2008 elections, electoral malpractices in these two regions and the concomitant effects of disputed results led to heightened tension in Ghana, culminating in the closure of many banks and shops on Dec. 30, 2008, in anticipation of widespread violence.

Extensive violence was avoided due to a combination of factors. Some were structural, such as the relative independence and resilience of the EC and the intervention of civil society. But some were more fortunate conjunctural factors, such as former President John Kufuor's release of a timely press statement on Jan. 1, 2009, calling on all parties to accept the forthcoming results when declared by the EC. However, although Ghana defied the odds and avoided political violence, the roots of the heightened tension remain unaddressed, and thus remain significant threats to national political stability as witnessed in the electoral disputes that accompanied the 2012 elections. The most notable of these unaddressed challenges relate to the existence of a significantly bloated voters' register that opportunistic political elites have persistently exploited to amass votes in their strongholds. This indicates that the latent threat of election-related violence in future elections could yet undermine Ghana's democratic gains. Prospects for the eruption of election-related violence were somewhat heightened by the contestations that characterized the 2012 presidential elections, as well as the ongoing inter-party divisions regarding the question of whether the current voter register is valid enough to form the basis for the forthcoming 2016 elections.

2.2 *Building Effective Democratic Institutions*

Democratic governance thrives on the basis of institutions established to check against possible abuse of power and protect individual rights and liberties. Ghana has made considerable progress in building democratic institutions, both state and non-state. But shortcomings persist, and excessive executive power and weaknesses in institutions of accountability are widely regarded as major democratic deficits.

In light of the gross human rights violations that characterized past military regimes in Ghana, the 1992 Constitution established several horizontal institutions of accountability aimed at broadening democracy and safeguarding human rights. These bodies include the Commission on Human Rights and Administrative Justice (CHRAJ), established to fight corruption and protect citizens' rights; the National Media Commission set up to promote freedom and independence of the media; the National Commission for Civic Education established to educate citizens about their civic rights and responsibilities; an independent Electoral Commission instituted to organize free and fair elections; and an independent judiciary.

Over the years, these institutions have contributed significantly to Ghana's democratic credentials by asserting their independence in various ways. In the 2008 elections, for example, the judiciary demonstrated its independence by turning down an *ex parte* motion filed by the ruling NPP, which sought to prevent the EC from declaring the election results until certain allegations of electoral fraud were investigated. The degree of independence demonstrated by the EC was equally admirable during the elections. Following the presidential run-off, both the NDC and NPP cried foul about alleged electoral malpractices and threatened to reject the results from certain constituencies in their opponents' regional strongholds. But after examining the evidence presented by both parties in support of their claims, the EC concluded that there was either inadequate documentation, or that the issues raised bordered more on criminality (e.g. intimidation by NDC activists of NPP party agents) rather than electoral malfeasance. Accordingly, the Commission found no evidence to invalidate the run-off results (see European Union Election

Observation Mission, 2009), and therefore declared the opposition NDC's candidate, John Atta Mills, the winner of the presidential elections. Similarly, since its establishment, the CHRAJ has investigated allegations of corruption involving high-level public officials, including the president and cabinet ministers, and it has even imposed sanctions on the latter.

Nonetheless, despite significant constitutional guarantees of rights, excessive executive hegemony weakens the effectiveness of formal oversight institutions, with adverse implications for human rights protection. For example, although the CHRAJ can investigate all allegations of human rights violations, only the politically appointed Minister of Justice and Attorney General has the powers to decide whether to prosecute cases recommended by the CHRAJ. Moreover, regarding the judiciary, the 1992 constitution fails to place a ceiling on the number of justices the president can appoint to the Supreme Court. The president's ability to appoint new justices to sit on specific cases that are of interest to the presidency makes the judiciary prone to executive manipulation (Abdulai, 2009).

This compromising of the independence of important rights-protecting bodies, such as the CHRAJ and the judiciary, has adverse implications for strengthening democratic institutions and consolidating democracy in Ghana. Not surprisingly, calls for constitutional amendments aimed at minimizing the powers of the president have been a recurrent theme among Ghanaian political commentators (see Ghana News Agency, 2008) and leading politicians in recent times.

Turning to non-state institutions, Ghana also boasts of a vibrant civil society and a free and independent media- thanks to the guaranteeing of associational rights and the relaxation of media censorship by the 1992 constitution. The strength of civic organizations is significantly felt during national elections, particularly the December 2008 elections. Since the return to multiparty democracy, civil society organizations (CSOs) have contributed significantly to promoting issue-based campaigning during national elections by, among others, organizing live televised debates for presidential and vice-presidential candidates to discuss key national development issues. CSOs have also played a major role in strengthening the credibility of elections results, especially through their deployment of several thousand election observers across the country. Unsurprisingly, the European Union Election Observation Mission report on the 2008 elections acknowledged the existence of 'a vibrant, mobilized and well-organized civil society in Ghana' (European Union Election Observation Mission, 2009). Private radio and television stations also contribute significantly to the transparency of elections by providing live reports of events at various polling stations across the country on voting day, by undertaking independent analysis of election results, and by displaying provisional results on television (e.g. Metro TV) and via the internet (e.g. Joy FM). These initiatives help make it difficult for any political party to manipulate election results, as has been the case elsewhere in Africa.

However, election reporting by some media outlets is often far from ideal. Indeed, some politically partisan radio stations often behave in irresponsible and unprofessional ways, engaging in the spread of unsubstantiated allegations. Such negative or unprofessional reporting styles contributed to the heightened tension that almost plunged the country into chaos during the 2008 elections. This has led some to call on government to hasten the passage of a broadcasting law so as to regulate the activities of radio stations and help prevent potentially destabilizing media reporting in future elections.[4]

Moreover, although Ghana is often praised as Africa's model for democratic governance, it needs to be recognized that increased electoral competition in Ghana has undermined the country's socio-economic development prospects in some significant ways. In particular, as ruling political elites have become increasingly vulnerable due, mainly, to the existence of a strong opposition party, the policy actions of ruling political parties tend to be geared towards distributional initiatives, designed to deliver resources and economic opportunities to higher and lower levels of the ruling coalition, as well as to deliver visible goods and services to as much of the population as possible. This has been the direct result of the short-term four-year election cycle, whereby only initiatives with potentially quick political gains get prioritized, as with the distribution of visible project spending and patronage. Unsurprisingly, there is now ample evidence of the existence of political budget cycles in Ghana's Fourth Republic. Since the return to multiparty democracy in 1992, there has been the tendency for governments to engage in inefficient and unproductive spending in order to meet myopic expectations from potential swing voters (Boakye, Dessus, Foday, and Oppong, 2012). Consequently, election years have often been characterised by huge budget deficits as a result of the authorities subsidizing things like fuel and utility prices, as well as using the public sector wage bill as a default means of employment in the run-up to elections (Whitfield, Thorkildsen, Buur, and Kjær, 2015). At the end of 2008, the

[4] See 'Media severely criticised over bad reportage', Available online at: http://ghanaelections2008.blogspot.com/2009/03/media-severely-criticised-over-bad.html

public sector wage bill-to-GDP ratio reached 11.3%, accounting for over 40% of recurrent expenditures, and 46% of all tax revenues (Coffey International Development, 2011: 47-8). The NPP government massively overspent in the run up to the 2008 elections, partly as a result of fuel subsidies. Thus, the NPP repeated history, exiting office in 2009 with the economy in chaos, just as Rawlings' NDC government had done in 2001. The NDC government led by President Mills had to return to the arms of the World Bank and IMF and undertake an 'austerity' budget (see Whitfield 2011). Incentives to overspend in election years are often driven by the perceived cost of losing power in a winner-takes- all political system.

2.3 *Economic Growth, Poverty Reduction and Inequality*

Ghana has recorded a strong growth performance during the past two decades. After more than a decade of stable annual growth in gross domestic product (GDP) at between 4 and 5 percent, growth began to pick up in the early 2000s and reached a steady rate of nearly 8 percent after 2006. There was then an impressive peak in 2011 mainly because of the discovery of oil and the rebasing of GDP. Since 2008, Ghana has grown more quickly than other African economies and, since 2010, more quickly than the average among lower-middle-income countries (Molini & Paci, 2015).

Rapid growth translated into accelerated poverty reduction, with both absolute and extreme poverty rates dropping dramatically in the last 25 years. Since 1991, the estimated national poverty rate has fallen by more than half, from 52.7 percent that year to 21.4 percent in 2012. The extreme poverty rate declined even more rapidly, dropping from 37.6 percent in 1991 to 9.6 percent in 2012.

Figure 1.1: Trends in poverty and extreme poverty, 1991-2012

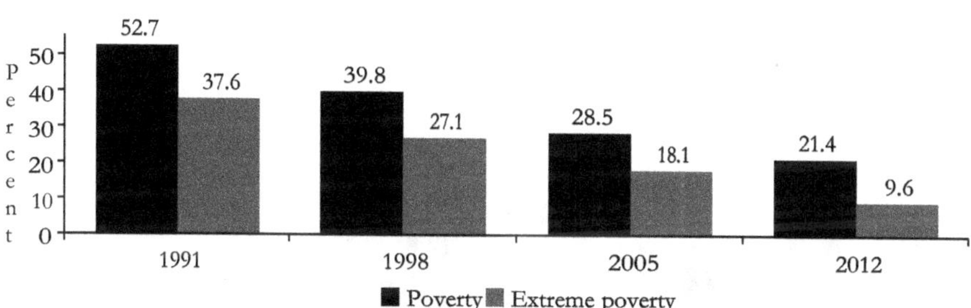

Source: Molini and Paci, 2015

Nonetheless, Ghana faces an equally intractable set of economic development challenges. A particularly important challenge of interest here relates to the problem of inequality. Although overall poverty levels in Ghana have declined, gross inequalities persist and continue to widen along three structural divisions. First, there is a persistently strong urban-rural dichotomy in poverty indicators, with deprivation being much higher in rural than in urban areas (Figure 1.2). This has been a long-standing problem throughout the post independent period. Second, poverty in Ghana continues to have important gender dimensions, with most indicators showing that women face higher levels of deprivation compared to men (Ghana Statistical Service, 2007). Third, the most marked of these inequalities is the persistent and widening gap between the three historically poorer northern regions and the rest of the country (Figure 1.2).

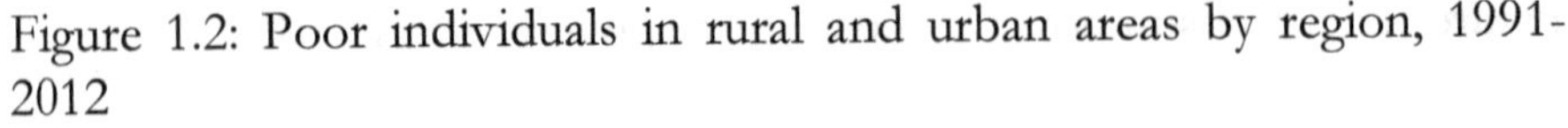

Figure 1.2: Poor individuals in rural and urban areas by region, 1991-2012

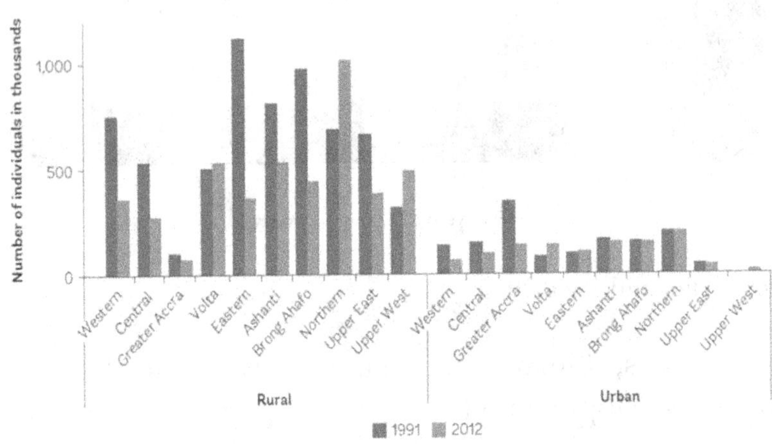

Source: Molini & Paci, 2015

Ghana is made up of 10 administrative regions, three of which (Northern, Upper East and Upper West regions) comprise northern Ghana, while the remaining seven are loosely categorized as constituting southern Ghana. Geographically, the severity and depth of poverty has remained highest in northern Ghana. The most recent Ghana Living Standards Survey (GLSS) undertaken in 2012 shows that current levels of extreme poverty in the three regions range between 21.3 percent of the population in the Upper East region to 45.1 percent in the Upper West region. By contrast, the national average is only 8.4 percent, with the lowest rate of 1.5 percent registered in Greater Accra, the nation's capital (Ghana Statistical Service 2014: 16).

In an analysis of data from the six rounds of the GLSS from 1991 to 2012, a recent World Bank commissioned study concludes that the north-south inequalities

> have grown over the last two decades to the extent that whereas both the poverty rate and absolute poverty numbers of the poor have declined in the more populous southern and central regions, the number of the poor has risen in the Northern Region and Upper West since 1991. As a result of these divergent trends, nearly 40 percent of the poor were living in the north in 2012, which had only 17 percent of the population' (Molini & Paci, 2015: 10).

These observations raise the critical question as to how far Ghana's recent growth and poverty reduction experience can be celebrated when its overall impact has been to make the relatively rich richer, and the poor poorer.

Figure 1.3: Rising inequality amidst poverty reduction in Ghana, 1992-2013

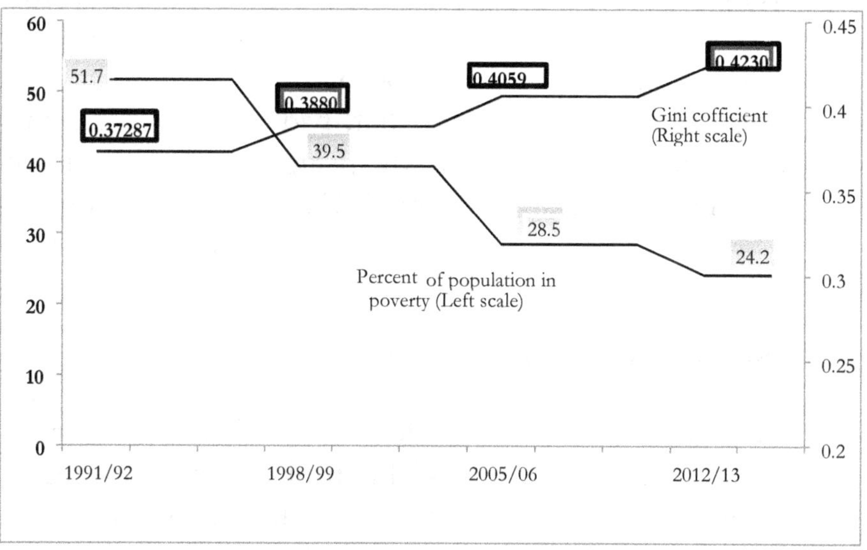

Source: Government of Ghana, 2014: 18

Another concern relates to the impact of the rising inequalities on Ghana's overall national development, particularly regarding the impact of growth on poverty reduction. While income poverty levels fell by 31.3 percentage points during the past 25 years, from 52.7 percent in 1991 to 21.4 percent in 2012, Ghana's Gini coefficient –a measure of income inequality –increased from 0.357 to 0.423 over the same period (Figure 3). In Ghana's recently adopted national social protection strategy, the Government of Ghana acknowledges these rising levels of inequality as a major problem, describing it as 'a dangerous sign that the poverty reduction effort is not being properly targeted at those who need it most' (Republic of Ghana, 2012: 22).

Results from the fifth Round of the Ghana Living Standards Survey (2005/06) revealed that if levels of inequality in Ghana remained unchanged during 1999-2006, the actual 10.4% decline in poverty during this period would have been 13.8% (Ghana Statistical Service, 2007: 34). In other words, the impact of growth on poverty reduction would have been much greater if it had not been offset by increasing inequalities. Other studies show that, had Ghana's economic growth not been accompanied by rising income inequality, Ghana would have achieved the MDG target of reducing poverty by half –vis-à-vis its 1990 level – as far back as 2006 (World Bank, 2007).

2.4 *Fighting corruption*

Since the return to multiparty democracy, Ghana has made significant attempts to address the problem of corruption. Most notable among these efforts are the establishment of anti-corruption institutions such as the CHRAJ and the Serious Fraud Office, as well as the promulgation of anti-corruption laws, including the Public Procurement Act in 2003 and the Whistleblowers Act in 2007. Indeed, the Global Integrity Initiative surveys have frequently rated Ghana among the few African countries that have a comprehensive legislative framework governing anti-corruption. However, there is strong public perception that corruption remains one of the greatest enemies to Ghana's socio-economic and political development prospects. Transparency International's Corruption Perception Index (CPI), which measures the perceived levels of public sector corruption across countries, has consistently scored Ghana's CPI below five (using a scale of 0 = highly corrupt to 10 = very clean) since the country's initial assessment in 1998. One reason is that although the institutional and legal frameworks for combating corruption have been strengthened, enforcement of anti-corruption laws in Ghana remains weak. Accordingly, the success of Ghana's anti-corruption reforms has been at best negligible, and government corruption remains a serious problem. Ghana has of course been consistently ranked on the CPI as relatively less corrupt than many other countries in sub-Saharan Africa. However, it needs to be emphasized that Ghana's relatively good ranking is not a result of the country being especially 'clean', but more due to its African peers being perceived as even more corrupt.

On coming to power in January 2001, the NPP government under former President John Kufuor declared a policy of 'zero tolerance for corruption', and the Kufuor administration's anti-corruption agenda appeared quite encouraging in its early years. The government repealed the criminal libel and seditious laws in July 2001, thus enabling allegations of corruption to be voiced, and subsequently prosecuted a sitting cabinet minister for causing financial loss to the state (Abdulai, 2009). Unfortunately, political will soon weakened, and by the beginning of Kufuor's second term in office in 2005, several surveys indicated that levels of corruption and bribery in Ghana were on the rise. For example, out of 900 respondents interviewed in a 2005 survey by the Ghana Integrity Initiative (GII), 90.1% (9 out of 10 respondents) considered corruption as a 'serious problem', while 61% perceived it to be 'worse' and 'much worse' (GII, 2005). Indeed, Ghanaian political commentators have subsequently not only accused the Kufuor administration of being especially corrupt, but have also identified the perception of growing levels of public sector corruption as a major factor in the NPP's electoral defeat in the December 2008 elections (Musah, 2009).

More recently, the last two rounds of the Afrobarometer surveys conducted in 2012 and 2014 found that large majorities of Ghanaians (ranging from 83% to 89%) perceive 'some', 'most', or 'all' police officers, national government officials, parliamentarians, judges and magistrates, tax officials of the Ghana Revenue Authority, chief executives of local government bodies, the President and officials in his office, local government representatives, and officials of the country's electoral management body to be involved in corruption (see Armah-Attoh, 2014; 2015). In the 2014 survey, three-fourths (75%) of Ghanaians felt that levels of corruption had actually increased over the past year, and 71% felt that the government had performed badly in fighting public sector corruption (Figure 1.4). These findings were made at a time when Ghanaians were crying foul over numerous corruption scandals involving public officials.

Figure 1.4: *Perceived changes in the level of corruption over the past year | 2014**

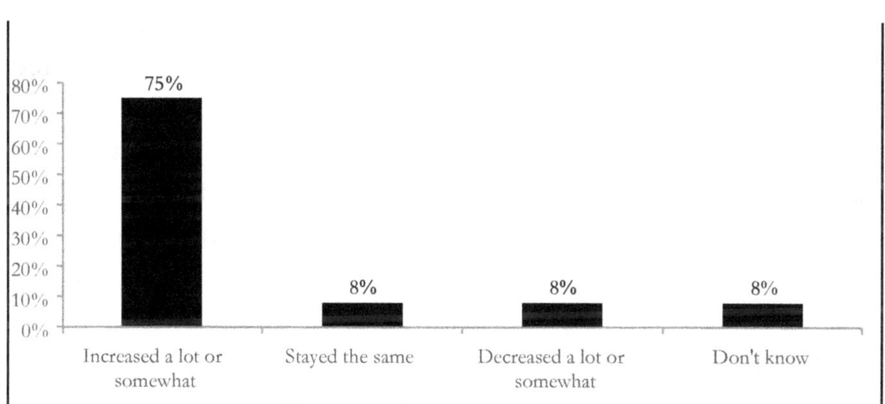

Source: Armah-Attoh (2014). *Respondents were asked: 'In your opinion, over the past year, has the level of corruption in this country increased, decreased, or stayed the same?'

One difficulty in controlling corruption in Ghana stems from its endemic nature, involving both petty and grand corruption among civil servants and sections of the political elite respectively. Under the NPP government, several corruption allegations involving high-level political figures were reported –including one involving Kufuor and his acquisition of a $3 million hotel registered in the name of his son, although subsequent investigations by the CHRAJ cleared him of any wrongdoing. Barely two years after the Atta-Mills-led NDC government came to power; at least three government ministers were forced to resign due to allegations of corruption of varying magnitudes. The Transparency International CPI at the time identified Ghana (alongside South Africa and Senegal) as one country where high-profile corruption scandals 'risk undermining political stability as well as the governments' capacity to provide effective basic services in sectors such as education, health and water' (Transparency

International, 2009). More recent major corruption scandals under the Mahama-led government have included those involving the Ghana Youth Employment and Entrepreneurial Development Agency (GYEEDA), the Savannah Accelerated Development Authority (SADA) project, Subah Info Solution, and the controversial Woyome judgement debate scandal. In addition, Parliament's Public Accounts Committee (PAC) sittings on the Auditor General audit reports continually reveal mismanagement and in some cases outright plundering of state resources by public officials (Armah-Attoh, 2014).

Corruption in Ghana is not just a problem among politicians. It is also widespread within the state bureaucracy, with Glover Quartey describing corruption among civil servants in particular as 'pervasive' (Quartey, 2009). The problem of corruption within the state bureaucracy has been attributed largely to issues of low salaries and poor conditions of service, with the government of Ghana itself recently acknowledging 'unacceptably poor conditions' in the public service (Government of Ghana, 2003). As one would expect, this significantly undermines the human capacity of the state bureaucracy, as the civil service finds it difficult to attract and retain professional staff. As a result, the state bureaucracy in Ghana is so weak that the government's ability to implement development programmes is severely curtailed (Killick, 2008). This weakness is partly evident in the poor delivery of key public services such as health, with the recorded infant mortality rate quite high at 71 per 1,000 births (National Development Planning Commission, 2008), and preventable diseases such as malaria still accounting for an extraordinary, and unacceptable 800,000 deaths per year among children under the age of 5 (Government of Ghana, 2007). Such figures are a stark reminder of the distance that Ghana still has to travel.

3. Conclusion

Ghana has made significant progress in institutionalizing multiparty democracy and enhancing the socio-economic well-being of *some* of its citizens in recent times. Beyond its historical record of five successful multiparty elections, Ghana boasts of a vibrant media and active civil society, while the promulgation of a liberal constitution and the existence of functional institutions of horizontal accountability now provide reasonable protection of civil and political rights. Considerable achievements have also been made within the economic sphere, with poverty levels reduced by half between 1992 and 2012.

So should Ghana now be held up as a model for Africa on the basis of these achievements?

Considering all the bad news in a continent where elections have often been marred by massive vote rigging, violence and spurious power-sharing agreements (as seen recently in Kenya and Zimbabwe), the praise of Ghana's democratic credentials is understandable. However, the intractable challenges faced by Ghana itself, including rising inequalities, high levels of corruption and excessive executive/presidential powers suggest the need for caution in depicting it as a model worthy of emulation by its African peers.

That Ghana has held five successful elections is unmistakably impressive by the standard of Sub-Saharan Africa. Yet, the 2007 bloody elections in Kenya, a country which had also up till then held successful elections, coupled with the fact that Ghana itself came very close to violence in its last two national elections in 2008 and 2012, underscore the fact that 'the number of successful and peaceful elections held in Ghana may not be a guarantee against the horrific ethnic conflicts that we have witnessed in certain parts of Africa' (Ayelazuno, 2009). This is particularly so in view of the fact that Ghana escaped widespread violence in the 2008 election not only purely due to structural factors, but also due to fortunate circumstantial occurrences. As a result, pro-democracy actors in Ghana cannot rest on their laurels with the satisfaction of considering the job finished.

Similarly, Ghana may have succeeded in spurring economic growth and reducing poverty in the last two decades, but this has been accompanied by a worsening in regional, geographical and gender inequalities. Failure to address these intractable challenges may retard Ghana's further developmental progress, and risk turning its so-called success into a rather hollow triumph.

References

Abdulai, A-G. (2009, Political will in combating corruption in developing and transition economies: A comparative study of Singapore, Hong Kong and Ghana. *Journal of Financial Crime*, 16 (4): 387-417.Abdulai, A-G., & Crawford, G. (2010), Democratic consolidation in Ghana: Prospects and challenges? *Democratization*, 17 (1): 26- 67

Afrobarometer (2009) Attitudes toward democracy in Ghana: A summary of Afrobarometer indicators, 1999-2008, available at: http: //afrobarometer.org/sites/default/files/publications/Summary%20of%20results/gha_r4_di.pdf [Accessed 13/02/16].

Armah-Attoh, D. (2014) Perceived corruption escalates, trust in institutions drops: A call for ordinary Ghanaians to get involved in the fight. Afrobarometer Dispatch No. 6. Accra: CDD-Ghana

Armah-Attoh, D. (2015), Corruption perceptions in Ghana: Different approaches reach similar conclusions. Available at: http://www.afrobarometer.org/blogs/blog-corruption-perceptions-ghana-different-approaches-reach-similar-conclusions [Accessed 13/02/16].

Ayelazuno, J. (2009), The 2008 Ghanaian elections: The narrow escape. Available at: http: //www.nai.uu.se/news/articles/ghanaian_elections_narrow/

Boakye, D., Dessus, S., Foday, Y., and Oppong, F. (2012) Investing the mineral wealth in development assets: Ghana, Liberia and Sierra Leone. Washington, D.C.: The World Bank

Coffey International Development (2011) Political economy of Ghana and thematic strategy development for STAR-Ghana. Inception Report for STAR-Ghana, Accra.

European Union Election Observation Mission (2009), Ghana Final Report: Presidential and Parliamentary Elections. Brussels: European Union

Ghana Integrity Initiative (2005), "Voice of the people" survey (Southern Ghana), Available at: http: //www.afrimap.org/english/images/documents/GhanaVoiceofthePeopleSurvey05.pdf.

Ghana News Agency (2008) CDD calls for conventions to curb executive discretion General News of Monday, July 28, 2008. Available at: http://www.ghanaweb.com/GhanaHomePage/NewsArchive/artikel.php?ID=147570

Ghana Statistical Service (2007), *Pattern and trends of poverty in Ghana 1991-2006*. Accra: Ghana Statistical Service

Ghana Statistical Service (2014), *Poverty Profile in Ghana: 2005-2013* Accra: Ghana Statistical Service

Government of Ghana (2003), *Ghana poverty reduction strategy (2003-2005): An agenda for growth and prosperity'.* Accra: National Development Planning Commission.

Gyimah-Boadi, E. (2009), Another step forward for Ghana. *Journal of Democracy* 20 (2): 138-152.

Jockers, H., Kohner, D., K., & Nugent, P. (2008) The successful Ghana election of 2008: A convenient myth? Ethnicity in Ghana's elections revisited. Munich Personal RePEc Archive (MPRA) Working Paper Series, Paper No. 16167.

Killick,T. (2008), What drives change in Ghana?', in E. Aryeetey and R. Kanbur (eds.), *The Economy of Ghana: Analytical Perspectives on Stability, Growth and Poverty.* London: James Currey, pp.20-35

Molini, V. & Paci, P. (2015). *Poverty reduction in Ghana: Progress and challenges.* World Bank, Washington, DC

Musah, J. (2009), Opinion: Why NPP lost election 2008', Available at: http://news.myjoyonline.com/features/200909/35529.asp.

National Development Planning Commission (2008), *The implementation of the growth and poverty reduction strategy (GPRS II), 2006 – 2009: 2007 Annual Progress Report*, Accra: National Development Planning Commission.

Quartey, Alex G. (2007) The Ghana civil service: Engine for development or impediment? *Ghana Speaks Lecture/Seminar.* Accra: Institute for Democratic Governance.

Radelete, S. (2010), *Emerging Africa: How 17 countries are leading the way.* Washington DC.: Center for Global Development.

Transparency International (2009), *Corruption perceptions Index 2009: Regional highlights: Sub-Saharan Africa*, p.2. Available at: http://www.transparency.org/policy_research/surveys_indices/cpi/2009/regional_highlights.

Whitfield, L. (2011), Competitive clientelism, easy financing and weak capitalists: The contemporary political settlement in Ghana, *DIIS Working Paper 27* Copenhagen: Danish Institute for International Studies.

Whitfield, L., Thorkildsen, O., Buur, L., Kjær, A. M. (2015) *The politics of African industrial policy: A comparative perspective* Cambridge: Cambridge University Press.

World Bank (2007), '*Ghana: Meeting the challenge of accelerated and shared growth*, Volume I: Synthesis Country Economic Memorandum, PREM 4, p.13, November 28, 2007. World Bank (2009), 'Ghana: Country Brief', available at: http://go.worldbank.org/QAKWTY7640

CHAPTER TWO

Social Exclusion, Adverse Incorporation and Spatial Poverty Traps in Africa

Abdul-Gafaru Abdulai

1. Introduction

Toward the end of the twentieth century, economic growth took off dramatically in many African countries, and there is now increasing talk of 'Africa rising'. In his influential book *Emerging Africa*, Steven Radelet categorizes a group of seventeen African countries as 'emerging' because their economic growth has been on a consistent upward trend since the mid-1990s (Radelet, 2010). Indeed, between 2000 and 2009, eleven African countries grew at an annual rate of 7 percent or more, which is considered sufficient to double their economies in ten years (UNECA, 2011, cited in Armah, 2013). Worryingly, however, available evidence shows that the impact of Africa's so-called impressive economic growth on *broad-based* poverty reduction has been disappointing. Two main reasons explain this. First, observers (e.g. Whitfield, Thorkildsen, Buur, and Kjær, 2015; Aryeetey, Owusu, and Mensah, 2009) have noted that Africa's impressive growth records have not been accompanied by the structural transformation of national economies. Within the region, only a few countries (e.g. South Africa and Mauritius) have created manufacturing industries that are internationally competitive and have diversified their exports away from dependence on a few primary commodities. The growth turnaround in the so-called emerging African economies has thus been driven largely by increases in international commodity prices, new discoveries of natural resources, and increased government spending fuelled by increases in foreign aid (Whitfield *et al.*, 2015). It is argued that this type of growth has not been accompanied by significant job creation, rising standards of living, and sustainable poverty reduction (Ibid).

Second, growth in Africa has generally not been inclusive in that significant segments of society have often been excluded, not only from the growth processes, but also from the distribution of the development largesse associated with economic growth. Consequently, even in countries where substantial progress has been made in terms of poverty reduction (e.g. Ghana, Uganda), this has often been accompanied by growing inequalities across regions in ways that undermine progress in broad-based development. This phenomenon has attracted considerable attention in the recent discussions on the sustainable development goals. Indeed across Africa, recent evidence points to the presence of wide spatial development disparities, with significant adverse implications for broad-based poverty reduction in the region. One study shows that Sub-Saharan Africa has the lowest growth-poverty elasticity in the world. Here, a 1 percent increase in growth reduces poverty by only 1.6 percent, compared with 3.2 percent in North Africa, and 4.2 percent in Eastern Europe and Western Asia. Thus, between 2000 and 2008, the proportion of people living on less than USD 1.25 a day declined slightly from 57 percent to 48 percent in Sub-Saharan Africa, in spite of the rapid economic growth in most countries in the sub-region during the period (Kanu, Salami, & Numaswa, 2013).

So what explains the persistent spatial poverty and inequality traps in Africa? Why have some regions within national space economies become and stayed poorer? Mainstream accounts of spatial poverty traps often put the blame on certain innate characteristics of poorer regions, while ignoring the implications of the ways in which such regions are incorporated into broader political formations. As Hickey and du Toit (2013: 134) put it 'poverty studies frequently fail to address the underlying processes that produce and reproduce poverty over time, preferring instead a descriptive focus on its correlates and characteristics'.

This paper combines the two-related concepts of adverse incorporation and social exclusion (AISE) to offer a political explanation regarding the deeper and more structural drivers of spatial poverty traps in Africa. While the concepts of social exclusion and adverse incorporation are both concerned with the role of inequalities in power in shaping the distribution of public resources, these concepts differ in their diagnoses of the roots of such inequalities. From the spatial perspective, the concept of exclusion sees relative deprivation as the product of some regions being 'left out' of broader socio-economic and political structures and processes. In contrast, adverse incorporation emphasises how such structures and processes can incorporate some ethno-regional groups in ways that are detrimental to their development (Wood, 2003; Hickey & du Toit, 2007; Moore, Grant, Hulme, & Shepherd, 208; Bird, Higgins, & Harris, 2010). These concepts represent two research traditions that have historically held conflicting claims (Jones, 2009), but recent research shows that the two can also operate in mutually reinforcing ways to underpin poverty and inequality (e.g. Hickey & du Toit, 2007; Mosse, 2010). The main interest in this paper is to show how and why political forms of exclusion and/or adverse incorporation shape socio-economic forms of exclusion in terms of the distribution of state resources, and how this in turn underpins spatial poverty traps.

The paper is organized as follows. Section 2 briefly reviews the literature on the meaning and causes of spatial poverty traps. Section 3 proposes a framework for understanding spatial poverty traps in Africa, based on the two related concepts of adverse incorporation and social exclusion (AISE). Section 4 demonstrates how an AISE framework can deepen our understanding of the structural drivers of spatial poverty traps, drawing evidence from selected countries in Sub-Saharan Africa. Section 5 concludes with the findings of the study.

2. Spatial Poverty Traps: Meaning and Causes

The Chronic Poverty Research Centre (2004) argues that spatial poverty traps 'emerge when the 'geographic capital' (the physical, natural, social, political and human capital of an area) is low and poverty is high, partly as a result of geographic disadvantage' As this definition suggests, most explanations of persistent spatial poverty traps emphasise location and agro-climatic conditions as the most crucial explanatory factor: 'location goes a long way to explaining why the people that live there are poor' (Ibid) Such residualist, power-blind forms of explanations feature prominently in accounts of why the Savannah regions in most Sub-Saharan African countries have disproportionate shares of extreme and chronic poverty (see Oduro, & Ayee, 2003). Writing on Ghana's historical north-south developmental divide, Ernest Harsch notes that:

> One hindrance is geography. The three northern regions are far from the ports, railways, markets, industrial centres and fertile farming areas that help stimulate greater economic and human development in southern Ghana (Harsch, 2008: 4).

These explanations often emphasise the poor agricultural potential associated with the 'bad geographies' of poorer regions as the reason for their poverty, with limited attention to the important observation that 'geography is not destiny' (Clark & Gray, 2012; Acemoglu & Robinson, 2012).[5] In order to explain the evolution and persistence of the spatial dimensions of poverty and inequality, economic geographers distinguish between first and second nature geography: while the former refers to some regions' favourable natural characteristics (for example soil type, proximity to rivers and so forth) in explaining their relative developmental fortunes, the latter relates to efficiency gains and agglomeration forces which usually amplify a region's initial advantage in terms of first nature geography (Krugman, 1991).

The wealth of empirical evidence points to the primacy of second nature geography in explaining uneven patterns of development. Based on a coordinated series of international case studies involving some 58 developing and transition economies, Kanbur and Venables (2005: 9) conclude that 'a key determinant of household well-being in a region, over and above household specific characteristics, is the quantity and quality of infrastructure in that region'. Unsurprisingly, in previously backward areas such as the Cerado and Northeast regions of Brazil and Thailand respectively, publicly targeted infrastructural investments have recently enabled both regions to conquer important world markets, defying previous claims that their 'challenging agroecological characteristics, remote locations, and high levels of poverty would prove impossible to overcome' (World Bank, 2009a: 23). These observations

[5] However, some scholars still explain the problem of regional inequalities in from the 'bad geography' perspective (for example, see Lall *et al.*, 2009).

imply that the relationship between physical geography and developmental outcomes is mediated by the distribution of public goods. To this extent, the neglect of politics, power relations and spatial inequality are problematic.

Indeed, growing evidence suggests that the often-power blind accounts of spatial poverty dynamics have rarely ever resulted in appropriate policy solutions to spatially unbalanced patterns of development in developing countries. Hickey (2013) has recently highlighted the largely depoliticised analysis of spatial inequality in Uganda's new National Development Plan, drawing attention to previous research that have already pointed to how such forms of analyses have led to inappropriate policy solutions for the country's poorer northern regions in the past. Similarly in a series of recent policy documents (see Republic of Kenya, 2011a; 2011b), the Government of Kenya notes how previous policies that sought to redress the country's spatial inequalities (in which the north is much poorer) were often misinformed by the 'bad geography' arguments and related approaches, with rarely any recognition that such inequalities are principally 'a political construct' (Republic of Kenya, 2011a: 13). Kenya's recent Vision 2030 policy document therefore emphasises the need to understand the challenges facing the poorer northern region as 'social and political in nature', ones that 'require more than technical solutions' (Republic of Kenya, 2011a: 18). While the benefits of the new political strategies proposed in this new policy document – which includes the redistribution of power and authority, as well as the establishment of a new Ministry of State for the Development of Northern Kenya – may be too early to assess on the ground, such observations do at least point to the failure of previous policy solutions that stemmed from the rather depoliticised interpretations of chronic poverty in the country's lagging regions.

In what follows, I argue that the two related concepts of adverse incorporation and social exclusion (AISE) hold a greater promise for understanding persistent spatial poverty traps in Africa.

3. Social Exclusion and Adverse Incorporation: A Framework for Understanding Persistent Spatial Poverty Traps

> Social exclusion and adverse incorporation are underlying causal processes that sustain inequity through the power relationships between people and key institutions, such as the state and the market (Jones, 2009: 12).

The term social exclusion was initially coined to describe various categories of people who were left out of state contributory benefits in Western Europe, but the term has since the 1990s been extended to encompass the multidimensional and relational aspects of deprivation and poverty (Moore *et al.*, 2008). From this multidimensional perspective, the concept of exclusion has come to denote situations in which a broad range of factors – from physical and mental disability to gender, unequal power relations, the nature of regional and spatial integration – prevent individuals from participating fully in social, political and economic life (du Toit, 2008; Koti, 2010). The notion of exclusion, from the spatial perspective, sees persistent inequality as essentially a product of some peoples' '…limited/inequitable opportunities and capabilities to participate in decision making, gain access to meaningful livelihood opportunities and social services due to discriminatory institutional practices in the political economic, social spheres...' (UNDP, 2007:12).

Although this is a multidimensional concept, encompassing social, economic, cultural and political dimensions, many analysts (e.g. Stewart, 2009; World Bank, 2005) have emphasised inequitable access to political decision-making structures as a particularly consequential dimension of exclusion. In a recent study on the politics of poverty and inequality, the United Nations Research Institute for Social Development (UNRISD) argues that poverty reduction is an inherently political enterprise, and draws attention to the central role of political inequalities in shaping the inequitable distribution of public resources and concludes that '…without political inclusivity there is little chance of implementing effective remedial policies for disadvantaged groups' (UNRISD, 2010: 82).

There are debates regarding the usefulness of the concept of exclusion in explaining relative deprivation in developing countries, especially Africa. Kabeer (2000) makes a strong case for the value addition of this concept, stressing that the idea of exclusion is particularly useful in poverty analysis where deprivation results from some people being 'set apart' or 'locked out' of participation in socio-economic and political development processes. In contrast, others emphasise the Western roots of this concept, and argue that the idea of exclusion is ill-suited for unravelling the factors that underpin poverty and inequality in developing countries. Gore (1994) notes that whereas the concept of exclusion was developed to describe 'pockets' of poverty faced by a small 'underclass' in industrialised countries, poverty in Sub-Saharan Africa is a mass phenomenon. This means that if being 'socially excluded' is synonymous with being left out in the formal economy, the notion of social exclusion will imply that nearly whole populations in Africa are 'excluded'.

Scholars have also criticised the overly-simplistic included/excluded dichotomy embedded in the concept of exclusion, arguing that persistent spatial poverty traps in much of sub-Saharan Africa stems not only from exclusion but also from people's incorporation into socio-economic and political life on disadvantageous terms. Associating the idea of social exclusion to the capability perspective of poverty, Sen (2000: 28-9) cautions against trying to explain all cases of capability deprivation in terms of exclusion. He notes that 'many problems of deprivation arise from unfavourable terms of inclusion and adverse participation, rather than what can be sensibly seen primarily as a case of exclusion as such'. Sen thus suggests the need to 'distinguish between the nature of a problem where some people are being *kept out* (or at least *left out*) and the characteristics of a different problem where some people are being included…in deeply unfavourable terms' (original emphasis). In fact, Gore (1994) argues that a conventional wisdom had emerged by the mid-1970s, 'that individuals and communities in Africa had been incorporated into the broader economy and society, and that what was problematical was their terms of incorporation' (not paginated).

Arising mainly from the above criticisms, one concept that has increasingly become prevalent in current development thinking has been the notion of 'adverse incorporation' (AI) – 'a situation in which people are included in social, political and economic spheres but on unfavourable terms' (Moore *et al.*, 2008:13). This concept challenges the widely held view that poverty is caused primarily by people being 'left out' in broader socio-economic, and political institutions and processes, while emphasising how unfavourable terms of incorporation into such institutions and processes can itself be the source of underdevelopment (CPRC, 2008a: 130).

Adverse incorporation sees development as a process by which some ethnic groups and regions may become and stay poorer precisely because of the way they are integrated economically, socially and politically into national, regional or global webs of interaction (Hickey & du Toit, 2007; Bird *et al*, 2010). There are some echoes here of the Marxist critique of capitalism, whereby persistent uneven development is seen as the outcome of the subordinate incorporation of peripheral regions into exploitative and imperialist economic networks. The notion of adverse incorporation, according to Bernstein (2007:1), thus has its 'roots in the definitive class relations and accumulation dynamics of capitalism more generally'.

Growing evidence has drawn attention to the possibility of people and indeed whole geographical regions being *both* socially excluded *and* adversely incorporated. Moore *et al.* (2008:13) have argued, for example, that migrant- labourers and their families in many parts of the world are not only often excluded from public services and the institutions of governance, but they are also, in most cases, simultaneously adversely incorporated into exploitative labour markets. This echoes Silver's (1994) argument that 'the excluded are simultaneously excluded and dominated' (quoted in Hickey & du Toit, 2007:5).

It is also important to recognise the complex ways in which processes of exclusion and adverse forms of inclusion can work in mutually-reinforcing ways in underpinning the spatial dimensions of poverty and inequality. One potential scenario is the way in which inequalities in political power among regional elites can shape the inequitable distribution of state resources. Notably in Sub-Saharan Africa where the highly personalised nature of political power has been well noted, the exclusion and /or adverse incorporation of a region into the polity can have important implications on the spatial distribution of patronage resources. Several analysts (e.g. Boone, 1994; Arriola, 2009) have argued that an important feature of politics in Africa has been the broad-based incorporation of ethno-regional spokespersons into their ruling coalitions, both as a means to discouraging potential rivals from coordinating other elites against them, and as a way of giving credibility to their promises to distribute patronage among political elites and the constituencies whom they represent.

Recent studies have established that the formal political representation of a region in government does not on its own translate into its capacity to influence resource allocation decisions (e.g. Abdulai & Hickey, 2016; Abdulai & Hulme, 2015). For example, it is unlikely that a deputy minister can have the same 'agenda-setting-power' as a minister with full cabinet status. This implies that even when ruling elites do not fully *exclude* particular ethno-regional groups from decision-making structures, they may still foster the *adverse incorporation* of elites from marginalised regions on relatively disempowering or unfavourable terms in ways that undermine their influence over resource allocation decisions and policy agenda more broadly in the interest of their constituents. In such contexts, it is possible for inequitable forms of political inclusion to undermine resource flows to marginalised regions, resulting in the exclusion of the poorest from the distribution of public resources. Underdeveloped regions, under such circumstances, may continue to lag behind through the interplay of processes of political adverse incorporation at the *elite level* and socio-economic forms of exclusion at the *mass level.*

This discussion suggests the need to think of adverse incorporation and social exclusion as potential complementary frameworks when seeking to investigate the social and political relations that make people poor and keep them in poverty (Green & Hulme, 2005). Such a combined approach is both necessary and feasible because both concepts share a preoccupation with politics, the historical nature of development problems as well as the multidimensional and relational nature of poverty. (Hickey & du Toit, 2013).

4. Social Exclusion, Adverse Incorporation and Spatial Poverty Traps in Africa.

This section utilises the analytical framework outlined above to explore the evolution and persistence of regional inequality in Sub-Saharan Africa (SSA).

Adopting an AISE approach to examining persistent spatial poverty traps demands that we look more closely at the relationships of power across multiple spheres – political, social and economic – and the ways in which such relationships shape both the reduction and reproduction of poverty. This section seeks to:

- show how the pursuit of the interests of colonial powers resulted in the simultaneous exclusion and adverse incorporation of some regions in Sub-Saharan Africa, and how this in turn contributed to laying a foundation for spatial poverty traps in the region; and
- explore the different ways in which regional elites have been incorporated into the polity and how these differential forms of political incorporation have contributed to shaping resource allocation outcomes and their underlying implications for regional inequality.

5. Colonialism and the Legacy of Spatial Poverty Traps in Africa

Although most contemporary African states were constructed under colonial rule, the foundation was in most cases laid by the consequences of European trade as well as political relations among kingdoms and tribes during the pre-colonial period (Osaghae, 2006). The advent of European trade, notably the slave trade, propelled 'tribal' wars that changed the face of pre-colonial state formations and ethnic relations in Africa, not least as it introduced new relations of 'superior-inferior' groups based on military strength and new forms of conquest and dominance (Ibid). Although colonial rule marked the end of slave raiding in many countries, the colonial state itself set the stage for uneven regional development in various ways. First, as part of a deliberate divide and rule strategy which sustained colonial rule, colonial powers systematically privileged certain ethnic groups over others (Chabal, 1992:131).

Second, given that the primary interest in colonization was to exploit the colonies rather than enhance their development, transport and communication infrastructure as well as the provision of basic social services (notably education) were 'very unevenly distributed in nearly all the colonies' (Boahene, 1987:101). Such resources were largely concentrated in areas where exploitable natural resources were available and in coastal areas where colonial powers typically built their administrative centres (van de Walle, 2009: 317).

Third, areas characterised by limited exploitable resources of interests to the colonial powers were not only generally excluded from public spending (Rothchild, 1969, 1984); the human capital of these regions were also typically exploited through their adverse incorporation into the wider economy as sources of cheap labour. For example, in Zambia, to the extent that the Bemba speaking groups were located in regions with relatively low agricultural potentials, they 'formed the bulk of the non-clerical, African labour force in the mines' (Dresang, 1974:1606). Historical accounts of the roots of the North-South inequalities in countries such as Nigeria and Uganda highlighted how the British colonial administration discouraged the production of cash crops in the North, mainly with the objective of recruiting cheap labour from these areas for export-oriented production in the South (see Mamdani, 1983). In sum, to the extent that the modernizing influences brought about by colonialism penetrated different ethno-regional groups in unequal degrees (Osaghae, 1994:142), this was both due to the simultaneous exclusion and adverse incorporation of some ethno-regional groups within the colonial economy.

It should be added that these two processes of exclusion and adverse incorporation tend to reinforce each other in underpinning high levels of deprivation among the marginalised ethno-regional groups. For example, the exclusion of such regions from productive investments, along with measures such as taxation played important roles in underpinning their adverse incorporation within the colonial economy as sources of cheap labour. Moreover, Lando and Bujra (2009: 5-6) highlight how colonial policies impoverished certain ethno-regional groups in Kenya through their adverse incorporation as labour reserves, emphasising that 'such policies were possible because ... institutions such as the Legislative Council (Legco) in which only white settlers were represented effectively "captured" public policy for the interest of this elite'. These observations point to the crucial role of political forms of exclusion in underpinning the socio-economic marginalisation of the populations concerned, via their disempowering terms of inclusion in other spheres of the wider political colonial economy.

6. But Why Has the Attainment of Political Independence in Sub-Saharan Africa Failed to Alter the Spatial Patterns of Poverty Created by Colonial Rule?

6.1. The Postcolonial Period: Addressing Uneven Development through Political Inclusion?

The differential patterns of incorporation discussed above played a pivotal role in shaping processes of postcolonial state formation in ways that set a tone for the continued dominance of the favoured regions during the immediate post-independent period. In particular, the selective development of educational systems impacted the regional patterns of human capital formations, laying a foundation for the socio-economic and political dominance of the regions favoured by colonial policies (Rothchild, 1985; Bening, 1990). Van de Walle (2009) has recently highlighted the ways in which dominant elites, who were often from the ethno-regional groups favoured by colonial policies, used political power to reinforce their initial socio-economic advantages after independence.

Uganda is one country whose experiences strongly illustrate these observations. Here, where Museveni's National Resistance Movement has been purportedly implementing an all-inclusive coalition government for over two decades now, Lindemann (2011b) has recently analysed the distribution of government positions among different ethno-regional groups for the period 1986-2008. With appointments broken down into three different categories: Cabinet, Deputy Ministers and the 'inner core' of political power, his findings show that the distribution of political, economic, and military power has historically been heavily biased in favour of ethnic groups from the south-western parts of the country, especially in the more consequential positions in the inner core (Ibid).[6] In contrast, elites from the historically underdeveloped Northern region were often assigned 'the most marginal positions'. This means that whereas they often 'received a proportional share of deputies', they were almost always 'greatly under-represented in Cabinet and almost entirely excluded from the inner core' (p.401).

These differential patterns of incorporation tended to constrain the influence of political elites from the North over government agenda, and thereby undermining the development prospects of the region. It is in light of some of these observations, along with the relatively unfavourable policies towards the North during both the colonial and post-colonial periods, that some analysts have emphasised the need to understand the persistently higher levels of poverty in Northern Uganda as a function of 'the region's "adverse incorporation" into the politics of state formation and capitalist development in Uganda over a prolonged period of time' (Golooba-Mutebi & Hickey, 2010: 1223).

These observations closely resonate with the experience of Côte d'Ivoire, a country also characterised by a serious socio-economic North-South divide. Although Côte d'Ivoire's relative political stability during her first two decades after independence has frequently been attributed to President Houphouët-Boigny's system of 'ethnic quotas' which ensured a 'fairly inclusive' government (Stewart, 2010a: 3; 2010b:149),

6 The 'inner core' was defined as comprising the President and key ministers responsible for Defence, Foreign Affairs, Internal Affairs, Finance, Planning and Economic Development, Commerce, Agriculture, Local Government, and Justice.

detailed analysis reveals a more nuanced picture. Langer (2005) has analysed data on the level of representation of various ethno-regional groups in government *vis-à-vis* their demographic sizes for the period 1980-2003. He did so paying particular attention to the Baoulé – the largest sub-group of the Akan and the ethnic group of both President Houphouët-Boigny and his successor, Konan Bédié. Although his findings point to what one could refer to as an all-inclusive government, as no major ethnic group was fully excluded, his data also pointed to a 'significant over-representation of the Akans'.

Moreover, in order to assess whether the inclusion of the various ethnic groups could be said to have translated into a more equal voice or decision-making powers, he presented data on the ethno-regional distribution of a set of key political positions – what he also termed 'the inner circle of political power'.[7] The results showed that the over-representation of the Akan and Baoulé was even 'more pronounced' in these key political positions. The conclusion then was that 'Houphouët-Boigny assigned the government positions of lesser importance to other ethnic groups' (Langer, 2005:9) – a clear form of political adverse incorporation. Moreover, Langer's analysis points to a close association between this skewed distribution of *real* political power and the ethno-regional patterns of well-being. Analysing data from the Demographic Health Surveys for the 1990s, he shows that both the Akan as a whole and the Baoulé in particular improved their relative socio-economic position considerably during 1994-1998, such

[7] These political positions included the President, Prime Minister, President of National Assembly, President of economic and social council, minister of security, minister of economy and finance, minister of defence, minister of mines and energy, minister of agriculture, minister of interior, minister of justice and minister of foreign affairs.

that the 'Akan's relative socio-economic prosperity was 40 per cent higher than Côte d'Ivoire's average' (Langer, 2005: 7).

The same story can be told of Kenya, where 'access to political power by the president's home determines the fortunes of that province and the resultant exclusion of other provinces' (Muhula, 2009:93; see also Stewart, 2010b). Analyses of the ethno-regional composition of governmental coalitions in postcolonial Kenya confirm that both the Kenyatta (1963-1978) and Moi (1978-2002) regimes disproportionately favoured their respective ethno-regional groups (i.e. Central and Rift Valley Provinces), especially with regards to the distribution of the upper echelons of government positions in the Cabinet, the Military, Diplomacy, and Public Service (see Nellis, 1974:14-15). Consequently, charges of tribal domination of President Kenyatta's ethnic groups (i.e. the Kikuyus) in the most 'juicy' government ministries were rife, with the Ministry of Commerce and Industry particularly seen essentially as 'a Kikuyu Ministry' (see Rothchild, 1969: 699-701). What is of particular interest has been the strong coincidence between the spatial distribution of government resources and patterns of access to political power in postcolonial Kenya. Under Kenyatta's rule in 1979, whereas the Central Province had only 766 people per hospital bed, 'politically excluded areas, like Nyanza, Western and North Eastern Provinces had an average of over 1000 peoples per bed' (Muhula, 2009: 95). Unsurprisingly, by the 1980s, child mortality levels among President Kenyatta's ethnic group (i.e. the Kikuyu) were on par with those of many industrialized countries (UNICEF, 1997, cited in Brockerhoff & Hewitt, 2000:34). Data for 1969 and 1970 point to similar patterns with regards to access to educational facilities and government expenditures on housing (see Rothchild, 1984:157; Alwy & Schech, 2004:271).

The Moi era brought similar advantages to the Rift Valley Province whose share of development expenditures for road construction remained disproportionately high during each year between 1979 and 1988 (Barkan & Chege, 1989), with similar advantages conferred on this Province in the area of Health (Ibid). It is not surprising, therefore, that by the end of the Moi administration in 2002, Rift Valley had about 6000 people per health facility, the least of any Province in Kenya (SID, 2007, cited in Muhula, 2009: 95). Variations in child survival followed a similar trend, whereby children of the ethnic group of President Moi, the Kalenjin, were 50 per cent less likely to die before age five years than others (Brockerhoff & Hewitt, 2000: 34). In sum, the historical data is clear that 'the distribution of public goods such as education facilities, health, water and physical infrastructure in Kenya has tended to follow patterns of access to political power' (World Bank, 2009b: 9).

Like Uganda and Cote d'Ivore, Ghana is also confronted with persistent and deepening regional inequalities in which the north (comprising the Northern, Upper East and Upper West regions) lags far behind in most development indicators. Indeed, data from the Ghana Living Standards Surveys shows that whereas the absolute number of the poor declined by some 2.5 million people in the South during 1991-2006, it increased by 0.9 million people in the North during the same period (World Bank, 2011: 5). Most scholars explain this problem in terms of certain innate characteristics of the north- the most notable of which is the region's fewer production potentials associated with its percieved 'bad geography' (Harsch, 2008; Lall, Sandefur, & Wang, 2009).

However, as Abdulai (2012) has recently argued, such explanations ignore the ways in which the north has been adversely incorporated into Ghana's political economy over a prolonged period of time. This included the subordination of the interest of the North to that of the South during the colonial period, both by excluding the former from public investments and through its adverse incorporation into the colonial economy as a pool of cheap labour. He argues instead that a key factor that explains the persistent north-south developmental disparities in contemporary Ghana has been the continuous exclusion of the historically poorer northern regions from a fair share of public spending; and that the socio-economic marginalisation of these regions has been underpinned principally by a weaker influence of northern elites on resource allocation decisions within a political environment that is driven by patron-client relations. The limited influence of northern politicians over resource allocation decisions is less of a function of their *exclusion* from decision-making structures, than a product of their *'adverse incorporation'* into the political system. This implies that taken at face value, the distribution of power within Ghana's successive ruling coalitions, since independence, has generally been characterised by regional inclusivity. However, Northern elites have largely been denied access to the inner core of power, undermining their influence over resource allocation decisions and broader policy agenda in the interests of their constituents. This problem reflects a longer-term trajectory over the post-colonial period, whenever the North was represented in the national government, it was always as a decidedly junior partner' (Ladouceur, 1979: 268).

One consequence has been that even social protection programmes designed with the formal objective of targeting the 'poor' often end up discriminating against the poorer Northern regions at the level of implementation. A typical example here has been the politics of Ghana's *HIPC Fund* which was established as part of the Poverty Reduction Strategy Papers. Despite a high level of government rhetoric of utilising HIPC debt relief to reduce regional inequalities through the provision of 'extra per capita expenditure for the three northern [poorer] Regions' (GoG, 2003: 44), a detailed analysis of the actual distribution of HIPC resources clearly points to the contrary. In the Ghana Poverty Reduction Strategy (GPRS I), the Ghanaian government planned to expend nearly half of HIPC resources in the poorer Northern regions, justifying this as a way of 'ameliorating the very high level of deprivation' in Northern Ghana (Ibid). Studies have shown, however, that it was the relatively prosperous Southern regions that actually enjoyed the highest per capita HIPC spending. During 2002-2005, average per capita HIPC expenditures in the North was only ¢7, 000 (US$ 0.8), compared to ¢30,000 (US$ 3.4) in the South. More strikingly, the per capita allocations for the poorest region, the Upper West in Northern Ghana (¢2,400 or US$ 0.3), was only 7% of that of Ashanti (¢33, 900 or US$ 3.8), one of the country's best developed regions (Abdulai, 2012).

The key explanatory factor here lies in the unequal power relations among regional elites, and the differential concentration of poverty and political power in the north and south of Ghana respectively. This means that whereas the incidence of poverty has been highest in the North, political power has mostly been concentrated in the South, and there has been a tendency of Southern elites to use their dominance over key state institutions in channelling public resources to their constituents (Abdulai, 2012; Akolgu & van Klinken,

2008). Having formulated the GPRS as a pre-condition for receiving HIPC debt relief, donors expected the distribution of HIPC resources to be guided by the equitable resource allocation criteria, as spelt out in the GPRS policy document. But as dominant Southern-based elites publicly side lined the GPRS formula and disbursed HIPC expenditures in ways that they believed would maintain their political power, the poorer Northern regions were marginalised in the actual distribution of HIPC resources. In contrast, Southern Ghana attracted far more than its planned share of HIPC funding, with the benefits heavily skewed towards the more politically dominant and economically advanced regions such as Ashanti and Greater Accra. Thus, whereas it was largely the poverty status of northern Ghana that made Ghana eligible for HIPC funding, that aid did not primarily benefit the poorer northern regions. Poorer citizens in the north therefore suffered from socio-economic exclusion in the distribution of HIPC resources because their political representatives were not part of the 'inner circle of political decision makers at the time.

7. Summary and conclusion

This chapter has made a case for the need to move beyond the often power-blind accounts of spatial poverty traps that tend to blame marginalized regions for their poverty. Instead, and utilizing the two related concepts of social exclusion and adverse incorporation, the analyses showed that politics and power relations have been central to the production and reproduction of spatial poverty traps in Africa. Post-colonial regimes laid a basis for uneven patterns of development in Sub-Saharan Africa, through the simultaneous exclusion of some regions from public investments and the adverse incorporation of those regions into the colonial economy as labour reserves. These processes contributed to uneven regional socio-economic development and a sense of comparative deprivation, along ethno-regional lines, that gave rise to conflicts over state power and resources after independence. Anxious to consolidate their hold onto power, postcolonial African regimes resorted to co-opting various ethno-regional political rivals into their ruling coalitions. Although this strategy played important roles in facilitating inter-elite co-operation and fostering regime stability, it did not play an equally important role in overcoming the colonial legacy of uneven development.

A key reason was the tendency of dominant elites to bolster their own legitimacy by assigning the most consequential decision-making powers to themselves, while fostering the inclusion of the historically marginalised regions on disempowering terms both by under-representing them *vis-à-vis* their demographic size, and by excluding them from the 'inner sanctums of political power' (Rothchild & Folley, 1988). Consequently, despite their inclusion, elites from the disadvantaged areas remained relatively powerless in influencing policy agenda in the interests of their constituents. This in turn undermined the equitable distribution of public resources, as those with access to real political power used their dominance over state institutions to consolidate their initial socio-economic advantages. The problem of unbalanced patterns of development in postcolonial Africa has therefore largely been a product 'of the intense political differences among the relatively advantaged and relatively disadvantaged subregions' (Rothchild, 1985:159).

These observations corroborate the value of the AISE framework which places considerable emphasis on (1) the need to problematise the value of inclusion; and (2) to explore the ways in which elite interests shape the design and actual functioning of state institutions (both formal and informal), and how this in turn influences development outcomes. Thus, from this perspective, the most important question to ask when thinking of the development prospects of lagging regions is not simply to probe whether they have been included or excluded from decision-making structures, but more importantly to examine the terms and conditions of their representation. Overall, then we concur with Hickey and du Toit (2013: 134) in their recent observation that the concepts of exclusion and adverse incorporation 'can significantly advance current understandings of chronic poverty, because they compel taking issues of causality seriously and relate these directly to social structures, relations, and processes. In particular, they force the examination of the multidimensional political and historical nature of persistent poverty'.

References

Abdulai, A-G. (2012), State elites and the politics of regional inequality in Ghana. PhD dissertation, University of Manchester, UK

Abdulai, A-G., & Hickey, S. (2016), The politics of development under competitive clientelism: Insights from Ghana's education sector'. *African Affairs*, 115(458): 44–72.

Abdulai, A-G., & Hulme, D. (2015), The politics of regional inequality in Ghana: State elites, donors and PRSPs', *Development Policy Review* 33(5): 529-553

Acemoglu, D., & Robinson, J., (2012) *Why nations fail: The origins of power, prosperity and poverty*. New York: Crown Business.

Akologo, S. Z., & van Klinken, R. (2008), Ghana: Why the North matters'. *Pambazuka News*, Issue 381, 6 June 2008.

Alwy, A., & Schech, S. (2004), 'Ethnic inequalities in education in Kenya', *International Education Journal* 5(2): 266-274.

Armah, B. (2013), Making sense of Africa's priorities for the post 2015 development agenda', *Development* 56(1): 114–122

Arriola, L. R. (2009), Patronage and political stability in Africa, *Comparative Political Studies* 42(10):1339-1362

Aryeetey, E., Owusu, G., Mensah, E. J. (2009), An analysis of poverty and regional inequalities in Ghana', *GDN Working Paper No. 27*, Global Development Network, October.

Barkan, J. D., & Chege, M. (1989), Decentralising the state: District focus and the politics of reallocation in Kenya', *The Journal of Modern African Studies* 27(3): 431-453.

Bening, R.B. (1990), *A History of Education in Northern Ghana, 1909–1976*. Accra: Ghana University Press.

Bernstein, H. (2007), Capital and labour from centre to margins, Keynote address for conference on Living on the Margins. Vulnerability, Exclusion and the State in the Informal Economy, Cape Town, 26-28 March 2007

Bird, K., Higgins, K., & Harris, D. (2010), Spatial poverty traps: An overview', *ODI Working Paper 321 and CPRC Working Paper 161* London: Overseas Development Institute, and Chronic Poverty Research Centre, University of Manchester

Boahene, A. A. (1987), *African perspectives on colonialism* Baltimore and London: The Johns Hopkins University Press.

Boone, C. (1994), States and ruling classes in postcolonial Africa: the enduring contradictions of power. In J.S. Migdal, A. Kohli, and V. Shue (eds.), *State power and social forces.* Cambridge: Cambridge University Press, pp.108-141

Chabal, P. (1992), *Power in Africa: an essay in political interpretation.* London: Macmillan and New York: St Martin's Press.

Chronic Poverty Research Centre (2004), The chronic poverty report 2004-2005' University of Manchester: Chronic Poverty Research Centre.

Clark, G., & Gray, R. (2012), Geography is not destiny: Geography, institutions and literacy in England, 1837-1863. *European Historical Economics Society Working Paper No. 15*, February 2012. Available at: http://ehes.org/EHES_No15.pdf.

Dresang, D. (1974), Ethnic politics, representative bureaucracy and development administration: The Zambian case, *American Political Science Review* 68(4): 1605-17.

du Toit, A. (2004), 'Social exclusion' discourse and chronic poverty: A South African case study, *Development and Change* 35(5): 987–1010.

du Toit, A. (2008) Living on the margins: The social dynamics of economic marginalisation', *Development Southern Africa*, 25(2): 135-150.

Escobal, J, & Torero. M. (2005), Adverse geography and differences in welfare in Peru. In Ravi Kanbur and Anthony J. Venables (eds.), *Spatial inequality and development.* Oxford: Oxford University Press, pp. 77-123

Ghana Statistical Service (2007), *Pattern and trends of poverty in Ghana 1991-2006* Accra: Ghana Statistical Service.

GoG (2003), *Ghana poverty reduction strategy 2003-2005: An agenda for growth and prosperity.* Accra: National Development Planning Commission.

Golooba-Mutebi, F. & Hickey, S. (2010), Governing chronic poverty under nclusive liberalism: The case of the northern Uganda social action fund, *Journal of Development Studies*, 46(7):1216-1239.

Gore, C. (1994), Social exclusion and *Africa south* of the *Sahara: A review* of the *literature'* Geneva: *International Institute for Labour Studies.*

Green, M., & Hulme, D. (2005), From correlates and characteristics to causes: Thinking about poverty from a chronic poverty perspective' *World Development* 33(6): 867–879.

Green, M., & Hulme, D. (2005), From correlates and characteristics to causes: Thinking about poverty from a chronic poverty perspective *World Development* 33(6): 867–879.

Groth, A. J., & Wade, L. L. (1984), Volume editors' introduction, in A. J. Groth and L. L. Wade (eds.), C*omparative resource allocation: Politics, performance and policy priorities* (Beverly Hills, London and Delhi: Sage Publications), pp.151-180.

Harsch, E. (2008), Closing Ghana's national poverty gap: North-south disparities challenge attainment of Millenium Development Goals', *Africa Renewal*, 23, No. 3, October 2008.

Hickey, S. & du Toit, A. (2013), Adverse incorporation, social exclusion, and chronic poverty'. In A. Shepherd and J. Brunt (eds.). *Chronic poverty: Concepts, causes and policy.* London: Palgrave Macmillan, pp.134-159

Hickey, S., & du Toit, A. (2007), Adverse incorporation, social exclusion and chronic poverty, *CPRC Working Paper 81*, Chronic Poverty Research Centre, University of Manchester

Hyden, G. (1985), Urban growth and rural development, in G. M. Carter and P. O'Meara (eds.), *African independence: The first twenty-five years.* Bloomington: Indiana University Press, pp.188-217

Jones, H. (2009), Equity in development: Why it is important and how to achieve it', *Working Paper 311* London: Overseas Development Institute)

Kabeer, N. (2000), Social exclusion, poverty and discrimination: Towards an analytical framework *IDS Bulletin*, 31(4): 83-97

Kanbur, R., & Venables, A. J. (2005), *Rising spatial disparities and development: Why do they matter?* Oxford: Oxford University Press.

Kanu, B.S., Salami, A.O., & Numaswa, K, (2014), Inclusive Growth: an imperative for African agriculture', African Development Bank (AfDB), Tunis.

Koti, F. T. (2010), 'Confronting sociospatial exclusion on the fringe of Africa's cities using participatory GIS: Lessons from

Athi River Town, Kenya', *Africa Today* 56(3): 62-82

Krugman, P.R. (1991), First nature, Second nature and metropolitan location', *NBER Working Paper No. 3740.*

Ladouceur, P. A. (1979), *Chiefs and politicians: The politics of regionalism in Northern Ghana.* London and New York: Longman Group Ltd.

Lall, S.V., Sandefur, J., & Wang, H. G. (2009), Does improving market access help de-industrialize lagging regions? Available at: http://siteresources.worldbank.org/DEC/Resources/84797-1257266550602/LallS.pdf [Accessed 19.08.15].

Lando, S., & Bujra, A. (2009), Class formation and inequality in Kenya, Paper for the Social Policy, Development and Governance in Kenya Programme, Development Policy Management Forum, Nairobi.

Langer, A. (2005), Horizontal inequalities and violent conflict: Côte d'Ivoire Country paper *Human Development Report office Occasional paper No. 32*, UNDP

Lemarchand, R. (1983), The state and society in Africa, in D. Rothchild and V. A. Olorunsola (eds.), *State Versus Ethnic Claims: African Policy Dilemmas* (Boulder, CO: Westview), pp.44-66

Lindemann, S. (2011), Just another change of guard? Broad-based politics and civil war in Museveni's Uganda, *African Affairs*, 110(440): 387-416

Mamdani, M. (1983), *Imperialism and fascism in Uganda.* London: Heinemann Education Books Ltd.

Moore, K., Grant, U., Hulme, D., & Shepherd, A. (2008), Very poor, for a long time, in many ways: Defining 'the poorest' for policy makers'. *CPRC Working Paper 124,* Chronic Poverty Research Centre, University of Manchester.

Mosse, D. (2010), A relational approach to durable poverty, inequality and power, *Journal of Development Studies,* 46 (7): 1156-1178.

Muhula, R. (2009), Horizontal inequalities and ethno-regional politics in Kenya, *Kenya Studies Review*, 1(1):85-105.

Mustapha, A. R. (2006), Ethnic structure, inequality and governance of the public sector in Nigeria, *Democracy, Governance and Human Rights Programme Paper Number 24.* Geneva: United Nations Research Institute for Social Development.

Nellis, J. (1974), The ethnic composition of leading Kenyan government positions, *Research Report No. 24 9* .Uppsala: The Scandinavian Institute for African Studies.

Oduro, A. & I. Aryee (2003). Investigating chronic poverty in West Africa. *CPRC Working Paper 28* Manchester: Chronic Poverty Research Centre.

Osaghae, E. E. (1994), Ethnicity in Africa or African ethnicity: The search for a contextual understanding, in U. Himmelstrand, K. Kinyanjui, and E. Mburugu (eds), *African perspectives on development: Controversies, dilemmas & openings.* New York: James Curry, pp.137-151.

Osaghae, E. E. (2006), Ethnicity and the state in Africa', *Working paper No.7.* Afrasian Centre for Peace and Development Studies.

Radelete, S. (2010), *Emerging Africa: How 17 countries are leading the way.* Washington DC.: Center for Global Development.

Republic of Kenya (2011a), Vision 2030 development strategy for Northern Kenya and other arid lands. Final draft, August 2011, Nairobi, Kenya.

Republic of Kenya (2011b), Draft sessional paper No… of 2011 on national policy for the sustainable development of Northern Kenya and other arid lands: Releasing our full potential, Version 7, Final Draft, 6 April 2011. Nairobi, Kenya.

Rothchild, D. (1969), Ethnic Inequalities in Kenya. *The Journal of Modern African Studies* 7(4): 689-711

Rothchild, D. (1984), Middle Africa: Hegemonial exchange and resource allocation, in A. J. Groth and L. L. Wade (eds.), *Comparative Resource Allocation: Politics, Performance and Policy Priorities*. Beverly Hills, London and Delhi: Sage Publications, pp.11-17.

Rothchild, D. (1985), State-ethnic relations in Middle Africa, in G. M. Carter and P. O'Meara (eds.), *African Independence: The First Twenty-Five Years*. Bloomington: Indiana University Press, pp.71-96.

Rothchild, D. & Foley, M. W. (1988), African states and the politics of inclusive coalitions, in D. Rothchild and N. Chazan (eds), *The Precarious Balance: State and Society in Africa*. Boulder and London: Westview Press, pp.233-264

Sen, A. (2000), *Social exclusion: Concept, application and scrutiny*, Social Development Paper No. 1, Asian Development Bank, available at: http://www.adb.org/documents/books/social_exclusion/Social_exclusion.pdf [accessed 24 May, 2010].

Stewart, F. (2009), Horizontal inequality: Two types of trap. *Journal of Human Development and Capabilities*, 10(3): 315 — 340

Stewart, F. (2010a), Horizontal inequalities as a cause of conflict: A review of CRISE findings, *Background Paper for World Development Report* 2011.

Stewart, F. (2010b), Horizontal inequalities in Kenya and the political disturbances of 2008: some implications for aid policy. *Conflict, Security & Development* 10(1): 133-159

Stewart, F., & Langer, A. (2007), Horizontal inequalities: Explaining persistence and Change', CRISE Working Paper No. 39, Oxford: University of Oxford, UK.

UNDP (2005), *Human Development Report 2005: International cooperation at a crossroads – Aid, trade and security in an unequal world*. New York: United Nations Development Programme.

UNDP (2007), *Ghana Human Development Report 2007: Towards a more inclusive society*. UNDP Ghana, Accra.

UNDP (2007), Empowering Rural Women and Alleviating Poverty by Strengthening the Local Shea Butter Industry in Northern Ghana, UNDP/Japan Partnership Fund, Project Document, UNDP-Ghana, Accra

United Nations Research Institute for Social Development (UNRISD) (2010), *Combating poverty and inequality: Structural change, social policy and politics*. Geneva: UNRISD.

van de Walle, N. (2009), The institutional origins of inequality in Sub-Saharan Africa.*Annual Review of Political Science*, 12:307-327.

Whitfield, L., Therkildsen, O., Buur, L. & Kjær, A M. (2015), *The politics of African industrial policy: A comparative perspective.* Cambridge: Cambridge University Press.

Wood, G. (2003), Staying secure, staying poor: the "Faustian bargain", *World Development,* 31(3):455-471.

World Bank (2005), *World Development Report 2006: Equity and Development* (Washington, D.C: The World Bank).

World Bank (2009a), *Awakening Africa's Sleeping Giant: Prospects for Commercial Agriculture in the Guinea Savannah Zone and Beyond* (Washington, DC: World Bank).

World Bank (2009b), Kenya: Poverty and Inequality Assessment, World Bank Poverty Reduction and Economic Management Unit, Africa Region

World Bank (2011), Tackling Poverty in Northern Ghana, Report No. 53991-GH. Washington D.C.: World Bank Africa Region.

PART II
CONTEMPORARY ISSUES IN MANAGEMENT DEVELOPMENT IN AFRICA

CHAPTER THREE

Corporate Governance, Shareholder Activism and Firm Performance in Ghana

Alex Kwame Abasi, Elikplimi Komla Agbloyor,
Joshua Yindenaba Abor

1. Introduction

Corporate governance is an extensive subject which pertains to the relationships among management (the agents), directors of a board, the owners of a firm (shareholders), and other stakeholders. It also refers to the social system and procedures for directing and controlling companies (World Bank, 2005). The corporation performs well when this relationship is well managed. However, the relationship turns sour at times. This is because the stakeholders have conflicting interests which might create problems. The parties that are particularly relevant to this study include Management, Board of Directors and Shareholders. The shareholders are the weakest in this relationship in terms of power and influence due to information asymmetry and moreover because they are not part of the daily management of the firm.

Though shareholders are the owners, however, since it is impossible for all of them to manage the firm at the same time, they employ managers to manage the firm on their behalf. This constitutes an agency contract. This employment contract has a potential risk of adverse selection and moral hazard.

Due to this possibility of adverse selection and moral hazard, there is the need for external monitoring because 'without external pressure from shareholders, managers may behave in ways that are sub- optimal for the shareholders' (Hillary & Oshika, 2003). This monitoring constitutes shareholder activism. Abor (2007) states that 'corporate governance is about supervising and holding to account those who direct and control the management' and the ultimate objective of shareholder activists/ activism is to hold the managers to account.

Shareholder activism can be defined as the actions taken by active investors who want to guard their investment to increase their wealth, by engaging managers who can meet their demands for reforms when managers are wasting resources (Brav, Jiang, Thomas & Partnoy, 2008; Gillan & Starks, 2000). The shareholders do this either by being hostile or using diplomatic means to ensure that good corporate governance systems are adopted and moral hazard minimized, so as to enhance firm performance.

Shareholder activism is a contemporary issue which has become significant because of its effect on the firm and similarly due to the media coverage it receives when it is launched. In addition, some studies show that activists play an influential role in improving corporate governance and ultimately, firm performance, though others find contrary results (Brav, Jiang, Thomas & Partnoy, 2008; Karpoff, 2001). Shareholder activism has become a necessary tool for shareholders as a result of the realization of the agency problem, where the owners of the firm are kept separate from the managers (Jensen & Meckling, 1976).

This separation of control and ownership leads to an agency problem which ought to be managed; yet managing it attracts agency costs which must be reduced. However, Grossman & Hart (1982) and Shleifer & Vishny (1997) posit that it is unprofitable for shareholders to hold their agents responsible because of the high monitoring cost plus the free riding problem.

The enquiry of whether activism increases shareholder value, and for that matter-, firm value, is an issue that has attracted varied opinions. This study reexamines the effect of active shareholder monitoring on managers, corporate governance and firm performance.

Though considerable research has been done on corporate governance issues and firm performance, very little has been done on shareholder activism (activism) and firm performance. Nonetheless, none of them used value-based metrics in their empirical examination. All of them used accounting-based performance measures (ROA) (Gantchev, 2013; Kandel, Massa & Simonov, 2011; Bechk, Frankes, Mayers & Rossi, 2009; Choi & Cho, 2003). This study therefore is the first to use Economic Value Added (EVA) and Market Value Added (MVA) to find the actual effect of shareholder activism on a firm`s performance.

Previous studies mostly adopted return on asset (ROA) as a measure of firm performance, which is not extensive enough because it does not capture costs of equity. As a result, these studies have produced mixed conclusions. There is therefore the need to use other superior measures of performance to establish the real effect of activism on the firm. Consequently, this study adopts Economic Value Added (EVA) and Market Value Added (MVA) as measures of firm performance, to reexamine the effect of shareholder activism on firm performance.

2. Literature Review

Investors are always concerned with recouping the principal amount plus the interest they will earn when parting with money. In most instances, they institute measures that will ensure that their investment is secure, and this forms a part of corporate governance. Some authors posit that 'corporate governance deals with the ways in which suppliers of finance to firms assure themselves of getting a return on their investment' (Shleifer & Vishny, 1997). Other studies such as Abor (2007) and World Bank (2005) look at it from a broader perspective and conclude that it tests the manner in which firms are directed, administered and controlled through different sets of processes, traditions and laws.

We notice, from the arguments above, that corporate governance takes different forms, but one fundamental and significant objective is to ensure the accountability of the managers in a firm by reducing the Principal-Agency problem. The governance system is such that, in order to safeguard shareholders who are the suppliers of the funds, 'internal and external corporate governance mechanisms are implemented to keep management`s interests in line with those of the shareholders'.

Examples of internal mechanisms are used to ensure board independence, by appointing or electing more non-executive board members, instituting incentive schemes to motivate managers to work in the interest of their principals, and appointing independent external auditors to scrutinize the work of the managers.

The external mechanism which is shareholder activism is normally 'triggered once internal mechanisms for checking management opportunism have failed, (Kyereboah-Coleman, 2007; Lillihook & Margolin 2008). Some previous studies show that good corporate governance has a positive nexus with firm performance, whereas other studies conclude otherwise.

Proponents of activism argue that it makes managers sit up and take good investment decisions, minimize waste, and take better tax decisions including tax avoidance strategies which minimize costs, which then enhance profitability (Lim, 2011; Greenwood & Schor, 2009). Davis (2002) states that managers have the discretion on dividend issues as well as on capital investment decisions which determines shareholder wealth thus making shareholders vulnerable. Consequently, to safeguard their interest, shareholders must improve on corporate governance which makes managers take good investment decisions that will enhance the firm`s performance. In Ghana, corporate governance issues are guided by the companies' code and the Corporate Governance Guidelines on Best Practices by the Securities and Exchange Commission (SEC). These guidelines seek ultimately to safeguard the interests of shareholders who are the owners of the firm, as well as to ensure that the interests of other stakeholders are not neglected. Nonetheless, shareholders can benefit from this guideline only if they actively monitor the operations of the managers (the agents).

Agency Theory: The agency theory was propounded by Berle & Means (1932) and Jensen & Meckling (1976). Jensen & Meckling (1976) defined the agency relationship as a contract between a principal and the agent, under which the principal engages the agent to perform some service on his/her behalf which involves delegating some decision making authority to the agent. They explain that, since shareholders are dispersed and cannot all manage the firm at the same time, they leave the firm in the hands of the managers, thus making it difficult to supervise these managers. This situation creates the agency problem. This agency problem emanates as a result of adverse selection and the moral hazard which occur because of the separation of ownership and control of the firm.

The "agency problem in corporate governance is due to management prioritizing its own benefits rather than shareholder value" (Lillihook & Margolin, 2008). This variance magnifies the difficulty that the financiers encounter in ensuring that their invested capital is not expropriated or wasted on negative net present value (NPV) projects, or less profitable projects (Kandel, Massa, & Simonov, 2011; Shleifer & Vishny, 1997).

Stern Stewart & Co. (2000) posit that mature firms normally generate large levels of free cash flow which leads to excess capital with the tendency to retain and then waste this capital, through overinvestment and diversification schemes. Therefore, the EVA performance metric guarantees that managers account for using equity just as they would have done for using debt without much trouble, by setting extensive covenants.

Shareholder Activism: The Securities and Exchange Commission of Ghana (SEC), in their corporate governance guideline book, encourages shareholders to 'demand acceptable standards of corporate governance from management of the firms they invest in'. The guideline also encourages all investors who are in the position to influence a firm to try to do so in order to boost compliance with corporate governance practices that have been put in place. This implies that the SEC encourages activism.

Gillan & Starks, (2000) define shareholder activists as 'investors who are dissatisfied with some aspect of a company`s management or operations, and so try to bring about change without a change in control'. This description suggests that shareholder activism is seen as a tool not (pursuing) / working at taking over but rather at bring amendments yet retaining management. This form of activism can be described as defensive activism (MacNei, 2010). Tirole (2005) states that 'active monitoring consists of interfering with management in order to increase the value of the investors` claim'.

In this definition, the interest is on EVA and MVA, that is increasing the firm`s value. This form of activism can also be described as defensive activism.

Another approach is where shareholders buy shares in firms in order to have control and put pressure on the management of companies to effect change (Lillihook & Margolin, 2008). This form of activism can be described as offensive activism. This means shareholder activism is normally initiated by dissatisfied shareholders who try to influence and improve the policies and strategies of their firm through negotiation, communication and pressure. The underlying concept in this definition is that this activity is triggered when shareholders are dissatisfied with the output from management and would want to change the results; and typically, this activity is undertaken by active shareholders.

Shareholder activism can therefore be defined as the actions taken by active investors who want to guard their investment to increase their wealth, by engaging managers to meet their demands for reforms when managers are wasting resources, and they do so either by being hostile or by using diplomatic means to ensure that good corporate governance systems are adopted and that the moral hazard is minimized so as to enhance firm performance (Brav, Jiang, Thomas & Partnoy, 2008 and Gillan & Starks, 2000). Thus, activism can be diplomatic or hostile. Brav *et al* (2008) state that hostile activism generates higher returns. They define hostility to include "threatened or actual proxy contest, takeover, lawsuit or public campaign that is openly confrontational".

Most incidents / examples of activism take the form of deliberations and negotiations behind closed doors, and so are normally hard to track. The activists can also take the 'Wall Street walk' (selling their shares) as a form of activism. These dissatisfied investors do not pressure management to change. However, they just dump their shares, which reduce share prices and affect the managers` income if it is tied to the share price (Emkuzheva, Paulini & Zymogliad, 2013). Such actions also send a signal to other investors, that the firm is underperforming. On the other hand, some investors, instead of taking the Wall Street Walk, may decide 'to continue to hold their shares and seek to induce changes within the firm', either with or without the intention of having control (Rennebook & Szilagyi, 2011).

Activists use many strategies and one of the contemporary tactics is the use of the social media where issues are sparked and discussed, and actions are taken. This can influence many shareholders to vote with their feet or taking the Wall Street walk or to win by proxy voting. Some firms are more vulnerable to activism than others. As an external control, activists typically 'target firms that underperform and also have weak governance structure' (Renneboog & Szilagyi, 2011). This monitoring is an external control and it comes with some costs.

***Incentive to Monitor*:** For monitoring to be effective, there should be the incentive to monitor. A shareholder`s incentive to actively monitor is determined by a trade-off between the private costs of monitoring which are fully paid for by the activist, and the public benefits of monitoring which are shared among all firm shareholders, thereby creating the free riding problem (Grossman & Hart, 1980; Shleifer &Vishny, 1986; Gantchev, 2013). So why do investors not simply take the Wall Street walk when they are dissatisfied with the performance of the firm since monitoring is expensive? The answer is that some investors do take the Wall Street walk but when the shareholder holds a majority of the stock, taking the Wall Street walk becomes an imprudent decision compared to the choice of staying and ensuring that management does the right thing to bring good returns to investors (Helwege, Intintoli, & Zhang, 2012).

This implies that once the majority shareholder starts a process of demand for reforms exiting is not an option. These shareholders are quite aware of their role as owners, therefore they will rather stay and fix the problem. So it is quite obvious that the impetus driving shareholder activism is financially driven with the objective of receiving better returns.

Chung & Talaulicar (2010) explain that shareholder activism can be categorized into two: those that are financially driven and those that are socially driven. Besides having the objective of improving profitability, shareholder activists also sometimes aim at 'influencing corporate management and boards in order to make corporations change in corporate social responsibility (CSR)'. The objective of socially driven activism is to achieve social benefits (Judge *et al*, 2010). The financially driven sort of activism targets the financial performance of firms and tries to pressure management to improve performance. The socially driven sort of activism is done by people who are concerned with the negative externalities of the operation of the firm. This study focusses on the financially driven form of activism. Gantchev (2013) states that, monitoring can only be effective when the net returns are positive. In other words if the returns generated from activism are greater than the costs incurred, shareholders will be incentivized

3. Nature of Shareholder Activism in Ghana

Activism takes a different form in Ghana. What actually happens is that institutional investors acquire stakes in firms with the intention of having board representation. The motive is to have control and influence policies relating to capital investment decisions. Normally, these investors put pressure on management, not publicly but through negotiations, either at the board level or at management meetings. Institutional investors in Ghana rarely take the Wall Street walk. As the head of equity of SSNIT puts it, 'exiting is not an option; we normally see to it that our objectives are achieved'. SSNIT stands for Social Security and National Insurance Trust, and it is one of the largest institutional investors in Ghana. Public announcement of activism only becomes an option when negotiations fail and some of the times firms in Ghana prefer that public agitation is avoided or activism is resolved quietly because of reputational issues.

Individual investors, on the other hand, acquire shares purposely for capital gains and to receive dividends, but not for the purpose of seeking control. These are usually minority shareholders who possess little power to influence management decisions. Exiting is not a problem to them because there are no shareholder unions in Ghana unlike in America where there is the United Shareholders Association (USA) and the People`s Solidarity for Participatory Democracy (PSPD) in Korea. Generally, individual investors in Ghana can be described as inactive/dormant investors because the majority of them do not monitor their managers.

The framework below shows that shareholders can be classified into dormant and active shareholders. Dormant shareholders typically do not actively monitor. They lose value for not being active, but benefit from the positive externalities that emanate from the active shareholders (shareholder activists). Active shareholders, on the other hand, use activism which involves using two tools to achieve their demands or objectives. One tool is the use of activism: private negotiation and/or public announcement, and the second tool is taking the Wall Street Walk.

Below is a conceptual framework that depicts the nature of activism in Ghana.

Figure 3.1

CONCEPTUAL FRAMEWORK

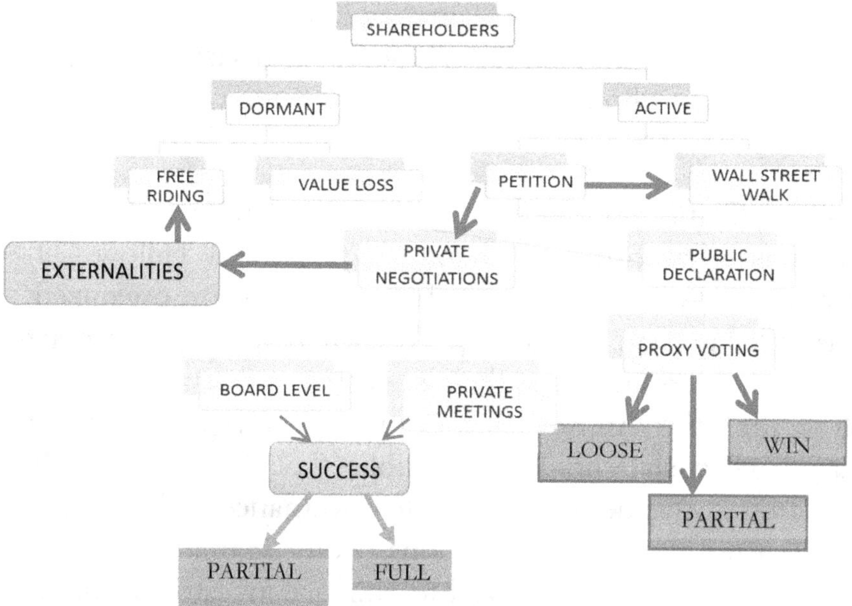

The framework shows that activism is a sequential process as was found by Gantchev (2013). It usually begins with petitions, then it progresses to private negotiations, either through private meetings or through deliberations at the board level. If these petitions are not addressed, these shareholders are likely to take the Wall Street Walk. Success can be achieved during private negotiations which can either be full success, thus the activists achieve all their objectives or partial success which is that some of their objectives are achieved.

If consensus is not reached, the activists progress to the next option of public declaration which is more hostile. At this point their intentions are made public and an Extraordinary General Meeting (EGM) is called. At the EGM, proxy voting is cast and the outcome can be a win, a partial win or a defeat / failure. But whatever the outcome may be at the final stage, its effect on corporate governance is positive. Managers will either implement reforms immediately or implement reforms later. This is consistent with Gantchev (2013) who posits that, 'activism begins as a sequence of escalating decision steps, in which an activist chooses a more hostile tactic only after less confrontational approaches have failed'

***Investor Conference*:** Due to the possibility of these disruptions a few firms in Ghana (Ecobank and Tullow Oil) now resort to meeting investors before AGMs are organized. This is called investor conference (IC) where managers interact with shareholders to know their concerns and try to address them before the AGM, because managers reputations get damaged when shareholders go public (Hill & Jones, 1992). This is an improvement in corporate governance and has been adopted after numerous agitations from shareholders. An investor conference is organized to enhance investor relations. The managers use investor conferences to listen to shareholders concerns and improve corporate governance and minimize shareholder activism.

Incidence of Shareholder Activism among the listed firms in Ghana:

Activism seems to be a new phenomenon in Ghana because its occurrence seems to have been very low at the start of this study (2007), and then began to increase till date as is shown by Figure 3.2 below. The data for the figure was obtained from SEC, SSNIT, Joy FM website, City FM website, Business and Financial Times website and Google search.

The figure shows the aggregate occurrence among all listed firms. Shareholder activism occurs when the shareholders agitate. Minutes from the annual general meetings (AGMs) and extra ordinary general meetings (EGMs) were made available by SEC and SSNIT for this study, which helped to realize the results in Figures 3.2 and 3.3. Moreover, information from the minutes of board meetings were gleaned and made available for this study. They have contributed to the realization of the results in Figures 3.2 and 3.3. In addition, a thorough search was done on the internet using google to detect any incidence of activism about any listed firm.

Figure 3.2

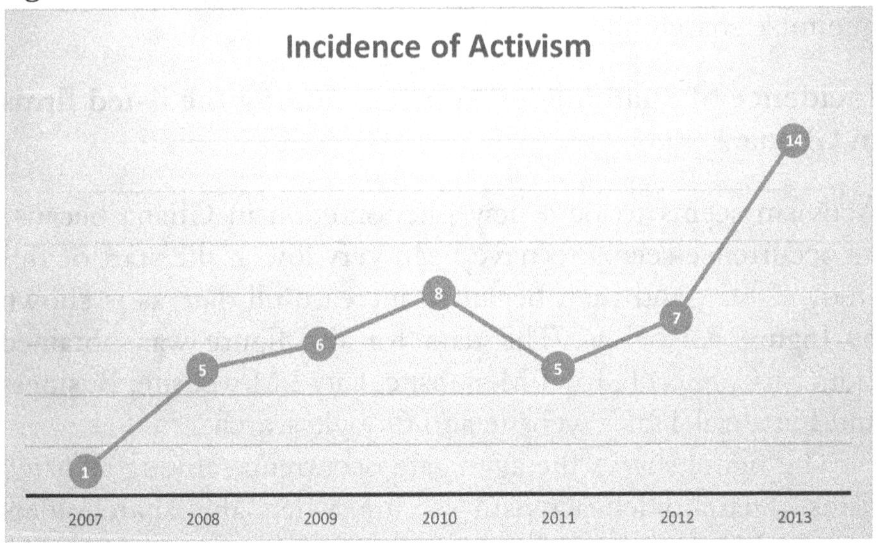

Source: *Field work, 2015*

The figure shows that only one (1) incident of activism was recorded in 2007, which increased to 5, 6 and 8 in 2008, 2009 and 2010 respectively. It then fell to 5 and 7 in 2011 and 2012 and then increased sharply to 14 cases in 2013. The Figure depicts that as activism started increasing in 2008, managers might have adhered to their demands and concerns, and this helped bring it down to 5 cases in 2011. However, it seems shareholders were becoming more aware of their rights, causing activism to sharply rise to 14 cases in 2013. This could be influenced by the SEC`s corporate governance guidelines that urge investors to be active in monitoring their firms to help in the building of a strong corporate governance system in Ghana.

Activism means actions taken by active investors, basically in the form of pressuring or engaging managers of their firm to meet their demands for reforms, when the managers are wasting resources. Incidences of activism capture the occurrence of these actions. Figure 3.3 below depicts the frequency of occurrence of activism for individual firms for the entire period of study, which is from 2007 to 2013.

Within this 7 year period, CFAO Ghana Ltd (CFAO), Clydestone Ltd (CLYD), Guinness Ghana Brewery Ltd (GGBL), Ghana Oil Company Ltd (GOIL), PZ Cussons Ghana Ltd (PZ), Social Security Bank (SSB), Sam Woode Ltd (SWL), and Transactions Solutions Ghana Ltd (TRANSOL) all experienced no incidence of activism. Standard Chartered Bank (SCB) experienced it once. Other firms like Accra Brewery Ltd (ABL), Aluworks Ltd (ALW), Ayrton Drug Manufacturing Ltd (AYRTN), Benso Oil Palm Plantations (BOPP), Cocoa Processing Company (CPC), EcoBank Ghana (EBG), Enterprise Insurance Company (EIC), Fan Milk Ltd (FML), Ghana Commercial Bank (GCB), Mechanical Lloyd Company (MLC) and Unilever Ghana Ltd (UNIL) all experienced it only twice.

Cal Bank (CAL), Produce Buying Company (PBC) and Unique Trust Bank (UT) experienced the phenomenon three times, and finally HFC Bank (HFC) and Super Paper Product Company (SPPC) recorded the highest incidence of activism in Ghana, four (4) times each, from 2007 to 2013.

This could mean that HFC bank and SPPC have poor corporate governance system, or that they underperformed compared to their peers. Helwege, Intintoli, & Zhang (2012) state that activists target firms that underperform or have weak corporate governance system.

Figure 3.3: Incidence of activism at the individual firm level

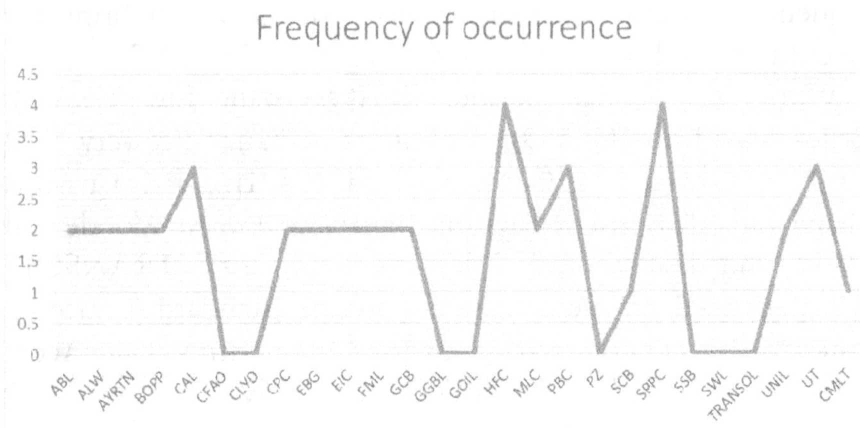

Source: *Field work, 2015*

The Presence of Sokaiya or Disturbatori in Ghana

Some of the corporate managers see activism from a different perspective. They do not view it as a tool to correct weak corporate governance; instead they see it as a threat and also as a group of investors who want to satisfy their self-interest by causing embarrassment to the managers. As a result, they resort to some techniques to suppress activism during the Annual General Meetings (AGM) and the principal technique they employ is called *Sokaiya* in Japan (Hilary & Oshika, 2008) and *Disturbatoris* in Italy (West, 2005). *Sokaiya* as a term refers to corporate extortionists who operate during AGMs.

Sokaiya or Disturbatoris can be described as deceptive shareholders who disrupt good corporate governance system. What they basically do is to intimidate the shareholders with genuine concerns, just to ensure that the meeting proceeds as planned. In Ghana, a careful study of minutes from AGMs provided by SEC shows the presence of *sokaiya/Disturbatoris.*

Unlike Japan, *sokaiya/Disturbatoris* in Ghana is practised by a few individual investors who do not form groups. These few *Disturbatoris* (bad investors) manage to acquire a small number of shares in several firms and use that to get access to their AGMs and then launch their attacks, or in most cases they resort to giving excessive praise to management just to create the impression that management is doing very well, and that they should keep up the good work. The minutes obtained from SEC shows cases where names of certain individuals run through the various minutes from firm to firm with almost the same approach: showering praise on management when other shareholders are complaining or are dissatisfied that management had done very little to better their fortunes. They do this to gain priority to speak, and by doing so they deny or prevent the genuine shareholder activists access to the platform to make their demands. Such behaviour is inimical to good corporate governance in Ghana.

4. Methodology

Two performance measures; Economic Value Added (E.V.A) and Market Value Added (M.V.A) methods have been estimated to find the impact of shareholder activism (activism) on shareholder value in Ghana. The study applied panel data technique to analyse the data. Hausman test was used to determine whether a fixed or random effect was appropriate for our estimation.

Population and Sample of the Study

The study population is all the listed firms in Ghana for the study period (2007 to 2013) because of availability of data and also because previous studies show that activism can create value and be an effective monitoring tool of publicly listed firms (Roman, 2013). There were 35 listed firms in Ghana as at May, 2015 and 5 delisted firms (GSE, 2015). Out of this population, 27 firms had data available for this study.

Sources of data

Data for measuring the dependent and the independent variable are obtained from the annual reports of the listed firms made available by GSE, and the Annual Reports Ghana website. Specifically the data were obtained from the income statement and the consolidated statement of the financial position. Share prices were obtained from the Ghana Stock Exchange (GSE). Corporate tax rates were obtained from the Ghana Revenue Authority (GRA). Both primary and secondary data were collected. The primary data were collected directly from investment officers and market analysts from SEC, SSNIT and SIC for the independent variable, ACT (activism). The secondary data were obtained from the annual reports of the listed firms, made available by the Ghana Stock Exchange (GSE).

Model Specification

This study seeks to find empirically whether activism has any effect on firm performance. Since the effect of activism on firm performance will be influenced by both time and firm specific effects, this study adopts panel analytical methods to accomplish the set objective.

Using panel data estimation is known to produce good results when the objective is to find relationships over time and across firms, because it has the dimensions of both time series and cross-sections (Brooks, 2008).

The general form of the panel data model according to Brooks (2008) can be specified as

$Y_{it} = \alpha + \beta X_{it} + \varepsilon_{it}$........................ (1)

Where: subscript i denotes the cross sectional dimension (firm) i = 1……..N and t denotes the time series dimension (time) t = 1………T;
Y_{it} is the dependent variable.

The model

To investigate whether activism has any effect on firm`s profitability and market value, the two models below are estimated;

$$EVA_{it} = \alpha_1 ACT_{it} + \alpha_2 BODS_{it} + \alpha_3 CEOT_{it} + \alpha_4 CEOD_{it} + \sum_{i=5}^{8} \varphi_i Controls_{it} + \lambda_t + \mu_i + \varepsilon_{it} \dots\dots\dots\dots\dots (2)$$

$$MVA_{it} = \beta_1 ACT_{it} + \beta_2 BODS_{it} + \beta_3 CEOT_{it} + \beta_4 CEOD_{it} + \sum_{i=5}^{8} \gamma_i Controls_{it} + \lambda_t + \mu_i + \varepsilon_{it} \dots\dots\dots\dots\dots (3)$$

α is the intercept term for all periods (t) and specific to a firm specific effect (i),
β is a k x 1 vector of parameters to be estimated on the independent variables.
X_{it} is a 1 x k vector of observations on the independent variables in the model which include the control variables.
λ_t is a proxy for control for time specific effect,
μ_i is a proxy for cross sectional heterogeneity.
$\alpha_1, \alpha_2, \alpha_3, \alpha_4$ and φ_i represent coefficient estimators in model (2) and

$\beta_1, \beta_2, \beta_3, \beta_4$ and γ_i represent coefficient estimators in model (3) and

ε_{it} is error term with zero mean and constant variance.

i represents each firm and t represents time.

Where: EVA_{it} in model (2) is the dependent variable; it represents Economic Value Added of firm i in year t. MVA_{it} in model (3) is the dependent variable; it represents Market Value Added of firm i in year t.

ACT_{it} is a dummy variable and a proxy for shareholder activism of firm i in year t, which takes the value of one when a firm experienced activism or zero otherwise.

This study adopts the estimation technique used by Brav, Jiang, Partnoy, & Thomas (2008), thus measuring activism as a dummy variable.

Data on Activism

The following methodology was used to capture incidence of activism in Ghana.

The first was that, minutes from AGMs were collected from the Securities and Exchange Commission (SEC). The SEC attends all AGMs of all listed firms and they take minutes. The minutes clearly explain what happened at the AGMs especially what happened between the shareholders and the management.

Particularly of interest to this study was to look for issues that constitute activism such as shareholder demands, agitations and expression of dissatisfaction etc. These issues put pressure on management to do better or take some decisions that hitherto were not among the agenda for implementation, and such omissions can also lead to some shareholders taking the Wall Street walk. Minutes for each firm, for each year, were reviewed and any incidence of activism was recorded.

The second technique used was a thorough search done on the internet using Google to identify any incidence of activism about any listed firm. The phrase, 'shareholders of' plus the name of the firm is googled and the results are screened. This is done for all firms under study to detect all reported cases during the period of study. Another search was done on the most reliable websites in the country including Joy FM website, City FM, Ghana News Agency website, Ghana web website, Business and Financial Times website, Daily Graphic Ghana website, Annual reports Ghana website, and Bank of Ghana website.

The third method used was personal interviews with some investment officers and the head of equity at SSNIT, and also the head of corporate planning at State Insurance Company (SIC).

$BODS_{it}$ is a proxy for board size which represents the number of board members on a firm`s board of directors. It is measured as the log of number of board members for firm i at time t (Abor, 2007; He & Sommer, 2006). Extant literature show that board size, as a corporate governance variable, has a positive effect on firm performance hence, it is included in this study (Kyereboah-Coleman, 2007; Adam & Mehran, 2010).

$CEOT_{it}$ is a proxy for CEO tenure which is the number of years a CEO stays in office. It is measured as the log of number of years a CEO stays in office (Abor, 2007). Information on CEO tenure was obtained from the annual reports of the various firms made available by GSE. CEO tenure is a corporate governance variable that affects firm performance and based on the findings of Kyereboah-

Coleman (2007), it is expected to enhance firm performance or have a negative effect on firm performance. This is because experience enhances knowledge and knowledge increase efficiency, but the CEO can also resort to empire building.

$CEOD_{it}$ is a proxy for CEO duality which is a dummy that takes the value of one when the CEO is also the board chairman or zero otherwise. The SEC recommends that the position of CEO and the board chair should not be vested in the same person, because the separation of the roles serves as a mechanism for ensuring that there is balance of power, increasing accountability and enhancing the capacity of the board for independent decision making. It also diminishes any excessive influence on management and the board.

Contrary to this concept is the stewardship theory which argues that the two positions should be vested in the same person, because occupying the two positions by the same person gives the CEO the chance to swiftly take decisions without the difficulty of too much bureaucracy. It is therefore expected to have either a negative or a positive relationship with firm performance (Kyereboah-Coleman, 2007).

Controls_{it} is a vector of control variables of firm i in year t.

Firm-Size; it is measured as the log of total asset (He & Sommer, 2006; Abor, 2007). It is expected to have a positive or negative relation. Firm size can have a positive relationship with performance if there is a good corporate governance system in place, and if the firm invests in only positive NPV projects and operate efficiently. However, firm size can also have a negative relation if the CEO, instead of investing in positive NPV projects, pursues empire-building objective, and when there is a bad corporate governance system.

Firm-Age; age in years (He & Sommer, 2006), it is measured as the log of years a firm has been in business. It is expected to have both a positive or negative relation with performance. It can have a positive relation with performance if it is able to generate wide acceptance of its products, and also because it is supposed to have acquired experience and have specialized in its area of operation. It has a negative relation with performance when its products are at their maturity stage of the products' life cycle, and has started to decline.

Overheads-Costs; are measured as the ratio of overhead expenses to total assets. It is expected to have either a negative or a positive relation with performance. This is because, if firms incur more costs, overheads ought to reduce their profitability, but if they are able to pass it on to consumers, it will have a positive relation with performance.

Firm-Risk; is measured as the standard deviation of return on asset (ROA). It is expected to have a positive relation with performance. It follows the risks-return relationship, thus the higher the risks, the higher the expected returns.

The methodology for calculating EVA is specified as follows: as adopted from Stern Stewart & Co. (2000), Shil & Dhaka (2009) and Vijayakumar (2011).

EVA = NOPAT – [(TA-CL) × WACC] .... (4)

NOPAT denotes net operating profit after tax, thus NOPAT = Earnings before interests and taxes (EBIT) – Corporate Tax

NOPAT=EBIT-Corporate Tax.. (5)

CE = (TA-CL)... (6)

Equation (6) represents capital employed, thus total asset minus current liability.

TA = total asset, CL = current liability, and WACC = weighted average cost of capital and it includes both the cost of debt and equity finance.

WACC is defined as;

$$\text{WACC}=[(r_E \times \frac{E}{V})] + [(r_D \times \frac{D}{V})(1 - T_c] \quad \text{.......................} (7)$$

Where $r_D = cost\ of\ debt, D = total\ debt,$
T_c= corporate tax rate, r_E = cost of equity, E = total equity, V = D + E.

Cost of debt was obtained using the Bank of Ghana (BoG) Policy rate from 2007 to 2013 to represent cost of debt for banks because they borrow from the BoG at that rate, whilst the one year Treasury bill rate from 2007 to 2013 is used to represent the cost of debt for the other firms because they borrow from the these banks not below this rate.
Cost of equity is computed using the Capital Asset Pricing Model (CAPM).
r_E = rf + β(rm – rf) ……………………………………………(8)
r_E= cost of equity for each firm
rf = risk free rate, is the one year Treasury bill rate, as obtained from the BoG website.
rm = GSE Composite index from 2007 to 2013, obtained from the Annual Report Ghana website.
β = beta, measures the sensitivity of a stock`s return to market returns.

Beta is computed using Data Regression method. Annual Percentage changes of the GSE composite index were computed for the period. Annual percentage changes of the firms` stock returns are also computed. These percentage changes of the stocks were then regressed on the percentage changes of the GSE composite index.
The betas obtained are then substituted into r_E = rf + β(rm – rf) to attain cost of equity for each firm for the entire seven year period of this study.
M V A = MVE – BVE ……………………………………(9).

Where MVE is the market value of equity and BVE is the book value of equity which is the capital invested.

MVA= (Number of common shares outstanding × share price) + (Number of preferred shares outstanding × share price) – book value of equity.

In order to capture variations in share prices within a particular year, we calculated the average share price for each firm and used that to proxy for the share price of a firm for a particular year.

The decision rule is that Value is added when MVA/EVA is positive and value is diminished when MVA or EVA is negative.

The Hausman test was conducted, and the results show that the Random Effect was appropriate for estimating both EVA and MVA. To ensure robust coefficients, the Breusch and Pagan Lagragian multipier test was conducted to detect heteroskedasticity and the Wooldridge test to detect Autocorrelation in panel data which are then corrected using Prais-Winsten regression.

5. Empirical Results

This section presents the results from the empirical estimations. We present the descriptive statistics, followed by the regression results:

Descriptive Statistics of dependent and independent variables:

Variable	Mean	Std dev	Minimum	Maximum
EVA	3.4739722	0.349856	0.14	10.76
MVA	17.95459	2.04842	12.1115	22.62815
ROA	0.0805172	0.1659419	-0.71	0.66
ACT	0.2386364	0.4274661	0	1
BOD SIZE	8.045455	2.203421	3	13
CEOT	2.943182	1.712862	1	7
CEOD	0.0733333	0.2615562	0	1
FIRM AGE	36.02841	21.79998	5	104
OVERHEADS COSTS	0.1618129	0.3160709	-0.17	3.58
FIRM RISK	0.1485227	0.3785024	0.01	2.54
FIRM SIZE	18.16667	2.274201	12.54	22.25

NB: EVA=NOPAT-[(TA-CL) x WACC]; MVA=MVE-BVE; ROA=PBT/TA; ACT is a dummy measured as 1 if the firm experience activism or 0 otherwise; BOD size is log of board size; CEOT is log of CEO tenure; CEOD is a dummy measured as 1 if CEO is the same as board chair or 0 otherwise; log of firm age; Overheads costs=ratio of overheads expenses to TA; Firm size=log of TA.

The table shows the summary of the descriptive statistics which comprises the mean, minimum, maximum, and standard deviation of the variables used in the study.

The natural log of Economic Value Added (EVA) had a mean value of 3. Activism had a mean of 0.23863664 indicating that on the average, the level of activism was 23% during the period of study. The descriptive statistics also show that the average ROA was 8%.

Board size had a mean of 8.045455, a minimum of 3 and a maximum of 13. The results also show that CEOs who double as board chairs represent only 7%, indicating that many firms in Ghana do not have their CEOs doubling as the board chairman.

5.1 Effect of Shareholder Activism on Firm Performance (EVA)

The internal performance measure that is of interest to this study is EVA, which has been proven to be a better performance measure (Stern, Stewart & Co., 2000). Hence if its regression result actually shows improvement in firm value influenced by activism, it can be concluded that certainly activism improves firm performance.

Variable	Coefficient
ACT	0.8519194**
	(0.385854)
BOD SIZE	2.286093**
	(1.085356)
CEOT	-0.1579169
	(0.1396179)
CEOD	1.645798
	(1.623698)
FIRM AGE	-0.7454808**
	(0.3410668)
OVERHEADS COSTS	-0.8085928
	(0.7522804)
FIRM RISK	5.282442
	(5.729171)
FIRM SIZE	0.0678833
	(0.1231384)
R-squared	0.6223
Wald chi2	146.48
Prob>chi2	0.0000

Significance Level: 1 %(***), 5 %(**) and 10 %(*). Standard errors are in parenthesis.

The regression results show that activism has a positive nexus with EVA (profitability) and is statistically significant at 5%. This denotes that incidences of activism pressures management to invest in positive NPV projects, and to adhere to good corporate governance principles which eventually improve firm performance proxied by (EVA). This finding is consistent with the findings of Strickland, Wiles & Zenner, 1996; Brav *et al*, (2008); Kandel, Massa & Simonov, (2011); and Roman, (2013) who also found that activism improves firm performance. But this result is contrary to the findings of Choi & Cho (2003) who did not find a positive association between activism and firm performance. However, they did not use EVA.

The implication of these results is that investors should be active and monitor managers because activism improves their wealth. Managers must also pay attention to shareholders` concerns as it improves firm performance and this explains why some firms organize investor conference for their shareholders so as to address their concerns before they go for their annual general meetings (AGM). This affords them more time to address shareholders' concerns and allow them to try to incorporate them in their plans, objectives and policies.

Board size also has a positive nexus with firm performance and it is significant at 5% denoting that a large board size increases firm performance as the members, coming from diverse backgrounds will bring their expertise together and take optimum investment decisions which will improve firm performance. It is also difficult for all of them to be loyal to the CEO, and so they are more likely to critically scrutinize investment options before approving them. This is consistent with the findings of Kyereboah-Coleman (2007) and Adams & Mehran (2010), but contrary to the findings of Eyenubo

(2013) who found a negative relation between bigger board size and firm performance, nonetheless none of them used EVA. Firm age has an inverse relation with EVA and is significant at 5%, which implies that as firms grow older they tend to be less profitable. This is because their investment opportunities might be diminishing, or using the product life cycle, their products might have reached their maturity and started to decline.

It could as well be that they generate excess capital and waste it through overinvestment. This is consistent with the findings of Stern Stewart & Co. (2000).

The result shows that activism actually improves firm performance. It increases the economic value that is added to their investment and so shareholders should be active monitors of managers to improve their wealth.

5.2 Effect of Shareholder Activism on Firm Performance (MVA)

The market value added (MVA) measures how much value has been added to the stock value of the firm at the stock market. This added value can be influenced by the incidence of activism as the stock market thrives on information. Here the dependent variable is changed from EVA to MVA and the independent variables are maintained so as to observe the effect of activism on MVA.

Variable	Coefficient
ACT	-0.1551878 (0.3084282)
BOD SIZE	0.3305175 (0.6257941)
CEOT	-0.2260936* (0.1212061)
CEOD	-1.901132 (1.397597)
FIRM AGE	1.036696* (0.5633267)
OVERHEADS COSTS	0.8201274*** (0.2187787)
FIRM RISK	7.0478* (3.668795)
FIRM SIZE	0.7322723*** (0.1346493)
R-squared	0.9795
Wald chi2	12956.77
Prob>chi2	0.0000

Significance Level: 1 %(***), 5 %(**) and 10 %(*)

After changing the dependent variable to MVA, which enabled a performance measurement to be done / undertaken at the stock market level the result is as depicted above. The dependent variable (MVA) measures firm performance at the stock market level. The regression result above indicates that activism (ACT) has an inverse relationship with firm performance at the stock market, but it is statistically insignificant. This could be because the stock market in Ghana is not informationally efficient.

CEO tenure is inversely related to MVA and statistically significant at 10%. This denotes that as CEOs stay in office for longer period they tend to focus less on value creation and possibly focus more on empire building and shareholders' respond to this. This is consistent with the findings of Abor (2007). Firm age is positively related to MVA and statistically significant at 10% denoting that as firms mature they win investors` trust and they buy and hold more of their shares which improve their share prices. The positive relationship here is contrary to the negative relationship found with EVA. The reason could be that the stock market is not informationally efficient, making stock traders, trade with the wrong information about the firm. Overheads costs are positively related to MVA and statistically significant at 1%, denoting that as operating expenses increase output also increases, thereby increasing profitability, but only if the firm is able to transfer the overheads costs to consumers. Firm risk is positively related to performance and statistically significant at 10%, denoting that the higher the risk the higher the returns. Thus as firms take more risks, they tend to generate more income and make more profit.

Firm size is positively related to MVA and statistically significant at 1%, denoting that large firms are more profitable because they are better able to take advantage of economies of scale. They are also able to invest in multiple products that generate multiple incomes, and implement efficient supply chain management system that eliminate waste, leverage global sourcing and enhance competitive advantage.

6. Conclusion and Implications

The subject of shareholder activism has become very vital in Ghana because the financial system is growing and people are investing in the economy and as a result, they will want to protect their investments. Shareholder activism has a positive effect on firm performance. It improves EVA and also improves corporate governance: therefore all stakeholders should be educated to understand activism and use it as a tool for improving firm performance when necessary. These findings posit compellingly that activism is good for the firm, it adds value to the firm, and therefore shareholders should be active and monitor managers of their firm because active monitoring enhances shareholder wealth.

Moreover, managers should not fight shareholders when shareholders are making demands, rather they should meet them (the shareholders), listen to their concerns and negotiate for a consensus. The implication is that an investor conference should be encouraged to address shareholders' concerns.

The SEC can mandate all listed firms to organize an investor conference at least once every year, to improve manager-shareholder relations so as to mitigate the agency problem and improve firm performance. There could be bidirectional link between shareholder activism and firm performance, hence it is recommended for further research.

References

Abor, J. (2007). Corporate governance and financing decisions of Ghanaian listed firms. *International Journal of Business in Society, Vol. 7, pp. 83-92.*

Adams, R. B. & Mehran, H. (2010). Corporate performance, board structure, and their determinants in the banking industry. *Federal Reserve Bank of New York Staff Reports, no. 330.*

Admati, A.R. & Pfleiderer, P. (2009). The 'Wall Street Walk' and shareholder activism: Exit as a form of voice. *The Review of Financial Studies, v 22, n 7.*

Becht, M., Franks, J., Mayer, C., & Rossi, S. (2009) Returns to shareholder activism: Evidence from a clinical study of the Hermes UK focus fund. *The Review of Financial Studies, Vol. 22, pp. 3093-3129.*

Black, B.S. (1998). Shareholder activism and corporate governance in the United States. *The New Palgrave Dictionary of Economics and the Law.*

Brav, A., Jiang, W., Partnoy, F., & Thomas, R, (2008). Hedge fund activism, corporate governance and, firm performance. *Journal of Finance,* 63, 1729-1773.

Brealey, R. A, Myers, S. C, & Allen, F. (2009). *Principles of corporate finance, Concise Edition.* New York*: McGraw-Hill/Irwin..*

Brooks, C. (2008). *Introductory econometrics for finance*, Second Edition. *Cambridge:* Cambridge University Press, (ISBN-13978-0-511-39848-3).

Choi, W. and Cho, S.H. (2003). Shareholder activism in Korea: An analysis of PSPD`s activities. *Pacific-Basin Finance Journal, 11, pp. 349-363.*

Chung, H. & Talaulicar, T. (2010). Forms and effects of shareholder activism. *Corporate Governance: An International Review, 18(4), 253-257.*

Davis, E.P. (2002). Institutional investors,corporate governance and the performance of the corporate sector. *Journal of Economic Systems, 26, 202-229.*

Eyenubo, A.S. (2013). The impact of a bigger board size on financial performance of firms: The Nigerian experience. *Journal of Research in International Business and Management, vol. 3(3), pp. 85-90.*

Gantchev, N. (2013). The costs of shareholder activism: Evidence from a sequential decision model. *Journal of Financial Economics, 107, pp. 610-631.*

Gillan, S.L. & Starks, L.T. (2000). Corporate governance proposal and shareholder activism; the role of institutional investors. *Journal of Financial Economics, 57, 275-305.*

Greenwood, R. & Schor, M. (2009). Investor activism and takeovers. *Journal of Financial Economics, 362- 375.*

Grossman, S.J. & Hart, O.D. (1982). Corporate financial structure and managerial incentives. *National Bureau of Economic Research, 107-140.*

He, E.& Sommer, D.W. (2006). Separation of ownership and control: Implications for board composition. *Journal of Management.*

Helwege, J., Intintoli, V., and Zhang A., (2012). Voting with their feet or activism? Institutional investors` impact on CEO turnover. *Journal of Corporate Finance, 18, 22-37.*

Hilary, G. & Oshika, T. (2003). Shareholder activism with weak corporate governance: Social presure, private cost and organized crime. *Electronic Journal of Contemporary Japanese Studies.*

Hill, C.W. & Jones, T.M. (1992). Stakeholder-agency theory. *Journal of Management Studies, 29:2.*

Jensen, M.C. & Meckling, W.H. (1976). Theory of the firm: Managerial behavior, agency costs and ownership structure. *Journal of Financial Economics, v. 3, n. 4, pp.305-360.*

Karpoff, J.M. (2001). The Impact of shareholder activism on target companies: A survey of empirical findings. *Journal of Financial Economics, 365-395.*

Kandel, E., Massa, M. & Simonov, A. (2011). Do small shareholders count? *Journal of Financial Economics*, 101, *pp. 641-665.*

Kyereboah-Coleman, A. (2007, November). Corporate governance and firm performance in Africa. *A paper presented at the International Conference on Corporate Governance in Emerging Markets.* Sabanci University, Istanbul, Turkey.

Lee, D.W. & Park, K.S. (2009). Does institutional activism increase shareholder wealth? Evidence from spillovers on non-target companies. *Journal of Corporate Finance, 15, 488-504.*

Lillihook, O. & Margolin, D. (2008). Shareholder activism: Can it be an effective governance mechanism? Stockholm School of Economics.

Lim, Y. (2011). Tax avoidance, cost of debt and shareholder activism: Evidence from Korea. *Journal of Banking and Finance, 35, 456-470.*

Manry, D. & Stangeland, D. (2003). The United Shareholders Association Shareholder *1000* and firm performance. *Journal of Corporate Finance, 9, 353-375.*

MacNeil, I. (2010). Activism and collaboration among shareholders in UK listed companies. *Capital Market Law Journal, vo. 5, NO. 4.*

O`Byrne, S.F. & Stern Steward & Co. (1996). EVA and market value. *Journal of Applied Corporate Finance, vol. 9, pp.116-125.*

Renneboog, L. & Szilagyi, P.G. (2011). The role of shareholder proposals in corporate governance. *Journal of Corporate Finance, 17, 167-188.*

Roman, R. A. (2013, August). Shareholder activism in banking. *Paper presented at the International Finance and Banking Society Conference.*

Shleifer, A. and Vishny R.W. (1997). A survey of corporate governance. *Journal of Finance, Vol. LII, NO. 2.*

Strickland, D., Wiles, K.W., Zenner, M. (1996). A requiem for the USA: Is small shareholder monitoring effective? *Journal of Financial Economics, 40, pp.319-338.*

Stern Stewart & Co. (2000). EVA andsStrategy. EVAluation. *Journal of Applied Corporate Finance.*

Tirore, J. (2005). The Theory of corporate governance. *Princeton University Press.*

Vijayakumar, A. (2011). Economic value added (EVA) and shareholder wealth creation: A factor analytic approach. *Research Journal of Finance and Accounting, vol.2, pp.22-37.*

West, J. (2005). EVA versus traditional accounting measures of performance as drivers of shareholder value- A comparative analysis. *Meditari Accountancy Research, Vol.13, 1-16.*

World Bank (2005). *Report on the observance of standards and codes (ROSC). Corporate Governance.* Ghana.

CHAPTER FOUR

Directors' Dealings and Operating Performances in Small Private Firms

Julius Aikins-Hawkson, Michael Graham and Alfred Yawson

1. Introduction

This chapter examines the relation between the use of the director's current account, as a means of owner-director remuneration, and the reported operating performance in small owner-managed firms. Closely-held small private (owner-managed) firms differ significantly from publicly listed-firms given the absence of separation of ownership from control noted in many large firms. Consequently the compensation incentive alignment and the competitive external labour market hypotheses, which feature prominently in remuneration-performance studies in large publicly listed-firms, are of little use to the decisions and incentives faced by the majority of closely-held small private firms. Indeed, evidence provided by Watson and Wilson (2005) for a sample of closely-held private U.K firms confirms that the two hypotheses are irrelevant, at least statistically, in determining board pay in owner-managed firms.

There is, at least, one convincing reason to further examine empirically the method of board remuneration practices in closely-held small private firms. Our motivation becomes clearer when we look beyond the principal-agent problem confronting the firm, and consider other stakeholder groups to be protected in the nexus of contracts that make up the firm. In the classic agency theory view, the principal and agent represent non-overlapping stakeholder groups, and the target groups to be protected are the shareholders. In this setting, conflicts mainly arise between professional managers and shareholders. Admittedly, this may also be the case in private firms with ownership concentrated in one or a few shareholders, where separation of ownership and control exists. In small owner-managed private firms, however, the owner and the manager usually represent an overlapping stakeholder group. In such firms the board may comprise the single owner-manager, the owner-director. A conflict between the owner-director and external stakeholders may, however, arise as the owner-director exhibits maximum opportunism to reduce obligations to external stakeholders, e.g., tax authorities.

The owner-director has complete discretion regarding how to allocate the firm's profit, e.g., between taking a market salary and making withdrawals of cash and goods, which are accounted for in the directors' current account. These cash flows, to the owner-directors, are substitutable in the sense that they accrue to the same individual. Still, the prospect of significant tax savings of one cash flow series, making withdrawals of cash and goods, relative to the other (taking a market salary) would suggest they are not perfect substitutes. The choice here, which is largely tax driven, may reflect the desire of the owner-director to attain and maintain an unobservable level of income stability or wealth to fund current and future consumption. This is supported by the tax morale literature which suggests that the self-employed have lower tax morale and the intrinsic motivation to pay taxes (see for instance Togler, 2004; Alm & Togler, 2006; and Priesto, Sanzo, & Suárez-Pandiello, 2006). Information asymmetry, a long-standing issue of concern for regulators and government agencies, suggests that corporate insiders have more information than outsiders, which enables the former group to benefit from the superior information set. This asymmetry raises the possibility that government agencies may not be able to price the firm's claims correctly. At the firm level, for example, an income-decreasing manipulation choice via directors' current account could be devised to reduce the firm's tax liability with lower reported earnings. Similarly the owner-directors may take advantage of the information asymmetry between the firm and external stakeholders to maximize their individual utility and reduce their tax liability. Utility maximization, in this context, refers to securing and maintaining an unobservable level of wealth. Along this line of reasoning, Watson and Wilson (2005) posit that owner-managers value inter-temporal stability in income to fund existing and anticipated consumption. Thus the owner-director's choice of compensation is likely to be influenced by factors related to the firm (e.g., profitability), as well as the institutional environment (e.g., tax rules).

In this paper we examine the use of directors' current account, a balance between a company and its directors in small owner-managed private firms, and reported operating performance. The director's current account is used to record directors' dealings in private firms. The Companies Act (2006) in the U.K mandates that if a debit balance stands on the director's account nine (9) months after the company accounting period, Corporation Tax Act 2010, s455 (formerly ICTA 1988, s419), a tax at the rate of 25% will be applied on the lower end of the amount outstanding at the year end and, 9 months after the year end. The firm is liable to pay this amount even if the company is making a loss, and there is no corporation tax due. Tax payable under section 455 is a temporary tax, and it is repayable to the company by HMRC nine months after the end of the accounting period in which the loan was repaid. Once the loan is repaid, the tax effect is nil. However, the time lag between the loan being repaid and tax being refunded can place a significant strain on the company's cash flow. This rule, however, does not apply uniformly across countries. For example, dissimilar to the U.K, a debit balance on a director's current account in Ghana does not attract automatic taxes, as there is no specific rule in the Companies Act of Ghana relating to taxation on the debit balance on the director's current account. This raises a strong possibility that owner-directors may exhibit self-serving opportunism to disadvantage the tax authority. For instance, an owner-director may withdraw monies from their company's account rather than take a market salary, which will attract a tax. Thus the mode of owner-director compensation may reflect the institutional environment.

Given this difference, the Ghanaian situation provides a representative test case on managerial opportunism in which the effect of directors' dealings in small owner-managed private firms on reported operating performance can be examined. The difference in the treatment of a debit balance on the director's current account between the U.K. and Ghana will also suggest that the Watson and Wilson (2005) sample cannot be used to investigate this unique type of owner-director opportunism. As noted by Watson (1991), decisions relating to directors' remuneration levels are impacted by the incidence of taxes, and *that close company directors' remuneration is likely to form part of a strategy designed to minimize their total tax liability* (p.86). Therefore taxable profits should be a significant explanatory variable with respect to remuneration levels. No empirical study, to our knowledge has examined this type of owner-director opportunism in small closely-held private firms. Additionally, we motivate this paper by noting evidence in the literature that suggests corporate financial choices are impacted by factors that relate to the characteristics of the firm, as well as to the institutional environment (see e.g., Guiso, Sapienza, & Zingales, 2004).

Using the hand collected data of small owner-managed private firms in Ghana during the period 2002 to 2009; we find that, indeed, directors' current account exerts significant and measurable influences on reported performance of small private firms. We find an inverse association between directors' current account and return on operating assets. Decomposing the operating performance into various components in the context of the Du Pont analysis, we find that a director's current account has a negative and significant impact on the operating profit margin, but shows no measurable effect on asset turnover. These results are robust to the inclusions of other variables known to influence performance (e.g., consultants, growth, liquidity, leverage and firm size). Our findings suggest that the owner-director attitude, possibly dictated by the characteristics of the firm, as well as to the institutional environment, can help explain reported profits in small private firms (Uhlaner, Floren & Geerlings, 2007). Our findings contribute to the empirical literature investigating the determinants of remuneration practices in small and closely held firms.

The rest of the paper is organized as follows. Section 2 presents the theory and hypothesis. Section 3 presents the data and sample construction. Section 4 presents the empirical results. Section 5 concludes the paper.

2. Hypothesis Development

A closely-held firm, in legal terms, is an incorporated business which is owned and controlled by less than six members and *close associates* (see Watson, 1991; and Watson & Wilson, 2005 for a more detailed discussion). By definition, there is a lack of separation of ownership from control in such firms; the owner and the manager represent an overlapping group and ownership and control are fused. In these firms the board may also consist of the single owner-manager. All the firm's cash flows accrue to the same individual, the owner-director, and agency problems as well as asymmetric information issues will not be relevant in the determination of pay. Owner-directors' pay can, however, still be assumed to be related to firm profits and they have complete discretion regarding how to allocate the firm's profit. We relate owner-director's pay at time *t*, D_t^*, to profits, P_t, by a fixed minimum level of pay, f_t, and a payout ratio, *r*, and present it as follows:

$$D_t^* = f_t + r(P_t). \qquad (1)$$

In this model, *r* forms the function of a number of factors including the number of directors and their marginal tax rates and reflects director(s)' current and anticipated minimum consumption requirements. The fixed minimum director pay level is unique to individual circumstances and consumption needs and vary across firms.

The model presented in equation (1), suggesting a positive relation between owner-directors remuneration and firm profitability, does not rely on the incentive alignment motivation proposed by the agency theory, because there is no obvious need to align the owner-director's pay with firm performance to mitigate agency problems. Rather it depends on an expected pay-out from the firm which aims at maintaining an unobservable level of wealth. Owner-directors have control rights over the cash flows of the firms and can decide to minimize this expected pay-out ratio, if it is reported as taxable income. Business owners represent their own interests and can use their control rights to maximize their personal welfare (Shleifer & Vishny, 1997; Fama & Jensen, 1983). In small owner-managed private firms these rights are largely restricted to the owner-director, which generally reduces the need to be opportunistic in the agency theory framework. However, owner-directors in small private firms can still exhibit self-serving opportunism to disadvantage external stakeholders. For instance, they can either forgo taking periodic salaries or take a lower salary and avoid paying the appropriate personal income tax. This opportunistic behaviour implies a non-declaration of income, thereby evading a level of personal income tax liability. Instead the owner-directors make withdrawals to maintain their inter-temporal stability in income to fund existing and anticipated consumption. We formally present this tax avoidance scheme via the use of the director's current account, basing our argument on tenets of the Hindriks & Gareth (2006) model of compliance.

The representative owner-director income level, D^*, is known to them as recipients, but unknown to the tax agency. In this model, the declared income, X, is assumed to be taxed at a constant rate t. The value of unreported income, D^*-X, is greater than or equal to 0 and the unpaid tax is $t[D^* - X]$. Under-declaration of income here may amount to making withdrawals of cash and goods from the firm instead of taking a market level salary. If owner-directors under-declare income without detection, their income level is given by $D^{*nc} = D^{*}. - tX$. If detected, a fine F is levied on the tax avoided, which gives an income level of $D^{*c} = [1-t]D^{*} - Ft[D^{*} - X]$.

Let the owner-director derive utility $U(D^{*})$ from the income D^{*}. After an income declaration of X is made, the income level D^{*c} occurs with probability p and the income level D^{*nc} with probability $1\text{-}p$. The representative owner-director, given such uncertainty, would choose the income declaration to maximize expected utility. When these facts are combined, the declaration X solves equation (2).

$$\max_{\{X\}} E[U(X)] = [1-p]\,U(D^{*nc}) + \ pU(D^{*c}). \tag{2}$$

The owner-director pay presented in equation (1) implicitly represents utility derived from declared income by the owner-director. Thus we can substitute equation (1) into the right-hand side of equation (2).

$$D^{*} \ = \ \max_{\{X\}} E[U(X)] = [1-p]U(D^{*nc}) + \ pU(D^{*c}) \tag{3}$$

From a theoretical viewpoint, an increase in the firm's profit before tax can equal the expected income of the owner-director in the extreme case, where the owner-director takes the entire firm's profit through the directors' current account. Practically, profit before tax may diverge from the owner-director's income as some income will have to be declared. Thus the firm may still report some income whilst the owner-director, at the same time, under-declares income to maintain an unobservable level of wealth. That decision can be said to depend on the degree of risk aversion of the utility function. Evidence in the literature suggests that the degree of absolute risk aversion decreases as income increases. We infer from this to suggest that the level of under-declared income increases as actual firm income rises.

Consequently, with decreasing absolute risk aversion, an increase in the owner director's income increases tax avoidance. In this case, the under reporting of the firm's operating income becomes a symptom of increasing the director's current account abuse. The central hypothesis of this paper is that there is an inverse relation between the use of director current account and the reported operating performance.

3. Data and Sample Construction

3.1. Data sources

Access to information is generally limited in the case of non-listed private firms. Consequently, we manually collected data from financial statements of Private Limited Companies, sourced directly from the annual reports filed with the Ghana Revenue Authority. Each registered private company is required under the tax law to file an audited financial statement with the Ghana Revenue Authority. This approach mitigates contaminations that financial statements of private firms might contain if they are sourced directly from them. We requested all financial statement of small firms, and those that are controlled by less than six members and *close associates* (see Watson, 1991), between 2002 and 2009. Following Streel and Webster (1990) and Osei, Baah-Nuakoh, Tutu, & Sowa (1993), small firms, as used in this paper, refer to firms with less than thirty employees. The authority was not forthcoming with the request, so it provided a sample of 45 selected private companies drawn from different industries in Ghana. The drawback here is that one cannot be entirely certain that the samples selected are truly random.

The private firms in our sample are a heterogeneous group. Table 1 present the industry and annual distribution of the sample. There are 219 firms per year observations distributed across 13 industries. By calculation / estimation (construction) there should be 405 firms per year observations for the empirical work undertaken. We are, however, unable to create a balanced panel, because financial statements could not be located for each firm in each of the 9 years in our sample period. The manufacturing and merchandizing sectors constitute the largest blocks in our sample, and represent 36.07% and 14.61%, respectively. This is followed by provision of services, constructions and entertainment, comprising 10.05%, 6.85% and 5.02%, respectively. The remaining 21% are distributed across 6 other industries. The sample size increases monotonically from 2002 (7.8%) to 16.9% in 2008, followed by a drop to 9.6% in 2009.

	Industry distribution		Annual distribution as a percentage of industry sample							
Industry name	Sample	% of sample	2002	2003	2004	2005	2006	2007	2008	2009
Construction	15	6.85%	6.7%	6.7%	13.3%	20.0%	13.3%	20.0%	20.0%	0.0%
Education	4	1.83%	0.0%	0.0%	0.0%	0.0%	25.0%	25.0%	25.0%	25.0%
Entertainment	11	5.02%	9.1%	9.1%	9.1%	9.1%	18.2%	18.2%	18.2%	9.1%
Farming	8	3.65%	0.0%	0.0%	12.5%	12.5%	25.0%	25.0%	12.5%	12.5%
Financials	8	3.65%	0.0%	0.0%	0.0%	0.0%	25.0%	25.0%	25.0%	25.0%
Information technology	8	3.65%	25.0%	12.5%	12.5%	0.0%	12.5%	12.5%	12.5%	12.5%
Manufacturing	79	36.07%	13.9%	13.9%	16.5%	20.3%	10.1%	10.1%	10.1%	5.1%
Merchandizing	32	14.61%	3.1%	6.3%	6.3%	15.6%	18.8%	18.8%	21.9%	9.4%
Oil and gas	9	4.11%	0.0%	0.0%	11.1%	11.1%	22.2%	22.2%	22.2%	11.1%
Printing	7	3.20%	0.0%	0.0%	0.0%	0.0%	28.6%	28.6%	28.6%	14.3%
Provision of services	22	10.05%	4.5%	13.6%	13.6%	18.2%	13.6%	13.6%	13.6%	9.1%
Real Estate	2	0.91%	0.0%	0.0%	0.0%	0.0%	0.0%	0.0%	50.0%	50.0%
Transport Services	14	6.39%	0.0%	0.0%	0.0%	7.1%	21.4%	21.4%	28.6%	21.4%
Total	219	100.00%	7.8%	8.7%	11.0%	14.6%	15.5%	16.0%	16.9%	9.6%

3.2. Variable selection

3.2.1. Dependent variables

We use profitability at the firm level as a dependent variable in this study. We assess the impact of directors' current account on return on net operating assets (ROA). ROA measures the ability to use the assets of a company to generate profits, and we define it as the net operating profit after tax scaled by the average of beginning and end of period net operating assets.

In the spirit of the Du Pont analysis, return on assets (ROA) can be decomposed into operating profit margin, operating assets turnover, and operating liabilities leverage. Operating profit margin is defined as net operating profit after tax scaled by total sales. Operating asset turnover, defined as total sales scaled by average operating assets at the beginning and end of the period in question, measures the firm's effectiveness in generating sales from its operating assets. How well these two aspects of operations are managed determines firm profitability. The operating liabilities' leverage ratio is defined as the operating leverage scaled by net operating assets, and the higher this ratio, the higher the return on net operating assets. The interaction of these three terms determines the return on net operating assets.

3.2.2 Independent variables

The key independent variable in this study is the director's current account which is used to record all transactions between the directors and the firm. Amounts due to the director are recorded as credit, while amounts owed by the director are recorded as debit. For example, loans given to the firm by directors are recorded as credit and considered additional investment by directors. On the other hand, directors may take loans from the business, which makes them creditors to their own firms. Furthermore, when directors withdraw goods from the business they become debtors to the firms, and these are recorded as debit and these add to the amount owed by the directors' to the firm. In addition, any 'private' payments made by the company to the director's family, friends, business partners or any person associated with the director are recorded in the directors' current account.

In this paper, we define a director's current account as the balance on the director current account scaled by total assets, and this constitutes the key independent variable tested in this study. As indicated above, there is a difference between the tax implications of this balance in the U.K. relative to Ghana. In the U.K, the tax code provides for a tax charge at the rate of 25% on the lower end of the amount outstanding at the year end, and nine months after the year end. Effectively, directors' current account in this regime should not create any conflicts between the directors and external stakeholders. The treatment of Directors Current Account by Tax authorities in Ghana is different from that of the UK. In Ghana, a debit balance on directors' account does not attract automatic taxes, as there is no specific rule relating to taxation on the debit balance on directors' current account. However, the Commissioner has authority to disregard or reverse any transaction that is geared towards tax avoidance. The Tax Commissioner does that by adding back such amounts to the declared profit. The reason being that had the money, or goods and services, not been loaned or withdrawn from company to the director, the company could have used it to generate profits, which could have become taxable. The commissioner is likely to add back such amounts to the profits declared, and taxed it with the added imposition of a fine for tax avoidance.

Prior studies show that board size is important in corporate decision making (John & Senbet, 1998; Kiel & Nicholson, 2003). In closely-held private firms, board size is usually small, as it is often made up of the owners. It is however important to determine whether board size has any impact on the operating performance of small firms. Prior studies argue that a large number of directors will subject the management and operations of the firm to a greater scrutiny and provide access to a wider range of resources (Kiel & Nicholson, 2003). It is not readily discernible if this argument holds for private firms. We use the number of directors in the private firm as a proxy for board size. Prior evidence shows that directors' compensation is typically linked to firm size (Dial & Murphy, 1995). In small firms it may be a bit of stretch to relate firm size to remuneration. The recent focus is on offering directors attractive compensations linked to firm performance (Bender, 2003; Thompson, 2005). Linking directors' compensation to firm performance appears realistic, because directors are ultimately responsible for corporate performance (Buchholtz, Lubakin, & O'neil, 1999; Eriksson & Lausten, 2000). Empirical research documents a positive association between executive compensation and firm performance (Eriksson & Lausten, 2000). It is, however, unclear whether attractive compensations can motivate directors in private firms to discharge their duties effectively. We measure director compensation as total director's remuneration scaled by total assets.

Small businesses rely on consulting firms for a number of services. For instance, many small businesses cannot afford to fund their own IT or HR departments, and these are contracted out to consulting firms. Consultants can also provide financial advice that will help the firm to develop a business plan, and get funding from a bank or other investor sources (Hustedde & Pulver, 1992). Small firms also rely on consultants for cost cutting and growth strategies. The use of consultants in private firms is consistent with Van Gils (2005) who shows that owner managers rely on other executives to augment their human capital in running the business. We use a dummy variable set equal to 1 if the firm engaged a consultant in the previous year, and zero otherwise. We also use control for growth, defined as annual change in sales; liquidity defined as current assets scaled by current liabilities; leverage defined as total debt scaled by total assets; and firm size measured as the log of total assets. These variables are included in the models as additional factors that can affect performance of small private firms.

3.2.3. Descriptive statistics and correlations

Table 2 reports the descriptive statistics for both the dependent and the independent variables. The mean and median returns on net operating assets are 0.007 and 0.018, respectively with a standard deviation of 0.276. The mean and median values for operating a profit margin are 0.28 and 0.239, respectively, with a standard deviation of 0.379. The mean (median) net operating asset turnover and operating liabilities leverage are 6.013 (2.812) and 2.252 (1.375) respectively. The standard deviations for these two asset turnovers and operating liabilities leverages are 12.755 and 3.499, respectively. The standard deviations in the performance measures show a clear variation in the distribution of these metrics across the firms in the sample. The mean values for consulting fee, directors remuneration and directors current account are 0.005, 0.007 and 0.154, respectively with standard deviations of 0.002, 0.029 and 0.358. The sample firms experience average (median) negative growth of -0.137 (-0.160) with a standard deviation of 0.435. The sample firms have mean (median) liquidity of 6.151 (1.198) with a standard deviation of 25.592. Even though the sample firms are well resourced, as indicated by high levels of liquidity, they also have high leverage. Indeed, the average (median) leverage is 0.749 (0.603) with a standard deviation of 0.947. The mean (median) size of these firms, measured as the log of total assets, is 12.491 (12.931) with a standard deviation of 2.77.

Table 4.2: Descriptive statistics

	Mean	Median	Standard deviation
Dependent variables			
Return on net operating assets	0.007	0.018	0.276
Operating profit margin	0.280	0.239	0.379
Net operating assets turnover	6.013	2.812	12.755
Operating liabilities leverage	2.252	1.375	3.490
Independent variables			
Directors remuneration	0.007	0.000	0.029
Directors current account	0.154	0.000	0.358
# of directors	2.908	2.000	1.303
Consulting fees	0.005	0.000	0.002
Growth	-0.137	-0.160	0.435
Liquidity	6.151	1.198	25.592
Leverage	0.749	0.603	0.947
Size (GHS'000)	3,954,241	412,838	10,646,773

The correlation coefficients are reported in Table 3, and, clearly, none of the magnitudes of the correlations is so large as to create multicollinearity problems. The largest correlations are 0.40, which is between size and number of directors, and 0.361 between firm size and the use of consultants.

Table 4.3: Correlations

		A	B	C	D	E	F	G	H
Director current account	A	1.000							
Director remuneration	B	-0.083	1.000						
# of directors	C	-0.319	0.001	1.000					
Consultants	D	-0.165	-0.058	0.175	1.000				
Growth	E	0.021	-0.116	0.070	0.063	1.000			
Liquidity	F	-0.001	0.197	-0.143	-0.096	-0.037	1.000		
Leverage	G	-0.259	-0.121	0.179	0.098	0.012	-0.068	1.000	
Size	H	-0.227	-0.196	0.400	0.361	0.054	-0.201	-0.006	1.000

4. Empirical Results

We examine the relation between director current account and operating performance in private firms by estimating the OLS model specified in equation (3):

$$Operating\ performance_{i,t} = \beta_0 + \beta_1(Directors\ current\ account)_{i,t-1} + \sum_{f=1}^{5} \beta_{3f} Control_{i,t} + \sum_{j=1}^{12} \beta_{4j}\ Industy_j + \sum_{y=2002}^{2009} \beta_{5y} Year_t + \varepsilon_{i,t}, \quad (3)$$

where the dependent variables are return on net operating assets, operating profit margin, operating assets turnover and operating liabilities leverage. In all the models we include industry dummies and yearly fixed effect to take account of annual and industry impact in operating performance. The standard errors are adjusted for heteroskedasticity and firm clustering to account for data dependence and any possible correlation in residual terms.

The results are presented in Table 4.4. Model (1) of Table 4.4 reports the regression estimates without other director characteristics. The results show a significant negative and statistically significant association between director current account (coefficient = -.0165, p-value = 0.029) and return on net operating profit. This basic model supports our hypothesis of a negative relation between director current account abuse and reported firm profitability. We argue that this negative relation is a symptom of increasing director current account and declining operating income. None of the control variables is significant with the exception of liquidity which is positive (coefficient = 0.001), and significant at the 10 percent level. In Model (2), we include director remuneration and board size as additional control variables. Director current account still retains its negative and significant impact on return on operating assets. The use of consultants has a negative impact, but it is statistically insignificant in the two estimated models.

Table 4.4: Return on net operating assets

	Model (1)	Model (2)
Director current account	-0.165**	-0.227**
	(0.029)	(0.031)
Director remuneration		0.320
		(0.542)
Number of directors		0.038
		(0.508)
Use of consultant	-0.003	-0.016
	(0.925)	(0.676)
Growth	-0.060	-0.035
	(0.201)	(0.511)
Liquidity	0.001*	0.001**
	(0.063)	(0.044)
Leverage	-0.029	-0.011
	(0.305)	(0.723)
Size	-0.008	-0.003
	(0.391)	(0.850)
Constant	0.204	0.127
	(0.105)	(0.658)
Industry dummy	Yes	Yes

Year dummy	Yes	Yes
R-squared	0.18	0.25
F-statistic	2.35***	2.45***
Observations	160	103

In Table 4.5, we examine the impact of directors' current account on the operating profit margin. In Model (1), we report a negative and statistically significant association between directors' current account and operating profit margin (coefficient of -.314 at the 5% significance level). In this model, the use of consultant has a significant negative impact on the profit margin whilst liquidity is still positively associated with profit margin. In Model (2), both director current account and use of consultants maintain the significant negative impact on the operating profit margin. Additionally, director remuneration is negative (coefficient = -3.116) and statistically significant at the 1 percent level ($p < 0.005$). These two findings indicate that firms with directors who withdraw resources from their firms in the form of loans and goods actually report poor performance, using operating profit margin as a measure of performance. In Model (2), we find a positive and significant association between board size and operating profit margin (coefficient = 0.218), statistically significant at the 5% level ($p <0.043$). In the estimated models, we also find a negative and significant relation between the use of consultants and operating profit margin. This finding is inconsistent with prior evidence that owner-directors in small business rely on the human capital of other executive team-members for business operations (Van Gils, 2005). Again, liquidity and firm size has a negative impact on operating profit margin.

Table 4.5: Operating profit margin

	Model (1)	Model (2)
Director current account	-0.314**	-0.444***
	(0.043)	(0.006)
Director remuneration		-3.116***
		(0.005)
Number of directors		0.218**
		(0.030)
Use of consultant	-0.242***	-0.210**
	(0.001)	(0.011)
Growth	0.032	-0.035
	(0.637)	(0.708)
Liquidity	-0.002***	-0.001***
	(0.004)	(0.006)
Leverage	-0.022	-0.039
	(0.435)	(0.148)
Size	-0.022	-0.060***
	(0.169)	(0.002)
Constant	0.617***	1.026**
	(0.001)	(0.024)
Industry dummy	Yes	Yes
Year dummy	Yes	Yes
R-squared	0.16	0.46
F-statistic	2.84***	2.72***
Observations	158	103

In Table 4.6, we examine the relation between director current account and operating asset turnover, the second component of return on operating assets. We perform this analysis because it is the interaction of asset turnover and profit margin that determines return on assets. The results presented in Model (1) and (2) of Table 4.6 are very different from those obtained in Tables 4.4 and 4.5. Director current account still maintains a negative coefficient, but it is statistically insignificant in both models. In Model (2) board size does not affect asset turnover as its coefficient is statistically insignificant. We find, however, that directors' remuneration is significant and positively related to asset turnover at the 1 percent level. Furthermore, the use of consultants is positive and statistically significant in both Models (1) and (2).

Table 4.6: Operating asset turnover

	Model (1)	Model (2)
Director current account	-2.403	-0.899
	(0.221)	(0.734)
Director remuneration		208.230***
		(0.000)
Number of directors		-6.963
		(0.226)
Use of consultant	8.471*	9.613**
	(0.061)	(0.047)
Growth	-2.318	-1.275
	(0.238)	(0.710)
Liquidity	-0.006	-0.022
	(0.773)	(0.279)
Leverage	-1.713*	0.418
	(0.083)	(0.732)
Size	-0.127	1.530
	(0.835)	(0.250)
Constant	15.628*	-12.660
	(0.084)	(0.444)
Industry dummy	Yes	Yes
Year dummy	Yes	Yes
R-squared	0.15	0.46
F-statistic	7.38***	8.34***
Observations	125	68

As return on operating assets are also affected by the amount of operating liabilities employed in the firm, we examine the effect of director current account on this component and report the results in Table 4.7. As long as operating liabilities do not hurt the reputation of the private firm, the more it is used, the better it is for the firm in terms of profitability. We find that director current account is insignificant in determining the amount of operating liabilities used in the firm. The reported results suggest that director remuneration has no measurable effect on operating liabilities. The number of directors has a negative (coefficient = -3.452) and significant impact ($p<0.054$) on operating liabilities leverage. However, the use of consultant has a significant positive impact on the use of operating liabilities in both Models (1) and (2). In all the estimated models, we also find a positive association between firm size and the use of operating liabilities leverage. Large private firms are able to use their size advantage to negotiate the payment period with suppliers, to take advantage of the credit offered in the normal course of business.

Table 4.7: Operating liabilities leverage

	Model (1)	Model (2)
Director current account	-0.438	-0.789
	(0.240)	(0.415)
Director remuneration		5.612
		(0.433)
Number of directors		-3.452*
		(0.054)
Use of consultant	2.973*	3.181*
	(0.069)	(0.099)
Growth	0.269	0.838
	(0.608)	(0.423)
Liquidity	-0.002	-0.003
	(0.625)	(0.530)
Size	0.350***	0.818**
	(0.007)	(0.014)
Constant	-0.353	-6.699
	(0.819)	(0.118)
Industry dummy	Yes	Yes

Year dummy	Yes	Yes
R-squared	0.23	0.30
F-statistic	2.37***	1.97**
Observations	124	67

5. Conclusion

In this chapter, we investigate the relation between the uses of directors' current accounts and reported operating performance in small owner-managed firms. Based on the literature, we hypothesize that the owner-directors exhibit maximum opportunism to reduce obligations to the tax authorities, through their use of the director's current account. The owner-director in Ghana may exhibit self-serving opportunism by, for instance, substituting cash withdrawal from the company for market level salary to disadvantage the tax authority, which has implications for reported firm performance. The Ghanaian case, therefore, offers a rich test case in which the effect of directors' dealings in private firms can be examined. We draw on the economic model of compliance which suggests that with decreasing absolute risk aversion, an increase in income increases tax avoidance. Given that the propensity to abuse the director current account increases as firm income rises, we posit a negative relationship between director current account and reported firm performance in small private firms.

Using a random sample of hand collected data on private limited companies in Ghana over the period 2002 to 2009; we find that the use of directors' current account has a negative influence on return on operating assets and operating profit margin. We explain the motive for the use of directors' account by directors of private limited companies to appropriate income to themselves to avoid paying taxes on them. We can therefore conclude that the effect of the abuse of director's account has an impact on the performance of small private companies in Ghana.

The findings have important implications for public policy regarding small firms. Small and medium sized enterprises are an important source of economic growth, and are credited with an essential role in employment creation in many economies. Thus they are put at the forefront of business policy making. The possibility of manipulating the financial performance variables of these enterprises would suggest that policy makers have to look at other benchmarks in a sustained attempt to assist these firms. The results of the study also have implication for the ongoing reforms at the newly constituted Ghana Revenue Authority. The Ghana Revenue Authority (GRA) was established by ACT 791, 2009 as an integrated Authority bringing together VAT (Value Added Tax) Service, Customs, Excise and Preventive Service (CEPS) and Internal Revenue Service (IRS) of Ghana. The Authority is undergoing reforms to make the integration meaningful and to increase revenue mobilization for Ghana. The findings in this paper will potentially motivate the GRA to adopt the UK system where the debit balance on the directors' current account of private limited companies attracts taxes.

References

Alm, J., & Torgler, B. (2006). Culture differences and tax morale in the United States and in Europe. *Journal of Economic Psychology,* 27, 224–246.

Brick, I. E., Palmon, O., & Wald, J. K. (2006). CEO compensation, director compensation, and firm performance: Evidence of cronyism? *Journal of Corporate Finance,* 12, 403-23.

Dong, M., & Ozkan, A. (2008). Institutional investors and pay: An empirical study of UK companies. *Journal of Multinational Financial Management,* 18, 16-29.

Doucouliagos, H., Haman, J. & Askary, S. (2007). Directors' remuneration and performance in Australian banking. *Corporate Governance, an International Review* 15, 1363-1383.

Duffhues, P. & Kabir, R. (2008). Is the pay-performance relationship always positive? Evidence from The Netherlands. *Journal of Multinational Financial Management* 18, 45-60.

Fama, E. F. & Jensen, M. (1983). Agency problems and residual claims. *Journal of Law and Economics,* 26, 327-349.Guiso, L., Sapienza, P. & Zingales, L. (2004). The Role of Social Capital in Financial Development," *American Economic Review,* 94, 526–556.

Hindriks, J., & Gareth D.M. (2006). *International public economics.* Place: The MIT Press.

Hustedde, R. J. & Pulver, G. C. (1992). Factors affecting equity capital acquisition: The demand side, *Journal of Business_Venturing,* 7, 363-374.

Jensen, M. (1993). The modern industrial revolution, exit, and the failure of internal control systems, *Journal of Finance,* 48, 831-880.

Jensen, M.C., & Meckling, W.H. (1976). Theory of the firm: managerial behavior, agency costs and ownership structure. *Journal of Financial Economics,* 3, 305-360

La Rocca, M., La Rocca, T., & Cariola, A. (2010). The influence of local institutional differences on the capital structure of SMEs: Evidence from Italy. *International Small Business Journal* 28, 234-257.

Main, B.G., Bruce A. & Buck, T. (1996). Total board remuneration and company performance. *The Economic Journal,* 106, 1627-1644.

Osei B, Baah-Nuakoh A, Tutu K.A, & Sowa N.K. (1993). Impact of structural adjustment on small-scale enterprises in Ghana', in Helmsing A.H.J and Kolstee T. H(eds), *Structural adjustment, financial policy and assistance programmes in Africa,* IT Publications. 51-70.

Pollard, J., (2003). Small firm finance and economic geography. *Journal of Economic Geography,* 3, 429-452.

Prieto, J., Sanzo, M.J., & Suárez-Pandiello, J., (2006). Análisis económico de la actitud hacia el fraude fiscal en España. Hacienda Pública Española, 177, 107–128.

Shleifer, A. & Vishny R.W.,(1997). A survey of corporate governance. *Journal of Finance,* 52, 737-783.

Stathopoulos, K., Espenlaub, S. & Walker, M. (2004). UK executive compensation practices: New economy versus old economy, *Journal of Management Accounting Research,* 16, 57–92.

Steel, W.F & Webster, L.(1990). Ghana's small enterprise sector: `Survey of adjustment response & constraints', Industry Series Paper 41, World Bank, Industry and Energy Department, Washington D.C

Torgler, B., (2004). Tax morale in Asian countries. *Journal of Asian Economics,* 15, 237–266.

Van Gils, A. (2005). Management and governance in Dutch SMEs. *European Management Journal,* 23, 583–589

Wan, T.W., Ong, C. H & Tung, P. K. (2000). Directors remuneration and profitability performance of listed companies in Singapore: A correlation and causality study. *Accounting Research Journal,* 13, 37-46.

Watson, R. (1991). Modelling directors' remuneration decisions in small and closely held UK Companies. *Journal of Business Financed Accounting,* 18, 85-98.

Watts, R.L.,& Zimmerman, J.L. (1978). Towards a positive theory of the determination of accounting standards, *The Accounting Review,* 53, 112-134.

Wirtz, P. (2011). The cognitive dimension of corporate governance in fast growing entrepreneurial firms. *European Management Journal,* 29, 431–447.

CHAPTER FIVE

Does Financial Inclusion Spur Financial Development in Africa?

Joseph Abor, Kofi A. Osei and Lord Mensah

1. Introduction

Financial inclusion is defined as the 'mechanism where households and businesses have access and can effectively use appropriate financial services. Such services, according to the Consultative Group to Assist the Poor (CGAP), must be provided responsibly and sustainably, in a well-regulated environment' (www.cgap.org/topics/financial-inclusion).

Financial development, on the other hand, is defined as the factors, policies and institutions that lead to effective financial intermediation and markets, as well as deep and broad access to capital and financial services (World Financial Development Report, 2012). The literature posits such financial services to include among others: bank deposits, all kinds of commercial loans, access to credit, a cheque facility, credit & debit cards, mortgages, insurance, transfers, pensions and investment schemes, payment and remittance services, and financial advice and consumer protection mechanism. Sarma and Pais (2008) noted that the financial inclusion objective is desirable for many reasons. First, it facilitates the allocation of productive resources; second, access to appropriate financial services can significantly improve the day-to-day management of finances; and third, an all-inclusive growth can help reduce the growth of informal sources of credit, which often tend to be exploitative.

It has been widely documented that developed economies have achieved an appreciable level of success in financial inclusion due to some active programmes implemented to advance its course. Some of these programmes include, but are not limited to: The Financial Inclusion Task Force (FITF) in the United Kingdom. This task force was constituted by the UK government in 2005 to monitor the development of financial inclusion; Community Reinvestment Act in the United States which required banks to offer credit throughout their area of operation and prohibited them from targeting only the rich neighborhood; The German Bankers Association voluntary code (1996) that promoted the 'Everyman current banking account' to facilitate basic banking transactions for its people.

The significance of financial inclusion is yet to gain scholarly attention in Africa. Until now, little has been known about the extent of financial inclusion levels in Africa, and the degree to which the disadvantaged groups, such as the poor, women, youth and the marginalized, are excluded from the formal financial system. Recently, a number of active works have progressed to help understand the level of financial inclusion in Africa. The FinScope survey by FinMark Trust indicates that most African economies record very low levels of financial inclusion. The Global Findex by Demirguç-Kunt and Klapper, (2012) shows that less than a quarter of adults in Africa have an account with a formal financial institution, whilst many adults in Africa still use informal methods to save and borrow. Further evidence shows that firms in Africa and other developing economies are less likely to have proper access to bank credit regardless of their size. This notwithstanding, the role technological advances, such as mobile money, innovation, and the creation of new delivery channels including 'mobile branches' or banking services, through third-party agents, have started to contribute in the financial access in Africa. An important observation was that, in 2011, mobile money achieved the broadest success in the whole of Africa, where approximately 14% of adults reported having used mobile money (Demirguc-Kunt & Klapper, 2012). In sum, the extent of financial inclusion in 2011, as revealed by the Global Findex, is that only 23% of adults in Africa have an account at a formal financial institution, implying that 77% are financially excluded. There is, however, a large variation into account ownership, which ranges from 42% in Southern Africa to 7% in Central Africa. In the Democratic Republic of Congo and the Central African Republic, more than 93% of adults are unbanked.

Knowing the low levels of financial inclusion in Africa and other developing economies, international bodies such as the Centre for Financial Inclusion (CFI), Alliance for Financial Inclusion (AFI) and the Global Partnership for Financial Inclusion (GPFI) have been tasked with the primary objective to advance financial inclusion for the world's poor. Specifically, the International Monetary Fund (IMF), the International Finance Corporation (IFC), the AFI and CGAP have been leading discussions on financial inclusion for households and SMEs in Africa. With more efforts to deepen financial inclusion, individual countries have pursued strategies to help promote an all-inclusive financial system to some extent. For example, in South Africa, a low cost bank account called 'Mzanzi' was launched in 2004 by the South African Banking Association to enable financially excluded people to have easy access in opening bank account. Reports indicate that this has been very beneficial for the South African economy. In Ghana, United Bank for Africa introduced the cashless account when they gained entry into the Ghanaian banking industry in 2002. UT Bank, Ghana introduced 'bank on wheels' in 2013 to enable banking services to be extended to the majority. Fidelity Bank introduced the opening of SMART account in 2014 to help get an account for individuals who do not meet the detailed requirements for having formal bank accounts.

Unlike the developed world, where financial inclusion has been assessed to trigger financial growth, little is known about Africa, where barriers exist for achieving an appreciable level of financial inclusion. This paper investigates whether financial inclusion necessarily spurs financial growth in Africa. In sum, we assess whether countries with a high financial inclusion success rate have developed financially, with focus on the banking sector. Subsequent sections are organized as follows: In Section 2, we review the literature. Section 3 discusses the source of the data and the methodology. In Section 4, we discuss the results and finally Section 5 provides the conclusion and the recommendation.

2. Literature Review

Midgley (2005) discusses financial inclusion from the perspective of universal banking and post offices in Britain. The study examines the policy background which led to the introduction of these services and the institutional role of the post office in Britain. The paper notes that universal banking was launched in UK in 2003, with three strategic objectives: modernize welfare payments, increase financial inclusion and provide a means of generating replacement business for the post office networks. Dev (2006) advances a paper that focusses on the issues and challenges of financial inclusion, and observes that although financial inclusion is important for improving the living conditions of those who cannot access the formal financial system, there are several factors that constrain the less privileged from using the mainstream financial system. He, however, advises banks to look at financial inclusion both as a business opportunity and as a social responsibility. Mor and Ananth (2007) in their case studies indicate that inclusive financial systems significantly raise economic growth, alleviate poverty, and expand economic activity. However, in their view, the provision of a financial inclusion service requires adherence to certain core design principles, irrespective of whether the provider is a bank or non-bank finance company. Subbarao (2009) also discusses financial inclusion challenges and opportunities. He asserts that financial inclusion is all about giving people the opportunity to build better lives for themselves and their children. That impulse, if given a chance, could contribute to sustained improvement in the quality of life at the community level and foster growth and poverty reduction at the national level. He further argues that financial inclusion is a win-win opportunity for the poor, for the bank and for the nation.

Chibba (2009) investigates the link between financial inclusion, poverty reduction and the millennium development goals (FI-PR-MDG nexus). He notes financial inclusion to offer incremental and complementary solutions to tackle poverty and inequality, to promote inclusive development and to address the MDGs. Sarma and Pais (2011) expand on the above study by examining the relationship between financial inclusion and human development. They identify country-specific factors that are associated with the level of financial inclusion. Specifically, they find GDP per capita to have positive association with financial inclusion; Income inequality to be negatively related to financial inclusion; Adult literacy is positively associated with financial inclusion; and Physical infrastructure, like a network of paved roads as highly positively significant in enhancing financial inclusion.

In the Ghanaian setting, Osei-Assibey (2011) explores the relationship between financial inclusion and poverty, by examining socio-economic factors underlying financial exclusion in Ghana. He found out that strong perception of access to finance difficulties, negative cultural or religious bias on credit use, and financial illiteracy are very important factors underlying voluntary self-exclusion.

On the India market, Bihari (2011) examines financial inclusion as an essential pre-condition to building a uniform economic development, both spatially and temporary, and to usher in greater economic and social equity. He intimates that access to financial services has a number of benefits to the individual, the community, and the country as a whole. Further, Lokhande (2011) conducts a study to highlight financial inclusion as an option for micro, small, and medium enterprises (MSMEs) in India. In line with Bradford (1993), some of the common challenges observed for the micro enterprises include undercapitalization, low ability to command loan finance due to insufficient collateral, lack of a track record or financial expertise, lack of broad based management skills, inadequate understanding of cash flow management, heavy dependence on the local market and limited number of customers, delay in receivables, obsolete technology and the high cost of loans. Ghosh (2012) investigates the factors that influence banking outreach (more or less financial inclusion). He uses time-series data on Indian states, covering the period 1973 to 2004. His analysis indicates a divergence across states in terms of the outreach of formal finance over timeand ceteris paribus. Further in India, Kumar

(2013) examines the status of financial inclusion and its determinants and finds that the supply side of inclusive efforts by branch network has an unambiguous beneficial impact on financial inclusion.

On financial development, Rewilak (2012) examines whether or not the incomes of the poor systematically grow with average incomes, and whether or not financial development enhances the incomes of the poorest quintile. His study uses a panel data that spans across observations from 1956 to 2008 and adopts the generalized method of moment (GMM) estimator. His findings complement a similar study that was carried out by Dollar and Kraay (2002). The study finds that by focussing on finance and using further measures of financial development, financial development might alleviate poverty, but not universally. They indicate that a 'one size fits all' model does not work as different regions react differently to financial development when income growth of the poorest quintile is considered.

Our study is modelled after the work of Sarma and Pais (2011), but it took into account the following variations: First, unlike Sarma and Pais (2011) which studied the relationship between financial inclusion and human development, our study focusses on how financial inclusiveness impacts on financial development. Also, due to lack of adequate data, Sarma and Pais (2011) compute index of financial inclusion (IFI) to aid their study, but our study uses a more comprehensive dataset, the novel Global Findex database from the World Bank, for our financial inclusion variable.

3. Data Source and Methodology

Data for the study consist of secondary data extracted from the Global Financial Inclusion (Global Findex) Database,

World Development Indicators (WDI), African Development Indicators (ADI) and World Governance Indicators (WGI), all published by the World Bank, and Chinn and Ito's Capital Account database. The Global Findex database offers us the data for a financial inclusion variable, which is the main predictor variable in our model. We obtained data for financial development (our dependent variable) from the WDI database. We obtained data for the control variable natural resource rent from the WDI database. The ADI database provides inflation data, whilst the WGI database providesdata for institutions. Finally, we obtained financial openness data from Chinn & Ito's Capital Account database. We obtained 2011 cross-sectional data of 42 African countries from the various data sources. We chose 2011 because the financial inclusion data (the main predictor variable in our study) obtained from the Global Findex database are available only for that year. The Global Findex dataset constitutes five main dimensions as proxies of financial inclusion (FI), namely: *Formal Accounts, Payments, Savings, Credit, Insurance.* Each dimension has several financial inclusion components. This study utilises fourteen (14) of these components, and they are *deposits, withdrawals, individual formal accounts, business accounts, accounts used to receive government payments, accounts used to receive wages, cheque payments, credit card, debit card, electronic payment, loan from a formal financial institution, health insurance,and mobile and formal savings.*

Financial development (FD) is the dependent variable specified in the model of this study, and it indicates financial development in the banking sector. It consists of banking sector development indicators such as M2/GDP, bank credit/GDP and private credit/GDP. *M2/GDP* represents money supply and quasi money. These comprise the sum of currency outside banks demand deposits other than those of the central government, and the time, savings and foreign-currency deposits of resident sectors other than the central government. *Bank Credit/GDP* represents domestic credit provided by banks. Domestic credits provided by the banking sector include all credits to various sectors on a gross basis, with the exception of credit to the central government, which is net. The banking sector includes monetary authorities and deposit money banks as well as other banking institutions where data are available. *Private credit/GDP* is defined as financial resources provided by financial corporations other than banks to the private sector, such as loan, non-equity securities, trade credits and other accounts receivable that establish a claim for repayment. Data for all indicators are from the WDI database of the World Bank website.

We postulate that financial development in a nation is a function of financial inclusion and other variables like inflation, institutional quality, financial openness and natural resource endowment in the nation. Generally, we can write: $\mathrm{FD} = g(\mathrm{FI}, \mathrm{Insti}, \mathrm{Infla}, \mathrm{FO}, \mathrm{NatRes})$. The specific equation is given by:

$$\mathrm{FD}_i = \alpha_i + \beta_1 \mathrm{FI}_i + \beta_2 \mathrm{Insti}_i + \beta_3 \mathrm{Infla}_i + \beta_4 \mathrm{FO}_i + \beta_5 \mathrm{NatRes}_i + \varepsilon_i \quad (1)$$

Where $i = 1, \cdots, 42$ specifying individual African countries. FD could be any of the financial development indicators stated above. The FI is the variable of interest obtained from the Global Findex, and it includes the 14 components stated above. We rely on the literature to choose the following control variables established to determine banking sector financial development; Institutional quality (Insti), Inflation

(Infla), Financial Openness (FO) and Natural Resource Rent (NatRes).

As noted above, the study uses fourteen proxies for financial inclusion, which might have common variations. We use Principal Components Analysis to condense the information contained in the fourteen proxies. That is to estimate the variables that capture the common variations among the fourteen components, with a minimal loss of information. This helped in determining the true FI variable to be used in the model(1). From the PCA analysis, we capture 'accounts used to receive wages (AcctRcvWages)' and 'individual formal accounts (IndivFormalAccount)' as the two major components among the fourteen. They explain as high as 69% of the variations among the fourteen components, and therefore, will be used as the proxies for financial inclusion the model.

Given our small sample size and to establish the robustness of our results, we use bootstrap technique to estimate our regression parameters of interest. Specifically, we resample from the residual in equation(1). That is, we estimate equation (1) above from the actual data and obtain the fitted values $\hat{FD}_i$ and the residuals, $\hat{\varepsilon}_i$. A sample of size $N = 42$ is generated from the residuals with replacements represented as $\hat{\varepsilon}_i^*$. The bootstrapped dependent variable is computed by adding the fitted values to the bootstrapped residuals, thus $FD_i^* = \hat{FD}_i + \hat{\varepsilon}_i^*$. Finally, we regress the new dependent variable on the original independent variable data to get the bootstrap coefficients $\hat{\beta}_j^*$. We repeat the process 10,000 times, and will generate 10,000 coefficients. A hypothesis test is performed on the distribution of the bootstrapped coefficients. The essence of the bootstrapping technique is to allow us not to make any strong distributional assumptions, since the analysis assumes the distribution of the actual parameters.

4. Results

Table 5.1 displays the descriptive statistics. As indicated in the Table, the mean level of financial depth (M2) was 38.22%, with an average bank and private credit of 33.58% and 26.52%, respectively, for the countries in the study. In addition, the descriptions from Table 5.1 indicate that the average money supply (M2), as a ratio of the Gross Domestic Product (GDP), was 38.22, with values ranging from a minimum of 12.05 to a maximum of 112.66 in the sample of countries in the study. Also, the mean bank credit of 33.58 has a minimum value -16.13 and a maximum value of 178.02. Finally, the average private credit is 26.52, and ranges from a minimum of 4.85 to a maximum of 144.68. The mean of the two main proxies of financial inclusion is 8.4 and 21.2 respectively. To analyse the parameters in turns, 'accounts used to receive wages', registers a mean of 8.4, and has a minimum value of 0.8 and maximum value of 26.7. 'Individual formal accounts' on the other hand, indicate a mean of 21.2 and has a minimum and maximum value to be 1.52 and 80.12 respectively. We measure inflation using the annual inflation rate from the ADI, which registers a mean of 6.72. The rates range from -4.9 to 21.4. The institution variable uses the rule of law estimate as a measure of institutional quality. It has a mean of 30.21 and ranges between 0 - 77.9, with higher levels of the index indicating institutional quality.

Table 5.1: Descriptive Statistics

Variable	Observtions	Mean	Standard Deviation	Minimum	Maximum
M2/GDP	37	38.218	22.011	12.052	112.655
Bank Credit/GDP	37	33.582	35.740	-16.134	178.018
Private Credit/GDP	37	26.519	27.419	4.849	144.680
Account used to receive wages	41	8.446	7.413	0.806	26.691
Individual formal account	41	21.192	16.013	1.522	80.123
Inflation	38	6.724	5.372	-4.895	21.350
Institution	41	30.207	19.699	0.000	77.934
Financial openness	41	-0.510	1.367	-1.864	2.439
Natural resource	39	14.831	17.712	0.006	73.676

Source: *Author's computation using data from Global Findex, Chinn & Ito Capital Account and World Development Indicators.*

Chinn and Ito's measure of financial openness indicates a mean of -0.51 and the index ranges from -1.86 to + 2.4. The higher the index, the more open a country is to cross-border capital transactions. Finally, the mean natural resource is 14.8, ranging from 0.006 to 73.7. From our analysis, it is observed that most African countries tend to have higher natural resources but the countries with unprecedented high natural resource rent are Congo Republic (73.7), followed by Mauritania (58.5) and then Gabon (50.6).

In Table 5.2, we use the 'accounts used to receive wages' as a measure of financial inclusion. The regression is estimated for all the three different measures of financial development. We find that, FI-accounts used to receive wages, is positive and significantly related to all the three measures of financial development. Accounts used to receive wages, which is our measure of financial inclusion is positive and significant at 1 percent in two of the three models, m2/GDP and private credit/GDP; and significant at 5 percent in the third model, bank credit/GDP. Specifically, if the number of accounts used to receive wages increase by 10 percent, financial development improves by between 16 to 25 percent in an economy. Thus, the results suggest that financial inclusion can lead to the development of the domestic banking sector. This assertion is credible because broadening the financial services base to enable the under privileged, the weaker sections of the society, the poor, the marginalized and the small and medium-sized firms to have easy access to financial services enlarges the sizeable accounts of the banking sector. This implies that African countries stand to benefit when deliberate efforts are made to pursue the financial inclusion phenomenon as a policy priority. One obvious benefit is to stimulate investment and growth in the economy and with an increased level of investment and economic growth, the economy is immune to financial repression. Thus, financial inclusion promotes the development of the domestic banking sector in Africa. This shows that an increase in the number of people who receive their wages through their formal accounts have a significant effect on financial development.

The control variables such as institutions and natural resources also have a significant effect on financial development. Whilst institutions have a positive effect, natural resources have a negative effect. Moreover, inflation has a negative effect on financial development; however, its negative effect is significant only in the third model or private credit.

Table 5.2: Cross-sectional regression with FI- Accounts used to receive wages

VARIABLES	(1) m2	(2) Bank credit	(3) Private credit
FI – Accounts used to receive wages	1.600***	2.525**	2.118***
	(0.560)	(1.032)	(0.704)
Inflation	-0.692	-0.726	-1.074**
	(0.663)	(0.844)	(0.505)
Financial openness	1.436	-0.646	-0.693
	(2.565)	(4.082)	(2.145)
Institution	0.315**	0.493**	0.498***
	(0.125)	(0.222)	(0.167)
Natural resource	-0.222*	-0.394*	-0.254**
	(0.110)	(0.223)	(0.122)
Constant	25.41***	7.146	4.306
	(5.503)	(10.54)	(7.012)
Observations	36	36	36
R-square	0.509	0.441	0.585
F statistics (5, 30)	6.18***	3.05**	5.97***

*standard errors are in parentheses. ***, **, * indicate significant at 1%, 5% and 10%*

Financial openness is found to have an insignificant effect on financial development in all the three models estimated. The insignificance of financial openness is not surprising, as it was observed from our descriptive statistics that almost all African countries included in our study do not have an open system that allows for cross-border capital transactions. In addition, institutional quality contributes significantly to financial development in all three models. Thus, an improvement in institutional quality improves the financial development of an economy. Specifically, an improvement in institutional quality by 10 percent leads to an improvement in financial development by about 3.2 to 5 percent, as reported in the results in Table 5.2. This implies that African countries that have institutions such as the court, the police or systems that ensure enforcement of laws and contracts between the banking sector and its clients tend to experience development in their banking sector accordingly. This signifies that, although increasing financial inclusion levels in an economy are critical, there is the need to regulate the activities involved. This is consistent with our expectation that strong institutions lead to higher development in the banking sector. The result also confirms the findings of Billmeier and Massa (2009) which note that institutions and macroeconomic stability have a positive impact on financial development.

In line with expectation, our results indicate that inflation reduces financial development in a nation as observed in model 3 of Table 5.2. The coefficient of inflation in the regression result for private credit/GDP is negative and significant at a 5 percent level of significance. The results indicate that an increase in the rate of inflation by 10 percent leads to a fall in financial development by 10.7 percent. This implies that the banking sector retards in development when inflationary levels are high. Inflation can lead to higher interest rates and cost of capital which tend to, consequently, exclude the less privileged and the smaller firms in the society due to price (price exclusion) from using the formal financial services. Our results indicate that high levels of inflation in an economy stifle the development of the economy's banking sector. This result is consistent with the findings of Yilmazkuday and Rousseau (2009) who also report that financial development loses much of its explanatory power in the presence of higher inflation. Lastly, the role of natural resources on financial development in the banking sector indicates negative and significant relation in all three models in our analysis. The results suggest that countries with natural resources are less likely to have an improved financial development. The sign is negative and significant at 10 percent in two of the three models, M2/GDP and Bank credit/GDP, and at 5 percent in the private credit/GDP model. Thus, an increase in a natural resources endowment by 10 percent leads to a fall in the rate of financial development by about 2.2 to 3.9 percent. This conforms to the resource curse paradigm and is also consistent with our view that resource-rich economies often fail to implement strong policies to develop (Holder & Bhattachayya, 2013). This therefore implies that higher natural resource rents have a higher propensity to hinder development in the banking sector of an economy. Our findings, however, agree with the findings of Holder and Bhattacharyya (2013), that resource rents are negatively related with financial development in countries with weak political institutions, but not in countries with sound political institutions. The R-square, which is the coefficient of determination in the model, indicates that between 44 percent and 59 percent of the variation in the domestic banking sector, development is explained by the independent variables used in the regression. The F-statistics indicates the overall significance of the regression model at 5 and 1 percent as reported in Table 5.2. The robust standard errors are reported in brackets, under the coefficients in the respective regression models.

Finally, to ensure robustness in our result we undertake the bootstrap approach to estimate the regression model. This is to enable us obtain the actual results of our study, since the earlier results could be based on asymptotic assumptions. Table 5.3 presents the results of the bootstrapped analysis, and we observe that the results confirm asymptotic regression results with the exception of the natural resource, which reported negative coefficients but which were not significant.

Table 5.3: Accounts used to receive wages bootstrap regression

VARIABLES	(1) m2	(2) Bank credit	(3) Private credit
FI – Accounts used to receive wages	1.600***	2.525**	2.118***
	(0.599)	(1.176)	(0.769)
Inflation	-0.692	-0.726	-1.074*
	(0.688)	(0.965)	(0.594)
Financial openness	1.436	-0.646	-0.693
	(2.758)	(4.379)	(2.323)
Institution	0.315**	0.493*	0.498***
	(0.147)	(0.266)	(0.193)
Natural resource	-0.222	-0.394	-0.254
	(0.145)	(0.270)	(0.159)
Observations	36	36	36

*Robust standard errors are in parentheses. ***, **, * indicate significant at 1%, 5% and 10%*

Using individual formal accounts as the main variable of interest in Table 5.4, we find FI to be positively related to financial development, indicating that an increase in the number of people who have accounts at formal financial institutions has a significant effect on financial development in the banking sector.

Additionally, control variables such as institutions and natural resources also have a significant effect on financial development. Institutions have a positive effect, whilst natural resources have a negative effect. Moreover, inflation has a negative effect on financial development. This is however only significant in the third model: private credit. Financial openness is found to have an insignificant effect on financial development in all the three models estimated, and this is probably due to the closed nature of capital accounts in African countries.

Table 5.4: Cross-section regression – FI-Individual formal accounts

VARIABLES	(1) m2	(2) Bank credit	(3) Private credit
FI – Individual formal account	0.790***	1.191**	1.062***
	(0.199)	(0.452)	(0.306)
Inflation	-0.493	-0.402	-0.813*
	(0.582)	(0.726)	(0.401)
Financial openness	0.0786	-2.654	-2.529
	(2.591)	(4.389)	(2.314)
Institution	0.260**	0.421*	0.421***
	(0.125)	(0.214)	(0.149)
Natural resource	-0.217*	-0.386*	-0.246*
	(0.115)	(0.225)	(0.124)
Constant	21.09***	1.074	-1.619
	(5.452)	(12.32)	(8.127)
Observations	36	36	36
F statistics (5, 30)	15.33***	3.18**	5.01***
R-squared	0.539	0.446	0.629

*standard errors are in parentheses. ***, **, * indicate significant at 1%, 5% and 10%*

Specifically, model 1 and 3 show that FI, measured as individual formal accounts, is strongly significantly related to financial development at 1% level. Model 2 shows significant relationship at 5% level. This suggests that an increase in the number of accounts with formal financial institutions in a given economy increases the financial development of that economy. The results confirm the findings in Table 5.2.

Again, we find a positive and significant relation between institutional quality measured by a rule of law index and banking sector development. Thus, an improvement in institutional quality improves financial development positively.

This is consistent with our expectation that strong institutions lead to higher financial development in the banking sector. The result also conforms to the findings of Billmeier and Massa (2009) who note that institutions and macroeconomic stability has a positive impact on financial development.

Natural resource, however, turns out to be negatively related to financial developments at the 10% significant level. Thus, an increase in natural resource endowment leads to a fall in the rate of financial development. This is consistent with our view that resource-rich economies often fail to implement effective policies to develop financially. Our findings agree with the findings of Holder and Bhattacharyya (2013), that resource rents are negatively related with financial development in countries with weak political institutions, but not with countries with sound political institutions.

Again, to ensure robustness in our result we undertook the bootstrap analysis of our asymptotic regression by replicating our regression results by ten thousand times. Table 5.5 below presents the results of the bootstrapped analysis. The Table shows consistency of results with the asymptotic assumption regression results, except the result of the natural resource variable which is still negative but not significant. Individual formal account has a positive and significant relationship with financial development, hence it could be concluded that financial inclusion promotes financial development.

Table 5.5: Individual formal accounts bootstrap regression

	(1)	(2)	(3)
VARIABLES	m2	Bank credit	Private credit
FI – Individual formal account	0.790***	1.191**	1.062***
	(0.231)	(0.515)	(0.339)
Inflation	-0.493	-0.402	-0.813*
	(0.631)	(0.854)	(0.489)
Financial openness	0.0786	-2.654	-2.529
	(2.779)	(4.706)	(2.537)
Institution	0.260*	0.421*	0.421**
	(0.141)	(0.255)	(0.170)
Natural resource	-0.217	-0.386	-0.246
	(0.141)	(0.270)	(0.158)
Observations	36	36	36

*Robust standard errors are in parentheses. ***, **, * indicate significant at 1%, 5% and 10%*

On the other hand, quality institutions are good, and they promote financial development in the banking sector as observed in the actual regression result above for all three Models. This suggests that whilst an effort is being made to promote financial inclusion, adequate policies should be put in place to reduce inflation, and at the same time strong institutions should be in place in order to achieve adequate financial development in the banking sector.

5. Conclusion and Recommendation

This study explored the impact of financial inclusion on financial development in the banking sector, using cross-sectional regression and bootstrap techniques. We used the PCA technique to obtain two main principal component indicators of the 14 financial inclusion indicators, namely: *'accounts used to receive wages' and 'individual formal accounts'* We further assessed the effects of principal component financial inclusion indicators on financial development in Africa. We estimated two regression equations, viz the asymptotic and the bootstrap versions for each FI indicator. The study found that financial inclusion (account used to receive wages and individual formal accounts) has a positive and significant effect on all the financial development indicators, namely; M2/GDP, private credit/GDP and bank credit. The results also show that the control variables such as institutions, natural resources and inflation also have a significant effect on financial development. Institutional quality has a positive effect on financial development. Natural resources and inflation on the other hand indicated a negative effect on financial development. In summary, the results of the study indicate that financial inclusion promotes the development of the domestic banking sector. We therefore conclude that financial inclusion spurs financial development in Africa, and, in this regard, the following recommendations are worthwhile.

It will be necessary for African countries that desire to develop their financial sectors to also pursue policies that will enable its people, especially those that have been marginalized, to be included in the banking sector. This is plausible because by broadening the financial services to enable usage by the under-privileged, small firms and the weaker sections of the society, enlarges the sizeable account for the banking sector.

Governments of African countries should express keen interest in promoting financial inclusion for their economies. Policy makers of African countries should have the financial inclusion agenda as one of its topmost priorities. The banks should be challenged to come up with strategies that will enable them to extend services to those who no have access to the formal banking services. Efforts should be made by the banks to educate the public on available products and how those products can be accessed with ease. In addition, people should be encouraged to use the formal banking sector, and also, commitments could be made to formalize the informal sector of financial institutions, to aid in the achievement of inclusive finance. All stakeholders should uphold policies that intend to promote financial inclusion.

The study also finds institutional quality to have a significant positive effect on financial development. This implies that as nations pursue the agenda of developing their financial sectors, it will also be imperative to enforce the laws of these nations, particularly in the banking sector. The autonomy of the Central banks in these countries should be enhanced, in order to make them initiate and implement policies which will eventually lead to the development of the economies financial sector

Finally, it is noteworthy that as the nations pursue financial development, efforts are made to control the levels of inflation. Our results indicate that inflation has an adverse effect on the level of financial development in a nation. There is therefore the need to put in prudent policies to reduce high inflation levels.

6. Limitations of the study and suggestions for Further Research

This study used a cross-sectional regression due to data availability, data collected were for a particular point in time, not over time. The data constraint therefore reduced the sample size for the study. This implies that results could have improved if the sample size had been larger by having data available over time and for more countries. It would therefore be beneficial to invest into data availability for future studies to be carried out. Future research could therefore focus on the possibility of a bi-directional causality between financial inclusion and financial development in developing countries.

References

Ardic, O. P., Heimann, M., & Mylenko, N. (2011). Access to financial services and the financial inclusion agenda around the world. A cross-country analysis with a new data set. *Policy Research Working Paper* 5537.

Bihari, C. S. (2011). Financial inclusion for the Indian scene. *SCMS Journal of Indian Management,* July to September, 2011. _PP illmeier, A., & Massa, I. (2009). What drives stock market development in emerging markets – institutions, remittances, or natural resources. *Emerging Markets Review* 10 (2009) 23-25.

Bradford, J. (1993). Banks and small firms: An insight into National Westminster Bank, *Quarterly Review,* retrieved December 30, 2010 from ww.fao.org.

Chinn, D. M., & Ito, H. (2006). What matters for financial development? Capital controls, institutions and interactions. *Journal of Development Economics, 81*, 163-192.

Chibba, M. (2009). Financial inclusion, poverty reduction and the millenium development goals. *European Journal of Development Research, 21*, 213–230.

Consolidated Group to Assist the Poor, *Website.*

Cull *et al.* (2012). Financial inclusion and stability: What does research show? Washington, DC: World Bank. *https://www.openknowledge.worldbank.org/handle/10986/9443* License: CC BY 3.0 Unported."

Dollar, D. & Kraay, A. (2002). Growth is good for the poor. *Journal of Economic Growth, 7,* 195-225,2002.

Demirguc-Kunt, A., & Klapper, L. (2012) Measuring financial inclusion. The global findex. *Policy Reserch working paer, 6025.*

Dev, M. S. (2006). Financial inclusion: Issues and challenges. *Economic and Political Weekly, 41* (41), 4310-4313.

Financial Development Report (2012) World Economic Forum.

FinMark Trust (2013). FinScope South Africa 2013 Survey Report

FinMark Trust (2012). FinScope Rwanda 2012 Survey Report

FinMark Trust (2012). FinScope Namibia 2012 Survey Report

FinMark Trust (2011). FinScope Swaziland 2011 Survey Report

FinMark Trust (2011). FinScope Losotho 2011 Survey Report

FinMark Trust (2010). FinScope Ghana 2010 Survey Report

FinMark Trust (2009). FinScope Botwana 2009 Survey Report

FinMark Trust (2009). FinScope Kenya 2009 Survey Report

FinMark Trust (2009). FinScope Zambia 2009 Survey Report

FinMark Trust (2008). FinScope Nigeria 2008 Survey Report

German Bankers Association Voluntary Code (1996).

Ghosh, S. (2012). Determinants of banking outreach: An empirical assessment of Indian states. *Journal of Developing Areas, 46* (2).

Guidotti, E. P., & Gregorio, D. J. (1994) Financial development and economic growth. *World Development, 23*(3), 433-448.

Holder, R., & Bhattacharyya, S. (2013). Do natural resource revenue hinder financial development? The role of political institutions. *World Development, 57*, 101-113.

Kumar, N. (2013). Financial inclusion and its determinants: Evidence from India. *Journal of Financial Economic Policy, 5*(1), 4-19.

Jentzsch, N. & Koker, D. L. (2012). Financial inclusion and financial intergrity: Aligned incentives. *World Development, 44*, 267-280.

Leeladhar, V. (2006). Financial inclusion, taking banking services to the common man. *Reserve Bank of India Bulletin,* January 2006.

Levine, R., Barth, R. J., & Caprio, J. G. (2004). Bank regulation and supervision: What works best. *Journal of Financial Intermediation, 13*, 205-248.

Levine, R., Loayza, N., & Beck, T. (2000) Financial intermediation and growth. Causality and causes. *Journal of Monetary Economics, 46*, 31-77.

Lokhande, A. M. (2011). Financial inclusion: Options for micro, small and medium enterprises. *Synergy (0973-8819),* Vol *9* Issue 2, p 39-50. 12p. http://connection.ebscohost.com/c/articles/64921834/financial-inclusion-options-micro-small-medium-enterprises

Midgley, J. (2005). Financial inclusion, universal banking and post offices in Britain. *Area, 37* (3), 277 – 285.

Mehrotra, N., Puhahendhi, V., Gopakumaran, G., & Sahoo, B. B. (2009). Financial inclusion – an overview; Department of Economic Analysis and Reasearch, Nantional Bank for Agriculture and Rural Development, Mumbai.

Mohan, R. (2006). Economic growth, financial deepining and financial inclusion, India. Something missing here

Mor, N., & Ananth, B. (2007). Inclusive financial systems: Some design principles and case study. *Economic and Political Weekly, 42* (13), pages…

Osei-Assibey, E. (2011). Financial inclusion and poverty; A study of socio-economic factors underlying financial exclusion in Ghana. *Doctorial Thesis,* Graduate School of International Development, Nagoya University, March, 2011.

Rewilak, J. (2012). Finance is good for the poor but it depends on where you live. *Journal of Banking and Finance, 37*, 1451-1459.

Sarma, M., & Pais, J. (2008). Financial inclusion and development: A cross country analysis, preliminary draft for presentation at the annual conference of the human development and capability association, New Delhi, 10-13 September, 2008.

Sarma, M., & Pais, J. (2011). Financial inclusion and development. *Journal of International Development, 23*, 613-628.

Sarma, M. (2010). Index of financial inclusion, discussion papers in economics, Centre for International Trade and Development, School of International Studies; Jawaharlal Nehru University, India.

Schydlowsky, D. (2012). Banking on financial inclussion. http://www.project-syndicate.org/commentary/the-benefits-of-financial-inclusion-by-daniel-schydlowsky.

Shafi, M., & Medabesh, H. A. (2012). Financial inclusion in developing countries, Evidences from an Indian State. *International Business Research, 5*(8).

Subbarao, D. (2009) Financial inclusion: Challenges and opportunities. http://www.bis.org/review/r091215b.pdf.

Swammy, V., (2013) Financial inclusion, gender dimension, and economic impact on poor households. *World Development, 56*, 1-15.

World Financial Development Report (2012). http://www3.weforum.org/docs/WEF_FinancialDevelopmentReport_2012.pdf, p 3

Yilmazkuday, H., & Rousseau, L. P. (2009). Inflation, financial development and growth: A triliteral analysis. *Economic Systems, 33*, 310-324.

CHAPTER SIX

Strategic Banking Competition Efficiency Nexus: A Perspective from Africa

Obi Berko O. Damoah, Emmanuel Carsamer and Kwasi Adjepong Darkwah

1. Introduction

In the strategic management literature, competition is regarded as one of the strategic variables because it determines the extent to which organisations achieve their strategic goals, including the degree of profit potential in an industry (see Eskandari, Miri, Gholami, Reza & Nia, S 2015). In the past two decades, the banking sector has experienced important changes in terms of regulatory structure and the functioning of the financial systems. These changes have affected the intensity of competition and efficiency. Consequently, the issue of whether more competition is good or bad for banking efficiency has been intensely debated among policymakers, regulatory institutions and academics (Barth, 2004; Beck., Coyle., Dewatripont., Freixas & Seabright, 2010; Martinez-Miera & Repullo, 2010; Wagner, 2010). Yet, the competition literature has little consensus on the issue. Some authors argue that competition reduces banks' profit and incentives (Hellman, Kevin & Stiglitz 2000). Researchers that belong to this school of thought hold that competition is considered to be a contributor to the instabilities that trigger challenges among banks in most countries. Martinez- Miera and Repullo (2010) also point towards a negative trade-off between competition and efficiency.

Other researchers (e.g. Beck, Demirguc-Kunt, & Levine, 2006; Boyd, De Nicolo, & Jalal, 2009) object to the preceding line of thinking and contend that competition, especially in the loan markets, reduces the risk of banks' portfolios. In this line of research, it is argued that a byproduct of competition is that it forces or compels banks to be stronger. To buttress this, Padoa-Schioppa (2001) claims that 'if banks were strengthened by the gymnastics of competition, the banking system would be stronger and more resilient to shocks'. Recent empirical evidence also supports the positive effect of competition on soundness of banks (Schaeck, Cihak, & Wolfe, 2009; Allen, Carletti, and Marquez, 2011).

This paper empirically analyses the relationship between banking competition, efficiency and soundness in Africa, by employing a dataset that covers many regions of Africa. In particular, it answers three related questions.First does competition contribute to bank soundness? Second, does a competitive environment increase efficiency? Is the mechanism through which competition affects efficiency and soundness as it is suggested in the industrial organization literature?

Some studies have examined one or two of the research questions above together, thereby contributing to our understanding of the issue (see Berger, Klapper, & Turk-Ariss, 2009; Beck, Coyle, Dewatripont, Freixas, & Seabright, 2010; Martinez-Miera & Repullo, 2010; Wagner, 2010). Yet, few studies test all the questions simultaneously.

In Africa, where the financial market is very (much) young, but being the main supporter of economic activities, makes it necessary to examine banking soundness in that continent. Furthermore, conducting this study in the developing economies is very important because the influence of globalization process coupled with the proposal for financial integration in some countries have heightened the perception of competition and soundness among banks (Borio & Zhu, 2008). A major contribution of the paper is that it uses a panel data to analyse the effect of banking-competition measures on two alternative measures of efficiency (cost and leverage efficiencies) in the African banking systems. The paper tests the validity of the Competition–Efficiency Hypothesis. It seeks to analyze how banks facing intense competition perform in terms of producing profit as well as being efficient.

In this paper, a new competition indicator developed in the industrial organization literature, Boone (2005, 2008), which is derived from the efficiency hypothesis proposed by Demsetz (1973), is applied. The index stresses that industry performance is an endogenous function of the growth of efficient firms. Thus, the indicator looks at the strength between cost efficiency and performance measured in terms of profitability. Following from the above literature, it is indicated that on the average the Boone indicator is more robust than other competition indices, suggesting that in terms of outputs the former is stronger than the latter in estimating the relationship between competition and efficiency. Overall, the paper seeks to empirically show the extent to which competition increases bank soundness and efficiency, and whether or not the effect is due to the decision that banks make to diversify their portfolios in response to the competition.

To achieve the objectives of the paper, the rest of the paper is organised as follows: Section 2 reviews both theoretical and empirical literature on the relationship between the banking sector's competition and efficiency. Section 3 specifies the measurement and construction of the key variables, data and econometric specifications. Section 4 discusses and presents the empirical results, and finally, Section 5 concludes and offers the implications of the study.

2. Theoretical & Empirical Literature

There are two approaches to the measurement of competition: the Structure-Conduct-Performance Hypothesis and the non-structural approach. The Structure-Conduct-Performance developed by Bain (1956) gained prominence in the early 1990s. The structure paradigm was investigated vigorously using the US' banking industry. Bain's (1956) Structure-Conduct-Performance hypothesis was criticized severely after it was applied, because of the econometric problem of endogeneity. The main opponent of it being Demsetz (1973) who argue that the positive relationship between rates of return and market concentration might not be the effect of market power on more concentrated markets, but rather of the consequence of differentials in efficiency among market participants. The critique led to the development of the Efficient Structure Hypothesis which states that performance brings about structure change that increases efficiency gains at the expense of less efficient ones.

The New Empirical Industrial Organization hypothesis was developed to address the deficiency of Efficient Structure Hypothesis. The New Empirical Industrial Organization hypothesis provides non-structural measures, such as the Lerner's (1934) Index, Iwata (1974), Bresnahan (1982) and Panzar and Rosse's (1987), H-statistic. This new approach believes that any dynamic behaviour of banks depends on the market structure in which they operate. Apart from the market structure influencing behaviour of banks, entry barriers, barriers on foreign ownership, and activity restrictions may also affect the behaviour of banks (Claessens & Laeven, 2004; Claessens, 2009). The commonly used non-structural measures are the Lerner's (1934) Index and the Panzar and Rosse's (1987) H-statistic. The Lerner's Index says that the larger the mark-up of price over marginal cost, the greater the realized market power. The H-statistic measures the extent to which changes in banking costs are reflected in changes in banking revenues. A novel index that is developed recently is the Boone's (2008) indicator which is applied in this study. The Boone indicator sees industry performance as an endogenous function of growth of efficient firms. Therefore, the study of competition in the banking sector and its relationship with bank efficiency are analysed based on the following hypotheses. First, competition enhances efficiency, and second, competitive banks will be sounder than non-competitive ones. These are in line with Schaeck and Cihak (2008).

The Competition–Efficiency Hypothesis suggests that increases in competition lead to increases in firms' efficiency and the evidence may come from different channels. According to Zarutskie (2013), banks respond to competition by specialization, through adjusting their lending technologies and focusing on certain types of loans. Dick and Lehnert (2010) report that competition raises lending efficiency and lowers banks' credit risk. Evanoff and Ors (2002) show that as competition increases, the incumbent banks respond by increasing their level of cost efficiency. For example, as deregulation heightens, it is argued that incumbent banks respond to threats of competition by improving their levels of efficiency (Jayaratne & Strahan, 1998; DeYoung., Hasan & Kirchoff, 1998; Evanoff & Örs, 2008).

Schaeck, Cihak, & Wolfe, (2009), reveal that banks hold higher capital buffers when operating in a more competitive environment. Berger, Klapper & Turk-Ariss (2009) maintain that competition disadvantages some banks, and find that banks with more market power have less risk of exposure during competition. For instance, the relationship between competition and the capitalization level suggests that when credit markets are competitive, market discipline coming from the asset side induces banks to hold positive levels of capital as a way to monitor and attract borrowers (Schaeck & Cihak, 2010; Allen *&* Song, 2005).

Recent studies are clear on the link between efficiency and soundness (Berger & DeYoung, 1997; Kwan & Eisenbeis, 1997). For instance, it is suggested that large banks tend to engage in credit rationing, because they have fewer but higher quality credit investments which enhances their financial soundness. Therefore, the extent of competition and the efficiency of lending decisions in banking are affected by information asymmetries. Dell'Ariccia and Marquez (2008) show that, banks generate proprietary information from lending activities which give an informational advantage over other less informed institutions. Banks respond to competition by reallocation of assets, for example through mergers and acquisitions; here, weak performing banks merge with well performing banks to maintain profits (Stiroh, 2000; Stiroh & Strahan (2003). This shows that competition creates reallocation of resources from weak to strong banks.

On the other hand, the Competition-Inefficiency Hypothesis states that competition leads to a decline in bank efficiency. The hypothesis is derived from the Quiet Life Hypothesis which argues that more market power could generate inefficiency. Monopoly power allows managers to enjoy a share of the monopoly rents in the form of discretionary expenses, or a reduction of their effort, which generates inefficiencies. The competition-fragility view suggests that monopolistic banks, operating in uncompetitive banking systems, may enhance profits and reduce financial fragility by maintaining higher levels of capital that protects them from external economic and liquidity shocks. Boot and Schmeijts (2006) perceive higher competition to be associated with less stableor shorter relationships between customers and banks, widening information asymmetries and requiring additional resources for screening and monitoring borrowers. So Weill (2013) provides support to a negative relationship between competition and efficiency in banking, in a study of 12 EU countries.

Empirical literature exists with regard to the relationship between competition and efficiency (see Boot & Schmeijts, 2006; Weill, 2013; Amidu & Wolfe, 2013; Schaeck., Cihak & Wolfe, 2009; Schaeck & Cihak, 2010). However, both at country and cross country levels, most of the studies are European based (Baltensperger & Dermine, 1990). Among the studies, few assess the evolution of banking competition in African countries after 2000s (Amidu & Wolfe, 2013). Besides, it is argued that the evaluation of the relationship between competition and bank efficiency, in African countries in the 2000s and beyond is rarely found in the literature (Schaeck, *et al.*, 2009; Schaeck & Cihak, 2010; Amidu & Wolfe 2013).

Yet, among the few empirical studies, Korsah, Nyarko, Tagoe, (2001) found that following the liberalization of the banking sector in Ghana, banks have become both more efficient and more profitable. In a related study, Hauner and Peiris (2005) examined the relationship between competition and efficiency, using data from Uganda after the financial sector reforms there. In that stud, the authors found that ever since the reforms were initiated the efficiency level among the banks increased because of the influences of competition. Another study that employed panel data using the enveloping analysis, Akoena, Aboagye, Antwi-Asare & Gockel (2012) found that in Ghana the technical efficiency of both large and small banks has improved, following competition. In a study by Buchs & Mathisen (2005), regarding the effect of competition and efficiency in the Ghanaian banking sector, the authors found that banks in Ghana operate under a non-competitive environment; which means that banks in Ghana operate under monopolistic condition. In Owusu-Antwi & Antwi (2013), the authors found contrary evidence with regard to competition, efficiency and soundness, after the financial sector liberalisation in Ghana. In that study the authors concluded that their test for a change in the competition status, as a result of the liberalization, was not significant, indicating that they found no evidence of variations in competition following liberalization. In addition, studies (e.g., Boot & Schmeijts, 2006; Weill, 2013; Amidu & Wolfe, 2013) found no increase in banking competition, because of the liberalisation. Finally, the empirical evidence on the competition-efficiency relationship is silent on the channel through which the banking sector competition affects efficiency. This gap is part of what our paper addresses.

3. Method & Data

Different measures of competition were used to examine its effects on efficiency and soundness. The competition index used in this study is an innovation in the industrial organization literature, proposed by Boone & Harrison (2005), and further developed by Boone (2008). This indicator is based on the efficient structure hypothesis that associates performance with differences in efficiency. Other measures, including H-statistics, the financial freedom index, bank activity restriction, and the efficiency adjusted Lener index, are employed to measure the degree of competition and to analyse its implication for bank efficiency and soundness. For instance, the banking freedom index constructed by Abiad, Detragiache, and Tressel (2010) is used as a measure of banking sector openness and the extent to which banks are free to operate their businesses. The liberalisation index ranges from 0 to 21, with highest score indicating fully liberalized. With these competition measures, this paper pays special attention to the Boone indicator because the originators consider it to be more robust than others (Dell'Ariccia, & Marquez, 2008). Based on Boone, Griffith, and Harrison (2005) and Van Leuvensteijn., Bikker., Rixtel & Sørensen (2007), the banking system- demand - curve in which bank i of country j produces a product (portfolio) q_i can be expressed as;

$$p(q_i, q_{j\neq i}) = a - bq_i - d\sum_{\substack{j=1 \\ j\neq i}}^{K} q_j, i = 1,2,...,\mathrm{N} \quad \text{.................................} (1)$$

Where N is the total number of banks in K countries.

The parameter a captures market size and b denotes the market elasticity of demand. The perception by consumers on different products , as close substitutes for each other, is represented by d. Assuming that each bank has the constant marginal cost c_i, it is assumed that $0 < c_i < a$ and $0 < d \leq b$. The profit maximization condition of a bank for optimal output q_i is expressed as:

$$\pi_i = \left[(a - bq_i - d\sum_{\substack{j=1 \\ j\neq i}}^{K} q_j) - c \right] q_i, i = 1,2,.., \text{N} \quad \text{.............................. (2)}$$

Assuming that $a > 1$, the first order condition with respect to output for equilibrium for N banks in K countries is given by:

$$a - 2bq_i - d\sum_{\substack{j=1 \\ j\neq i}}^{K} q_j - c_i = 0, i = 1,2,..., N \quad \text{..............................}$$

(3)

The general first order condition for equilibrium for N banks in K countries that have positive output level is specified as:

$$q(c_i) = \frac{\left[\left(\frac{2b}{d} - 1 \right) a - \left(\frac{2b}{d} + N - 1 \right) c_i + \sum_{j=1}^{K} c_j \right]}{[2b + d(N-1)] \left(\frac{2b}{d} - 1 \right)} \quad \text{.............................. (4)}$$

Equation (4) specifies a linear relationship between output and marginal cost, and according to Schaeck and Cihak (2011), profits depend on marginal cost in equation (2) in a quadratic way. If profits π_i is defined as a variable excluding entry costs θ, then an entry decision of a prospective bank will be $\pi_i \geq \theta$ in equilibrium. Thus a bank only enters a market if and only if this condition holds. According to Boone (2008), these properties increase competition in two different ways. One, competition increases when the products offered by different banks become close substitutes and banks aggressively interact ($d \uparrow, \text{d} < \text{b}$). Second, competition becomes intense when entry costs decline. Performance of the most efficient firms usually improves under these regimes (Boone, 2008).

Assuming downward sloping relationship between profits, π_i and marginal costs, c_i, it follows that higher marginal cost means lower margins per unit of output for a given price. In addition, if higher marginal cost leads to higher prices, output is reduced and the market share declines. The profit elasticity which measures profit response to changes in marginal cost is calculated by regressing profit (π) on marginal cost. Since marginal costs are not observed directly, average cost is used as a proxy for the empirical estimation for bank i as follows:

$$\pi_{it} = \alpha + \beta In(c_{it}) \quad \text{.......................................} (5)$$

In this study, the Boone indicator is used to show how competition affects bank soundness. Hence we estimate a category of panel data models of the form:

$$W_{ijt} = \alpha + \beta B_{jt} + \gamma X_{ijt} + \delta C_{jt} + \varepsilon_{ijt} \quad \text{................................} (6)$$

Where W_{ijt} measures bank soundness for bank i in country j at time t, β_{jt} is the Boone indicator at time t, and X and C are vectors of bank and country specific variables as control for other factors that affect bank soundness, and ε_{ijt} denote the errors term.

The bank's return on assets (ROA) is regressed on average cost to obtain information on how much profitability covaries with cost. The intuition is that an increase in cost reduces profits in all markets; the same percentage increase in a more competitive market leads to a greater decline in profits, because banks are punished more harshly for being inefficient. Since the indicator measures the extent to which differences in efficiency are reflected in performance differences, ROA is regressed on average cost to check how much performance covaries with cost. Therefore, the Boone indicator that expresses the reduction of profits that arise from cost inefficiencies, plus some bank specific factors to allow for heterogeneity and varying effect of competition on soundness over time is empirically expressed as follows:

$$\pi_{ijt} = \alpha + \sum_{t=1}^{T} \beta_{jt} d_{jt} In(c_{ijt}) + \sum_{t=1}^{T-1} \gamma_{jt} d_{jt} + \mu_{ijt}, i = 1, 2, ..., \text{N}; \text{j} = 1, ..., \text{K} \text{ ......(7)}$$

Where N is the total number of banks, K is the total number of countries, π_{ijt} are the profits of bank i in country j at time t as a proportion of total assets; c_{ijt} is an average variable costs; d_{jt} is a time dummy, which is 1 in year t and otherwise zero, and u_{ijt} is the error term. Profits increase for banks with lower marginal costs (β <0). The basis for this is that an increase in competition raises profits of the more efficient banks relative to the less efficient ones. The larger the β in absolute value, the stronger the competitive indicator. Average cost of bank i is measured as a share of total income. Average costs comprise interest and personnel expenses, administrative and other operating expenses. Income consists of interest income, fee income, other operating income, commission and trading income. Equation (7) is estimated using a Generalized Moment Methods (GMM) estimator, whereby one year's lagged values of the explanatory variables were used as instruments. The benefits of the two-step GMM estimator relative to a traditional instrumental variables estimator, come from the use of the optimal weighting matrix, the over identifying restrictions, and the relaxation of the *i.i.d.* assumption. The estimated coefficients for the Boone indicator are expected to be negative and significant.

4. Other Variables Description

The dependent variables used are bank soundness from equation (6) and bank efficiency. For a measure of bank efficiency, the study estimates cost efficiency using stochastic frontier techniques (see Owusu-Antwi & Antwi, 2013), leverage which is used as alternative measure of efficiency, and for soundness the Z-score is calculated as:

$$Z = \frac{(ROA + E / A)}{\sigma ROA} \quad \dots\dots\dots\dots\dots\dots\dots\dots\dots\dots\dots (8)$$

where ROA is return on assets of bank i in country j , E/A denotes the equity to asset ratio and σROA is the standard deviation of return on assets. Here, a two-year rolling time window for the σROA is used to allow for variation in the denominator of the Z-score. This approach ensures that the Z-scores are mainly moved by changes in the levels of capital and profitability.

The Z-score combines both banks' capital, profits and the risk banks face, measured by the standard deviation of returns. Actually the Z-score is used to measure the number of times standard deviations of a return realization has to fall till equity is depleted (Demirguc-Kunt & Huizinga, 2010; Turk-Ariss, 2010). The index essentially measures the accounting distance to default for a given bank. A higher Z-score implies a lower probability of insolvency, providing a direct measure of soundness that is superior to analysing something like leverage.

Besides, this study uses a number of control variables that affect the relationship of interest. The control variables include bank-specific characteristics and the macroeconomic environments. For bank-level controls, logarithm of total assets is employed as a proxy for bank size- as larger banks are frequently subjected to too-big to- fail policies. Asset growth is included to account for differences in risk preferences and bank growth. Following Laeven and Levine (2007) better diversified banks are assumed to be less risky, so here diversification is controlled for and measured by their revenue diversification index. The higher the quality of management, the higher the interest margins that the bank imposes since high quality management translates into a profitable composition of assets and a low cost composition of liabilities. The ability to generate quality assets is used as a proxy for quality of management. A ratio of total loans to assets (loan/assets) is used as a proxy for credit risk. Inflation, financial development, exchange rates and GDP growth are included in the regression to account for differences in macroeconomic environments. Inflation is the rate of inflation based on the consumer price index. GDP growth measures business cycle fluctuation. The study employs the respective countries' broad based money supply to GDP as a measure of monetary policy, because monetary policy affects bank lending and subsequently banks profitability. The local currencies per US' dollar is included as a measure of risk of expropriation. It measures the degree to which the individual country's laws protect and enforce monetary policy.

5. Data Sources

The bank level's micro data used in this study come from the most recent Bank scope and macro-country level data obtained from the World development indicator. The data frequency is annual consisting of 329 banks across 29 developing African countries for eight year period, from 2002 to 2009. Mostly, unconsolidated balance sheet data are preferred as appropriate, even though at times the study has had to depend on consolidated statements, because of data unavailability. The sample includes all commercial banks, cooperative banks, development banks, savings banks, real estate and mortgage banks for which annual data is available for the study period during the years 2002–2009. To ensure that banks that are important players in the deposit and/or loan markets are not omitted; medium and long term credit banks and specialized government institutions are included in the sample. The banking freedom index was obtained from the Heritage Foundation (2010).

6. Estimation Strategy: The Dynamic Panel Model

A regression approach based on the dynamic panel model is the framework used for testing the relationship of interest. It first analyses whether the banking competition decreases (or increases) cost efficiency, second, whether the effect of competition on bank soundness is via efficiency channel. The empirical models which investigate these relationships are:

$$E_{ij,t} = \lambda_0 + \lambda_1 E_{ij,t-1} + \lambda_2 \beta_{jt} + \lambda_3 (mktsh_{it} * loang_{it}) + \sum_{j=4}^{k} \lambda_j X_{ijt} + \sum_{g=3}^{p} \lambda_g D_{ijt} + \mu_{it} \quad \text{.................(9)}$$

$$Z_{ij,t} = \lambda_0 + \lambda_1 Z_{ij,t-1} + \lambda_2 \beta_{jt} + \lambda_3 (mktsh_{it} * loang_{it}) + \sum_{j=4}^{k} \lambda_j X_{ijt} + \sum_{g=3}^{p} \lambda_g D_{ijt} + \gamma_{it} \quad \text{................(10)}$$

$$\mu_{it} = \varepsilon_i + v_t + e_{it}$$

$$\gamma_{it} = \varepsilon_i + v_t + e_{it}$$

$$E[\varepsilon_i] = E[v_t] = E[\varepsilon_i v_t]$$

Where $E_{ij,t}$ denotes cost efficiency/leverage and $Z_{ij,t}$ represents soundness of bank i in country j at time t. We estimate the cost efficiency using stochastic frontier techniques. The $E_{ij,t-1}$

and $Z_{ij,t-1}$ are the observation on the same bank i in the same county in the previous year. The β_{jt} is the Boone indicator of country j at time t, which is the degree of banking competition of a bank i in country j in period t. Given that lower values of the Boone indicator signify more competition, it is expected that an inverse relation between the Boone indicator and the dependent variables exist. The interaction between market share and the loan growth of bank i in country j at period t is presented by $(mktsh_{it} * loang_{it})$, the variables X_{iJt} and D_{ijt} are a set of k variables controlling the bank-specific variables, and macroeconomic variables. The λ's are the parameter vectors and μ_{it} *and* γ_{it} are observed time-invariants. Here the disturbance term has two components: the ε_i is an unobserved time-invariant bank-specific effect, and v_t is the disturbance term. The application of the standard Ordinary Least Squares (OLS) in estimating Equations (8) and (9) is impossible because $E_{ij,t-1}$ and $Z_{ij,t-1}$ are correlated with fixed effects in the error term which gives rise to a dynamic panel bias. Moreover, there is evidence to suggest that OLS produce biases when an attempt is made to control for unobserved heterogeneity and simultaneity. Also, the influences on a bank's efficiency could cause it to adjust competition strategies. Therefore, the estimation strategy used to deal with possible endogeneity issues in Equations (8) and (9) is the Blundell and Bond (1998), and Alvarez and Arellano (2003) method of systems of equations in both first difference and levels. It is indicated that the system GMM estimator combines the standard set equations in first-difference with a suitable lagged level as instruments, and an additional set of equations in levels with suitably lagged first differences as instruments. Generally, linear difference and system GMM estimators have one–and–two step variants. The two-step System GMM, correct standard error, small-sample adjustments, and orthogonal deviation are employed (Windmeijer, 2005). The two step variant uses residuals from the one-step estimates and is asymptotically more efficient than the one-step.

7. Results & Discussion

The validity of the Boone indicator as a measure of competition is analysed in two ways: First, an analysis was done to test if its theoretical assumptions hold, and second, an examination was carried out regarding how the index moves with other characteristics of competition. The theoretical assumptions state that competition increases, according to the Boone model, under the two regimes: more aggressive interaction and declines of entry costs, or presence of product substitutes. The proxies for banks' potential aggressive competition and the decline of entry costs are the index of activity restrictions, and the proportion of rejected applications for bank licenses relative to the number of applications received. To capture information on product substitutes, the efficiency adjusted Lerner index was used because market power influences stock market investments, hence serving as close substitutes for bank products.

In this analysis the correlations of the Boone indicator with the other variables was first analysed. The correlations of the Boone indicator with the other variables were tested. To investigate substitutability of competition measures, the Boone indicator was then regressed on each one of the other variables. Here an estimated coefficient of determination (R^2) of 0.6 indicated that the measures could be perfect substitutes. The results are reported in Tables 1 and 2 below. The correlation coefficient between the Efficiency adjusted Lerner index and H-statistics, the Entry restriction and the Boone index were positive, while some were statistically significant, indicating that the indices seem not to measure the same concept of competition.

Table 6.1: Correlation Matrix of Competition Measures

Variable	Boone Index	H statistics	Activity Restriction	Banking Freedom	Capital Req. Super	Supervisory Power	Ent Den
Boone Indicator	1						
H statistics	0.0871	1					
Activity Restriction	-0.1904	-0.071	1				
Banking Freedom	-0.269**	-0.0784	0.3528***	1			
Efficiency Adjusted Lerner Index	0.1229**	0.241**	-0.1348	0.221**	1		
Supervisory Power	-0.0301	0.165***	-0.047	0.0402	0.438**	1	
Entry Restriction	0.165***	0.142	-0.432***	0.228**	0.328**	0.320	1

Table 6.2: Boone Indicator and Other Competition Measures

Dependent Variables	**Boone Indicator Coefficient**	**t stats**	R^2
H statistics	-2.376	9.623	0.67
Activity Restriction	-1.881	13.356	0.36
Banking Freedom	-6.689	10.163	0.45
Capital Requirement Supervision	-104.643	4.434263	0.70
Supervisory Power	-2.726	18.191	0.67
Entry Restriction	-1.264	12.843	0.25

The Boone indicator is regressed on the other measures of competition.
All estimated coefficients are significant at 1% level

However, other measures such as activity restriction, banking liberalization and supervisory power of government correlate negatively with the Boone indicator, implying that they are on course of measuring the same concepts. In this case, the indicator is intuitively measuring competition, especially, with those that have a negative correlation, suggesting strong competition when regulators impose restrictions as well as when applications for bank charters are rejected. The negative relation between the Financial Freedom Index and the Boone indicator indicates that competition is higher in systems with more freedom. This suggests that conventional indices are likely to underestimate the degree of competition in the banking market. These results justify the alternative use of various specifications in the analysis.

Moreover, the regression of the Boone indicator on the capital requirement supervision index indicates 70 percent of the information contained in the Boone indicator is also reflected in the capital requirement supervision. Also the regression of the Boone indicator on banking freedom index and H-statistics explained 45 and 67 percent respectively. The standard ordinary least square regression of the indicator on all other features of competition shows that the Boone indicator highlights about 70 percent of the information that is contained in these variables. This evidence reinforces the decision to use the Boone indicator for the study purpose, because it captures a broad variety of other characteristics of competition. Thus, this analysis indicates that the theoretical assumptions of the indicator are well reflected in empirical regularities.

Table 6.3 shows summary statistics of the key variables used in this study, and in general the data contains outliers and positive values.

Table 6.3: Descriptive Statistics

Variables	Obs	Mean	SD	Min	Max
Z-Score	2495	42.25023	78.09015	-21.0645	1243.713
Total Asset	2495	2078.617	7288.956	0.208	123213.8
Asset growth	2495	0.21654	0.231674	-0.99153	0.998076
Revenue Diversification	2495	0.387463	0.202884	5.58E-05	0.999199
Loan Loss provision to Total Asset	2495	0.045679	0.066288	0.000268	0.810345
Herfindahl-Hirschman index	2495	0.478223	0.140336	0.175939	0.992284
GDP per capita	2495	0.053549	0.039339	-17.70	0.274617
Boone indicator	2495	-0.46375	-0.46375	0.463747	7.8478
Loan growth	2495	0.505266	0.193511	-0.177	0.50496
Market share	2495	0.110485	0.134376	4.98E-05	0.916125
Inflation	2495	62.04659	62.04659	62.04659	24411.03
exchange Rate	2495	105.29756	10.529756	10529756	6.72E+09
Monetary Policy	2495	19.15528	19.15528	19.15528	975
Profit before tax	2495	42.43475	42.43475	42.43475	120.4627

The positive values make the use of a logarithmic or square root transformation valuable / useful, in order to achieve normality easily. All bank-specific variables are averaged by the banks during the period 2002–2009. The figures from the Boone indicator vary by more than 100% across the regions, with African banks on average pricing their product at 27% over and above marginal cost. Similarly, total assets and banks' soundness have the highest mean and in line with it, the asset growth rate is huge at 21% per annum. Loan growth is significantly strong at 50% and GDP grows about 5% per annum. But other macroeconomic factors such as exchange rates and inflation appeared to be poor. For instance, the average inflation rate is 62%, and this poses a great threat to banks' strategic planning in the region.

However, banks in Africa are doing well because bank-specific variables, such as profit in terms of ROA and Z-score, are at a favorable level. For instance, annual profit is pegged at 42% which is very high, comparatively. Regarding other bank-specific variables, banks are averagely performing in terms of size which is more than $2078.61 million. On the average, the data signal on average performance for banks in the region.

7.1 The Effect of Competition on Banks Soundness

This sub-section analyses the empirical results with the aim of examining the effect of competition on bank soundness as well as examining other sources of bank soundness in the developing African banking industry. To begin, Table 6.4 presents the results of the regressions that use bank specific variables and macroeconomic variables, accounting for the level of development and the monetary policy stance.

Following Demirguc-Kunt and Huizinga (2010), the estimated results include country and yearly fixed effects, and the clustering of the errors at the bank level. Three varieties of competition that are estimated are: the Boone indicator, the H-Statistics and efficiency adjusted Lerner. Columns 1, 4, 7, 8 and 9 relate to the Boone indicator, Columns 2 and 5 relate to the H- Statistics, whilst Columns 3 and 6 relate to efficiency-adjusted Lerner. Here the panel data models with random effects are in columns (1), (2) and (3) in Table 6.4. Columns (1) and (4) contain bank-specific variables to control for characteristics of the banking system and a time trend. The negative sign at the one percent level for the Boone indicator strongly supports a reallocation effect of profits from inefficient banks to efficient ones to contribute to sound banking activities and this underscores that competition increases banks' Z-scores via the efficiency channel. In the other columns, when the GDP growth and the exchange rate were incorporated, the estimated coefficients of the Boone indicator increased.

The empirical results revealed that banks operate with lower Z-scores in a concentrated banking system. The inverse relation between the Herfindahl Hirschamn Index and the Z-scores suggests that banks in more concentrated systems are more likely to be considered too big-to-fail. In fact, institutions like that may operate in a less sound manner. Consequently, these banks operate at lower capital ratios than would be appropriate, considering their risk profiles. Similarly, the revenue diversification index has a positive and significant relationship with the bank soundness, indicating that Z-scores increase in diversification. It is accepted in this study that the Boone indicator is endogenous, because more weak institutions may try to survive by increasing risk through the offering of risky loans which in itself is a sign of increased competition. This result indicates that banks that specialize in generating non-interest income tend to have a higher market power, hence higher profit.

It was also found that the size of the bank is positively related to Z-scores, suggesting that larger banks tend to have more market power. The result is consistent with the argument that larger banks are efficient, gaining economies of scale and scope and producing at lower cost which enables them to have higher margins (Amidu & Wolfe, 2012). Another significant factor that affects bank soundness is the loan loss provision which measures quality of management. The negative sign variable means that a large loan loss provision cripples the bank investment which indicates that banking managers are inefficient. The results thus suggest that banks with efficient and high quality management have higher Z-scores.

The macroeconomic variables (GDP growth and exchange rate) have a different degree of impact on the soundness of banks. The exchange rate does enter sound banking negatively, but insignificantly throughout the specification. This means the exchange rate level decreases sound banking as currency depreciates. Thus, monetary policy impacts significantly on sound banking in developing economies. The GDP growth coefficient is positive and significant as expected on the dependent variable. For instance, a 1% increase in the level of economic development leads to an average of about 13% - 52% increase in the level of sound banking.

To address presence of bias (ness) in the study, the 2SLS estimator was used. Both the Financial Freedom and an interaction term of market share and loan growth were used as instruments for the competition indicators. The indicators remained significantly negative with no physical change in magnitude in columns (4) to (6), in Table 6.4, indicating a possible absence of bias (ness) in our previous estimates. The two models were tested using the Durbin-Wu-Hausman test for exogeneity of the indicators. The results of the tests are significant and rejected the exogeneity of the indicators, thereby accepting that an instrumental variable approach is necessary.

To check for Heterogeneous responses to competition, the main components of the Z-scores were used to examine whether the beneficial effect of competition on soundness was basically attributable to the effects of competition on capitalization on returns, or on the volatility of profits. Columns (7) – (9) show the results. These regressions indicated an inverse relationship of the Boone indicator, with all three components of the Z-score. Yet, the estimated coefficients of the variable remained significant at conventional levels, with similar magnitudes of their coefficients. In all, these findings imply that competition, via the efficiency channel, principally drives Z-scores higher through incentives to hold higher capital ratios and reallocations of profits. This gives a better intuition of the Boone indicator as a measure of competition.

Since the focus remains on the endogeneity of the Boone indicator, Amemiya's (1982) two-stage quantile estimator was followed. First, predicted values for the Boone indicator were generated by regressing the Boone indicator on the interaction term of the bank's market share and loan growth, on its Financial Freedom, and on the exogenous variables. Second, the Z-score was regressed on the predicted value for the Boone indicator and the exogenous variables. The hypothesis that the transmission mechanism from competition through the efficiency channel on soundness depends on the soundness of the banks in question was validated in the quantile regression analysis. Table 6.5 reports the results from the two-stage quantile regression for the 10th, the 25th, the 50th, the 75th, and the 90th quantile of the distribution of the Z-score. From Table 6.4, The Random Effect (RE) model R^2 of 0.041 in the first column shows that 4.1% of the differences in a bank's soundness can be explained by the model. Also the RE model R^2 of 0.054 in the second column shows that 5.4% of the differences in a bank's efficiency can be explained by the model.

Table 6.4: The Impact of Competition on Bank Soundness

ble del setup	Random	Effects		Two-Stage	Least squares			2SLS	2SLS
	RE	RE	RE	2SLS	2SLS	2SLS	2SLS		
acteristi									
							Capital	ROA	SDroa
otal)	-9.123***	-0.201***	-7.1028***	-7.362***	-7.432***	-6.77***	0.0081***	0.0016***	-1.153***
	(-1.812)	(-0.0139)	(-1.568)	(-0.977)	(-0.687)	(-1.371)	(0.0028)	(0.0004)	(-0.139)
growth	0.968	0.0211*	2.0781	3.226	2.963	-5.94***	0.0011	0.0012	2.101
	(9.116)	(0.0118)	(9.249)	(9.404)	(3.698)	(-1.285)	(0.0009)	(0.0043)	(2.032)
nue sificatio ex	17.743	0.0025**	0.086 *	0.071*	-12.99***	17.543	0.0001***	0.027	1.912
	(12.38)	(0.0424)	(11.715)	(13.07)	(-4.695)	(13.68)	(0.0300)	(0.006)	(1.486)
loss /Total s	-95.63***	-83.26***	-91.521**	-73.27**	74.42	-85.53**	0.0002***	-0.113***	-29.04***
	(-36.90)	(-40.461)	(-37.88)	(-35.43)	(48.628)	(-36.733)	(0.082)	(-0.016)	(-5.437)
ndahl hamn	2.835	0.1086	5.4629	1.929	1.486	1.8123	1.117	1.325	0.26984
	(16.076)	(0.0936)	(17.79)	(13.471)	(1.586)	(15.646)	(0.879)	(1.289)	(0.0963)
o on.									
growth		0.0032**	0.0003***		0.0002***	0.0001***	0.001***	1.54E-6***	0.0001***
		(0.212)	(0.742)		(0.1028)	(0.623)	(0.0014)	(1.41E-06)	(0.086)
nge		-0.00091	-0.0537*		-1.084***	-0.0283	-2.12E-05	-0.0007**	-0.0004
		(0.0026)	(0.031)		(0.4059)	(0.0299)	(7.20E-06)	(0.0003)	(0.0005)
petition									
tistics e tor	-6.540***		21.382 (16.128)	21.382	3.536 (3.152)		-0.006***	-0.0033***	-0.001***
	(0.623)			(1.039)			(0.002)	(0.0006)	(0.022)
ency ted r		0.0723*				0.0210**			
		(3.168)				(0.089)			

Time effect									
Time trend	0.089*	0.121	0.0269***	0.0058	0.0271***	0.0096	3.7505	1.59E-05	0.003**
	(0.055)	(1.891)	(8.400)	(0.006)	(0.0040)	(0.008)	(1.35)	2.66E-06	0.0008
Country Dummies	YES	Yes	Yes	Yes	Yes	Yes			
Obs	2560	2560	2560	2549	2549	2549	2549	2549	2549
Number of Banks	329	329	329	329	329	329	329	329	329
Wald Model chi	121.04***	136.52***	93.02***	71.21***	81.08***	84.56***	109.88**	130.97***	10.62**
Hansen chi				7.341**	8..962**	6.476***	21.1***	1.4195	1.2072
R2	0.041	0.054	0.0765	0.058	0.2164	0.113	0.177	0.114	0.073

Note: *, ** and *** are significance at 10%, 5% and 1% level respectfully. RE and 2STLS are the random effect and two stage least squares estimation respectively. In parenthesis is the standard errors. For columns 1-6, the dependent variable is Z score.

To understand the underpinnings of the negative relationship between the Boone index and the Z-score, the components f, Z-score are used as dependent variable.

Table 6.5: The Effect of Competition on Bank Soundness-Quartile regression estimates

Model setup	10%	25%	50%	75%	90%
Competition indicator					
Boone indicator	-0.741***		-1.529***	-2.651***	
	(-0.252)		(-0.581)	(-0.944)	
Efficiency Adj. Lerner		0.0472**			
		(0.293)			
Bank freedom					5.697
					(4.496)
Bank-specific variables					

Total assets (log)	-0.834***	-1.125***	-2.523***	-5.462***	-13.74***
	(-0.258)	(-0.305)	(-0.535)	(-0.765)	(-2.199)
Asset growth	0.474	0.265	1.172	18.05*	9.506
	(1.809)	(2.337)	(4.235)	(10.01)	(22.86)
Diversification index(rev)	-8.747***	-10.99***	-26.99***	0.0997*	3.189
	(-2.604)	(-3.305)	(-5.142)	(6.807)	(13.39)
Loan loss provisions/Total assets	0.0387**	-27.55**	-6.807***	13.46	53.07
	(12.77)	(-12.55)	(-13.32)	(22.74)	(65.39)
Country-specific variables					
Herfindahl Hirschman index	-6.173***	-2.129***	-4.6309***	14.84	3.275
	(-3.664)	(-3.796)	(-6.320)***	(9.686)	(36.65)
GDP growth	0.0592*	0.0819*	0.0753*	0.0639*	0.092144*
	(0.160)	(0.183)	(0.429)	(0.408)	(1.092)
Monetary Policy	-0.0029***	-0.003***	-0.0041**	-0.007***	-0.011***
	(-0.0013)	(-0.0011)	(-0.0009)	(-0.0009)	(-0.0028)
Time effect					
Time trend	0.0003***	0.0006***	0.0008***	0.0028**	0.0006*
	(0.0006)	(0.0007)	(0.0015)	(0.0028)	(0.0109)
Country dummies	Yes	Yes	Yes	Yes	Yes
Obs	2549	2549	2549	2549	2549
number of banks	329	329	329	329	329
F test model/wald model	0.044	0.033	0.043	0.055	0.079

Note: *** $p<0.01$, **$p<0.05$, * $p<0.10$. In parenthesis is the standard errors and the dependent variable

From Table 6.5, the coefficient of competition remains negative and significant across the quantiles. We reject the null hypothesis for the equality of the coefficients, using the F-test for each quantile, and conclude that relying on only one measure of central tendency may be insufficient to evaluate the effect of competition. Therefore, the result brings to the fore that the health of banks influences how a competition increasing policy may affect soundness in the relevant banking market. Second, the results seem to highlight those banks at the lower tail-end of the distribution of the Z-score benefit less from competition as reflected in the magnitude of the coefficient of the competition indicators. The intuition is that a fragile institution is likely to have a low capital ratio, lower and more volatile profits, and is likely to operate at higher costs. Such a situation will make it harder for small institutions to survive the increasing competition than more efficient banks.

7.2 *Efficiency*

The attention here is to show the empirical relations between the Boone indicator and efficiency. Table 6.6 reports the results of random effect and dynamic panel data models and suggest that competition increases cost efficiency. Column (1), (4) and (7) in table 6.5 contain the Boone indicator and a time trend, while the remaining columns include bank-specific variables and controls for characteristics of the banking systems, and macroeconomic variables for government policy direction. The negative sign at the one percent level for the Boone indicator strongly confirms the positive link between competition, efficiency, and soundness. The intuition underscores competition to covariate with banks' Z-scores in the efficiency channel. The critical issue is that competition and efficiency are endogenous because the direction of causality is a priori not clear.

Table 6.6: The Effect of Competition on Efficiency

Variable	OLS	OLS	2SLS	2SLS	cost	cost
Competition Indicator						
Boone	0.0004***	0.0008***	-0.113***	-0.127***	-0.202***	
	(-0.0014)	(-0.0015)	(-0.024)	(-0.030)	(-0.027)	
Efficiency(-1)					0.480***	0.00068***
					(0.0687)	(0.0136)
Bank Specific Characteristics						0.000461***
log (Total Asset)		0.00045***		0.0003***		(0.0833)
		(0.0016)		(0.034)		
Market Share		0.0004***		0.0005**		
		(0.0196)		(0.0026)		
Asset growth		0.0177		0.0409**		
		(0.0112)		(0.2495)		-0.0687***
Country specific variables						(-0.0573)
GDP growth		0.0009***		0.00084***		0.0306**
		(0.0007)		(0.028)		(0.0027)
Herfindahl Hirschamn Index		-0.021***		-0.089***		
		(-0.0174)		(-0.059)		0.0099**
Monetary policy		0.072*		0.003**		(0.00102)
		(0.00359)		(0.0002)		
Time Effect						
Time trend	0.000859***	-2.43E- 0.00025***	0.0005***	4.74E- 0.00026***		
	(0.003)	3.85E-06	(.31E-05)	0.00012		
Obs	2557	2557	2515	2515	1320	1320
number of banks	29	29	29	29		
r2	0.043	0.155994				
hansen J test	n/a	n/a	37.17***	130.45***		

Anderson test	n/a	n/a	21.37***	61.27***		
F model test /Wald x2	9.116***	37.59***	n/a	n/a	49.14***	57.72***
BP test	0.8765	0.6785	n/a	n/a	n/a	n/a

Note: OLS, 2SLS and Cost are ordinary least squares, two stage least squares and cost efficiency.
The dependent variable for columns 1-4 is the leverage (total liability to total asset). Cost efficiency is generated from a stochastic frontier analysis. In parenthesis is the standard error.
Anderson and Hansen tests test for the relevance of instruments, BP test tests for serial correlation and F model test tests for the fitness of the model. *** $p<0.01$, ** $p<0.05$, * $p<0.1$

First, competition is usually considered to provide incentives to increase efficiency; and second, more efficient banks may compete more aggressively. To ameliorate this issue, the dynamic panel data estimator is employed using lagged values of Financial Freedom and lagged values of an interaction term between market share and loan growth as instruments for the competition. The Financial Freedom index is an excellent instrument for the Boone indicator, because the supervisory power of the state is considered as an interference that affects competition.

Moreover, the analysis indicates a strong association between the efficiency index and the Boone indicator. The interaction term of the bank's market share with loan growth was used because it increases whenever the market share or loan growth or both increase. Such direct correlations signal stiff competing institutions which mean any astronomical growth of one bank might have an (expectational) assumed / anticipated effect on the competitive banking market. The Boone indicator again has inverse and significant relations with efficiency. When we incorporate GDP growth (log) and the monetary policy, the effect of the Boone indicator significantly increases implying that strong macroeconomic environment might affects soundness and competition through increased economic activity.

Our Durbin-Wu-Hausman test, which verified whether the two-step estimator was necessary and whether the instruments satisfied the exclusion restrictions, rejected the exogeneity of the Boone indicator. The Anderson test verified the relevance of our instruments, and we also passed the Hansen test.

8. Conclusion and Implications

This paper contributes to literature by providing empirical evidence on how bank competition affects soundness and efficiency using a panel dataset of 329 banks during 2002–2009 and employing panel random effect, the dynamic panel analysis and two stages least square regressions. The study analysed the mechanism by which competition affects soundness and efficiency. As there is no consensus in the literature regarding how best to assess the degree of bank market competition (Berger., KlapperTurk & Ariss, 2009), three different specifications of competition indices were constructed: First a novel measure of competition by Boone (2008), second the Pansar and Rosse H-statistics index from the Heritage Foundation, and third the Lerner efficiency adjusted index to investigate the competitive environment of the sample banks and then use the results to assess whether the effect of competition via the efficiency channel on soundness depends on the regulation in the banking industry. This paper demonstrates that on the average, the Boone indicator is larger than that of the H statistics and efficiency adjusted index, indicating that the last two have underestimated the degree of bank market competition.

The values from the various specifications of the competition index suggest that competition motivates banks to improve cost efficiency, and that competition motivates successful banks to reallocate profits from inefficient ones to more efficient ones. Also, the Boone indicator appeared to be robust since it captures about 70 percent in the variation of many other features of banking competition. This result supports the argument that larger banks are efficient, well-resourced and enjoy economies of scale and scope and have the ability to produce at lower cost that enables them to have high profits. Similarly, diversifying into sources of income activities enhances bank soundness. Asset size and its growth, highly stimulates soundness and efficiency. Third, the result also shows that the resilient macroeconomic environment does not only increase the cost efficiency level of banks, it also rewards soundness. The results thus provide support to the existing findings, that banks tend to specialize in more competitive environments and it is believed this can be attributed to their power to process soft information loans.

9. Implications of the Study

On the policy and practical implication, the fact that the level of bank competition affects bank soundness and efficiency to some extent should be of high relevance to policy makers, regulatory authorities and bank owners. The paper's policy recommendation is that since a high degree of promoting competition does seem to have benefits for efficiency and soundness, the policy makers and regulatory authorities should introduce guidelines that enable banks to have a considerable level of bank market competition. Considerable bank competition is needed, because little competition will negatively affect bank soundness and hence efficiency (Liu,

Molyneux, & Wilson, 2010). Second, policymakers need to consider that any action that raises competition in the banking sector can affect the soundness of the institutions in a heterogeneous way. Thus a regulatory initiative that allows a moderate level of bank competition, which promotes profits for growth purposes must be pursued. In terms of practical implications, bank managers must put mechanisms in place to absorb and safeguard competition that will give rise to more cost inefficiency. With regard to market participants, they should be educated on the benefits of competition, by being advised that a sizeable amount of their investment should be directed towards banks with considerable cost efficiency.

Finally, the findings of this paper show that competition in itself is not detrimental to bank activities, but the level and the application of it could affect bank risk-taking behaviour. Therefore, regulatory and supervisory authorities should co-ordinate to put in place an equilibrium regulatory framework that will allow banks to have an average level of competition that is robust and consistent with any competition policy. The analysis in this study can be deemed as the partial equilibrium analysis because it did not account for contagion among banks coming from failed inefficient institutions. The literature reviewed, mostly after the 2008 financial crisis, indicated that banks are linked through credit derivatives and because the study did not test for such effects, further studies can consider a general equilibrium approach to the issue.

References

Abiad, A., Detragiache, E., and Treseel, T., (2010). *A new database of financial reforms.* IMF Staff Papers No. 57, pp. 281– 302.

Adi, B. (2015). An evaluation of the Nigerian telecommunication industry competitiveness: Application of Porter's five forces model, *World Journal of Social Sciences*, 5, 3, 15-36

Akoena, S. K., Aboagye, A. Q. Q., Antwi-Asare, T. O. & Gockel, A. F. (2012). *A study of bank efficiencies in Ghana,* Oxford: CASE

Alvarez, J., & Arellano, M. (2003). The time series and cross-section asymptotics of dynamic panel data estimators. *Econometrica*, Vol.71, 1121–1159.

Allen, F., Carletti, E. & Marquez, R. (2011). Credit market competition and capital regulation. *Review of Financial Studies Vol.* 24, 983-1018.

Allen, F., & Song, W. L. (2005). Financial integration and EMU. *European Financial Management,* Vol. 11, 1, 7–24.

Amemiya, T. (1982). Two stage least absolute deviations estimators. *Econometrica*, Vol. 50, 689–711

Amidu, M., & Wolfe, S. (2012). The impact of market power and funding strategy on bank interest margins. *European Journal of Finance*, 1–21.

Amidu M. & Wolfe, S. (2013). Does bank competition and diversification lead to greater stability? Evidence from emerging markets. *Review of Development Finance* Vol.3, 152–166

Bain, J. (1956). *Barriers to new competition.* Cambridge, M A.: Harvard University Press.

Baltensperger, E., & Dermine, J. (1990). European banking: Prudential and regulatory issues. In J. Dermine (Ed.), *European banking in the 1990s.* London: Blackwell.

Barth, J. R., Gerard, C., Jr., & Levine, R. (2004). Bank supervision and regulation: What works best? *Journal of Financial Intermediation*, Vol.13, 2, 205–248.

Buchs, T., & Mathisen, J. (2005). *Competition and efficiency in banking behavioral evidence from Ghana.* IMF Working Paper WP/05/07. International Monetary Fund.

Beck, T., D. Coyle, M. Dewatripont, X. Freixas, & P. Seabright, (2010). *Bailing out the banks: Reconciling stability and competition. An analysis of state-supported schemes for financial institutions*, CEPR Report, London, UK.

Beck, T., Demirguc-Kunt, A., & Levine, R., (2006). Bank concentration, competition and crisis, first result. *Journal of Banking and Finance*, Vol. 30, 1581–1603.

Berger, A., Klapper, L., & Turk-Ariss, R. (2009). Bank competition and financial stability. *Journal of Financial Services Research*, 35, 99–118.

Berger, A., & De Young, R. (1997). Problem loans and cost efficiency in commercial banks. *Journal of Banking and Finance*, Vol.21, 849–870.

Blundell, R. W., & Bond, S. R. (1998). Initial conditions and moment restriction in dynamic panel data models. *Journal of Econometrics,* Vol. 63, 113–134.

Boot, A. W., & Schmeijts, A. (2006). The competitive challenge in banking. In L. Renneboog (Ed.), *Advances in corporate finance and asset pricing* (pp. 133–160). Amsterdam: Elsevier.

Boone, J., (2008). A new way to measure competition. *Economic Journal Vol.* 118, 1245-1261.

Boon, J. R. & Harrison. (2005). Measuring competition. AIM Research Working Paper 022-August-2005.

Borio, C. & Zhu, H. (2008). *Capital regulation, risk-taking and monetary policy: A missing link in the transmission mechanism.* BIS working paper No. 268.

Boyd, J. H., De Nicolo, G., & Jalal, A. (2009). *Bank risk taking and competition revisited, new theory and evidence.* Working paper WP/09/143 IMF.

Bresnahan, T. F. (1982). The oligopoly solution concept is identified. *Economics Letters*, Vol.10, 87–92.

Claessens, S., & Laeven, L. (2004). What drives bank competition? Some international evidence? *Journal of Money, Credit, and Banking,* Vol. 36, 562–583.

Claessens, S. (2009). Competition in the financial sector: Overview of competition policies. *World Bank Research Observer*, 24, 1, 83–118.

Demsetz, H. (1973). Information and efficiency: Another viewpoint. *Journal of Law and Economics*, Vol.10, 1–22.

DeYoung, R., I. Hasan, & B. Kirchhoff, (1998). The impact of out-of-state entry on the cost efficiency of local commercial banks. *Journal of Economics and Business* 50.

Dell'Ariccia, G. & R. Marquez (2008). Can cost increases increase competition? Asymmetric information and equilibrium prices. *Journal of Economics*, Vol. 39, 144-162.

Demirguc-Kunt, A., & Huizinga, H. P. (2010). Bank activity, and funding strategies: The impact on risk and return. *Journal of Financial Economics*, 98, 3, 626–650.

Dick, A., & Lehnert, A. (2010). Personal bankruptcy and credit market competition. *Journal of Finance*, 65, 655–686.

Eskandari, M. J., Miri, M., Gholami, S., Reza, H.,& Nia, S. (2015). Factors affecting the competitiveness of the food industry by using Porter's five forces model case study in Hamadan province, Iran. *Journal of Asian Scientific Research*, 5, 4, 185-197

Evanoff, D., & Örs E. (2008). The competitive dynamics of geographic deregulation in banking: Implications for productive efficiency. *Journal of Money, Credit, and Banking*, Vol. 40, 897 – 928.

Evanoff, D., & Örs, E. (2002). *Local market consolidation and bank productive efficiency.*

Federal Reserve Bank of Chicago Working Paper 02-25.

Hauner, D. & S. J. Peiris, (2005). *Bank efficiency and competition in low-income countries: The case of Uganda*, IMF Working Paper WP/05/240, African Department, Washington D. C.

Hellman, T. F., Kevin Murdoch, K., & Stiglitz, J. E. (2000). Liberalization, moral hazard in banking and prudential regulation: Are capital requirements enough? *American Economic Review*, Vol. 90, 1, 147–165.

Iwata, G. (1974). Measurement of conjectural variations in oligopoly. *Econometrica*, Vol.42, 947–966.

Jayaratne, J. & P.E. Strahan, (1998) Entry restrictions, industry evolution, and dynamic efficiency: Evidence from commercial banking, *Journal of Law and Economics Vol.*41, 239-273.

Koetter, M., Kolari, J., & Spierdijk, L. (2008). *Efficient competition? Testing the "quiet life" of US banks with adjusted Lerner indices.* Working Paper: Gröningen University.

Korsah, K., Nyarko, E. K., & Tagoe, N. A. (2001). Impact of financial sector liberalization on competition and efficiency in the Ghanaian banking industry. *International Labor Organization Research paper, 01-2,* 1-51.

Kwan, S., & Eisenbeis, R.A. (1997). Bank risk, capitalization, and operating efficiency. *Journal of Financial Services Research,* Vol. 12, 117–131.

Laeven, L., & R. Levine (2007) Is there a diversification discount in financial conglomerates? *Journal of Financial Economics,* Vol. 85, 331–367

Lerner, A. P. (1934). The concept of monopoly and the measurement of monopoly power. *The Review of Economic Studies*, Vol. 1, 3, 157–175.

Liu, H., Molyneux, P., & Wilson, J. O. S. (2010). *Competition and stability in European banking: A regional analysis.* Istituto Luigi Einaudi per gli Studi Bancari Finanziari e Assicurativi (I stein), working Paper 2010, no. 10.

Martinez-Miera, D. & Repullo, R. (2010) Does competition reduce the risk of bank failure? *Review of Financial Studies Vol.*23, 3638-3664.

Meon, P., & Weill (2005). Can a merger in Europe help banks hedge against macroeconomic risk. *Applied Financial Economics*, 15, 5, 315–326.

Owsus-Antwi, G. & Antwi, J (2013). Do financial sector reforms improve competition of banks? An application of Panzar and Rosse model: The case of Ghanaian Banks. *International Journal of Financial Research*, 4, 3, 43-61.

Padoa-Schioppa, T. (2001). Competition and supervision in the banking industry: A changing paradigm? *European Finance Review*, Vol. 5, 1–5.

Panzar, J. C., & Rosse, J. N. (1987). Testing for monopoly equilibrium. *Journal of Industrial Economics*, Vol. 35, 443–456.

Schaeck, K., & Cihak, M. (2008). How does competition affect efficiency and soundness in banking? New empirical evidence, ECB Working Paper Series No. 932, European Central Bank

Schaeck, K., Cihak, M., & Wolfe, S., (2009). Are competitive banking systems more stable? *Journal of Money Credit and Banking.* Vol. 41, 711–734.

Schaeck, K., & Cihak, M., (2010). *Competition, efficiency and soundness in banking: An industrial organisation perspective,* European Banking. Centre Discussion Paper No. 2010-20S.

Stiroh, K.J., (2000). *Compositional dynamics and the performance of the US banking industry.* Federal Reserve Bank of New York Staff Report No. 98.

Stiroh, K.J. & Strahan, P. E., (2003). Competitive dynamics of deregulation: Evidence from US banking. *Journal of Money, Credit, and Banking Vol.* 35,801-828.

Turk-Ariss, R. (2010.) On the implication of market power in banking: Evidence from developing countries. *Journal of Banking and Finance* Vol. 34, 765–775.

The Heritage Foundation Index of Economic Freedom (2010). *The link between economic opportunity and prosperity'.* The Heritage Foundation and DowJones and Company, Washington, DC, USA.

Van Leuvensteijn, M., J.A. Bikker, A. van Rixtel, and C. Kok Sørensen (2007), 'A new approach to measure competition in the loan markets of the euro area', ECB Working Paper Series No. 768.

Wagner, W., (2010) Loan market competition and bank risk-taking, *Journal of Financial Services Research Vol.* 37, 71-81.

Windmeijer, F. (2005). A finite sample correction for the variance of linear efficient two step GMM estimators. *Journal of Econometrics,* 126, 1, 25–51.

Weill, L. (2013). Bank competition in the EU: How has it evolved? *Journal of International Financial Markets, Institutions and Money,* Vol. 26, 100–112.

Zarutskie, R. (2013). Competition, financial innovation and commercial bank loan portfolios. *Journal of Financial Intermediation* http://dx.doi.org/10.1016/ j.jfi.2013.02.001.

CHAPTER SEVEN

Strategic Planning and Corporate Performance: An Exploratory and Comparative Study of Leading Ghanaian firms

Daniel F. Ofori, Obi Berko O. Damoah and Freda Addu

1. Introduction

Studies concur that strategic planning has become one of the basic management tools that is gaining attention among practitioners, educators, researchers and policy makers (Whittington & Cailluet, 2008; Rigby & Bilodeau, 2011). It is confirmed that the popularity of strategic planning transcends organisations and industries (Liu, Siguaw & Enz, 2008). Why do firms develop strategic plans? According to Damoah (2016), among the main motivations behind a strategic plan are: acting as a tool for managing competition; serving as a device for raising funds; acting as the main internal and external communication tool; being used as the major performance management tool; being used as a key reward management tool; and being used as a risk management tool. According to Wheelen and Hunger (2006), strategic planning assists firms to attain an appropriate match and/or fit, and to form a defence against influences from both the external and the internal environment. Furthermore, strategic planning brings together all business units' strategies within an overall corporate strategy, and acts as a control tool for a performance review and progress towards the attainment of objectives (Aldebayyat & Anchor, 2008).

Moreover, firms undertake strategic planning because in so doing they are able to identify and exploit future marketing opportunities, as well as enhance internal communication among all constituents in the firm (ibid). David (2009) contends that strategic planning prevents firms from being taken by surprise, concerning rapid changes in the operating arena. Schraeder (2002) sees strategic planning as a means of providing organizational members with information about its future direction. Baker (2003) argues that strategic planning elicits commitment from employees, as well as serving as some sort of a monitoring mechanism to ensure that individuals in organisations do not deviate from the objectives of the firm. To help them decide whether or not to fund possible projects, donor organisations are attracted to firms that possess strategic plans (Shraeder, 2002).

Technological revolution, rapidly escalating competition and strategic maneuvering, deregulation, extreme emphasis on pricing, quality and satisfaction of customers, and the increasing focus on innovation following the globalization process are also among the reasons why strategic planning has become popular in organisations. According to Jain (1993) such changes are too complex for organisations to be marshalled through an intuitive management style. The essence of strategic planning, therefore, is to match an organisation's capabilities and competencies with the competitive conditions of the external environment, and achieve its performance objectives (Hopkins & Hopkins, 1997; Wheelen & Hunger, 2006; Thompson, Strickland & Gamble, 2008).

Various themes have been explored in the strategic management field, for example, strategy-as-a-practice (Whittington, 2006); strategic workshops (Johnson, Prashantham, Floyd & Bourque, 2010), strategic meetings (Jarzabkowski & Seidl, 2008); Strategic activities (Vaara & Whittington, 2012); strategic planning and performance

(Suklev & Debarliev 2012), among others. Of these themes, the strategic planning-performance relationship is among the constructs that has received significant research attention, yet its empirical foundation is still divided.

A number of studies have found a positive relationship between planning and firm performance. For example, by using the configuration theory and the resource-based view to understand the effect of strategic planning and firm performance, Sarason and Tegarden (2003) found partial support with regard to the positive relationship between strategic planning and firm performance. Using a sample from Turkey, Efendioglu and Karabulut (2010), established a significant correlation between strategic planning and firm performance. In another study by Delmar & Shane (2003), the authors also confirmed a positive relationship between firm performance and strategic planning. Dibrell., Craig & Neubaum (2014) also found that a formal strategic plan impacts positively on firm performance. Again, using a sample from Zimbabwe, Chavunduka, Chimunhu & Sifile (2015) found support for the existence of a positive relationship between strategic planning and firm performance. Other studies establishing a positive relationship, include, but are not limited to Bracker and Pearson (1986); Pearce, Robbins, and Robinson (1987); Rhyne (1986); Miller and Cardinal (1994); Hopkins and Hopkins (1997); Brews and Hunt (1999); Aldehayyat and Twaissi (2011); Suklev and Debarliev (2012). Other studies that have looked at the relationship but did not find any positive correlations, include Glaister and Tatoglu (2006); Ghobadian, O'Regan, Thomas and Liu (2008); Gică and Negrusa 2011).

In Ghana, a few studies have examined the strategic planning practices among organisations (Asamoah, 2006; Atttiogbe, 2007; Tetteh and Ofori, 2010; Debrah, 2012;

Damoah, 2016), yet only a few interrogate the link between strategic planning and corporate performance. This study therefore aims at shedding light on the debate from a Ghanaian viewpoint. To achieve the purpose of the study, the rest of the paper is structured as follows. Section 2 looks at the theoretical and empirical literature as well as the development of hypotheses. Section 3 focusses on method and operationalisation of variables. Finally, Sections 5 and 6 present data analysis, results, conclusion and implications of the study.

2. Theoretical Framework

This sub-section seeks to clarify the key concepts that inform the hypotheses examined in this study.

2.1. Defining Strategic Planning

Schendel and Hofer (1979) defined strategic planning as a series of rational sequences that include the mission statement of an organisation, its long-term goals, the outcome of environmental analyses, its strategy formulation, implementation, and strategic monitoring, review and evaluation. According to Ketokivi and Castañer (2004), strategic planning consists of specific processes that involve strategic activities, namely: an annual analysis of performance goals, and the development of budgeting as well as translating priorities into resource allocation decisions. According to Hopkins and Hopkins (1997), strategic planning is defined as the process of employing systematic standards and detailed investigations to formulate and execute, including the monitoring and review, as well as the evaluation of a strategic plan, leading to a formal documentation of expectations of /for stakeholders (p.637).

Following Wolf and Floyd (2013), a strategic plan is a deliberate, periodic process and/or series of activities that create a structured method of strategy formulation, implementation and control. Also it is argued that strategic planning is concerned with selecting and implementing the strategic initiatives of an organization (Jarzabkowski & Balogun, 2009). Notwithstanding the diverse opinions expressed above, this study is based on the operationalisation strategic planning by Wolf and Floyd (2013), because of its clarity and detail.

2.2. Firm Performance

Company performance is presented as a multidimensional concept and so its measurement is difficult (Falshaw & Tatoglu, 2006). In the strategic management literature, researchers have looked at firm performance from two perspectives, namely financial and non-financial measures (Venkatraman & Ramanujam, 1986; Chavunduk, Chimunhu & Sifile, 2015). According to researchers (Shrader, Taylor & Dalton, 1984; Miller & Cardinal, 1994; Hopkins & Hopkins, 1997; Baker, 2003), the most widely used surrogate in the field is financial measures, which include sales, revenue and return on earnings (ROE). Others are profitability, market value and return on assets (ROA). Satisfaction of employees, customers, shareholders and the reputation of the business are among the non-financial measures (Ong & Teh, 2009; Santos & Brito, 2012). Haber and Reichel (2005) argue that financial performance and non-financial performance are the same as objective and subjective performance measures, respectively. Of the financial measures, those that are mostly applied are *return on assets* (ROA), *and return on equity* (ROE) (Falshaw & Tatoglu, 2006; Ong & Teh, 2009).

This study uses the financial performance measures based on ROA and ROE, and examines the relationship between financial performance and formal strategic planning as one of the hypothesis informing the study.

2.3. Strategic Planning Formality and Firm Performance

In line with Sukley and Debarliey (2012), a strategic planning formality implies the extent to which management deliberately undertakes strategic planning activities such as having a team that formally concentrates on strategic planning activities, allocating of quality management time to strategic planning, and deliberately developing short and long-term objectives. Strategic planning formality in this study follows this line of thinking. On the empirical front, researchers (Glaister, Dincer, Tatoglu, Demirbag & Zaim, 2008; Kraus, Harms & Scwarz, 2006; Suklev & Debarliev, 2012) have established that strategic planning formality has a positive relationship with firms' performance. In the light of the theoretical, empirical and the intuitive appeal between planning formality and firm performance, this study seeks to extend this hypothesis.

2.4. Strategic Planning Intensity and Firm Performance

It is also argued that the degree of intensity organisations apply to strategic planning differs. Researchers, for example, Robinson and Pearce (1998) and Chavunduk *et al.* (2015) define strategic planning intensity as the extent to which senior management possess strategic planning expertise, as well as the extent to which they believe that strategic planning impacts positively on firm performance. The theoretical assumption is that a higher degree of strategic planning intensity will impact positively on firm performance, possessing of expertise in-house planning-performance and belief among senior management. In light of this, this present study examines this theoretical assumption.

3. Empirical Literature

The following paragraph summarises a sample of empirical studies. Thune and House (1970) and Herold (1972) found, for example, that formal planners outperformed informal planners. Firms that use strategic planning formality have been found to exhibit a more superior long-term financial performance than non-formal strategic planners. Baker and Leidecker (2001) reported a positive relationship between planning and performance. Furthermore, using a structural equation model, Glaister, Dincer, Tatoglu, Demirbag & Zaim (2008) also confirmed a positive link between planning and firm performance. By contrast, some studies found a contradictory relationship. Using a longitudinal study of 61 Fortune and 1000 corporations, Leonatides and Tezel (1980) established no consistent relationship between planning and financial performance. Second, Boyd (1991) synthesised 29 empirical studies based on 2,496 organizations, and found the positive effect of planning on performance to be weak. Third, Hopkins and Hopkins (1997) failed to find a positive relationship between planning and performance. Whilst the empirical front of strategic planning and performance remains divided, the trend from extant studies show that the positive effect of strategic planning and firm performance seems more plausible, relative to the contrary argument. Following from the theoretical assumption of the concepts discussed above, coupled with the positive effects of the empirical findings, the following hypotheses are posed:

H1 There will be a positive significant correlation between strategic planning and firm performance

H2a: Strategic planning formality will positively correlate with firm performance;
H2b: Strategic planning intensity will positively correlate with firm performance:
H3a: Strategic planning intensity will depend on managerial factors, namely;

- Strategic planning expertise in the firm
- Planning-performance beliefs by managers

H4: There will be significant differences between indigenous and internationally connected firms in Ghana, with regard to strategic planning practices.

4. Methodology

4.1. Data, Population and Data Collection Instruments

This section presents the data, population and the data collection instrument employed in this study. The study draws on leading firms from the Ghana Club 100 companies (GC 100) consisting of an annual compilation of the top 100 companies in Ghana. The eligibility criteria for the GC 100 listing include: (1) being a limited liability company; (2) having cumulative net profits that are positive for the most recent three year period, up to the date of assessment and (3) being a company with government share ownership of not less than 50%, unless it is listed on the Ghana Stock Exchange. This study combined two consecutive lists of the GC 100, namely the 2005 and the 2008 as its sample frame. Structured questionnaires were administered. The combination of the 2005 and 2008 lists of the GC 100 produced 74 companies appearing on both. Out of this list, 35 companies located within the Accra-Tema Metropolis were purposively selected and used for the study. The sample of 35 was drawn from multi- sectors as shown in Figure 7.1 below.

Figure 7.1: Sample's Industries

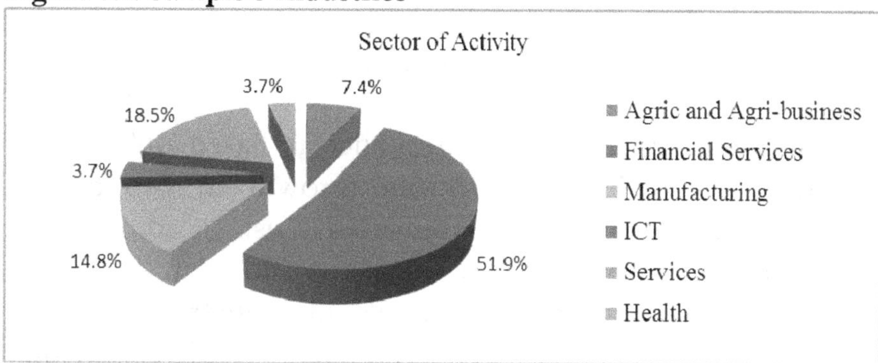

Source: Survey Data, 2010

From Figure 7.1 above, the financial service firms dominate the sample, whilst the ICT sub-sector are among the least firms represented in the sample

4.2. Analytical Method & Descriptive Statistics

Responses from the questionnaire were coded and analyzed using the Statistical Package for Social Sciences (SPSS). The Person Correlation, One way analysis of variance (ANOVA) and a chi-square test are the main statistical tests employed to examine the hypotheses. Out of the total, 77.8% of the respondents had post graduate qualifications with the remaining (22.2%) being first degree holders. 22.2% of the respondents had been in their current positions for between 6 and 10 years; 18.5% of them had been in their current positions for over 10 years. 40.7% had been in their current position for between 2 and 6 years. 8.5% of the respondents had occupied their current position for less than 2 years. 59.3% were locally owned (that is 100% Ghanaian ownership) while the remaining 11 (40.7%) were internationally connected (that is, they have international linkages with a parent company resident outside Ghana). A majority of the respondents were senior executives.

4.3. Operationalisation of Variables

As indicated earlier, firm performance is based on financial measures, using ROE, ROA and growth in profitability. Strategic planning was measured using the mean aggregate/composite score of the Boyd and Reuning-Elliot's (1998) seven indicator strategic planning instrument. They include (1) annual goals, (2) trend analysis, (3) competitor analysis, (4) long-term goal, (5) on-going evaluation, (6) short-term annual plans and (7) mission statement. Planning expertise was measured on a frequency of responses, depending on whether it is neutral, high and/or very high. Planning and performance beliefs were measured by ascertaining whether or not management believes that strategic planning results in superior performance. Lastly, planning intensity was measured on frequency of responses, based on the time a firm allocates to planning. Planning formality is measured based on the extent to which strategic planning practices are based on the formality of designing a mission statement and formulation of long term goals, among others. Locally owned Ghanaian firms and internationally connected companies are defined using a dummy variable where 1 represents wholly local and internationally owned companies.

5. Results & Analysis

Using the mean aggregate/composite score of the Boyd and Reuning-Elliot's (1998) seven indicator strategic planning instrument, strategic planning was found to be negatively correlated to all the performance measures except return on equity (ROE). The composite index of strategic planning was developed to measure the extent to which the firms benefit from strategic planning activity. This was done by averaging the degree of emphasis scores for the seven strategic planning tools, as presented in Table 7.1. So *H1* was partially supported and not fully supported. Also from Table 7.2a, *H2a* concerns strategic planning formality; here it was found to be positively correlated with all the performance measures, except with return on assets (ROA). Consequently, *H2a* was largely supported. Tables 7.1 and 7.2a are presented below.

Table 7.1: Correlations between strategic planning and performance

	Strategic planning	ROA	ROE	Growth	Overall
Strategic planning	1.000	-0.025	0.158	-0.121	-0.142
ROA		1.000	0.626	0.566	0.638
ROE			1.000	0.636	0.756
Growth				1.000	0.922
Overall					1.000

Source: Survey Data, 2010

Table 7.2a: Correlation between strategic planning formality and performance

	Planning Formality	ROA	ROE	Growth	Overall
Planning Formality	1.000	-0.044	0.058	0.081	0.104
ROA		1.000	0.626	0.566	0.638
ROE			1.000	0.636	0.756
Growth				1.000	0.922
Overall Performance					1.000

Source: Survey Data (2010)

With regard to *H2b,* the finding indicates that, strategic planning results in superior performance only when managers engage with some degree of strategic planning intensity, such as formulating a mission statement, long-term objectives, conducting internal and external analysis, evaluating strategic options, and implementing strategic options, among others. Overall, it is shown that the correlation between performance variables (ROA, ROE and growth) and the various strategic planning activities are all significantly positively correlated. This therefore means H2b is supported. The results are shown in Table 2b below.

Table 7.2b: Correlation table for strategic planning intensity and firm performance measures

	1	2	3	4	5	6	7	8	ROA	ROE	Growth	Overa
1	1.000											
2	0.251	1.000										
3	0.268	0.618	1.000									
4	0.350	0.390	0.783	1.000								
5	0.306	0.533	0.568	0.391	1.000							
6	0.268	0.436	0.538	0.421	0.709	1.000						
7	0.293	0.201	0.414	0.374	0.606	0.581	1.000					
8	0.567	0.682	0.820	0.725	0.810	0.771	0.683	1.000				
ROA	0.180	0.088	0.213	0.036	0.107	0.244	0.050	0.183	1.000			
ROE	0.017	0.246	0.201	0.022	-0.020	0.043	-0.052	0.092	0.626	1.000		
Growth	0.111	-0.099	0.072	-0.050	0.007	0.071	0.024	0.029	0.566	0.636	1.000	
Overall	0.092	-0.070	0.109	-0.015	0.055	0.191	0.135	0.098	0.638	0.756	0.922	1.000

Source: Survey Data, 2010

1. Company Mission
2. Long term objectives
3. External Environment
4. Internal Environment
5. Evaluating strategic options
6. Implementing strategic options
7. Controlling strategic options
8. Aggregate Strategic Planning Intensity

With regard to *H3a* and *H3b,* it was found, at the 5% significance level that strategic planning intensity significantly depends on the level of expertise of the firm and strong planning-performance beliefs among the sample firms respectively. Tables 7.3 and 7.4 present these findings. This therefore means *H3a* and *H3b* are supported.

Table 7.3: Strategic planning intensity, and strategy planning belief and strategic planning level of expertise

			Strategic Planning Level of Expertise			Strategic Planning Performance of belief			
			3	4	5	3	4	5	**Total**
Aggregate Intensity	3	Count	2	1	0	2	0	1	3
		% within Aggregate Intensity	66.7%	33.3%	0%	66.7%	0%	33.3%	100%
	4	Count	1	7	5	1	4	8	13
		% within Aggregate Intensity	7.7%	53.8%	38.5%	7.7%	30.8%	61.5%	100%
	5	Count	0	7	4	0	2	9	11
		% within Aggregate Intensity	.0%	63.6%	36.4%	0%	18.2%	81.8%	100%
Total		Count	3	15	9	3	9	18	27
		% within Aggregate Intensity	11.1%	55.6%	33.3.%	11.1%	22.2.%	66.7%	100%

Source: Survey Data, 2010

Table 7.4: Chi-square Test Results

	Strategic Planning Level of Expertise			**Strategic Planning Performance of belief**		
Statistics	Value	df	Asymp. Sig. (2-sided)	Value	df	Asymp. Sig. (2-Sided)
Pearson Chi-Square	11.228	4	0.024	11.797	4	0.019
Likelihood Ratio	9.001	4	0.061	9.252	4	0.055
Linear-by-Linear Association	3.736	1	0.053	5.448	1	0.020
No. of Valid Cases	27			27		

Source: Survey Data, 2010

Whilst Table 7.3 above shows the summary of the responses with regard to planning expertise and performance, the main analysis is confirmed in the chi-square test. From Table 7.4 above, The Pearson chi-square *t*-statistic and *p*-value for the dependency of strategic planning intensity and on the strategic planning level of expertise in the firm were 11.228 and 0.024, respectively. ($N = 27$, $df = 4$, $\alpha = 0.05$) indicating a level of significance at 5% significance level. Hence H3a is therefore supported. Also, the Pearson chi-square *t*-statistic and *p*-value for the dependency of strategic planning intensity and on a strategic planning performance belief among management were 11.797 and 0.019, respectively (N = 27, df = 4, α = 0.05) indicating a level of significance at 5% significance level. Hence *H3b* is therefore supported.

H4 focusses on the extent to which locally and internationally connected firms differ in strategic planning practices. From Table 7.5 below, the one –way ANOVA analysis reveals that there is no significant difference between local and internationally connected firms regarding their emphasis on areas of strategic planning (e.g. formulation of mission and long-term goals) [F (1, 25) = 0.498, P=0.487]. The results further show that no significant difference is observed between local and internationally connected firms on their views about the strategic planning process (which aspect of the strategic planning process to start from), [F (1, 25) = 0.121, P=0.731]. Further, results indicate that there is a significant difference between local and internationally connected firms regarding their use of tools and techniques of strategic analysis, [F (1, 25) = 4.070, P=0.055]. Finally, the results indicate that there are no significant differences between local and internationally connected firms, in their extent of commitment [F (1, 25) = 0.504, P=0.484]. In conclusion, the one way analysis of variance (ANOVA) results show that, with the exception of the use of strategic planning tools, there is no statistically significant difference between local and internationally connected firms with regard to strategic planning practices. Therefore, *H4* is not fully supported. Table 7.5 below presents the results of the One-way ANOVA.

Table 7.5: Differences in strategic planning between local and internationally connected firms.

One-Way ANOVA

	Source	SS	Df	MS	F	P-Value
A: Differ in their emphasis on areas of strategic Planning	Between variation	0.224	1	0.224	0.498	0.4869
	Within variation	11.245	25	0.450		
	Total variation	11.469	26			
B: Differ in their views about the strategic Planning process	Between variation	0.045	1	0.045	0.121	0.7311
	Within variation	9.229	25	0.369		
	Total variation	9.274	26			
C: Differ in their use of tools and techniques of Strategic analysis	Between variation	2.814	1	2.814	4.070	0.0545
	Within variation	17.284	25	0.691		
	Total variation	20.098	26			
D: Differ in their commitment to strategic activities	Between variation	0.212	1	0.212	0.504	0.4843
	Within variation	10.496	25	0.420		
	Total variation	10.707	26			

Source: Survey Data, 2010. * 10% significance level

6. Discussion

As indicated in the analysis, with the exception of ROE, strategic planning was found to be negatively correlated with the other performance measures. Thus, no significant relationship between strategic planning and performance was established, except for ROE. The results supports Boyd

(1991) and Hopkins and Hopkins (1997), but contradicts Baker & Leidecker (2001) and Glaister *et al.* (2008) who found positive relationship. The outcome of this hypothesis presents a mixed picture and a lack of consensus as regards the true impact of strategic planning on corporate performance. An explanation, according to Powell (1992), is that if all companies in an industry plan ahead, strategic planning would no longer be a competitive advantage but rather a competitive necessity. Other views, with regard to the negative relationship, could imply that planning that is executed is yet to yield its benefit to the firm, and therefore it is sometimes too early for planners to judge the planning outcomes. This assumption reflects Boyd (1991), who intimated that strategic decision making today may show up positively on the firm's financial statements in later years, and so the lack of instant financial gain in terms of positive ratios should not deter managers. For instance, Brews and Hunt (1999) contend that a lapse of time is required before the performance effect of a strategy shows up.

H2a predicted that strategic planning formality will positively and significantly correlate with organizational performance, while *H2b* predicted that strategic planning intensity will positively and significantly correlate with organizational performance. Both hypotheses are supported. *H2a* adds to the empirical support of the perceived inherent value in formalized strategic planning, as a way of improving corporate performance. Though, it appears, increased emphasis on formal strategic planning could be an effective means of improving strategic performance, the relationship is quite weak, clearly indicating that more needs to be done to consolidate the relationship. The support of *H2b* implies that managements of firms in Ghana are intensifying their strategic planning activities. The correlation between aggregate strategic planning intensity and the performance measures all registered positive relationships, indicating that the higher the intensity with which managers engage in planning, the better the performance results. The results suggest that it is not whether strategic planning firms in Ghana are able to achieve their performance objectives, but rather whether they engage in planning with the intensity needed to achieve their performance objectives.

H3a proposed that the intensity with which firms in Ghana engage in strategic planning depends on the planning - performance beliefs of managers. From the analysis above, this hypothesis was supported. *H3b* also predicted that the intensity with which Ghanaian firms undertake strategic planning depends largely on the level of expertise available to conduct the planning exercise. The findings indicate that, by all accounts, this is largely the case thereby supporting *H3b.* This finding is not surprising, given the positive views the respondents expressed on strategic planning and their high educational background. The latter also corroborates Higgins and Vincze (1993) who posit that firms' competence in strategic planning may determine the degree to which firms become involved in the planning process. This finding further suggests that it is not whether managers in Ghana engage in strategic planning with intensity, but whether they possess the requisite expertise or competence to do so, as well as whether they believe that planning with intensity results in improved performance. While this finding corroborates Hopkins and Hopkins (1997), it also contributes to the relatively scant literature in Ghana on the effects of strategic planning expertise.

H4 tests whether or not variations with regard to view, emphasis, tools and commitment to strategic planning exist between wholly local and internationally connected firms. The results indicate that with the exception of the use of tools and techniques of strategic analysis, there are no significant differences in the nature and practice of strategic planning between the two groups, which is between wholly local firms and internationally connected firms. So, this hypothesis was largely rejected as there was insufficient evidence to support it. Overall, it is evident that strategic planning is now considered as a basis for all the organisations' efforts and decisions. It implies that Ghanaian businesses, both internationally connected and local, apply strategic planning tools.

7. Conclusion and Implications

The study finds support for the planning-performance relationship discussed in extant literature. It is evident from the findings that strategic planning is a critical component of management and governance of companies in Ghana, for both wholly locally owned and internationally connected firms. Firms in Ghana employ strategic planning as one of their management tools. The results show that firms in Ghana deliberately engage in the formulation of mission statements, long-term objectives, and annual goals. Overall, it is shown that this behaviour is connected to their performance.

From the results, the study has the following implications. For practitioners, the results imply that firms must continue to embrace strategic planning, yet the practice of strategic planning must not be based on intuition, but must be formal and explicit. In so doing organisations stand to benefit from the outcomes of strategic planning activities. Second, for a strategic planning practice to positively influence firm performance, management must continuously intensify the intensity of the planning exercise. What this means is that strategic planning exercises must include few but detailed activities, such as formulating vision, mission, annual goals, and long-term goals, among others.

Furthermore, senior management has a critical role to play if strategic planning practices are to yield significant impacts on organisational outcomes. The results imply that senior management must first show a firm belief that strategic planning will influence the company's performance in a significant way. They must also ensure that the company has in-house expertise to drive strategic planning in the firm.

Although the empirical front of strategic planning and firm performance continues to be divided, there are several benefits to having a strategic plan. Therefore, government ministries, departments and agencies responsible for private sector development must support firms in strategic planning training and ensure that the management of every company possesses a strategic plan to unify organisational efforts, show the staff where the company is heading as well as the specific tasks staff are to perform, if they are to achieve the set organisational ends.

8. Limitations and Suggestion for Future Studies

The study's limitations include the limited sample of organisations, the limited sectors examined and the limited time and scope employed. It was further limited by the quantitative approaches which did not allow for an in-depth examination of reasons for the choices made. Future research could improve the results by employing a larger sample size, as well as the use of more qualitative instruments to tease out reasons for organisational strategic planning cycles, approaches and comparisons between historical results.

References

Aldehayyat, J. S., & Anchor, J. R. (2008). Strategic planning tools and techniques in Jordan: Awareness and use. *Strategic Change*, Vol. 17,pp. 281-293. Available at www.interscience.wiley.com DOI:10.1002/jsc.833.

Aldehayyat, J. S., & Twaissi, N. (2011).). Strategic planning and corporate performance relationship in small business firms: Evidence from a Middle East country context. *International Journal of Business and Management*, 6(8), 255-263.doi:10.5539/ijbm.v6n8p255.

Asamoah, O. E. (2006). *Impact of strategic planning on performance of district assemblies in Ghana: Case study of Ahanta West District Assembly. Unpublished*, A Thesis Submitted to the School of Management, Blekinge Institute of Technology, Sweden in Partial Fulfillment of the Requirement for the Degree of Masters of Business Administration.

Attiogbe, E. J. (2007). *An evaluative and comparative study of strategic planning in public universities in Ghana: The case of University of Ghana, Kwame Nkrumah University of Science and Technology and University of Cape Coast. Unpublished*, A thesis presented to the University of Ghana for the award of a Master of Philosophy in Business Administration (Human Resource Management Option).

Baker, G. A. (2003). Strategic planning and financial performance in the food processing sector. *Review of Agricultural Economics*, Vol. 25, No. 2, pp. 181-192.http://www.jstor.org/stable/1349849. accessed on 28/10/09.

Baker, G. A., & Leidecker. (2001). Does it pay to plan? Strategic planning and financial performance. *Agribusiness*, Vol. 17(3), 355-364.

Boyd, B. K. (1991). Strategic planning and financial performance: A meta-analytic review. *Journal of Management Studies*, Vol. 28, No. 4, pp. 353-374.

Boyd, B. K., & Reuning-Elliot, E. (1998). A measurement model of strategic planning. *Strategic Management Journal*, Vol. 19, No. 2, pp181-192.http://www.jstor.org/stable/3094063 28/10/09.

Bracker, J. S., & Pearson, J. N. (1986). Planning and financial performance of small, mature firms. *Strategic Management Journal*, 7(6):503-522.http://www.jstor.org/stable/2486136 Accessed: 06/04/2010 17:17.

Brews, P. J., & Hunt, M. R. (1999). Learning to plan and planning to learn: Resolving the planning school Learning school debate. *Strategic Management Journal*, Vol. 20, No. 10, pp. 889-913.http://www.jstor.org/stable/3094154 28/01/10.

Chavunduka, D., Chimunhu, P., & Sifile, O. (2015). Strategic planning intensity and firm performance: A case of Zimbabwe Mining Development Corporation. *European Journal of Business Management*, 7,5,12-18.

Damoah, O. B. O. (2016). *Exploring strategic planning from a practitioner viewpoint: A post-graduate edition.* Accra, Ghana: Digibooks.

Debrah, K. P. (2012). *The effect of strategic planning on the performance and operations of the Agricultural Development Bank.* A Master's Thesis, University of Science and Technology, Kumasi, Ghana, Unpublished

David, F. R. (2009). *Strategic management: Concepts and cases.* 12th Edition. Upper Saddle River, New Jersey: Pearson Prentice Hall .

Delmar, F., & Shane, S. (2003). Does business planning facilitate the development of new ventures? *Strategic Management Journal*, 24,1165-1185.

Dibrell, C., Craig, J. B., & Neubaum, D. O. (2014). Linking the formal strategicplanning process, planning flexibility, and innovativeness to firm performance. *Journal of Business Research*, 67(9),2000-2007.

Efendioglu, A. M., & Karabukut, A. T. (2010). Impact of strategic planning on financial performance of companies in Turkey. *International Journal of Business and Management*, 5,4, 3-12.

Falshaw, R. J., & Tatoglu, K. W. (2006). Evidence on formal strategic planning and company performance. *Management Decision*, Vol. 44, No. 1, pp. 9-30.Available at www.emeraldinsight.com/0025-1747.htm (10/02/10).

Ghobadian, A., O'Regan, N., Thomas, H., & Liu, J. (2008). Formal strategic planning, operating environment, size, sector and performance. *Journal of General Management*, 34(2), 1-20.

Gica, O. A., & Negrusa, A. L. (2011). The Impact of strategic planning activities on Transylvanian SMEs – an empirical research,. *Procedia Social and Behavioral Sciences*, 24, 643-648.doi:10.1016/j.sbspro.2011.09.084.

Glaister, K. W., Dincer, O., Tatoglu, E., Demirbag, M., & Zaim, S. (2008). A causal analysis of formal strategic planning and firm performance: Evidence from an emerging country. *Management Decisions*, Vol. 46, No. 3, pp 365-391.Emerald Group Publishing Limited. www.emeraldinsight.com/0025-1747.htm accessed: 16/11/09.

Hopkins, W. E., & Hopkins, S. A. (1997). Strategic planning-financial performance relationship in banks: A causal examination. *Strategic Management Journal*, Vol. 18, No. 8,pp 635-652.http://www.jstor.org/stable/3088180. accessed: 28/10/09.

Hopkins, W. E., & Hopkins, S. A. (1997). Strategic planning–financial performance relationships in banks: a causal examination. *Strategic Management Journal*, 18(8):635-652.

Jarzabkowski, P., & Balogun, J. (2009). The practice and process of delivering integration through strategic planninig. *Journal of Management Studies*, 46,1255-1288.

Kraus, S., Harms, R., & Schwarz, E.J. (2006). Strategic Planning in Smaller Enterprises: New Empirical Findings. *Management Research News*, 29 (6), 334-344.

Liu, Z., Siguaw, J. A., & Enz, C. A. (2008).). Using tourist travel habit and references to assess strategic destination positioning: The case of Costa Rica. *Cornell Hospitality Quartely*, 49,3,258-281.

Miller, C. C., & Cardinal, L. B. (1994). Strategic planning and firm performance: a synthesis of more than two decades of research. *Academy of Management Journal*, 37(6):1649-1665.

Miller, C. C., & Cardinal, L. B. (1994). Strategic planning and firms performance: A synthesis of more than two decades of research. *The Academy of Management Journal*, Vol. 37, No. 6, pp. 1649-1665.. http://www.jstor.org/stable/256804 accessed 28/10/2009.

Pearce , J. A., Freeman, E. B., & Robinson, R. B. (1987). The tenuous link between formal strategic planning and financial performance. *Academy of Management Review*, Vol. 12, No. 4, pp. 658-675.

Pearce, J. A., Robbins, D. K., & Robinson, R. B. (1987). The impact of grand strategy and planning formality on financial performance. *Strategic Management Journal*, 8(2):125-134.

Rhyne, C. L. (1986). The relationship of strategic planning to financial performance. *Strategic Management Journal*, Vol. 7, No. 5, pp 423-436.

Rhyne, L. C. (1986). The relationship of strategic planning to financial performance. *Strategic Management Journal*, 7(5):423-436.

Rigby, D., & Bilodeau, B. (2011). *Management tools and trends.* ??: Bain & Company.

Sarason, Y., & Tegarden, F. (2003). The erosion of the competitive advantage of strategic planning. *Journal of Business and Management*, 9(1),1-21.

Schraeder, M. (2002). A simplified approach to strategic planning: Practical considerations and an illustrated example. *Business Process Managment Journal*, Vol. 8, No. 1, pp 8-18.. Available at http://www.emeraldinsight.com/1463-7154.htm (September 5, 2009).

Shrader, C. B., Taylor, L., & Dalton, D. R. (2009). Strategic planning and organisational performance: A critical appraisal. *Journal of Management*, Vol. 10, No. 2, pp. 149-171.http://jom.sagepub.com/cgi/content/abstract/10/2/149 05 Sept 2009.

Song, M., Zhao, Y. L., Arend, R. J., & Subin, I. M. (n.d.). Strategic Planning As A Complex And Enabling Managerial Tool. . *Strategic Management Planning*.

Sukley, B., & Debarliev, S. (2012). Strategic planning effectiveness comparative analysis of the Macedonian context. *Economic and Business Review*, 14(1), 63-93.

Tetteh, E.N. & Ofori, D.F. (2010). An exploratory and comparative assessment of the governance arrangements of universities in Ghana. *Corporate Governance*, 10(3), 234-248.

Thompson, A. A., Strickland, A. J., & Gamble, J. E. (2008). *Crafting and executing strategy: The quest for competitive advantage: Concepts and cases.* New York: 16TH Edition- McGraw- Hill International Edition.

Venkatraman, N., & Ramanujam, V. (1986). Measurement of business performance in strategy research: A comparison of approaches. *The Academy of Management Review*, Vol. 11, No. 4, pp 801-814.www.jstor.org/stable/258398 accessed on 30/11/09.

Whittington, R., & Cailluet, L. (2008). The craft of strategy. *Long Range Planning*, 41,241-247.

Wolf, C., & Floyd, S. W. (2013). Strategic planning research: toward a theory driven agenda. *Journal of Management*, (March), 1–35.

CHAPTER EIGHT

The Effect of Internal Audit Quality on Earnings Management of Listed Firms in Ghana

Joseph Mensah Onumah, Mohammed Amidu and Augustine Donkor

1. Introduction

Earnings management (EM) has become a topical issue in both academia and practice due to the numerous corporate scandals over the years (Enron, WorldCom, Arthur Anderson, Aldelphia & Parmalat). These scandals have caused an increase in academic research in EM (Prawitt, Smith & Wood, 2009; Al-khabash & Al-Thuneibat, 2008; Cohen, Dey & Lys, 2008; Davidson, Goodwin-Stewart & Kent., 2005; Chung, Firth & Kim, 2002), creating awareness of its presence and possibly attempting to find ways to deal with it, which strengthens the position to examine the concept in the context of our environment, which is not seen to have witnessed any research in this area. Parfet (2000) and Jacksonh and Pitman (2001) assert that the possibility of management engaging in EM is high, because accounting standards (IFRS and GAAP) used in financial reporting allow management a wide scope of alternatives to treating the same transaction or event. Such managerial discretion can result in the possibility of management engaging in EM (Al-khabash & Al-Thuneibat, 2008). The need to deal with such phenomenon has resulted in an increased emphasis on the need for stronger corporate governance (CG) to ensure improved financial reporting quality (Cohen *et al.*, 2004; Rezaee, Olibe & Minmier, 2003;

Herdman, 2002). This, to Barac and Van Staden (2009), has led to the proliferation of CG guides and codes. Davies and Schlitzer (2008) adds that to restore investor-confidence in regulatory frameworks, thereby leading to greater transparency and accountability in corporate affairs, there is the need for CG guides and codes. Compliance to these regulatory frameworks is as good as instituting them; therefore the need for mechanisms to aid in their compliance in order to achieve a good CG. CG has focussed its attention on the role of maintaining transparency and accountability in financial reporting (Al-Shetwil, Ramadili, Chowdury & Sori, 2011), possibly to counter the rising number of corporate scandals. As a result, there has been the introduction of the internal audit function (IAF) as the fourth cornerstone of CG, alongside management, external auditing and the audit committee (Al-Shetwil *et al.*, 2011; Gramling, Maletta, Schneider & Church, 2004; Cohen *et al.*, 2008) to improve financial reporting quality (FRQ). High quality auditing is more likely to restrict EM (Healy & Palepu, 2001; Kim, Chung & Firth, 2003a). IAF plays an important role in the quality of work of external auditors, IAF is further seen as an additional third party that monitors management actions (Okafor & Ibadin, 2009) and the only partner of management involved in the day-to-day running of the company. If IAF is of high quality, it will be in a good position to identify the possible biases (opportunistic behaviour) exhibited by management in the course of executing their duties.

There is no demand for accounting discretion in a perfect market because there is no role for financial disclosures (Watts & Zimmerman 1978, 1986; Holthausen & Leftwich, 1983). But Sun and Rath (2008) asserts that capital markets are imperfect (information asymmetry and agency conflicts) as such financial reporting is necessary for capital market efficiency. Countries with weaker and inefficient capital markets therefore require high quality financial reports. Ghana is noted to have one of the weakest and most inefficient capital markets (Frimpong, 2008; Ayentimi, Mensah & Naa-Idar, 2013), but with more growth potentials. Quality financial information available in the market will therefore help grow capital markets (Healy & Palepu, 2001), whereas financial irregularities (such as EM practices) will possibly collapse the market. IAF quality plays a key role in the provision of such quality financial information (Prawitt *et al*, 2009; Prawitt, Sharp & Wood, 2012; IIA, 2003). Assessing the state of IAF quality in Ghana is paramount for its impact on financial reporting quality. The mechanisms of CG (including IAF) which ensure that managers of companies act in the best interest of shareholders and other stakeholders are relatively inactive in Ghana (Mensah, 2002), hence the possibility of management engaging in EM practices in Ghana. A report by the Centre for Policy Analysis - Ghana (CEPA) in 2005, hinted that the activities of IAF in the public sector are not strong in Ghana. Onumah and Krah (2012) add that while the effectiveness of IAF in the Ghanaian public sector is hampered, research on the quality of IAF in the private sector of Ghana seems to be lacking. The relative inactivity and almost a nil research available on the joint conceptual areas of IAF and EM in Ghana, as well as the weak and inefficient capital market, which can be influenced by quality financial reports, connote the need to arouse some activity in the area. The study therefore assessed the state of IAF quality in Ghana and the possible relation between IAF quality and EM of listed non-financial institutions in Ghana.

The rest of the paper is organised as follows: Section (2) reviews existing literature, Section (3) discusses the data used in the study and also details the model specification, a proxy for internal audit function, the definition of the main variables used in the analysis and the other control variables. Section (4) contains the discussion of the empirical results and section (5) summarizes and concludes the paper

2. Literature Review

The Organization for Economic Co-operation and Development (OECD, 1999) defines CG as a system by which business corporations are directed and controlled. Messier, Glover and Prawitt, (2008: p.36) adds that CG is 'a system consisting of all the people, processes and activities to help ensure proper stewardship over entities' assets'. La Porta, Lopez-de-Silanes, Shleifer and Vishny (2000) in another way sees the concept as a set of mechanisms through which outside investors protect themselves against exploitation by the insiders. To Shah, Zafar and Durrani (2009), better governance is supposed to lead to better corporate performance by preventing the exploitation of controlling shareholders and ensuring better decision-making, cases which make the subject of CG important. The agency theory underpins the need for effective CG in organisations. Jensen and Mecklin (1976) assert that the agency theory explains how public corporations exist, given the assumption that managers do not bear the full wealth effects of the decisions. Shleifer and Vishny (1997) also refer to the theory as one that helps to deal with difficulties financiers have in assuring themselves that their funds are not expropriated by managers, and therefore calling for mechanism to help deal with such issues. Shleifer and Vishny (1997) add that CG mechanisms provide shareholders some assurance that managers will strive to achieve outcomes that are in the shareholders' interests.

Good governance requires that organisations are governed in accordance with the governance principles of transparency, accountability, responsibility, participation, fairness and independency. It is indicated that 'a good CG structure helps ensure that management properly utilizes the enterprise's resources in the best interest of absentee owners, and fairly reports the financial condition and operating performance of the enterprise' (Lin & Hwang, 2010: p.59). IAF is seen to enhance the ability of CG to ensure quality financial reporting (Prawitt *et al.*, 2009; Al-Shetwil *et al.*, 2011). Norman Rose and Rose (2010) add that IAF is an important component of CG because it is a key player in the day-to-day corporate integrity, sound reporting and anti-fraud activities. The functions of IAF were expanded by IIA in their definition of the concept as 'an independent, objective assurance and consulting activity designed to add value and improve an organisation's operations' (IIA, 1999). Christopher, Sarens and Leung (2009) assert that this expansion essentially involves the provision of additional services, which are initiated by the board and management as a means of ensuring that accountability and transparency requirements of board and management are met. Ramamoorthi (2003) further adds that the focus of IAF in recent years has seen a massive shift to one that promotes and supports effective organisational governance. This, to Prawitt *et al.* (2008), allows IAF to perform work that is relevant to the host entities' financial reporting processes. The quality of IAF is paramount and is often assessed based on IAS 610. The standard posits five main components for constructing the IAF quality; objectivity, professional experience, professional certification, training and the nature of work performed relating to financial reporting.

It is worth noting that IAF may affect financial reporting quality by first affecting all the components of CG, as depicted in the CG mosaic by Cohen *et al.* (2004). Thus, Norman *et al.* (2011) suggest that IAF impacts CG and FRQ by being independent from management, serving as an assurance service provider to the board through the audit committee and providing reports that external auditors can rely on for their audits (Felix, Gramling, & Maletta, 2005). Literature asserts that external auditors rely on internal auditors for quality auditing (Mihret & Admassu, 2011) and this is influenced by the quality characteristics of internal auditors (Gramling *et al.*, 2004). To Norman *et al.* (2010), the primary role of audit committee is to ensure 'high quality financial reporting', and they do this by relying on IAF (Gramling & Hermanson, 2006).

High quality auditing enhances CG, financial reporting quality and reduces EM (Cohen *et al.*, 2004); an audit committee also has a constraining effect on earnings manipulation (Cohen *et al.*, 2004; Lin & Hwang, 2010) and an effective board negatively relates to EM (Klein, 2002; Xie *et al.*, 2003). IAF ensures the effectiveness of all these functions and, as a result, can affect EM when it is of high quality (Prawitt *et al.*, 2009).

According to Healy and Wahlen (1999: p.368), EM is 'when managers use judgment in financial reporting and in structuring transactions to alter financial reports to either mislead some stakeholders about the underlying economic performance of the company or to influence contractual outcomes that depend on reported accounting numbers'. Good CG enhances the reliability of financial reports (Cohen *et al.*, 2004) and reduces the possibility of EM (Rezaee *et al.*, 2003). IAF contributes to enhanced CG performance and therefore can reduce EM. These reviewed researches and studies have highlighted the concept of CG, the strengthening position of the IAF and the EM issues as evolved by management. It is the context of Ghana which is missing in the literature and which this study hopes to contribute to.

3. Research Methodology

Sample and Selection Criteria

Non-financial firms listed on the Ghana Stock Exchange (GSE) from 2007 representing the IFRS years of Ghana's adoption formed the sample of the study; in all, 15 firms were selected as the sample for the study (these 15 firms are those listed before 2007 and had a substantive IAF). The study used non-financial firms as there is no common construct for assessing financial reporting quality of both financial and non-financial firms together. Also, the number of listed financial firms for the period of the study is very much limited. To achieve the objectives of the study, two constructs are measured; EM and IAF, where EM is the dependent variable and measured by the discretionary accrual method, with data gleaned from the annual reports of sampled firms from 2007 to 2012. IAF is the independent variable for the study, its data were collected through a survey strategy using questionnaires.

Measurement of Variables

Internal Audit Function Quality

The study adapted the composite measure of IAF quality by Prawitt *et al.* (2009). This measure is pinned upon IAS 610 which prescribes the factors external auditors must take into consideration when assessing the quality and effectiveness of internal auditors. The measure therefore assesses the competence, the objectivity and the nature of work performed by internal auditors relating to financial reporting. These three components are expanded further to five characteristics. The study measures competencies of internal auditors based on professional experience, professional certifications and training (of internal auditors). The study assigned one (1) to experience if the average number of years of internal auditor's practice exceeds the mean number of years of the sample; otherwise zero (0) is assigned. Professional certification was proxied on whether the internal auditors hold professional certificate for their practice as auditors. With this, the study assigned one (1), if the internal auditors hold professional certificates; otherwise zero (0) is assigned. Training of internal auditors was measured based on the average number of training hours per year of internal auditors. The study assigned one (1) if this measure is above the mean hours of training of the sampled firms, otherwise zero (0) is assigned.

The objectivity of internal auditors is also based on who the internal auditor reports to; is it to management, or to the board through the audit committee of the board. The study assigned one (1) if internal auditors report to the board, otherwise zero (0). Reporting to management, according to Balkaran (2007), undermines the IAF's independence and objectivity and therefore affects the quality of IAF. Assessing the quality of internal auditors in relation to EM required the study to take into consideration the nature of work of internal auditors to financial reporting. Prawitt *et al.* (2009) asserts that a well-funded IAF will work effectively towards quality financial reporting; ISA 610 requires external auditors to consider the work of internal auditors but with a caveat that the work must be of high quality, and internal auditors' perception on the percentage of their work that relate to financial reporting. These are therefore used to measure the nature of an internal auditor's work towards financial reporting. The study assigned one (1) when the released budget is more than 50% of budgeted amount, assigned one (1) when external auditors uses the work of internal auditors, assigned one (1) when the perception of internal auditors out of a scale of 5, recorded above three; otherwise zero (0) is assigned to all the situations. The nature of the auditor's work towards financial reporting is assigned one (1) when the three measures record above their average; otherwise zero (0) is assigned.

To form the composite measure for IAF quality, each variable is dichotomised to one (1) and zero (0). The five variables representing the components of IAF quality were then added to create IAF quality. A score of zero (0) meant a low IAF quality and a score of five (5) meant a high IAF quality.

Earnings Management

The discretionary accrual model (Jones, 1991) was adopted to measure EM in this study, because it has been proven to be the ideal method (Rezaee & Roshani, 2012; Al-Shetwil *et al.*, 2011; Prawitt *et al.*, 2008). Specifically the study adopted the modified Jones model (Dechow, Sloan & Sweeney, 1995) because it had been used extensively in prior literature and accepted as an appropriate measure for discretionary accruals estimation (Kent, Routledge & Stewart, 2010; Collins, Pungaliya & Vijh, 2012). To use this model, total accruals (TAC) and non-discretionary accruals (NACC) are estimated in order to determine the discretionary accruals (EM).

In computing for total accruals, the cash flow approach is adopted. Even though the balance sheet approach has been used in the majority of prior studies (e.g. Jones, 1991; Dechow *et al.*, 1995), Collins and Hribar (2002) argue that the balance sheet approach is identified as not including some other non-current accruals, such as overstated provisions for restructuring costs and loan losses or warranty costs, but only takes into account depreciation and amortization. The latter study further argues that the frequency and magnitude of errors introduced when using the balance sheet approach can be more substantial than the cash flow approach. In line with these, total accruals (TAC) were measured based on the cash flow approach as;

$$TAC_{it} = EbXA_{it} - Oc_{it} \text{ -- (1)}$$

Where: $EbXA_{it}$ is defined as earnings before extraordinary and abnormal items of a given firm i in year t and OC_{it} is the operating cash flow of a specific firm i in year t. Non-discretionary accruals are then estimated as the fitted values based on the equation

$$NACC_{it} = \beta_0 + \beta_1\left(\frac{1}{A_{it-1}}\right) + \beta_1\left(\frac{\Delta REV_{it} - \Delta AR_{it}}{A_{it-1}}\right) + \beta_3\left(\frac{PPE_{it}}{A_{it-1}}\right) + \epsilon_{it} \text{------ (2)}$$

Where:

-TAC_{it} / A_{it-1} is non-discretionary accrual (NACC), ΔREV is change in operating revenues, ΔAR is change in account receivables and PPE is gross property, plant and equipment.

In line with the work of Healy (1985) and DeAngelo (1986), discretionary/abnormal accruals (DAC) were calculated as the difference between TAC and NACC. Accordingly, the DAC was the residual from the above regression and derived as follows:

$DAcc_{it} = TAC_{it} - NACC_{it}$ -- (3)

Empirical Framework

To assess the extent to which IAF Quality affects EM, the regression model is tested:

$$DAcc = \beta_0 + \beta_1(IAFquality) + \beta_1(ACeffectiveness) + \beta_3(EAquality) + \beta_4(Size) + \beta_5(Leverage) + \beta_6(ROA) + \beta_7(MBV) + \beta_8(CFO) + \epsilon_{it} \text{--- (4)}$$

Where; 'IAFquality' is internal audit function quality which was measured using a composite measure of five (5) variables (professional experience, professional certification, training, line of reporting and the internal audit size). Audit Committee Effectiveness (ACeffectiveness) was also measured based on a composite measure of three variables (size, independence and financial expertise) and External Audit Quality (EAquality) measured using dummy variable based on whether the firm uses Big4 audit firm or not.

The study controls for a number of variables of which prior studies have shown to affect the relationship between IAF quality and EM (Al-Shetwil *et al.*, 2011; Rusmin, 2010; Prawitt *et al.*, 2009; Becker, 1998). The study controls for firms size on assertions that larger firms are more inclined to management earning because of operational complexities (Lobo & Zhou, 2006). Klapper and Love (2004) are of the opinion that such large firms have better corporate governance mechanisms which are expected to deal with such complexities. The study further controls, for the effect of leverage on EM (Rusmin, 2010), performance on EM, cash flows on EM and firm value on EM.

4. Empirical Results

The results indicate that discretionary accruals (a proxy for EM) recorded an overall mean of 0.219, with a standard deviation of 0.217 and a minimum and maximum of practices hovering around 0.0014 and 0.9254, respectively. This indicates the prevalent of EM practices in Ghana. This results is in line with Agyekum, Aboagye–Otchere and Bedi (2014). The engagement of EM among firms in Ghana (as seen in Fig.8.1) was high in 2007, but consistently fell until 2010, and then increased again. This indicates that as Ghana adopted IFRS initially, the practice of EM kept falling until 2010, and increased again from 2011 onwards. On industry lines, the Distribution and Trading Industry over the years had reducing levels of EM practices recording an average of 0.1401 with the Printing, Publishing and ICT Industry recording the highest average level of EM practices of 0.3333.

Figure 8.1: EM Levels in Ghana over years

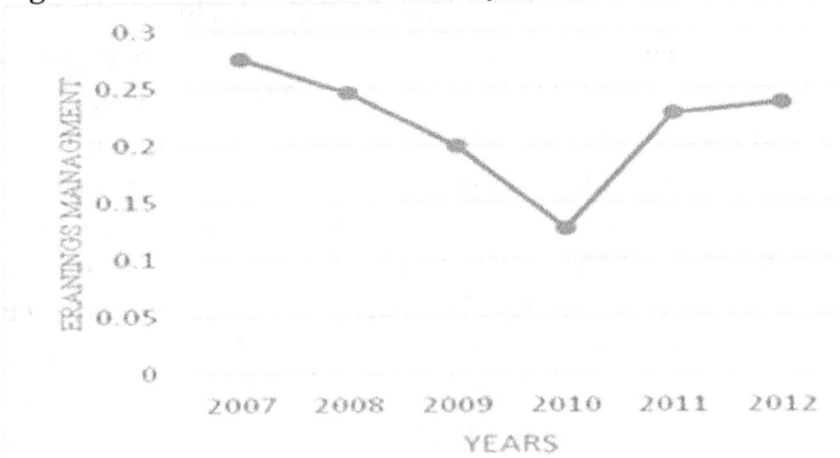

Figure 8.2: IAF Quality at Industry Levels

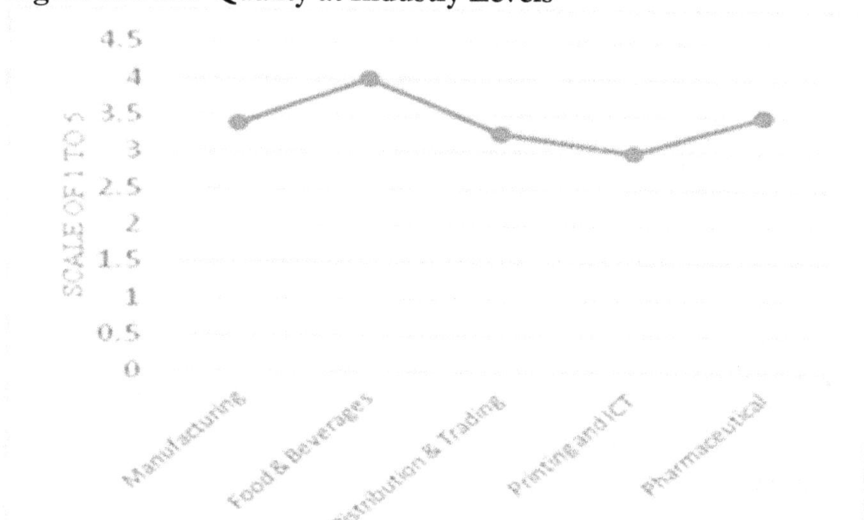

Figure 8.3: EM practices across Industries

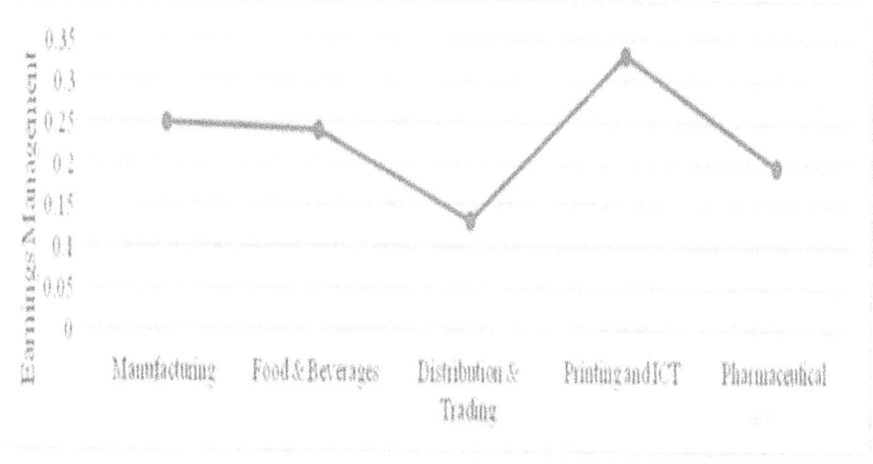

The results of the study indicate that with a quality scale of 1 to 5, the quality level of IAF of listed firms was on average of 3.4. This does indicate that the quality levels of IAF of listed firms can be considered as moderately high. Thus, on a scale of 0 (weak) to 5 (high), the IAF quality of listed firms recorded a mean of 3.4, with a spread between 2 and 4, which was significant at a 1% significant level, with t-test computed at 40.09. From Figure 2, the Food and Beverage Industry is identified with the highest level of IAF quality, with Printing, Publishing and ICT recording the lowest measure.

4.1 *Correlation and Regression Results*

The correlation between the dependent variable EM and the independent variables were not very strong per Table 8.3. All the CG variables were negatively related with EM, as expected according to the agency theory. CG variables per the agency relationship are expected to reduce management opportunistic behavior (Klein, 2002). Control variables over times have often had different relationships with the measure of EM across studies (Stubben, 2010; Prawitt *et al.*, 2009). Firm size and return on assets were also negatively related to EM, while firm value, leverage of the firm and cash flow from operating activities, positively related to EM.

Table 8.1: Descriptive Statistics

Variable	Mean	Std. Dev.	Min	Max
Earnings Management	0.219	0.217	0.0014	0.9254
IAF Quality	3.4	0.83	2	4
Firm Size	76.73	77.97	0.89	289.27
Cash Flow Volatility	7.02	16.53	-44.70	61.59
External Audit Quality	0.71	0.46	0	1
Audit Committee Effectiveness	2.87	0.50	1	3
Leverage	0.60	0.24	0.08	1.00
Performance	0.088	0.142	-0.31	0.38
Firm Value	4.49	15.35	-16.37	141.83
t-test (IAF Quality)	40.09	P value <	0.000	

Source: Research Study, 2014

Table 8.2 represents the Random Effects regression results, which were chosen based on the Hausman Specification Test.

The results indicated that the coefficients were not significantly different (Chi square = 5.78 with a probability of 0.6721 – Table 8.4). The regression results show an overall R-square of 34.88% and a Wald chi-square value of 43.39. This indicates that the independent variables of the model explain just about 34.88% of the dependent variable (EM), significant at a 1% significance level. The R-squared obtained could be considered high when compared to that in other studies on EM (Lev, 1989; Stubben, 2010; Ali, Salleh & Hassan, 2008; Rahman & Ali, 2006; Davidson *et al.*, 2005; Saleh, Iskandar & Rahmat, 2005), which studies recorded an adjusted R-squared between 12.8% and 28%. These indicate that the overall R-square obtained is consistent with prior studies on EM.

Table 8.2. Regression Results

Model	Coefficient
IAF Quality	-0.3629*
	(0.2172)
Aceffeciveness	-0.0208
	(0.0455)
EAquality	-0.0637
	(0.0528)
Size	-0.0538*
	(0.0321)
Performance	-0.2810**
	(0.1404)
Firm Value	0.1263***
	(0.0388)
Leverage	0.0021
	(0.0118)
CFO Volatility	0.3408***
	(0.0797)
Constant	0.6835***
	(0.2401)
R square	
Within	0.3610
Between	0.1179
Overall	0.3488
Wald Chi-square (8)	43.39
Prob. > Chi^2	0.0000
No. of Observation	90

Notes: The dependent variable is the EM, measured using discretionary accruals (DAC). IAF Quality is the measure for the quality levels of internal audit function. Aceffeciveness proxies for audit committee effectiveness and EAquality measures external audit quality, based on whether the firm uses "Big four audit firm" or not. Natural logarithm of total assets measures size of the firm. ROA is the proxy for firm performance, firm value is measured by market to book value ratio and leverage is measured by the ratio of total debt to total asset. Standard deviation of Cash Flow from operating activities was used as a proxy to measure CFO volatility. Standard errors are reported in parentheses.

**Statistical significance at 10% level. **Statistical significance at 5% level.*
****Statistical significance at 1% level.*

From Table 8.2, the results show a negative and significant relationship between IAF quality and EM, as predicted in other works (Al-Shetwil *et al.*, 2011; Prawitt *et al.*, 2009) and the agency theory. This was at a 10% significance level. This presupposes that high quality IAF mitigates the tendency of management's opportunistic behaviour to engage in EM. This can possibly explain the reason the Printing, Publishing and ICT industry recorded the highest level of EM practices (Fig. 8.3) because it recorded the lowest level of IAF quality among the industries listed on the GSE (Fig. 8.2). This is consistent with the agency theory which posits that there is the need to monitor management to reduce their tendency of engaging in illicit activities. It is however inconsistent with the works of Davidson *et al.* (2005), Ratsula (2010) and Al-Shetwil *et al.* (2011) which studies, even though they found a negative relationship between IAF quality and EM, were findings that were not significant. Again, the result is consistent with Klein's (2002) assertion that monitoring systems attributable to CG, when effective in reducing management's capacity to manage earnings.

Table 8.3: Correlation Matrix of the Independent Variables

	EM	IAFQ	ACEFF	EAQ	SIZE	ROA	FIRMV	LEV	CFOv
EM	1.00								
IAFQ	-0.11	1.00							
ACEFF	-0.10	0.12	1.00						
EAQ	-0.13	0.32	0.22	1.00					
SIZE	-0.20	-0.14	0.31	0.22	1.00				
ROA	-0.19	0.08	0.01	-0.04	0.29	1.00			
FIRMV	0.21	-0.19	0.19	-0.17	0.40	0.21	1.00		
LEV	0.10	-0.14	-0.01	0.27	-0.10	0.33	-0.02	1.00	
CFOv	0.42	0.18	0.04	-0.24	-0.14	0.05	-0.01	-0.10	1.00

Table 8.4: Hausman's Test for Model 1 (Dependent Variable = Discretionary Accruals)

Variable	Fixed Effect	Random Effect	Difference	Std. Error
IAF quality	-0.35006	-0.36294	0.012887	-
Aceffectiveness	-0.02418	-0.02077	-0.003418	0.0014297
EAquality	-0.06225	-0.06375	0.001492	-
Size	-0.04877	-0.05376	0.004989	0.0050966
Performance	-0.30323	-0.28098	-0.022249	0.011735
Firm Value	0.129817	0.126392	0.003425	0.0028532
Leverage	0.002636	0.002066	0.000571	0.0001934
CFO Volatility	0.346822	0.340786	0.006036	0.0174988

Test: Ho: Difference in coefficients not systematic
Chi square (8) = 5.78
Prob. > chi square = 0.6721

The study found a negative insignificant relationship between audit committee effectiveness and EM. This result is not consistent with the agency theory and CG mechanisms, and further not consistent with literature asserting that the committee is an important component of CG that ensures quality financial reports (PwC, 1999: p.7; Bansal, 2005: p 129; Krishnan, 2005; Norman *et al.*, 2010). However, the result is consistent with Rahman and Ali (2006) and Prawitt *et al.* (2009). The quality of External Auditing was also not significant but was negatively related to EM as in the works of Davidson *et al.* (2005) and Ali *et al.* (2008), but inconsistent with a lot of other literature which found a negative significant relationship between audit quality and EM (Kent *et al.*, 2010; Chen *et al.*, 2009).

Size of a firm has negative significant relationship with EM. This was consistent with the works of Davidson *et al.* (2005), Al-Shetwil *et al.* (2011), Rahman and Ali (2006) and Xie, Davidson and DaDalt (2003). Performance of the firm (ROA) also had a negative significant relationship with EM practices, indicating that in periods of higher earnings there is less need for EM and vice versa (Davidson *et al.*, 2005; Prawitt *et al.*, 2009; Al-Shetwil *et al.*, 2011). Firm value (MBV) on the other hand recorded a positive significant relationship with EM. This was consistent with Davidson *et al.* (2005), but inconsistent with Prawitt *et al.* (2009). Leverage of firms was positively related to EM as expected, but was insignificant. The volatility in cash flow on the other hand was found to be positive and significant, relating to EM practices. This is consistent with the findings of Hribar and Nichols (2007) and Prawitt *et al.* (2009).

5. Conclusion

This study examined IAF quality and how it relates possibly with EM. The data were from 2007 to 2012. The results of the study affirm the assertion of agency theory, that there is the need for monitoring mechanisms in agency relationships. Thus all the CG monitoring components (IAF, Audit Committee and External Auditing) negatively related to the practices of EM and therefore the need to put in measures to enhance them.

IAF quality in Ghana was found to be moderately high and negatively related to EM practices, implying that the higher the IAF quality, the lesser the practice of EM. EM practices, on the other hand, were also found to be high and consistent among firms in Ghana. The practice was found to be prevalent among industries that had IAF quality, less than the average measure of IAF in the study. This supports the assertion that high quality IAF has the potential of dealing with EM practices in Ghana. This finding has implications on policy, thus it presupposes that Ghana should rethink its position on internal auditing in the private sector, and make it a compulsory unit of every listed firm, rather than stick to its current state, this change is necessary in order to follow current international practices (Sarbanes, 2002).

The study recommends that other studies be conducted to assess the exact effect of IFRS adoption on EM practices in Ghana, since the study's results project that IFRS adoption caused EM practices in Ghana to fall at the early stages of the adoption but started rising afterwards. It is the view of the study that further studies be conducted to assess various means in improving the quality of IAF both in the public and the private sector of Ghana. With a negative relationship between firm size and performance with EM, the study recommends that further studies ought to be conducted to seek to establish the reasons for EM practices in Ghana, other than the known reasons globally.

References

Agyekum, A. A. B., Aboagye–Otchere, F., & Bedi, I. (2014). Earnings management and corporate governance: the Ghanaian experience. .*International Journal of Management Practice*, *7*(4), 309-323.

Ali, S. M., Salleh, N. M., & Hassan, M. S. (2008). Ownership structure and earnings management in Malaysian listed companies: the size effect. *Asian Journal of Business and Accounting*, *1*(2), 89-116.

Al-khabash, A. A., & Al-Thuneibat, A. A. (2008). Earnings management practices from the perspective of external and internal auditors: evidence from Jordan. *Managerial Auditing Journal*, *24*(1), 58-80.

Al-Shetwi1 M., Ramadili S. M., Chowdury T. H. S., & Sori Z. M., (2011). Impact of internal audit function on financial reporting quality: Evidence from Saudi Arabia. *African*

Journal of Business Management Vol.5 Issue27, pp. 11189-11198

Ayentimi, D. T., Mensah, A. E., & Naa-Idar, F. (2013). Stock market efficiency of Ghana stock exchange: An objective analysis. *International Journal of Management, Economics and Social Sciences (IJMESS), 2*(2), 54-75.

Balkaran, L. (2007). A solid reporting line. *The Internal Auditor,* 64(1), 96–97.

Bansal P. (2005). Evolving sustainably: A longitudinal study of corporate sustainable development. *Strategic Management Review* 26(3): 197–218.

Barac, K., & Van Staden, M. (2009). The correlation between perceived internal audit quality and defined corporate governance soundness. *African Journal of Business Management, 3*(13), 946-958.

Chen, Q., Kelly, K., & Salterio, S. (2009). Does auditing deter potentially fraudulent earnings management? An experimental investigation. *An Experimental Investigation (November 30, 2010).* Type of publication??

Christopher, J., Sarens, G., & Leung, P. (2009). A critical analysis of the independence of the internal audit function: Evidence from Australia. *Accounting, Auditing & Accountability Journal, 22*(2), 200-220.

Chung, R., Firth, M., & Kim, J.B. (2002). Institutional monitoring and opportunistic earnings management. *Journal of Corporate Finance* Vol. 8, pp. 29-48.

Cohen D. A., Dey A., & Lys T. Z. (2008). Real and accrual-based earnings management in the pre and post-Sarbanes-Oxley periods. *Accounting Review*, Vol. 83 Issue3, pp. 757-787.

Cohen, J., Krishnamoorthy, G. & Wright, A. (2004). The corporate governance mosaic and financial reporting quality. *Journal of Accounting Literature*, 23, 87-152

Collins, D. & Hribar, P., (2002). Errors in estimating accruals: Implications for empirical research. *Journal of Accounting Research*, Vol. 40, Issue 1, p105-135.

Collins, D., Pungaliya, R., & Vijh, A. (2012). The effects of firm growth and model specification choices on tests of earnings management in quarterly settings. *Available at SSRN 1823835*.

Davidson, R., Goodwin-Stewart, J., & Kent, P. (2005). Internal governance structures and earnings management. *Accounting & Finance*, *45*(2), 241-267.

Davies, M., & Schlitzer, B. (2008). The impracticality of an international "one size fits all" corporate governance code of best practice. *Managerial Auditing Journal*, *23*(6), 532-544.

DeAngelo, L., (1986). Accounting numbers as market valuation substitutes: A study of management buyouts of public stockholders. *The Accounting Review*, Vol. 41, pp. 400-420.

Dechow, P. M., Sloan, R.G, & Sweeney, A., (1995). Detecting earnings management. *The Accounting Review*, Vol. 70, No. 2, April, pp. 193-225.

Felix, W. L., Gramling, A. A., & Maletta, M. J. (2005). The influence of non-audit service revenues and client pressure on external auditors' decisions to rely on internal audit. *Contemporary Accounting Research*, *22*(1), 31-53.

Frimpong, J. M. (2008). Capital market efficiency: An analysis of weak-form efficiency on the Ghana stock exchange. *Journal of Money, Investment and Banking*, (5), 5-12.

Gramling, A. A., & Hermanson, D. R. (2006). What role is your internal audit function playing in corporate governance? *Internal Auditing-Boston-Warren Gorham and Lamont Incorporated-*, *21*(6), 37.

Gramling, A., Maletta, M. J., Schneider, & Church, B. K. (2004). The role of the internal audit functions in corporate governance. *J.Account. Lit.*, Vol. 23, pp.194-244.

Healy, P. M. (1985). The effect of bonus schemes on accounting decisions. *Journal of Accounting and Economics*, *7*(1), 85-107.

Healy, P. M., & Palepu, K. G. (2001). Information asymmetry, corporate disclosure, and the capital markets: A review of the empirical disclosure literature. *Journal of Accounting and Economics*, *31*(1), 405-440.

Healy, P., & Wahlen, J. (1999). A review of the earnings management literature and its implications for standard setting. *Accounting Horizons*, Vol. 13, Issue 4, Dec pp. 365-384.

Herdman, R. (2002*). Making audit committees more effective.* Speech at Tulane Corporate Law Institute, March 10. Available at: http://www.sec.gov/news/speech/spch543.htm.

Holthausen, R. W., & Leftwich, R. W. (1983). The economic consequences of accounting choice implications of costly contracting and monitoring. *Journal of Accounting and Economics*, *5*, 77-117.

Hribar, P., & Craig Nichols, D. (2007). The use of unsigned earnings quality measures in tests of earnings management. *Journal of Accounting Research*, *45*(5), 1017-1053.

Hribar, P., & Craig Nichols, D. (2007). The use of unsigned earnings quality measures in tests of earnings management. *Journal of Accounting Research*, *45*(5), 1017-1053.

IIA (1999). *A vision for the future: Professional practices framework for internal auditing,* The Institute of Internal Auditors Research Foundation, Altamonte Springs, FL

IIA (2003). Internal audit reporting relationships: Serving two masters. *The IIA Research Foundation*

Jacksonh, S. B., & Pitman, M. K. (2001). Auditors and earnings management. *The CPA Journal, 71*(7), 38. ??

Jensen, M. C, & Meckling, W. H. 1976. Theory of the firm: Managerial behavior, agency costs and ownership structure. *Journal of Financial Economics*, 3: 305-360

Jones, J. (1991). Earnings management during import relief investigations. *Journal of Accounting Research*, Vol. 29, No. 2, pp. 193-223.

Kent, P., Routledge, J., & Stewart, J. (2010). Innate and discretionary accruals quality and corporate governance. *Accounting & Finance*, *50*(1), 171-195.

Kim, J. B., Chung, R., & Firth, M. (2003a). Auditor conservatism, asymmetric monitoring and earnings management. *Contemporary Accounting Research* Vol. 20 Issue2, pp.323-359

Klein, A. (2002). Audit committee, board of director characteristics and earnings management. *Journal of Accounting and Economics* Vol. 33 Issue3, pp. 375-400.

Krishnan, J. (2005). Audit committee quality and internal control: An empirical analysis. *The Accounting Review* 80 (2), 649–675.

La Porta, R., Lopez-de-Silanes, F., Shleifer, A., & Vishny, R. (2000). Investor protection and corporate governance. *Journal of Financial Economics*, *58*(1), 3-27.

Lev, B. (1989). On the usefulness of earnings and earnings research: Lessons and directions from two decades of empirical research. *Journal of Accounting Research, 27, 153–192 (Supplement)*

Lin, J. W., & Hwang, M. I. (2010). Audit quality, corporate governance, and earnings management: A meta-analysis. *International Journal of Auditing, 14*(1), 57-77.

Mensah, S. (2002). Corporate governance in Ghana: Issues and challenges. In *African Capital Markets Conference, December, Accra, Ghana.*

Messier, W. Jr., Glover, S., & Prawitt, D. (2008). *Auditing and assurance services: A systematic approach,* 6th Edition, New York, NY: McGraw-Hill Irwin,

Mihret, D. G., & Admassu, M. A. (2011). Reliance of external auditors on internal audit work: a corporate governance perspective. *International Business Research, 4*(2), p67.

Norman, C. S., Rose, A. M., & Rose, J. M. (2010). Internal audit reporting lines, fraud risk decomposition, and assessments of fraud risk. *Accounting, Organizations and Society, 35*(5), 546-557.

OECD (1999). *OECD Principles of corporate governance,* Organisation for Economic Cooperation and Development, Paris.

Okafor, C., & Ibadin P. (2009). The imperatives of internal audit in Nigerian banks: Issues and prospects. *Global Journal of Social Sciences* 8, (2): 21-27.

Onumah, J. M., & Krah, R. Y. (2012). Barriers and catalysts to effective internal audit in the Ghanaian public sector. *Research in Accounting in Emerging Economies, 12*, 177-207.

Parfet, W. U. (2000). Accounting subjectivity and earnings management: A preparer perspective. *Accounting Horizons, 14*(4), 481-488.

Prawitt, D. F., Sharp, N. Y., & Wood, D. A. (2012). Internal audit outsourcing and the risk of misleading or fraudulent financial reporting: Did Sarbanes-Oxley get it wrong? *Contemporary Accounting Research, 29*(4), 1109-1136.

Prawitt, D. F., Smith, J. L., & Wood, D. A. (2009). Internal audit quality and earnings management. *The Accounting Review, 84*(4), 1255-1280.,

Prawitt, D., N. Sharp, & Wood, D., (2008). *Does internal auditing affect the external audit fee?* Working Paper, Brigham Young University, Texas A&M University, Brigham Young University

PricewaterhouseCoopers (1999). *Audit committees: Good practices for meeting market expectations.* New York, NY: PricewaterhouseCoopers.

Rahman, R. A., & Ali, F. H. M. (2006). Board, audit committee, culture and earnings management: Malaysian evidence. *Managerial Auditing Journal, 21*(7), 783-804.

Ramamoorthi, S. (2003). *Internal Auditing: History, Evolution and Prospects.* The Institute of Internal Auditors Research Foundation.

Ratsula, O. P. (2010). *The interplay between internal governance structures, audit fees and earnings management in Finnish listed companies.* Accounting Master's thesis, Department of Accounting & Finance, Alto University School of Economics

Rezaee, F., & Roshani, M. (2012). Efficient or opportunistic earnings management with regards to the role of firm size and corporate governance practices. *Interdisciplinary Journal of Contemporary Research in Business, January, 3*(9).

Rezaee, Z., Olibe, K. O., & Minmier, G. (2003). Improving corporate governance: The role of audit committee disclosures. *Managerial Auditing Journal, 18*(6/7), 530-537.

Saleh, N. M., Iskandar, T. M., & Rahmat, M. M. (2005). Earnings management and board characteristics: Evidence from Malaysia. *Jurnal Pengurusan*, *24*(4), 77-103.

Sarbanes, P. (2002, July). *Sarbanes-oxley act of 2002.* In The Public Company Accounting Reform and Investor Protection Act. Washington DC: US Congress.

Shah, S. Z. A., Zafar, N., & Durrani, T. K. (2009). Board composition and earnings management an empirical evidence from Pakistani listed companies. *Middle Eastern Finance and Economics*, *3*(29), 30-44.

Shleifer, A., & Vishny, R. W. (1997). A survey of corporate governance. *The Journal of Finance*, *52*(2), 737-783.

Stubben, S. R. (2010). Discretionary revenues as a measure of earnings management. *The Accounting Review*, *85*(2), 695-717.

Sun, L., & Rath, S. (2008). Fundamental determinants, opportunistic behaviour and signalling mechanism: An integration of earnings management perspectives. *International Review of Business Research Papers*, *4*(4), 406-420.

Watts, R. L., & Zimmerman, J. L. (1978). Towards a positive theory of the determination of accounting standards. *Accounting Review*, 112-134.

Xie, B., Davidson, W. N., & DaDalt, P. J. (2003). Earnings management and corporate governance: the role of the board and the audit committee. *Journal of Corporate Finance*, *9*(3), 295-316.

CHAPTER NINE

Social Marketing Interventions on Domestic Energy Conservation in Ghana

Ernest Yaw Tweneboah-Koduah, and Weetsa Marian Adinku

1. Introduction

Energy conservation has become a very critical issue at this time of Ghana's economic and social development. Many countries are undergoing energy conservation measures by lowering their consumption levels and using energy saving appliances (Bichard and Thurairajah, 2013). There has been varying opinions on radio talk shows and social media on Ghana's energy crisis (Arko, 2013) as to how the government can solve Ghana's energy crisis. Hospitals, businesses and domestic consumers have suffered considerably from power cuts. Irrespective of efforts by governments to increase the amount of energy produced in Ghana, the country is still struggling to supply reliable power to it consumers, which is a major constraints to Ghana's economic growth (Energy Group Africa Region, 2013). The continued disruption in the supply of power in Ghana has had significant adverse effects on national output, foreign exchange reserves, and tax revenues. This has led to an investment of about US$2.2 billion in gas infrastructure and power-barge by the government of Ghana (MOFEP, 2014). This money could have been spent in other productive sectors of the economy.

The blame for the power cuts has been alluded to several reasons: low levels of water in the Volta Lake and droughts, gas shortage as a result of damage to the pipelines of the West

Africa Gas Pipeline Project (Brew-Hammond and Kemausuor, 2007; Gyabaah, 2011; Centre for Policy Analysis, 2007). In almost all the ongoing public debates, the critical issue of energy conservation, which is essential for preventing future energy crisis and ensuring sustainable power supply in the country, is barely mentioned (Arko, 2013). In Ghana, households form the bulk of energy consumers, accounting for 73 per cent of the total power generated in the country. This is followed by the mining sector (13%), 7% for the Northern Electrification sector and another 7 % for the rest of the consumers (Arko, 2013). Social marketing seeks to change the knowledge, attitudes and ultimately the behaviour of individuals and groups (Andreasen, 2003). Social marketing is increasingly recognised to be an effective tool to change people's behaviour, providing a fuller appraisal and understanding of marketing process and outcomes (Dibb and Carrigan, 2013).

Energy conservation is typically defined as a reduction in the total amount of energy consumed (Gillingham, Newell, & Palmer, 2009). It also refers to reducing energy usage or the practice of decreasing the quantity of energy used (Fuseini, 2011). Since 2005, the Ghana Energy Foundation has brought out many social marketing intervention programmes for the efficient use of energy, including the distribution of fluorescent bulbs that consumes less energy than the incandescent bulbs (Energy Foundation, 2008). This is as a result of Ghanaians use of many electrical gadgets such as TV's in multiple rooms, microwaves, computers, ipads and mobile phones that are constantly on charge (Nsakie-Kassim 2010). Many Ghanaians associate energy conservation and efficiency with the use of expensive technology such as solar panels and wind turbines because of the lack of concise and clear communication on how to conserve energy in homes and companies (Nsakie-Kassim, 2010). Considerable amounts of energy can be saved through behavioural change, which can only be realised through effective social marketing interventions.

When examining how individuals change or modify their behaviours, the Transtheoritical Model (TTM) allows implementers to understand when particular shifts in cognitions, intentions, and behaviours occur, and how they occur (Cismaru, Lavack, Hadjistavronpoulos and Dorsch, 2008). The transtheoretical model which has been used in several interventions (Matsudo, 2002; Prochaska, 2004; Reger, 2002) hypothesise, that behavioural change unfolds through a series of stages. Therefore, it is critical to understand and identify the stage an individual is in before a successful change intervention can be designed and applied (Stead, Hastings and McDermott 2007). From initial studies of smoking, the TTM rapidly has expanded to include investigations and applications to a broad range of health and mental health behaviours, mammography and cancer screening, medication compliance, HIV testing intentions, unplanned pregnancy prevention, pregnancy and smoking, sun exposure and physicians practising preventive medicine (Tweneboah-Koduah, 2013; Prochaska, Spring, and Nigg, 2008).

Irrespective of the numerous applications and benefits of the transtheoretical model to social marketing interventions, little empirical research has been conducted on the model's application to energy conservation behaviour in Ghana. In Ghana, the limited research carried out on energy conservation has concentrated mostly on the need for energy conservation and the amount of energy consumed yearly (Dramani and Tewari, 2013). To fill this gap, the transtheoretical model, serves as the theoretical underpinning for this study, to understand how it could be employed to design an effective social marketing campaign for energy conservation in Ghana.

2. Literature Review

French & Blair-Stevens, (2010) define social marketing as the systematic application of marketing alongside other concepts and techniques, to achieve specific behavioural goals, for the social good. Social marketing has become a powerful tool for social change, outlining its domain around voluntary behavioural change (Andreasen, 2002). Over the past two to three decades, marketers and public health experts have developed and refined this thinking, learning particularly from international development efforts, where social marketing was used to inform family planning and disease control programmes (Manoff, 1985). Social marketing has been sufficiently used as a tool in pursing health education practice, such as mental health, HIV/AIDs, malaria, breastfeeding, condom use and many others (Whitelaw, 2010). Countries such as Australia have used social marketing to try and solve or minimise its energy use, by advocating for energy conservation and consumptions (Gray and Bean, 2010).

Academics in the 1980s and 1990s defined social marketing programmes as containing the following elements: consumer orientation (Lefebvre and Flora, 1988; Andreasen, 1995), exchange (Lefebvre, 1996; Leather & Hastings, 1987) and a long term planning approach (Andreasen, 1995). This was further developed by Andreasen (2002) who identified six benchmarks for genuine social marketing interventions: 1) behaviour change, 2) consumer research, 3) segmentation and targeting, 4) use of the marketing mix of products, price, place, and promotion (McCarthy, 1960), 5) exchange, and 6) consideration of competition. These criteria inform practitioners with the knowledge of knowing if their interventions fall under social marketing. The implementers of social marketing use the media in communicating their interventions to the target market. Therefore, the next section discusses the social marketing media.

3. Social Marketing Media

The channels used by the implementers of social marketing interventions include television, radio, newspapers and internet (Petrella, Speechley, Kleinstiver and Ruddy 2005). According to the authors, television was most frequently observed, with 58.9% of the test respondents, versus 48.4% of control respondents ($P < .01$). Radio showed a difference, with 28.6% (test) versus 19.5% (control) ($P < .01$), billboard with 25.9% (test) versus 16.0% (control) ($P < .03$). These mediums were found to have a significant value which is lower than 0.05. Juwaheer, Vencatachellum, Pudaruth, and Saib (2012) posit that radio and billboards are effective communication mediums in which information can be delivered to target audience. Iqbal's (2013) study on selecting an appropriate source of media, shows that billboards was one of the most efficient and effective ways of causing a positive response, when intending to change behaviour.

According to Sweenzy, Soutar and Mazzarol (2012) 'word of mouth' (WOM) messages had a greater effect on people's willingness to use a service and this is increasingly becoming recognised as an important promotional tool, particularly within a professional services environment where credibility and quality plays a critical role in consumers' choice (Sweenzy, Soutar & Mazzarol, 2008). Furthermore, McDonnel (2005) and Nielsen, (2007) conclude that modern consumers have become less attentive to traditional advertising. This has influenced organisations to reduce their expenditure on traditional advertising and revisited WOM as a powerful marketing tool (Kilby, 2007). Based on the above literature, the following hypotheses are formulated.

> Hypothesis 1: Television has no positive and significant impact on people's behavioural change with respect to energy conservation.
> Hypothesis 2: Radio has no positive and significant impact on people's behavioural change with respect to energy conservation.
> Hypothesis 3: flyer/billboard has no positive and significant impact on people's behavioural change with respect to energy conservation
> Hypothesis 4: word of mouth has no positive and significant impact on people's behavioural change with respect to energy conservation

The persuasive impact of messages depend both on factors associated with information, such as the type, structure and arguments, and on the recipient's personal, socio demographic and psychological factors, such as age, gender, education, attitudes, values, and beliefs (McGuire, 1981). Readiness to change behaviour is one of the recipient-related factors that may influence the way an individual interacts with information concerning that behaviour (Bar-Ilan, Shalom, Shoham, Baruchson-Arbib, and Getz, 2006). If people lack knowledge about the implications of wasting energy, they may lack motivation to alter unhealthy habits to which they are accustomed. Hence, increased knowledge of these risks and benefits can be considered a precondition for change (Bandura, 2004; Bar- Ilan *et al.*, 2006). However, increased knowledge alone does not necessarily lead to improvements in behaviour (Sligo and Jameson, 2000). Hussaini and Majid (2014)'s studies assert that households' energy use have three major issues that are associated with energy conservation and efficiency, these are: the architectural issue, appliance efficiency issues, and human behavioural issues. Consequently, the human dimension to energy analysis as well as technology based improvements in energy efficiency are significantly influenced by human social behaviour, which in turn is influenced by the level of education, the awareness and the social status of individual users of the energy. However, Stephenson, Barton, Carrington, Gnoth, Lawson, and Thorsnes, (2010) posit that consumer energy behaviour can be understood at its most fundamental level by examining the interaction between cognitive norms (beliefs, understanding,) material culture (income, accommodation status) and energy practice (practice, processes).

Mathieson, Peacock and Chin (2001) describe age as a measure of personal resources or perceived behavioural control. Honold (2000) argues that user capabilities are usually a result of demographic indices (user's age, educational background and income) or situational experiences. Morris and Venkatesh (2000) and Brigman and Cherry, (2002) argue that age reduces perceived behavioural control because self-efficacy and cognitive skills decrease as people grow older. They also argue that age increases the effect of subjective norms, because older workers have a greater need for affiliation. Matheison *et al.* (2001) argue that education level could be positively associated with perceived behavioural control, because it could reflect users' level of internal capabilities, such as technical skills and intelligence. The theory of planned behaviour would then predict that education level should influence usage directly, beyond its effect (Matheison *et al.*, 2001). Like age, education level should also be associated with self-identity and subjective norms. Nonetheless, if users' conceptions of energy conservation change as they receive further education, the educational level should directly affect usage behaviour (Sparks & Shepherd, 1992). Users' education level may also influence subjective norms, for example, by creating social expectations that one will conserve energy in certain ways. Moreover, the influence of the educational level on usage via perceived behavioural control will be positive (Mathieson *et al.* 2001), whereas the influence via social norms and self-identity, however, may be positive or negative, depending on the context. Tweneboah-Koduah (2013) found a statistically significant difference between the marital status of Ghanaians and their act to use condoms to protect themselves against HIV/AIDS. Based on the review of the literature, the following null hypotheses are formulated:

> Hypothesis 5: There will be no significant difference between respondents' energy conservation behaviour and their current level of education.
> Hypothesis 6: There will be no significant difference between age groups of respondents and their energy conservation behaviour.
> Hypothesis 7: There will be no significant difference between respondents' income and their energy conservation behaviour.

This research adopts the Transtheoretical model (TTM) by Prochaska, DiClemente, and Norcross (1992) to analyse the role of social marketing interventions on domestic energy consumption in Ghana. The transtheoretical model allows social marketers to view human intentional behaviour change (DiClemente, 2007). This model was adopted to analyse the stages of change of Ghanaians when it comes to energy conservation. TTM states that individuals may pass through several stages of change when they are trying to modify their behaviour. Each stage represents a constellation of tasks that create the foundation for the movement forward in the process of change (Di Clemete, 2007). These stages include pre-contemplation, contemplation, preparation, action, maintenance, termination, and relapse (Prochaska *et al.*, 1992). During the pre-contemplation stage, the individual does not admit or recognise that the behaviour is a problem, and there is no intention to change the behaviour any time within the next 6 months. For instance, they do not know about energy conservation and have no intention of conserving energy. Over time, as the individual realises that the behaviour is a problem, through social marketing interventions, the individual moves into the contemplation stage (Tweneboah-Koduah, 2013). In the contemplation stage, the individual intends to change his/her behaviour in the next 6 months. They are more aware than pre-contemplators of the pros and cons of changing their behaviour. The preparation stage occurs when the individual becomes ready to initiate change in the very near future, usually measured as the next month. At this stage, the individual makes changes to his or her behaviour or changes to his or her environment that will facilitate behavioural change. Individuals who have successfully changed their behaviour for a period of 1 day to 6 months are said to be at the action stage. The maintenance stage follows the action stage and is the period when the individual integrates the behavioural change into his or her life and attempts to prevent relapse. The termination stage will occur only when it is certain that the problem behaviour is extinguished and will not return, and when former temptations are no longer a threat. TTM specifies how a person can be classified as being in each of these stages of change (i.e., pre-contemplation, contemplation, preparation, action, maintenance and termination), as well as what can be done to make people feel more vulnerable so that they will move from the pre-contemplation stage to a later stage (Prochaska *et al.*, 1992).

4. Research Methodology

This research employs a quantitative research method to determine the inferences that can be made about some characteristic, attitude, or behaviour of the population (Creswell, 2009). The population of the research constitutes all residents of high income and low income suburbs in the Accra Metropolitan Assembly. A stratified sampling technique was employed to ensure that each population element (residents in East-Legon and La-Bawulashie) was represented (Gunnar, 2000). The study followed a three-step process by partitioning the population into sub-groups or strata (high income and low income) areas, and by using a simple random sampling technique to select East-Legon (high income) and La-Bawulashie (low income) suburbs in Accra. Based on the demographic (outlook) indices such as buildings and road infrastructure, East-Legon is considered as an affluent middle class area, whereas La-Bawulashie as a lower class standing area. The two communities are well known in the Accra Metropolitan Assembly (Grant & Yankson, 2013). The respondents were selected by the use of a stratified sampling technique to ensure that each population element was represented. The selection of the sample size for the survey is based on the cost basis approach, since there was limited external funding for this research. In this case, the size of a sample depends on the acceptable sample error balanced against the cost for that sample size (Burns & Bush, 2010). It is always important to note that the cost of research should not exceed the value of the information expected from the research (Burns & Bush, 2010). If the researchers decided to double the sample size to 600 respondents, for instance, the additional cost might have exceeded the additional information expected. The sample error at 95% confidence level for 300 and 600 will give statistical accuracy of +/–5.7% and +/-4.0%, respectively.

A 5-point Likert rating scale was used to measure the constructs of the transtheoretical model (TTM) of pre-contemplation (no intention to take action within the next 6 months), contemplation (intention to take action within the next 6 months), preparation (intention to take action within the next 30 days, and have taken some behavioural steps in this direction), action (changed overt behaviour for less than 6 months), maintenance (changed overt behaviour for more than 6 months), and termination (no temptation to relapse and 100% confidence). The researchers avoided questions that were confusing or improperly worded and designed the questionnaire so as to obtain the required information in an unbiased manner. Before giving out questionnaires to respondents, the researchers informed them that they were not obligated to answer any questions that would make them uncomfortable. The researchers provided respondents with adequate information about the purpose of the research, and confidentiality at the point of giving them the questionnaire. The questionnaire was administered to 300 respondents in East-Legon and La-Bawulashie in Greater Accra Municipality, Ghana. In all, 256 respondents returned their completed questionnaire, but 240, representing 80% of the total number of questionnaires distributed, were found usable for analysis.

Statistical analysis techniques such as mean and frequencies, factor analysis, multiple regression, and analysis of variance (ANOVA) were employed to analyse the data. Any time the sign value in the ANOVA table was greater than 0.05, the researchers did not waste time inspecting the mean for difference. However, if the sign value was 0.05 or less, the differences between the different categories of the respondents are significant. In such cases, post ad hoc procedures such as Duncan's multiple range test was used to identify the pair or pairs of groups where the mean was significantly different (Garee, 1997). To know how different groups differ, the mean of each group was used and the group mean helped to know on average the views of all groups.

5. Analysis of Findings

This study sought to understand the domestic energy consumption behaviour of Ghanaians using the transtheoritical model (TTM) proposed by Prochaska *et al.*, (1992). In this section, the study presents the profiles of the respondents and the findings on the various stages that the respondents go through in their energy consumption behaviour, from precontemplation to termination and possible relapse.

The study collected responses from 240 respondents from the East-Legon and La-Bawulashie suburbs in the Accra Metropolitan Assembly, of which 55.8% were male and 44.2% were female. In terms of age, 49.8% of the respondents were between the ages of 18 and 30 years, and 50.2% of the respondents were above 31years. 75% of the respondents had their education up to tertiary level. Only 25% had education below SSS/A-Level. From this, it can be concluded that a large number of the respondents had more than basic education and could thus understand social marketing interventions on energy conservation in Ghana. Regarding the occupational status of respondents, 74.7% of respondents were employed/self-employed, 25.3 % were unemployed/retired. This connotes that the bulk of respondents were employed and had the potential of being able to pay their electricity bills and as such, their views could be of high relevance. In terms of consumers' monthly income, 49.2 % of respondents earned more than GH¢ 1,000. 4.9 % of respondents earned less than GH¢100 and 35.3% earned between Gh¢100- ¢1,000 and only 10.6% had no income. It can be concluded that the majority of the respondents had an income. 85.8 % of respondents where Christian, 10% were Muslims and only 4.2% had no religion or belonged to the traditional religion.

Regarding the stage of change of the respondents energy conservation behaviour, the study found 26 (11%) of the respondents in the precontemplation stage, 15 (6%) in contemplation stage, 11(4.6%) in preparation stage, 29 (12%) in action stage, 73 (30.4%) in maintenance stage, and 86 (36%) in the termination stage. This suggests that very few Ghanaians have reached the termination stage when it comes to their energy conservation behaviour, while the majority of them are still in the earlier stages.

There were six principal statements measuring the various forms of media through which energy conservation interventions were conveyed to the target audience. These span radio, television, seminars/workshop, word-of-mouth, flyers/billboard and the internet. However, in the case of behavioural change, with respect to the current intervention being measured, there were three variables measuring that component (see table 9.2). As such, an exploratory factor analysis was required to check if there was the need to reduce the variables to ascertain the ones which best measures behavioural change. The variables measuring this construct (by using energy saving appliances, by switching off appliances when not in use, by ironing in bulk) were factors analysed. Prior to the extraction of factors, the Bartlett test of Sphericity (Approx. Chi-square= 411.681, df. 3, sig. 0.000) and the KMO measure of sampling adequacy (Value of .715) confirmed that there was significant correlation among the variables to warrant the application of an exploratory factor analysis. Only variables whose Eigen values were equal to or greater than 1 were selected (Malhotra & Birks, 2007). In addition, variables with loadings of at least 0.5 and factors with a reliability threshold of 0.7 (Hair, Black, Babin, and Anderson, 2010) were selected for the analysis. In the exploration, all three (3) variables were factor analysed in an attempt to identify the best measures of the latent construct called behavioural change. The results revealed that the variables measuring the factor were found to explain altogether a satisfactory 81.242% of the total variance in explaining behavioural change (see table 9.2).

Table 9.1: KMO and Bartlett's Test

Kaiser-Meyer-Olkin Measure of Sampling Adequacy.		.715
	Approx. Chi-Square	411.681
Bartlett's Test of Sphericity	Df	3
	Sig.	.000

Table 9.2: Total Variance Explained

Component	Initial Eigenvalues			Extraction Sums of Squared Loadings		
	Total	% of Variance	Cumulative %	Total	% of Variance	Cumulative %
1	2.437	81.242	81.242	2.437	81.242	**81.242**
2	.364	12.138	93.380			
3	.199	6.620	100.000			

Extraction Method: Principal Component Analysis.

In Table 9.3: The internal reliability of the three variables were analysed through Cronbach's coefficient alpha. Only factors that meet the minimum value of 0.6, as postulated by (Hair *et al.*, 2010) were accepted. Also, in order to test the value of the variables that loaded onto the factors, the item–to total correlation- was set above 0.3 (Parasuraman. Zeithaml, and Berry 1988).

Table 9.3: Reliability of scales for behavioural change

Variables	Loadings	No. of Items	Cronbach's alpha
		3	.883
I have been using energy saving appliances	.933		
I switch off appliances when not in use	.893		
I help save energy by for instance, ironing in bulk	.877		

From the Cronbach's alpha coefficient results, it is clear that all the scales for the independent variables, as well as those for the dependent variable, exceeded the conventional acceptable 0.6 value. These were computed into a composite construct (Behaviour Change) to be used as dependent variable for a multiple regression analysis.

In Table 9.4 multiple regressions was undertaken to test and validate hypotheses 1 to 6 of the study. Results from the multiple regressions were used to analyse the relationship between the media platforms used to convey social marketing interventions and behavioural change.

Table 9.4: Relationship between Communication Media and Behavioural Change

	S.E	*B*	T	Sig.
(Constant)[a]	.229		9.555	.000
Radio	.064	.312	4.303	.000
Television	.064	.215	2.923	.004
Seminar/workshop	.078	-.155	-2.198	.029
Word of mouth	.061	.036	.548	.584
Flyer/billboard	.067	-.025	-.345	.730
Internet	.063	.134	1.993	.047
R .711			S.E of estimate	.17870
R-Square .692			F-statistics	52.400
Adj. R-Square .573			Prob. (F-stats.)	.000

[a]Dependent variable: Behavioural Change

Behavioural change was used as the dependent variable, whilst the independent variables were represented by radio, television , seminars/workshops, word-of-mouth, flyers/billboards and the Internet. Table 9.4 presents a summary of the multiple regression least squares results for the dependent and independent variables.

The results from the regression indicate that there is a strong and significant reliability between variables used for the model to represent social marketing intervention media (F = 52.400, Prob. F-stats <0.05). From table 6, it can be found that R Square value= .692. Expressed as a percentage, it is found that the model consisting of independent variables (radio, television, seminars/workshops, word-of-mouth, flyers/billboards and the Internet) explains 69.2% of the variance in social marketing intervention media, an important indication of the relevance of the model. The adjusted R-Squared is 0.573, and this, according to Hair *et al.*, (2006) is good for exploratory studies which test any phenomenon without theoretically established scales.

On the individual results, radio was found to have the greatest impact on consumers' behavioural change as far as social marketing interventions on energy conservation is concerned (β =0.312, t=4.303, p=0.000, < 0.05). This means that the bulk of the sampled respondents formed positive energy conservation habits based on the interventions they heard on radio. The second media contributor to consumer behavioural change was television (β =0.215, t=2.923, p=0.004, < 0.05) implying that the sampled respondents were also impacted to some extent by the social marketing interventions via television. The third medium, which influenced consumers' behavioural change with social marketing interventions on energy conservation, was the Internet (β =0.134, t=1.993, p=0.047, < 0.05). Although seminars/workshops were significant, Internet had a negative relationship in the current study (β = -.155, t= -2.198, p=0.029, < 0.05). This is an indication that the sampled respondents believed that, though seminars and workshops were good avenues for educating consumers on social marketing interventions (measured by significance), they considered them either unavailable or not patronised. In another dimension, word-of-mouth (β =0.036, t=0.548, p=0.584, > 0.05) and flyers/billboards (β = -.025, t= -.345, p=0.730, > 0.05) were statistically not significant in the current study. Remarkably, the latter even had a negative relationship, an indication that this medium was also not available or least impacting on communicating social marketing interventions on energy conservation to consumers.

Table 9.5: Age versus Stages of change in Social Marketing Interventions

ANOVA						
		Sum of Squares	**Df**	**Mean Square**	**F**	**Sig.**
Pre-contemplation	Between Groups	1.127	4	.282	.166	.956
	Within Groups	397.802	234	1.700		
	Total	398.929	238			
Contemplation	Between Groups	2.138	4	.534	.517	.723
	Within Groups	241.795	234	1.033		
	Total	243.933	238			
Preparation	Between Groups	4.639	4	1.160	1.395	.236
	Within Groups	194.541	234	.831		
	Total	199.180	238			
Action	Between Groups	.608	4	.152	.116	.977
	Within Groups	307.869	234	1.316		
	Total	308.477	238			
Maintenance	Between Groups	7.461	4	1.865	.819	.514
	Within Groups	532.883	234	2.277		
	Total	540.343	238			
Termination	Between Groups	4.878	4	1.220	.498	.737
	Within Groups	572.636	234	2.447		
	Total	577.515	238			

In addition, the study used the analysis of variance (ANOVA) to understand if there is a significant difference between age, education and income on the respondents' behaviour towards energy conservation. This was done by using the various stages as the independent list versus the demographic variables. The

ANOVA results in Table 9.5 show that age is not significant in all the stages. Thus respondents' ages do not affect their stage of energy conservation.

Table 9.6: Education versus Stages of change in Social Marketing interventions

ANOVA						
		Sum of Squares	Df	Mean Square	F	Sig.
Pre-contemplation	Between Groups	59.978	3	19.993	13.825	.000
	Within Groups	335.492	232	1.446		
	Total	395.470	235			
Contemplation	Between Groups	1.726	3	.575	.558	.643
	Within Groups	239.168	232	1.031		
	Total	240.894	235			
Preparation	Between Groups	2.811	3	.937	1.163	.325
	Within Groups	186.964	232	.806		
	Total	189.775	235			
Action	Between Groups	6.450	3	2.150	1.702	.167
	Within Groups	293.058	232	1.263		
	Total	299.508	235			
Maintenance	Between Groups	14.004	3	4.668	2.078	.104
	Within Groups	521.094	232	2.246		
	Total	535.097	235			
Termination	Between Groups	28.680	3	9.560	4.091	.007
	Within Groups	542.168	232	2.337		
	Total	570.847	235			

Regarding education, the study found that education is significant at the Pre-contemplation and Termination Stages. Education had no significant impact on contemplation, preparation, action and maintenance stages (see table 9.6).

Table 9.7 shows the post hoc analysis results of pre-contemplation and termination, which have a significant relationship with education. On average, the respondents, irrespective of their education, disagree (2.08), but agree that they are at the precontemplation stage. However, respondents with tertiary education are less likely to agree that they are at the precontemplation stage (1.80) as compared to respondents with no formal education (3.44).

Table 9.7 Post-Hoc Analysis: Education

		N	Mean	Std. Deviation
Precontemplation	Noformal education	9	3.44	1.740
	JSS	12	2.75	1.765
	SSS/A'Levels	38	2.87	1.614
	Tertiary	177	1.80	1.013
	Total	236	2.08	1.297
Termination	Noformal education	9	2.44	1.667
	JSS	12	3.33	1.670
	SSS/A'Levels	38	2.97	1.533
	Tertiary	177	3.71	1.512
	Total	236	3.53	1.559

At the termination stage, on average, all the respondents, irrespective of their education, agreed (3.53) that they have reached the termination stage. However, those who have no formal education are less likely to agree (2.44) that they are at the termination stage. Meanwhile, respondents with education up to tertiary level are more likely to agree (3.71) on being at the termination stage. The findings of the data analysis show that educational level can affects consumers' progression to the termination stage: the higher the educational level of respondents the more knowledge gained about energy conservation. This leads to the practice of energy conservation. On the other hand, respondents with less/no education, may have limited knowledge on social marketing interventions, and on energy conservation, therefore, energy conservation is hardly practised or not practised at all.

In Table 9.8, when the various stages were examined with income levels of respondents, it was found that the maintenance and the termination stages were significant as far as social marketing interventions on energy conservations are concerned. Based on the positive significant difference at pre-contemplation and termination stages, a post- hoc procedure was also used to determine the mean difference within maintenance and termination Stages.

Table 9.8: Income versus Stages of Social Marketing interventions

ANOVA						
		Sum of Squares	Df	Mean Square	F	Sig.
Pre-contemplation	Between Groups	13.213	5	2.643	1.526	.183
	Within Groups	377.425	218	1.731		
	Total	390.638	223			
Contemplation	Between Groups	5.950	5	1.190	1.128	.346
	Within Groups	229.889	218	1.055		
	Total	235.839	223			
Preparation	Between Groups	4.450	5	.890	1.127	.347
	Within Groups	172.104	218	.789		
	Total	176.554	223			
Action	Between Groups	7.734	5	1.547	1.178	.321
	Within Groups	286.248	218	1.313		
	Total	293.982	223			
Maintenance	Between Groups	57.838	5	11.568	5.624	.000
	Within Groups	448.377	218	2.057		
	Total	506.214	223			
Termination	Between Groups	28.276	5	5.655	2.346	.042
	Within Groups	525.612	218	2.411		
	Total	553.888	223			

In Table 9.9, a Post-Hoc analysis shows income is significant only at maintenance and termination stages. On average, the respondents, irrespective of their income level, are more likely to be neutral (3.16) about whether they are at the maintenance stage when it comes to practising energy conservation. However respondents who earn between GH¢1,000- GH¢15,000 and over ¢15,000 are more likely to agree (3.80 and 3.40, respectively) that they are more at the maintenance stage than their counterparts in other income groups. On the other hand, respondents who earn less than a GH¢ 100 and respondent who earn 'no income' are less likely to disagree (1.73 and 2.63, respectively) in being at the maintenance stage. This finding shows that respondents with higher incomes are more likely to practice energy conservation because they might be paying electricity bills, and respondents with low incomes or no income are less likely to practise energy conservation because they may not pay the bills.

Table 9.9 Post-Hoc Analysis: Income

		N	Mean	Std. Deviation
Maintenance	Less than GH 100	11	1.73	1.104
	GH 101 - GH 500	34	3.29	1.315
	GH 501- GH 1000	45	2.76	1.721
	GH 1001-GH 1500	40	3.80	1.418
	Over GH 1500	70	3.40	1.408
	No income	24	2.63	1.209
	Total	224	3.16	1.507
Termination	Less than GH 100	11	2.64	1.804
	GH 101-GH 500	34	3.47	1.542
	GH 501-GH 1000	45	3.33	1.692
	GH 1001-GH 1500	40	3.95	1.431
	Over GH 1500	70	3.64	1.485
	No income	24	2.88	1.569
	Total	224	3.48	1.576

At the termination stage, all the respondents are more likely to agree (3.48) in being at the termination stage. However, respondents who earn income between GH 1001 -GH 1500 and over are more likely to agree (3.95, 3.4 respectively) in being in the termination stages than their counterparts who earn less income. This seems to suggest that respondents with no or less income are more likely to be wasteful when it comes to energy conservation in Ghana.

6. Discussion of Findings

This is an exploratory study that utilises the TTM to understand the domestic energy conservation behaviour of Ghanaians. The study found respondents in all the stages: Pre-contemplation, Contemplation, Preparation, Action, Maintenance and Termination. This finding is consistent with previous studies such as (Tweneboah–Koduah and Owusu-Frimpong, 2013) who posit that consumers can be found in all these stages, when trying to undergo a social behaviour change process. Matsudo, 2002; Prochaska, 2004; and Reger, 2002; emphasise that behavioural change unfolds through a series of stages, for that reason interventions must identify the stage individuals are in before any further interventions can be implemented. Therefore, a generic intervention cannot be applied to all the stages of change. The study found 36% of the respondents at the termination stage, 30.4% at the maintenance stage and 12% at the action stage. Further, 4.6% were found at the preparation stage, whereas 6% were at the contemplation stage, with 11% at pre-contemplation. This suggests that the majority of Ghanaians have taken action or gone beyond the action stage, but only 36% of the respondents have reached the termination stage when it comes to their energy conservation behaviours. The study also suggests that 11% of the respondents are uninformed or unaware about the consequences of not conserving energy in Ghana (Prochaska, *et al.*, 2008). The study is consistent with Naar-King, *et al.*, (2007) who used the transtheoretical model to access substance use in HIV-positive youth and focussed on the use of alcohol and marijuana. Regarding alcohol use, the majority of respondents were at the maintenance (42%) and precontemplation stages (26%). In addition, the test for marijuana showed that the majority of respondents were found at the maintenance (61%) and precontemplation (25%) stages.

Regarding respondents' energy conservation behaviour and their level of education, age and income, the ANOVA results revealed that education is significantly related to the respondents' energy conservation behaviour at both the precontemplation and termination stages. The respondents with tertiary education are more likely to disagree that they are in the precontemplation stage than their counterparts with no formal education, who are likely to agree that they are in the precontemplation stage. On the other hand, the respondents with tertiary education are more likely to agree that they are at the termination stage than their counterparts with no formal education, who disagree that they have reached termination. This suggests that social marketing interventions on energy conservation in Ghana have much more influence on those who are educated than those with no education. This is because those with no/less education receive a lot of information, but synthesise information much slower than those with higher educational levels. Therefore, the null hypothesis, which indicates that there is no significant difference between educational level and respondents' energy conservation behaviour, is rejected. This finding is consistent with Matheison *et al.* (2001) and Tweneboah-Koduah and Owusu Frimpong (2013) who argue that educational level could be positively associated with perceived behavioural controls, because it could reflect the users' level of internal capabilities, such as technical skills and intelligence. The results show that income is significant at the maintenance and termination stages. Respondents with less/no income are more likely to be careless when it comes to energy usage than their counterparts who earn Gh1,500 and above. This may be due to respondents with no/less income not paying electricity bills, whilst those with higher income paying their bills. This seems to suggest that respondents with no or less income are more likely to be wasteful when it comes to energy conservation in Ghana. Therefore, the null hypothesis, which indicates that there is no difference between income and energy conservation behaviour of respondents is rejected. The study, however, found no significant difference between age and energy conservation behaviour of the respondents at all the stages of TTM. Therefore, the null hypothesis, which indicates that there is no significant difference between age and energy conservation behaviour of the respondents, is accepted. This finding is consistent with a prior study done by Dempsey *et al.*, (2011), who found that age had no such associations with the transtheoretical model constructs and age of respondent did not bring about knowledge of intention to use pills. Naar-king *et al.*, (2007) also found that age was not significant to any study variable in their study of the transtheoretical model and substance abuse in HIV-positive youth.

Among the mediums used to communicate social marketing interventions on energy conservation, radio was seen to have the most significant impact on social marketing interventions on energy conservation in Ghana, followed by television. This finding is consistent with Tweneboah-Koduah 2013; and Petrella *et al.*, 2005. They assert that the radio is more accessible to consumers when a social marketing message needs to reach target audiences.

7. Recommendation and Limitation

This study recommends that social marketing strategies must be adapted for the stage at which each target audience is found (Andreasen, 1995). To be effective, interventions should focus upon specific behaviours, and perhaps, not surprisingly, the most effective interventions will be those directed at a single behaviour rather than at multiple behaviours (Fishbein, 2000). Social marketing professionals should see their roles as working at a particular level of intentions or employing a specific type of behavioural change strategy. To influence respondents move from precontemplation to contemplation, social marketing campaigns on energy conservation should inform Ghanaians about the consequences of not conserving energy in Ghana. The interventions should also identify barriers which may impede understanding of the recommended behaviours.

To have Ghanaians move from the preparation and contemplation stages to the action and maintenance stages, social marketers must increase perceived benefits, social pressure and behavioural control as well as decrease the perceived cost of conserving energy in Ghana (Andreasen, 1995). Social marketers who seek to influence Ghanaians to conserve energy should target Ghanaians irrespective of their age with the same intervention, since there is no significant difference between age groups and energy conservation behaviours. And those with primary and no formal education should be targeted differently, to move them from the precontemplation to the termination stage. It is also recommended that social marketing interventions should be designed to influence Ghanaians with less or no income to influence them to conserve energy. The implementers of social marketing interventions on energy conservation in Ghana should focus on Radio and TV as mediums of communicating social marketing interventions since the study found them to be the most effective mediums of communicating interventions on energy conservation behaviours in Ghana.

Finally, the implementers of social marketing interventions on energy conservation should use social approval to encourage those Ghanaians who have reached termination to continue their behaviour of energy conservation. This study is limited in that it interviewed respondents in only East Legon and La-Bawulashie in the Greater Accra Municipality, and is, therefore, not representative of all Ghanaians. It is therefore recommended that future research should cover all regions in Ghana to determine the most effective media that can best inform the public on energy conservation. The study is also limited to the extent that it employed only the TTM to understand the energy usage among Ghanaians, even though; there are a number of other behavioural change models. Therefore, it is recommended that future research should employ an integrative behavioural prediction model to understand energy usage among Ghanaians.

References

Agyarko, K. (2010). *Energy efficiency drive the story of Ghana*, Energy Commission.

Andreasen, A. (1995). *Marketing social change: Changing behaviour to promote health, social development, and the environment.* ., San Francisco, CA.: Jossey-Bass

Andreasen, A. R. (1994). Social marketing: Its definition and domain. *Journal of Public Policy & Marketing, 13* (1), 108-114.

Andreasen, A. R. (2002). Marketing social marketing in the social change marketplace. *Journal of Public Policy and Marketing, 21* (1), 3-13.

Andreasen, A. R. (2003).The life trajectory of social marketing: Some implications. *Marketing Theory, 3* (3), 293-303.

Arden, M. A., & Armitage, C. J. (2008). Predicting and explaining transtheoretical model stage transitions in relation to condom-carrying behaviour". *British Journal of Health Psychology, 13* (4), 719-735.

Arko, C. (2013). Energy conservation, key to sustainable use in Ghana. Ghana News Agency, @ www. ghananewsagency.com, retrieved – 15/09/2013

Bandura, A. (2004). Health promotion by social cognitive means. *Health Education & Behaviour, 31* (2), 143-164.

Bar-Ilan, J., Shalom, N., Shoham, S., Baruchson-Arbib, S., & Getz, I. (2006). The role of information in a lifetime process: A model of weight maintenance by women over long time periods. *Information Research, 11* (4), 11-4.

Belch, G. E., & Belch, M. A. (2003). *Advertising and promotion: An integrated marketing communications Perspective.* The McGraw–Hill.

Bernhardt, J. M., Mays, D., & Hall, A. K. (2012). Social marketing at the right place and right time with new media. *Journal of Social Marketing, 2* (2), 130-137.

Bezjian-Avery, A., Calder, B., & Iacobucci, D. (1998). New media interactive advertising vs. traditional advertising. *Journal of Advertising Research, 38*, 23-32.

Bichard, E., & Thurairajah, N. (2013). Behaviour change strategies for energy efficiency in owner-occupied housing. Construction Innovation: *Information, Process, Management, 13* (2), 165-185.

Block, L. G., & Keller, P. A. (1998). Beyond protection motivation: An integrative theory of health appeals. *Journal of Applied Social Psychology, 28* (17), 1584-1608.

Brew-Hammond, A., & Kemausuor, F. (2007). Energy for all in Africa—to be or not to be?. *Current Opinion in Environmental Sustainability, 1* (1), 83-88.

Brigman S. & Cherry KE. 2002. Age and skilled perfor mance: Contributions of working memory and process ing speed. *Brain and Cognition* 50: 242–256.

Burns, A. C. and Bush, R. F. (2010*), Marketing research, 6th ed.*, Prentice Hall, Upper Saddle River, New Jersey: Pearson Education, Inc. .

Callaghan, R. C., Taylor, L., & Cunningham, J. A. (2007). Does progressive stage transition mean getting better? A test of the ranstheoretical model in alcoholism recovery. *Addiction, 102* (10), 1588-1596.

Cismaru, M., Lavack, A. M., Hadjistavropoulos, H. & Dorsch, K. D.(2008). Understanding health behaviour: An integrated model for social marketers. *Social Marketing Quarterly*, *14* (2), 2-32.

Creswell, J. W. (2009), *Research design: Qualitative, quantitative, and mixed approaches, 3rd* ed. . Thousand Oaks, California: Sage publications.

Costello, A. B. & Osborne, J. W. (2005). Best practices in exploratory factor analysis: Four recommendations for getting the most from your analysis. *Practical Assessment Research & Evaluation*, *10* (7), 1-9

Dann, S. (2010). Redefining social marketing with contemporary commercial marketing definitions. *Journal of Business Research*, *63* (2), 147-53.

Dempsey, A. R., Johnson, S. S., & Westhoff, C. L. (2011). Predicting oral contraceptive continuation using the transtheoretical model of health behaviour change. *Perspectives on Sexual and Reproductive Health*, *43* (1), 23-29.

Derbaix, C., & Vanhamme, J. (2003). Inducing word-of-mouth by eliciting surprise: A pilot investigation. *Journal of Economic Psychology*, *24* (1) 99-116

Diamantopoulos, A., O'Donohoe, S., & Lane, J. (1989). A comparison of advertising practices within the accounting profession, *The Service Industries Journal*, *9* (2) 280-296

Diamantopoulos, A., O'Donohoe, S., & Lane, J. (1990). Modelling advertising decisions by accountants: A path analysis. *The British Accounting Review, 22* (1), 3-26.

Dibb, S., & Carrigan, M. (2013). Social marketing transformed: Kotler, Polonsky and Hastings reflect on social marketing in a period of social change. *European Journal of Marketing, 47* (9), 1376-1398.

DiClemente, C. C. (2007). Mechanisms, determinants and processes of change in the modification of drinking behaviour. *Alcoholism: Clinical and Experimental Research, 31* (s3), 13s-20s.

Dramani, J. B., & Tewari, D. D. (2013). Electricity end-use efficiency in Ghana: Experience with technologies, policies and institutions". *Mediterranean Journal of Social Sciences, 4* (13), 669.

Energy Commission. (2010). *National energy statistics.* Accra, Ghana: Energy Commission

Energy Foundation (2008). Towards *energy efficient economy: annual report and financial statement.* Ghana: Energy Foundation

Field, A. (2005) *Discovering statistics using SPSS* (2nd edition), London: Sage .

Foux, G. (2006). Consumer-generated media: Get your customers involved. *Brand Strategy, 8*, 38-39.

French, J., & Blair-Stevens, C. (2010). Key concepts and principles of social marketing. In French J; Blair S. C; McVey D; & Merritt R. (eds). *Social marketing and public health: Theory and practice,* .Oxford: Oxford University Press:

Fuseini, I., (2011) Towards efficient lighting and appliance market: The case of Ghana, ee Global 2011, Energy efficiency global forum, April 12-14, 2011 Brussels, Belgium.

Garee M. L. 1997. Statistics don't lie if you know what they'r really saying, *Marketing News*, 31(19), 11.

Gillingham, K., Newell, R.G. & Palmer, K. (2009). *Energy efficiency economics and policy.* Discussion Paper, DP 09-13. Washington,D.C.: Resources for Future

Gray, D. M., & Bean, B. (2011). Can social marketing segmentation initiatives be used to increase household electricity conservation?". *Journal of Nonprofit & Public Sector Marketing, 23* (3), 269-305.

Gunnar K.(2000). The level-based stratified sampling plan. *Journal of the American Statistical Association* 95: 1185–91.

Hair, J. F., Black, W. C.; Babin, B. J., & Anderson R. E., (2010). *Multivariate data analysis (7th ed).* Eagelewood Cliffs: Prentice Hall.

Hussaini, I. U., & Majid, N. H. A. (2014). Human behaviour household energy use and the implications of energy efficiency delivery: A case of Bauchi, Nigeria. *International Journal of Energy Sector Management, 8* (2), 230-239.

Iqbal, H. (2013). Selecting an appropriate source of media as an effective source of promotion and communication from ATL and BTL modes of advertising. *International Review of Basic and Applied Sciences, 1* (2), 25 34.

Juwaheer, T. D., Vencatachellum, M. I., Pudaruth, M. S., & Saib, M. M. S. I. (2012). Social marketing efforts to boost blood donor rate in developing countries–A case study of Mauritius. *ZENITH International Journal of Multidisciplinary Research, 2* (6), 58-74.

Kilby, N. (2007). Market shift opens door to word of mouth. *Marketing Week, 30* (38), 12-?.

Kotler, P., & Zaltman, G. (1971, July). Social marketing: An approach to planned social change. *Journal of Marketing, 35* (3), .3-12

Leathar, D. S., & Hastings, G. B. (1987). Social marketing and health education. *Journal of Services Marketing, 1* (2).,49-52.

Lefebvre, C. (2009). Integrating cell phones and mobile technologies into public health practice: a social marketing perspective. *Health Promotion Practice, 10* (4), 490-494.

Lefebvre, R.C. (1996). 25 years of social marketing: Looking back to the future. *Social Marketing Quarterly*, Special Issue: 51-58.

Lefebvre, R.C., Flora, J. A. (1988). Social marketing and public health intervention. *Health Education Quarterly, 15* (3): 299-315.

Malhotra, N. K., Birks, D. F., Palmer, A., & Koenig-Lewis, N. (2003). Market research: An applied approach. *Journal of marketing management, 27*, 1208-1213.

Mangos, N. C., Lewis, N. R., & Roffey, B. H. (1997). Marketing accounting services: An inter-country and ethical comparison. *Marketing Intelligence & Planning, 15* (1), 11-18.

Mangos, N. C., Roffey, B. H., & Stevens, J. A. (1995). Research note: marketing accounting services: a cross-cultural comparison. *International Marketing Review, 12* (6), 68-81.

Manoff, R. K. (1985), *Social marketing: New imperative for public health*, Eastbourne, N.Y.: Praeger,

Matheison K.; Peacock E.; & Chin, W.W. (2001). Extending the technology acceptance model: The influence of per- ceived user resources. *The Data Base for Advance in Information Systems* 32: 86–112.

Matsudo, V.; Matsudo, S.; Andrade, D.; Araujo, T.; Andrade, E.; de Oliveira, L. C., & Braggion, G. (2002). Promotion of physical activity in a developing country: The AgitaSa˜o Paulo experience, *Public Health Nutrition, 5* (1), 253-261.

McCarthy, E. J. (1960). *Basic marketing: A managerial approach.* Homewood: Irwin.

McDonnell, F. (2005), Integrating word of mouth marketing, paper presented at the International Word-of-mouth Marketing Conference, 6-7 October, Hamburg, in Andres,N. (Ed.), Proceedings of the 1st International Word-of-Mouth

Marketing Conference, Brand Science Institute, Hamburg, Germany.

McGuire, W. J. (1981). Theoretical foundations of campaigns. In R. E. Rice & J. W. Paisley (Eds.), *Public communication campaigns* (pp. 41–70). Beverly Hills, CA: Sage.

Michie, S., & Abraham, C. (2004). Interventions to change health behaviours: Evidence-based or evidence-inspired?. *Psychology & Health, 19* (1), 29-49.

Migneault, J. P.; Adams, T. B., & Read, J. P., (2005). Application of the Transtheoretical Model to substance abuse: Historical development and future directions. *Drug and Alcohol Review, 24* (5), 437-448.

Miller, W. R., & Rollnick, S. (2002). *Motivational interviewing: Preparing people for change. New York*: Guildford

Ministry of Finance and Economic Planning (2014), Ghana Government 2015 Budget, Minstry of Finance and Economic Planning, Ministries-Accra, Ghana.

Morris M,& Venkatesh V. 2000. Age difference in technol ogy adoption decision: Implications for a change work- force. *Personal Psychology* 53: 375–403.

Naar-King, S.; Wright, K.; Parsons, J. T.; Frey, M., Templin, T., & Ondersma, S. (2006). Transtheoretical model and substance use in HIV-positive youth. *AIDS care, 18* (7), 839-845.

Nielsen (2007). Trust in advertising, a global Nielsen consumer report, October, available at: www.nielsen.com/solutions/TrustinAdvertisingOct07.pdf (accessed 18 April 2014).

Nsakie-Kassim, L., (2010). Energy and environmental issues in Ghana @ www.energyblogspot.com/2006/06/money-at-home-html. Posted: 1/06/2010, retrieved 18/09/2013.

Parasuraman, A., Zeithaml, V.A. & Berry, L.L. (1988), SERVQUAL: A multiple-item scale for measuring consumer perceptions of service quality, *Journal of Retailing, Vol.* 64, Spring, pp. 12-40

Petrella, R. J.; Speechley, M.; Kleinstiver, P. W., & Ruddy, T. (2005). Impact of a social marketing media campaign on public awareness of hypertension. *American Journal of Hypertension, 18* (2), 270-275.

Prochaska J.O, & DiClement C. C. 1982. Transtheoretical therapy: Toward a more integrative model of change *Psychotherapy, Theory, Research, and Practice,*19, 276-288.

Prochaska, J. J., & Sallis, J. F. (2004). A randomized controlled trial of single versus multiple health behaviour change: Promoting physical activity and nutrition among adolescents. *Health Psychology, 23*, 314-318.

Prochaska, J. J., Spring, B., & Nigg, C. R. (2008). Multiple health behaviour change research: An introduction and overview. *Preventive Medicine, 46* (3), 181-188.

Prochaska, J.O.; DiClemente; C.C., & Norcross, J.C. (1992). In search for how people change. *American Psychologist, 47*(9), 1102-1114.

Reger, B.M (2002). A community campaign using paid media to encourage walking among sedentary older adults. *Preventive Medicine, 35*, 285-292.

Rowley, J. (2001). Remodeling marketing communications in an internet environment. *Internet Research, 11*(3), 203-212.

Rust, R.T.; Moorman, C., & Bhalla, G. (2011), Rethinking marketing, *Harvard Review,* September, available at: http://hbr.org/product/rethinking marketing/an/R1001F P DFENG(accessed 10 June, 2014).

Silverman, G. (2011*). Secrets of word-of-mouth marketing: How to trigger exponential sales through runaway word of mouth.* AMACOM Div American Mgmt Assn.

Singer, E. A. (2007). The transtheoretical model and primary care: The times they are a changing. *Journal of the American Academy of Nurse Practitioners, 19* (1), 11-14.

Singer, E. A. (2007). The transtheoretical model and primary care:'The times they are a changin'. *Journal of the American Academy of Nurse Practitioners, 19* (1), 11-14.

Sligo, F. X., & Jameson, A. M. (2000). The knowledge—behaviour gap in use of health information. *Journal of the American Society for Information Science, 51*(9), 858-869.

Smith, W. A. (2006). Social marketing: An overview of approach and effects. *Injury Prevention, 12* (suppl 1), i38-i43.

Sparks, P; Shepherd, R.(1992). Self-identityandthetheoryof planned behaviour: Assessing the role of identification with 'green consumerism'. *Social Psychological Quarterly* 55: 388–399.

Staats, H. J.; Wit, A. P., & Midden, C. Y. H. (1996). Communicating the greenhouse effect to the public: Evaluation of a mass media campaign from a social dilemma perspective. *Journal of Environmental Management, 46* (2), 189-203.

Stead, M.; Gordon, R.; Angus, K., & McDermott, L. (2007). A systematic review of social marketing effectiveness. *Health Education, 107* (2), 126-140

Stephenson, J.; Barton, B.; Carrington, G.; Gnoth, D.; Lawson, R., & Thorsnes, P. (2010). Energy cultures: A framework for understanding energy behaviours. *Energy Policy, 38* (10), 6120-6129.

Stevens, R.; Loudon, D.; McConkey, C., & Dunn, P. (1992). Accountants and advertising: Image vs. need. *The National Public Accountant*, September, 46-51.

Sweeney, J. C.; Soutar, G. N. & Mazzarol, T. (2012). Word of mouth: Measuring the power of individual messages. *European Journal of Marketing*, Vol. 46, No. 1/2, pp. 237-257.

Sweeney, J. C.; Soutar, G. N., & Mazzarol, T. (2008). Factors influencing word of mouth effectiveness: Receiver perspectives. *European Journal of Marketing, 42* (3/4), 344-364.

Tootelian, D., & Gaedeke, R. (1990). Marketing of professional services as applied to tax professionals: representation of the client, public, or profession. *Journal of Professional Services Marketing, 6* (11), 17-52.

Tweneboah-Koduah, E, Y., & Owusu-Frimpong, N. (2013). Social marketing on AIDS: Using transtheoretical model to understand current condom usage among commercial drivers in Accra, Ghana. *International Journal of Voluntary Sector Marketing,* 1-20.

Tweneboah-Koduah, E. Y. (2013). *The role of behavioural change theory in social marketing interventions on HIV/AIDS in Ghana,* Phd Thesis, London Metropolitan University, London, UK.

Velicer, W. F.; Prochaska, J. O.; Bellis, J.M.; DiClemente, C.C.; Rossi, J.S.; Fava, J. L., & Steiger, J. H. (1993). An expert system intervention for smoking cessation. *Addictive Behaviours, 18,* 269-290.

Whitelaw, N. (2010). System change and organizational capacity for evidence-based practices: Lessons from the field. *Generations, 34* (1), 43-50.

Wilhite, H.; Nakagami, H.; Masuda, T.; Yamaga, Y. & Hanada, H. (1995). *A cross cultural analysis of household energy-use behaviour in Japan & Norway.* Conference Proceedings of European Council for an Energy Efficient Economy (ECEE) 1995 Summer Study Panel 4: Human Dimensions, available at: www.eceee.org/conference-proceedings/ (accessed 16 April 2014).

Wilson, C., & Dowlatabadi, H. (2007). Models of decision making and residential energy use. *Annual. Rev. Environ. Resources.*, 32, 169-203.

Wilson, G. T., & Schlam, T. R. (2004). The transtheoretical model and motivational interviewing in the treatment of eating and weight disorders. *Clinical Psychology Review, 24,* 361–378.

World Bank (2013). *Energizing Economic Growth in Ghana: Making the Power and Petroleum Sectors Rise to the Challenge.* June.

CHAPTER TEN

Philanthropic and Corporate Models of Hospital Governance in Ghana: A Comparative Study

Patience Aseweh Abor

1. Introduction

Private hospitals are a key component of the healthcare delivery system of many countries. In Ghana, the government has created an enabling environment to encourage the private sector's participation in the healthcare delivery system. The private sector currently represents about 55% of healthcare delivery in the country (MOH2012), and is regulated by the Private Hospitals and Maternity Homes Board established by Act 1958 (No. 9) as amended. The main healthcare providers in the private sector are the mission-based providers, which consist of the Christian and Muslim hospitals, and the private medical and dental practitioners. The mission-based providers are mainly private-not-for-profit establishments, whereas the medical and dental practitioners are private-for-profit.

Eldenburg, & Krishnan, (2003) argue that for-profit organizations are interested in maximizing the present value of their profits, and the purpose of their corporate governance is clear on this. The governance structure manages the process of maximizing this objective function through incentives and by the monitoring of the top management. However, in nonprofit organizations, it is not at all apparent what the managers are supposed to maximize. Eldenburg, .Hermalin, .Weisbach, & Wosinska (2004) assert that the literature has expressed differing views. For instance, Alchian and Demsetz (1972) suggest that nonprofit organizations will tend to exist in places where more shirking is 'desired,' while Fama and Jensen (1983a, b) emphasize that donors' utility is often an important consideration in nonprofits' decisions. Both of these arguments are special cases of the general proposition that nonprofits maximize some function other than the present value of profits. The identity of this function is not obvious, nor is it obvious how this objective function is chosen inside an organization (Eldenburg *et al*, 2003). It could be argued that the objective of the organization would have implications for its governance structure.

Taylor (2000) explains that a hospital board is ultimately accountable to the organization's ownership. With respect to church-owned, government-owned or military hospitals, there is, in fact, an owner. Many other hospitals owned by 'corporations' have their own boards and the owners may be board members or non-board members. The board's responsibility of hospitals owned by a 'corporation' other than a denomination or government is mainly to the hospital's mission and values (Drucker, 1990, Bader, 1991).

This study examined the healthcare governance of private hospitals in Ghana. Specifically, we compared the governance structures of not-for-profit (mission-based) and private-for-profit hospitals. Previous studies have concentrated on the differences in the governance forms of religious and secular not-for-profit hospitals (Alexander, Morlock, & Gifford, 1988), and the governance forms of health systems and health networks.

Alexander, Lee, Shoou-Yih., and Bazzoli,(2003), differences in governance structures of public hospitals in different countries (Ditzel.,Štrach and Pirozek 2006) and differences in the governance structures of public and private hospitals, (Eeckloo, Herckb, Hulleb & Vleugelsa 2004; Abor, & Abekah-Nkrumah, 2008). In spite of the clear distinction in the objectives of private-not-for-profit hospitals and private-for-profit hospitals, none of these studies looked at the differences in these two ownership types of hospitals. This current study departs from previous ones in the sense that it focusses on comparing the differences in governance structures of private-not-for-profit and private-for-profit hospitals.

The study specifically compared the hospital board characteristics and practices of mission-based not-for-profit and private for-profit hospitals. It also compared the skill level of the boards of mission-based and private for-profit hospitals.

The next Section reviews existing literature in relation to hospital ownership types and governance forms. Section 3 describes the methodology used for this study. Section 4 discusses the empirical findings. Finally, Section 5 concludes the study.

2. Literature Review

2.1 Hospital Ownership and Governance Models

The major ownership types of hospitals include for-profit, non-profit, and public ownership. The non-profit hospitals are normally owned by religious groups and non-governmental organizations. Both non-profit and public hospitals have non-profit making motives. For-profit ownership, on the other hand, entails shareholders who expect a return on their investment. Therefore, for-profit hospitals are expected to reward their shareholders in the form of dividends, by generating short- term and long-term profits. Non-profit hospitals, though they need short-term surpluses to finance their operations (Chang & Tushman, 1990), are mainly responsible to their communities to provide the necessary quality services rather than to generate long-term profits. The existing literature suggests that not-for-profit firms have different objective functions other than profit maximization. The objective function may include issues regarding maximizing quality, quantity and/or prestige, helping to fulfill demand for local public goods or to meet the needs in the community, or to maximize the well-being of specific important constituencies, such as the medical staff or the consumers (Newhouse, 1970; Pauly & Redisch, 1973; Weisbrod, 1988; Frank & Salkever, 1991; Ben-Ner & Gui, 1993; Lakdawalla & Philipson, 1998). Consequently, whereas for-profit and non-profit hospitals both attempt to generate short-term profit margins, for-profit hospitals' financial responsibility to their shareholders is likely to result in higher long-term profitability than for hospitals in the non-profit sector. Certainly, for-profit chains would be expected to show higher operating margins than non-profit hospitals because of the financial interests of their stakeholders.

Gregg (2001) also argues that together with a clear ownership structure, non-profit healthcare institutions also lack the principle of maximization of profit. However, in corporations, profitability and share value constitute the most important criteria to assess decisions. Eeckloo *et al.* (2004) suggest that in hospitals, the objectives are less unequivocal and often contradictory. The main objective is of course to provide qualitative specialized care. But next to this, hospitals must also pay attention to the accessibility of this care and the financial equilibrium of the hospital's exploitation.

The ownership type of the hospital has implications for the form of governance system adopted by the hospital. In a for-profit context, a well-defined relationship between ownership and control is the predominant aim of any model of corporate governance. This relationship is generally referred to as the 'accountability' of management and board of directors towards shareholders. Governance of non-profit hospitals starts from a totally different situation: since there are no real owners, the emphasis has shifted from the shareholders to the stakeholders. As healthcare is a social good, each group of stakeholders merits recognition of its interests, and not merely because of its contribution to the added value of other groups (Eeckloo *et al.*, 2004).

The governance forms of not-for-profit and for-profit hospitals can be looked at along the philanthropic and corporate models of governance. The philanthropic board model is typically associated especially with non-profit organizations. The corporate model on the other hand is associated with the commercial sector and therefore can be found in for-profit hospitals (Johnson, 1986). Some healthcare experts have argued that the philanthropic model, with its emphasis on asset preservation and constituent representation, has worked well and thus needs only minor modifications to become adaptive to the current environmental conditions facing hospitals (Umbdenstock, Hageman, & Amundson 1990; Griffith, 1988). Others, however, have broadly questioned the capacity of the traditional, voluntary board model to meet the new strategic challenges posed by a competitive healthcare environment (Barrett & Windham, 1984; Delbecq & Gill, 1988; Shortell, 1989; Weiner & Alexander, 1993a). Alexander *et al.* (1988) explain the main differences between philanthropic and corporate boards with respect to board size, heterogeneity, inside directors, CEO participation on board, CEO accountability to board, limit to consecutive terms, board compensation, and strategic activity. These differences are presented in Table 10.1 and discussed in the subsequent paragraphs.

Table 10.1: Governing Board Types

Philanthropic Model	Corporate Model
Large board size	Small board size
Wide range of perspectives and Backgrounds	Narrow, more focused range of perspectives and backgrounds
Less corporate representation on board	Greater corporate representation on board
Less physician representation on board	Greater physician representation on board
Numerous participants in new board member selection	Few participants in new board member selection
Constituent/community representation criteria for new board member selection	Skills/expertise criteria for new board member selection
Less management influence in new board member selection	Active management participation on Board
Little management participation on board	Greater management influence in new board member selection
No limit to consecutive terms for board members	Limit to consecutive terms for board Members
No compensation for board service	Compensation provided for board Service
Emphasis on asset preservation	Emphasis on strategic activity
Large number of standing committees	Small number of standing committees
Less active strategic committees	More active strategic committees

Source: Adapted from Alexander *et al.* (1988), page 317 and Weiner and Alexander (1993a), page 328.

Board size is the number of board members on the board. Philanthropic boards are often depicted /portrayed by a large number of members and they tend to represent a wide range of interests (Pfeffer, 1972). Historically, the major role of hospital trustees has been to maintain or enhance the legitimacy and prestige of the institution within the community, as well as to attract resources to the hospital from the surrounding environment (Alexander *et al.*, 1988).

Corporate boards, on the other hand, are usually smaller in size and tend to focus as a function of the narrower constituencies to which the organization is responsible (Zald, 1969; Mace, 1971; Ewell, 1987). Gu (2010) suggests that hospital governance models are changing, shifting from a large, largely philanthropic model to a smaller 'corporate' model.

The heterogeneity of the board is considered in terms of age, gender, racial or ethnic background, area of residence, and occupation of the board members. The range of perspectives and backgrounds on philanthropic boards are much broader than corporate boards in the sense that they tend to (influence) attract / incorporate a wide range of constituencies and stakeholders. Corporate boards, however, tend to focus on fewer shareholders (Pfeffer, 1973, 1972; Johnson, 1986). It then stands to reason that philanthropic boards are more likely to have more members with diverse characteristics in terms of age, gender, racial or ethnic background, area of residence and occupation than corporate boards. The more business-like orientation of corporate boards is particularly likely to be reflected in greater occupational homogeneity (Alexander *et al.*, 1988).

Inside directors are management members who are on the board. Philanthropic boards are normally made up of fewer inside directors because of their emphasis on environmental linkages and community relations (Deegan, 1982; Morlock & Alexander, 1986). Corporate boards often comprise of a large number of inside directors, since they have knowledge and understanding of the internal working of the organization. Greater insider representation on the board is also seen as a form of reward to a manager, and to achieve greater correspondence between organizational operations and policymaking (Juran, 1966; Mace, 1971).

CEOs tend to play a more significant role on corporate boards than they do on philanthropic boards. This is mainly because CEOs of philanthropic organizations mostly share power with other professional and management groups, thus diluting their influence on the boards (Zuckerman, Barrett, & Shortell, 1979; Alexander & Morlock, 1985). CEOs of corporate organizations have traditionally held more power vis-a-vis the boards and the businesses because of their ultimate authority over all aspects of running the organization (Mizruchi, 1983). Strong executive influence on the board is considered important in improving the linkage between policymaking and operations, lessening the conflict between management and board members, and facilitating selection of directors whose views are consistent with the philosophy of the organization (Johnson, 1986; Alexander *et al.*, 1988).

Corporate boards tend to make a clearer distinction between policymaking and operations of the organization than their philanthropic board counterparts do (Vance, 1968; Mace, 1976). They are more likely to see their role to include formulation of institutional policy and strategic decision-making, with delegation of responsibility and authority to the CEO for daily operations. This distinction of the board's strategic role and the CEO's operational responsibilities improves the board's monitoring of the CEO's activities and hospital performance. Routinely formal CEO evaluations by the board are seen as an important method of monitoring and improving CEO performance, as well as indirectly establishing stronger linkages between operations and policymaking (Ewell, 1972; Alexander & Morlock, 1985; Alexander *et al.*, 1988).

The term of the board is how long board members are allowed to serve on the board. In the corporate board model, there are often limitations placed on the number of consecutive terms board members may serve, to keep the board from becoming too conservative/ set in its ways and cautious (Pfeffer, 1973; Johnson, 1986; Kovner, 1978). On the other hand, philanthropic boards tend to be self-perpetuating bodies. This means, board members of philanthropic boards may serve on the board indefinitely or in other cases are allowed to select their successors (Ewell, 1982; Alexander *et al.*, 1988).

In terms of board compensation, philanthropic boards have traditionally avoided compensating board members. This is mainly due to the voluntary nature of board service (Johnson, 1986). Corporate boards, on the other hand, normally pay board fees to their members for board service. Although corporate board members are only rarely fully compensated for the value of their time, it is considered that even a token gesture in this regard strengthens the bond between the corporate board member and the organization (Rehm & Alexander, 1986; Ewell, 1982; Alexander *et al.*, 1988).

With respect to a board's strategic activity, philanthropic board members are likely to view themselves as trustees concerned with preserving the assets of the organization and fulfilling its fiduciary responsibilities. In the corporate board model, board members often focus on establishing an overall policy direction for the organization (Prybil & Starkweather, 1976; Kaufman, 1979; Ritvo, 1980). Alexander *et al.* (1988) argue that, in the current healthcare climate, for instance, corporate boards are more likely to be concerned with the hospital's competitive position.

2.2 Existing Empirical Literature

In terms of empirical literature, very few studies exist on hospital governance of for-profit and non-profit hospitals (see Alexander *et al*, 1988; Judge & Zeithaml, 1992; Weiner & Alexander, 1993; Eeckloo *et al*, 2004; Alexander,. Weiner &. Bogue 2001) and these studies focus on North America and European hospitals.

Alexander *et al* (1988) find that religious and secular not-for-profit hospitals are not only more likely than state, county, and municipal hospitals to restructure along corporate lines, but are also more likely to alter their governance practices after / in line with / according to corporate restructuring. Alexander and Scott (1984) suggest that government hospitals experience less discretion than private and voluntary hospitals to alter their internal structure or patterns of service delivery. Judge and Zeithaml (1992) compared the board's strategic role in non-profit hospitals with that in for-profit industrial firms and found that non-profit hospital boards are generally more involved in the strategic decision process than the for-profit hospitals. This could be the due to the 'goodwill' or voluntary nature of non-for profit hospital boards, that makes these board members more committed to their duties and obligations to the hospitals they govern.

Weiner and Alexander (1993) hypothesize that Government hospitals are subject not only to most of the external controls confronting voluntary, not-for-profit hospitals, but also to additional public and political controls. If it is true. that these greater institutional pressures constrain the capacity of government hospitals to adapt to increasing market pressure, then private not-for-profit hospitals are more likely to exhibit the corporate model of governance than are publicly owned (government) hospitals. They found that privately owned hospitals are more likely to exhibit corporate governance forms than publicly owned one. Eeckloo *et al* (2004) also found numerous differences between private and public hospitals, especially with respect to professional background, time spending and partition of competencies.

Alexander *et al* (2001) also compared the data of two national surveys on hospital governance conducted in 1989 and 1997. They found that hospital boards tend to serve more as a source of continuity than as the leading edge of change. In another study, Alexander *et al* (2003) found that the governance forms of health systems and health networks do not differ substantially on structure and composition. The vast majority of both types of organized delivery systems have incorporated governing boards, high proportional representation by affiliate organizations, and similar board size. Ditzel *et al* (2006) analysed the public hospitals in New Zealand and hospitals in the Czech Republic and discussed their findings in light of D. W. Taylor's nine principles of 'good governance'. They found that, while some similarities exist, the key difference between the two countries was that while many forms of 'ad hoc' hospital governance exist in Czech hospitals, public hospitals in New Zealand are governed in a 'collegiate' way by elected District Health Boards. The study found that some of the principles of 'good governance' existed in the Czech hospitals and many more were practised in New Zealand. According to Eldenburg *et al* (2003), the structure of ownership has a large impact on hospital governance. They explain that the governance in different organizational forms function differently from one another.

Following from the review of the relevant literature, we hypothesize that given the different ownership types, mission-based hospitals and for-profit hospitals will have different objectives and therefore will exhibit different governance systems.

3. Methodology

This study sought to compare the governance structures of mission-based and for-profit hospitals in Ghana. The sampling process involved in selecting a representative part of the population for the purpose of determining parameters or characteristics of the whole population (Cooper & Schindler, 2010). The study population for this study included mission-based and for-profit hospitals. Data for this analysis were obtained from a field survey that was conducted across the country and were collected from both primary and secondary sources. Primary data were obtained by the use of questionnaire and interviews with top management of the hospitals, while secondary data were obtained from existing hospital records, board minutes and other strategic documents of the hospitals. Out of one hundred and twenty (120) mission-based and for-profit hospitals sampled, sixty-seven (67) completed questionnaires were received made up of 31 mission-based and 36 for-profit hospitals. The resulting response rate of 56% was quite reasonable for a survey of this type considering that empirical studies involving surveys have been known to generate far less percentage response rates. This is in line with the rule of thumb of the choice of $n = 30$ for a boundary between small and large samples and for the purpose of estimating a mean, 30 observations are enough (see Hogg & Tanis, 2011).

The composition of the overall sample of hospitals is indicated in Table 10.2. Not-for-profit or mission hospitals represent 46.3% of the total sample of hospitals while private for-profit hospitals represent 53.7% of the sample of hospitals used in this study.

Table 10.2: Composition of the Sample of Hospitals

Hospital Type	Frequency	Percent	Cumulative
Not-for-profit hospitals	31	46.3	46.3
For-profit hospitals	36	53.7	100
Total	67	100	

Measurement of governance structures was based on a broad range of hospital governance attributes. These attributes are classified into two dimensions of hospital governance, and they include: the hospital board characteristics and practices, and skill level of the board and management. A comparison of the governance structures and practices of mission-based or not-for-profit and private-for-profit hospitals was done using Analysis of Variance (ANOVA).

4. Analysis and Discussion of Results

4.1 Hospital Board Characteristics and Practices

Table 10.3 presents the mean values of hospital and board characteristics of mission-based hospitals and private for-profit hospitals. Not-for-profit hospitals are larger with a mean bed size of approximately 68, while for-profit hospitals have a mean bed size of approximately 35. Again not-for-profit hospitals are the older with a mean age of approximately 29 years, while for-profit hospitals have a mean age of approximately 25 years. In terms of location, the results indicate that about 82% of not-for-profit or mission-based hospitals are located in the national capital, Accra, with less than 18% located outside Accra, and with respect to private hospitals 69% of the hospitals are located in the national capital, while 31% are located outside the national capital.

Table 10.3: Mean Values across Forms of Hospitals

Variable	Not-for-Profit Hospitals	For-Profit Hospitals	ANOVA
Hospital size	68.13	34.60	32.58***
Hospital age	29.01	25.07	5.53**
Location	0.82	0.69	0.23
Presence of hospital board	1	0.8	19.25***
Board size	7	4.53	50.56***
Board composition	0.62	0.54	3.27*
Medical staff on board	0.29	0.43	13.68***
Board leadership structure	0.36	0.61	8.35***
Board diversity	0.39	0.41	0.01
Frequency of board meetings	3.28	5.38	3.98**

Note: ***, **, and * mean significant at 1, 5, and 10 percent level respectively. Hospital board is a dummy variable and is defined as 1, where the hospital has a board in place and 0 where the hospital has no board. Board size is defined as the number of board members. Board composition is defined as the proportion of outside board members on the board. Board participation by medical staff is the proportion of medical staff on the board. Board leadership structure is a dummy = 1, if the CEO is the board chair, and 0 if otherwise. Board diversity is defined as the proportion of females on the board. Frequency of board meetings is the number of board meetings in the year. Hospital size is defined as the number of hospital beds. Hospital age is defined as the number of years the hospital has been in existence. Location is a dummy variable = 1, if the hospital is located in the national capital, and 0 if it is located outside the national capital.

In examining and comparing the characteristics of hospital boards across the forms of hospitals, the results indicate that in terms of the presence of hospital board all the not-for-profit or mission-based hospitals sampled have a board. About 80% of the for-profit or private hospitals have a hospital board in place. Considering the profit orientation of private hospitals, they may see the need to have a governing board to provide direction for the hospital, especially when most of these hospitals tend to be owner-managed.

The results show statistically significant difference between the mean board size of mission-based hospitals and private-for-profit hospitals. Out of the number of hospitals with a board, not-for-profit hospitals have a board size of approximately 7, while for-profit or private hospitals have a board size of approximately 5. Not-for-profit hospitals have board size that falls within the range recommended in literature, as indicated on Table 4, but that of private for-profit hospitals falls below the recommended range. Bader (1991) suggests that in health systems with several boards, the system works best with lean governing boards having the average of seven to ten members.

Mission-based hospitals have a significantly higher proportion of non-executive directors represented on the board (62%) than private hospitals with a mean of 54%. Both mission-based and private hospitals have more than half outside or independent directors on their hospital board. This is consistent with best practice which suggests that the board should be composed of a majority non-executive board members.

Private hospitals have a significant higher percentage of medical staff on the board (43%) than not-for-profit or mission hospitals which report a mean percentage of medical staff of 29%. In terms of board participation of medical staff, the results indicate that both forms of hospitals have medical staff represented on their board. This finding complies with best practice, as shown on Table 10.4.

With respect to board leadership structure, the results indicate a statistically significant difference between the sample groups. About 36% of the mission hospitals have the CEO also doubling as the board chair. In Ghana, the majority of mission-based and public hospitals maintain a board typology, where the CEO's position is separate from that of the board chair. Such a board structure complies with best practice. In the case of for-profit or private hospitals, the majority (61%) of them have their CEO also serving as the board chair. The majority of private hospitals in Ghana having the CEO also serving as the board chair, may be attributed to the fact that most of these private hospitals are owner-managed, and the owner-manager may also want to serve as the chair-person of the hospital board in order to maintain control. The board leadership structure of most private hospitals does not comply with best practice, but it is due to the reason that the CEO plays a more significant role on corporate boards of private hospitals than they do on philanthropic boards of mission hospitals (Zuckerman *et al.*, 1979). This phenomenon is however contrary to what is suggested by Meyer and Rowan (1977) that decoupling governance structures from activities would allow a hospital, for example, to respond to competitive market pressure by emphasizing strategic activities, while at the same time adhering to institutional demands for consistent representation by retaining an occupationally heterogeneous board.

With regards to board diversity, the results, as indicated on Table 10.3, signal that private for-profit hospitals have a higher female representation on the board, though not significant with a mean of 41%, while not-for-profit hospitals have a mean of 39% female representation. Interestingly, both forms of hospital have female representation on their board, but in both the hospital types, board diversity or percentage of females on the hospital board is less than 50%. This finding was unexpected, given the depth of literature on the resource dependency theory and the stakeholders theory that suggest that the heterogeneity of board is considered a perspective of the philanthropic board (mission not-for-profit) model, while the corporate board (private for-profit) models tends to focus on fewer shareholders (Pfeffer,1973,1972). It is also contrary to the assertion that philanthropic boards are more likely to have members with diverse characteristics in terms of age, gender, ethnic and area of residence than corporate boards (Alexander *et al.*,1988).

Table 10.4: Best Practices in Healthcare Board Governance

Board Characteristics	Best Practice	Not-for-profit Hospitals	For-profit Hospitals	All
Board size	Between 7 and 10 board members.	✓	×	×
Board composition	Board should be composed of majority non-executive directors.	✓	✓	✓
Board participation by medical staff	The board should have medical staff representation.	✓	✓	✓
Board leadership structure	The role of CEO should be separated from that of board chair.	×[a]	×[b]	×[a]
Board diversity	There should be female representation on the board	✓	✓	✓
Frequency of board meetings	The board should hold a minimum of four meetings in a year.	×	✓	✓

✓ means does comply.

× means does not comply.

×[a] Less than 50% of the hospitals have CEO also acting as board chair.

×[b] Over 50% of the hospitals have CEO also acting as board chair.

Board meetings are very useful for the board to receive important information that helps it evaluate the performance of the firm through these meetings. A board's authority is exhibited in the number of times it meets (Eeckloo *et al.*, 2004). This means a board cannot be called a board with the mandate to make decisions and take action, when it does not meet. In differentiating between good and great boards, it was concluded that exceptional boards make meetings matter (Board Source, 2005). It stands to reason that frequent board meetings are important to ensure the board's effectiveness. The board of directors of for-profit or private hospitals has the higher frequency of board meetings. On the average, they meet about 5 times in a year. Not-for-profit or mission-based hospitals have a lower frequency of board meetings. They meet about 3 times in a year. The results indicate that the boards of not-for-profit hospitals fall short of the required number of meetings, while the boards of private-for-profit hospitals meet more frequently than the board of not-for-profit hospitals. The extant literature suggests a minimum of four meetings in a year. Apart from mission-based hospitals, the boards of private for-profit hospitals generally hold the required number of meetings as recommended. The results also suggest that board meetings are based on prepared agendas, and that minutes are taken at all board meetings. Agendas are driven by and aligned with the annual board goals and work plan and those agendas and previous minutes are sent to members ahead of board meetings.

Using a likert-type scale to ascertain the level of involvement of the board in the activities of the hospitals, the results show that boards of private for-profit hospitals (with a mean of 4) are more involved than not-for-profit hospitals (4.3). The relative active boards of the private for-profit may be attributed to the profit motive of such hospitals. Board members have a responsibility to deliver value to the shareholders. This finding corroborates the findings with respect to frequency of board meetings.

4.2 *Skill Level of the Board and Management*

This study provides interesting findings with respect to the skill level of board and management of mission-based not-for-profit, and of private for-profit hospitals. The findings indicate that all board members of both mission-based and private hospitals have a university degree. With respect to the skill level of management, the results also show that all members of the management team of mission-based hospitals have a university degree, while 92% of members of management team of private hospitals have a university degree. All sampled mission-based hospitals have a qualified hospital administrator. In the case of private hospitals, 55% engage a hospital administrator, but only 23% tend to be qualified.

Table 10.5: Skill Level of Board and Management

	Not-for-Profit Hospitals	For-Profit Hospitals
Skill of Board	100%	100%
Skill of Management	100%	92%
Hospital administrator	100%	55%
Skill of hospital administrator	100%	23%

5. Conclusion and Implications

Private hospitals are a key component of the healthcare delivery system of many countries and hospital boards play an important role in the governance of these hospitals. The main aim of this study was to examine the healthcare governance structures of private and mission hospitals in Ghana. To achieve this, an empirical based investigation was conducted using questionnaires and interviews.

The results of this study reveal that hospital governance configuration only conforms partially to either corporate or philanthropic governance typology. This finding supports a suggestion by Weiner and Alexander (1993) that the corporate philanthropic distinction must be understood as an ideal conception, rather than as an accurate depiction of hospital governance forms in practice.

The results, however, reveal that mission hospitals tend to be dominantly philanthropic, while private hospitals have board structures that fit closely with the corporate model of governance. The results show that, regardless of ownership form, most hospitals have a governing board in place. However, the characteristics of these boards differ depending on the core mission of the hospitals, as a result of the difference in the underlying philosophies of these hospitals. For instance, the number of females, the proportion of non-executive directors represented on the board, and the percentage of medical staff on for profit hospitals were clearly different from the number of such members on a not- for-profit hospital. The results also indicate a significant difference in the leadership structure, with less than half of all mission hospitals having the CEO also doubling as the board chair.

Interestingly, even though the results indicate that both forms of hospital have female representation on their board, board diversity or percentage of females on the hospital board is less than half. Also, the results indicate that while the boards of private-for-profit hospitals meet more frequently, the boards of not-for-profit hospitals fall short of the required number of meetings.

Finally, the findings also indicate that all board members of both mission-based and private hospitals have the necessary educational background of at least a university degree. This holds same for the skill level of management, where all members of the management team of mission-based hospitals have a university degree, while the majority of members of the management team of private hospitals have a university degree. The results also show that all mission-based hospitals have a qualified hospital administrator, while more than half of private hospitals, engage hospital administrators. Thus, prevailing governance structures of hospitals in Ghana are characterised by a mix of corporate and philanthropic natures.

This study offers empirical evidence of the governance configuration revealed in the categorization of hospitals in Ghana, as well as the skill level of the management teams. Future research on hospital governance is however necessary to test a possible hybrid (a mix of corporate and philanthropic) models of governance boards and how these will change over time as hospitals boards face new and more complex challenges.

References

Abor, P. A., Abekah-Nkrumah, G. & Abor, J. (2008). An examination of hospital governance in Ghana, *Leadership in Health Services Journal*, 21(5), 47-60.

Alchian, A. & Demsetz, H. (1972). Production, information costs, and economic organization, *American Economic Review*, 62, 777– 795.

Alexander, J. A., Weiner, B. J. & Bogue, R. J. (2001). Changes in the structure, composition, and activity of hospital governing boards, 1989–1997: Evidence from two national surveys. *The Milbank Quarterly*, 79(2), 253–279.

Alexander, J. A., Morlock, L. & Gifford, B. (1988). The effects of corporate restructuring on hospital policymaking, *Health Services Research*, 23(2), 311-27.

Alexander, J. A., Lee, S. Y. D., & Bazzoli, G. J. (2003). Governance forms in health systems and health networks. *Health Care Management Review*, 28(3), 228-242.

Bader, B. S. (1991). Five keys to building an excellent governing board, *Hospital Trustee Association of Pennsylvania, Rockville, MO.*

Barrett, D. & Windham, S. (1984). Hospital boards and adaptability to competitive environments, *Health Care Management Review*, 11-20.

Ben-Ner, A. & Benedetto Gui, B. (1993). *The nonprofit sector in the mixed economy.* Ann Arbor: University of Michigan Press.

Cooper, D. R. & Schindler, P. S. (2010). *Business research methods*, New York: McGraw-Hill, 11th Edition.

Deegan, A. (1982). Hospital planning: Board member, administration and physician, *Hospital and Health Services Administration*, 27(2), 6-21.

Delbecq, A., & Gill, S. (1988). Developing strategic direction for governing boards, *Hospital & Health Service Administration*, 33(1), 25-35.

Ditzel, E., Štrach, P. & Pirozek, P. (2006). An inquiry into good hospital governance: A New Zealand-Czech Comparison, *Health Research Policy and Systems*, 4(2), 1-10.

Drucker, P. F. (1990). *Managing the non-profit organization*, New York: Harper-Collins,

Eeckloo, K., Van Herck, G., Van Hulle, C. & Vleugels, A. (2004). From corporate governance to hospital governance: Authority, transparency and accountability of Belgian non-profit hospitals' board and management, *Health Policy*, 68, 1-15.

Eldenburg, L., & Krishnan, R. (2003). The influence of ownership on hospital financial performance Strategies. In *Organizational Economics of Health Care Conference.*

Eldenburg, L., Hermalin, B. E., Weisbach, M. S. & Wosinska, M. (2004). Governance, performance objectives and organizational form: Evidence from hospitals, *Journal of Corporate Finance*, 10, 527– 548.

Ewell, C. (1982). Wonder boards: How to build strong governing bodies 12 ways, *Trustee*, 35(10), 33-37.

Fama, E. & Jensen, M., (1983a). Agency problems and residual claims, *Journal of Law and Economics*, 26, 327– 349.

Fama, E. & Jensen, M., (1983b). Separation of ownership and control, *Journal of Law and Economics* 26, 301– 325.

Frank, R. G. & Salkever, D. S. (1991). The supply of charity services by nonprofit hospitals: Motives and market structure, *RAND Journal of Economics*, 22(3), 430-445.

Gregg S. (2001). The art of corporate governance: A return to first principles. *Centre for Independent Studies*, 100.

Griffith, J. (1988). Voluntary hospitals: Are trustees the solution?' *Hospital & Health Services Administration*, 33(3), 295-310.

Hogg, E. A. & Tanis, R. V. (2011). *Probability and statistical inference*, 8th Edition,Pearson Prentice Hall

Johnson, T. (1986). Improving board effectiveness in hospitals: Can the corporate model help? *Working Paper*, University of Pennsylvania, Philadelphia.

Judge, W. Q. & Zeithaml, C. P. (1992). An empirical comparison between the board's strategic role in nonprofit hospitals and in for-profit industrial firms. *Health Services Research*, 27(1), 47–64.

Juran, J. & Londen, J. (1966). *The corporate director.* New York: American Management Association.

Kaufman, K., Shortell, S., Becker, S., & Neuhauser, D. (1979). The effects of board composition and structure on hospital performance, *Hospital and Health Services Administration*, 24(1), 37-62,

Kovner, A. (1978). Improving community hospital board performance, *Medical Care,* 16(1), 79-89.

Lakdawalla, D. & Philipson, T. (1998). Nonprofit production and competition, *National Bureau of Economic Research Working Paper 6377.*

Mace, M. (1971). *Directors: Myth and reality.* Boston: Harvard University Press.

Meyer, J. W. & B. Rowan, (1977). Institutional organizations: Formal structures as myth and ceremony, *American Journal of Sociology*, 80, pp. 340-363.

Mizruchi, M. (1983). Who controls whom? An examination of the relation between management and boards of directors in large American corporations, *Academy of Management Review*, 8(3), 426-435.

Morlock, L. & Alexander, J. (1986). Models of governance in multihospital systems: Implications for hospital and system-level decision making, *Medical Care*, 24(12), 1118-1135.

Ministry of Health (2012). *Annual Report: Ghana private sector health sector development policy,* Accra

Newhouse, J. P. (1970). Toward a theory of nonprofit institutions: An economic model of a hospital, *American Economic Review,* 60, 64-74.

Pauly, M. V. & Redisch, M. (1973). The not-for-profit hospital as a physicians' cooperative, *American Economic Review,* 63(1), 87-99.

Pfeffer, J. (1972). Size and composition of corporate boards of directors: The organization and its environment. *Administrative Science Quarterly*, 17, 218-228.

Pfeffer, J. (1973). Size composition and function of hospital boards of directors: A study of organizational environment linkage, *Administrative Science Quarterly,* 18(3), 349-364.

Prybil, L., & Starkweather, D. (1976). Current perspectives on hospital governance, *Hospital and Health Services Administration* , 21, 67-75.

Rehm, J., & Alexander, J. (1986). Governing board compensation revisited, *Trustee,* 39(4), 24-27.

Ritvo, R. (1980). Adaptation to environmental change: The board's role, *Hospital and Health Services Administration,* 25(1), 23-37.

Shortell, S. (1989). New directions in hospital governance, *Hospital & Health Services Administration,* 34(1), 7-23.

Taylor, D.W. (2000). Facts, myths and monsters: Understanding the principles of good governance, *The International Journal of Public Sector Management*, 13(2), 108-115.

Umbdenstock, R. J., Hageman, W. & Amundson, B. (1990). Five critical areas for effective governance in not-for-profit hospitals, *Hospital & Health Services Administration,* 35(4), 481-492.

Vance, S. C. (1968). *The corporate director.* Homewood, IL: Dow Jones, Irwin,.

Weiner, B. J., & Alexander, J. A. (1993). Corporate and philanthropic models of hospital governance: A taxonomic evaluation, *Health Services Research*, 28(3), 325–55.

Weisbrod, B. A. (1998). *The nonprofit economy,* London: Harvard University Press

Zald, M. N. (1969), The power and function of boards of directors: A theoretical synthesis, *American Journal of Sociology*, 75(1), 97-111.

Zuckerman, H., Barrett, D. & Shortell, S. (1979). *Evaluating the performance of multi-institutional systems: The role of governance and organizational structure, in multi-institutional hospital systems,* Chicago: Hospital Research and Educational Trust.

CHAPTER ELEVEN

Improving Quality of Care in Ghana's Hospitals: Views of Patients and Health Care Providers

Aaron Asibi Abuosi

1. Introduction

Quality of care is an important objective for health sectors in developing countries for a variety of reasons. From the perspective of patient rights, patients from all socio-economic levels, who seek healthcare, deserve correct and courteous treatment, safe medical conditions, and sufficient information on their health status and treatment options (Williams, Schutt-Aine & Cuca, 2000, Reinhardt & Cheng, 2000, WHO, 2006, Robyn, Sauerborn & Bärnighausen, 2013). Providing high quality services, it has been argued, can also result in increased utilization of health services, readiness to contribute to financing health, compliance with prescription, and a reduction in the risk of self-treatment (Kaseje, Spencer & Sempebwa, 1987, McCombie, 1996, Akin & Hutchinson, 1999, Leonard, Mliga & Mariam, 2002, Kamuzora & Gilson, 2007, Tipke, Diallo, Coulibaly, Störzinger, Hoppe-Tichy, Sie & Müller, 2008, Robyn *et al.*, 2013). Andaleeb (2001) argues that the tendency for some people in developing countries to seek health care abroad, despite the overwhelming personal costs and inconveniences of going abroad, conveys a message that they want quality services.

Interest in research on quality of care in developing countries has increased over the past two decades (Baltussen & Ye, 2006). Assessments of quality of care commonly include a variety of approaches, such as direct observation of patient-provider interaction surveys, provider interview surveys, patient-perspective surveys and facility assessment surveys (Franco, Franco, Kumwenda & Nkhoma, 2002, Kogan, Holmboe & Hauer, 2009, Onishi, Gupta & Peters, 2010, Robyn *et al.*, 2013). Studies on quality of care from patients' perspective have been conducted through household surveys (Haddad & Fournier, 1995, Pretorius & Greeff, 2004), exit interviews (Newman, Gloyd, Nyangezi, Machobo & Muiser, 1998, Van Duong, Binns, Lee & Hipgrave, 2004), mystery clients (Maynard-Tucker, 1994, Mamdani & Bangser, 2004), and focus groups (Haddad, Fournier, Machouf & Yatara, 1998a, Stekelenburg, Kyanamina, Mukelabai, Wolffers, Roosmalen & Van., 2004, De Allegri, Sanon & Sauerborn, 2006, Robyn, Hill, Souares, Savadogo, Sie & Sauerborn, 2011).

Most studies in developing countries have examined perceptions of quality of care from the perspective of patients (Abuosi & Atinga, 2013, Baltussen, Yé, Haddad & Sauerborn, 2002, Baltussen & Ye, 2006, Haddad *et al.*, 1998a, Haddad, Fournier & Potvin, 1998b, Turkson, 2009). However, not many studies have examined quality from either patients' or providers' perspectives, or from both.

Haddad, Potvin, Roberge, Pineault and Remondin (2000) argue that assessment of quality of care may be enhanced by including patient and professional (health care provider) perceptions of quality. Brown and Swartz (1989) also argue that though client assessments are important, the provider's view, when combined with the client's perspective, can provide additional insight into areas where change is needed. The authors are also of the view that since providing quality services is the responsibility of healthcare providers, any study on perceptions of quality focussing on only patients is lopsided, and may fail to address quality concerns comprehensively, especially where patients and providers' perceptions of quality of care are at variance. This study therefore sought the views of both patients and providers on ways quality care could be improved in Ghana's hospitals.

2. Literature Review

Mashego and Peltzer (2005) studied community perception of quality of primary health care services in a rural area of the Limpopo Province, South Africa, using focus group discussions. Perceived quality was discussed within the categories of conduct of staff, technical care, health care facility, health care organization, drugs, and waiting time. The study identified drug availability, interpersonal skills and technical care as the three main areas with poor perceived quality, and therefore recommended that priorities for enhancing perceived quality of primary health care should particularly focus on these three areas.

A study by Baltussen *et al.* (2002) on users' opinion on the quality of care of primary health care services in rural Burkina Faso found that respondents were relatively positive on items related to health personnel practices and conduct, and to health care delivery, but less so on items related to adequacy of resources and services and to financial and physical accessibility. In particular, the availability of drugs for all diseases on the spot, the adequacy of rooms and equipment in the facilities, the costs of care and the access to credit were valued poorly. The study concluded that improving drug availability and financial accessibility to health services were the two main priorities for health policy action.

Juma and Manongi (2009) conducted exit interviews with adult patients or caregivers of children and conducted focus group discussions with community members in the Kilosa District Hospital in Central Tanzania. The authors found that provider-patient interactions, timely services, supply of medicines and favouritism were the major factors affecting quality of service at the hospital. Cost of service was perceived to be reasonable, provided medicines were available.

In Afghanistan, Hansen, Peters, Viswanathan, Rao, Mashkoor and Burnham (2008) found that clients' perceived quality of primary care services was higher when health workers were more thorough in taking patient histories, conducting physical examinations, and communicating with patients. Clients' perceived quality was also higher when the health worker providing care was a doctor. However, perceived quality was lower when the wait before being seen by a provider was long.

Sharma and Narang (2011) investigated user perception regarding service quality and how that varied between different healthcare centres and according to the demographic status of patients in India. They found that 'healthcare delivery' and 'financial and physical access to care' significantly impacted the perception among men, while among women it was 'healthcare delivery' and 'health personnel conduct and drug availability'. The study observes that, with improved income and education, the expectations of the respondents also increased. It was not merely the financial and physical access that was important, but the manner of delivery, the availability of various facilities, and the interpersonal and the diagnostic aspect of care that also mattered to the people with enhanced economic earnings.

In Ghana, a review of previous research reports on quality of care commissioned by the Health Research Unit (HRU) of the Ghana Health Service (GHS) in 2006 found that clients were dissatisfied with long waiting time, poor staff attitudes, illegal charges, high cost of care, dirty environment and limited avenues to seek redress (GHS, 2007). The review also found a number of shortcomings common to the institutions studied. These included inadequate numbers of skilled staff, unreliable and inadequate supply of water and electricity, inadequate equipment, shortage of logistics, low drug availability, and gaps in provider knowledge. In many health facilities, standard managerial practices that ensure effective use of (limited) resources were not universally practised. The GHS (2007) review is generally consistent with much of the findings of Turkson (2009) who assessed clients' perceptions of the quality of healthcare delivery in a rural district in Ghana. The participants, who were out-patients at health centres and hospitals, perceived poor attitude of some health workers, long waiting times, high cost of services, inadequate staff, policy of payment for health services, frequent referrals to hospitals, and lack of ambulances at facilities as being detrimental to an effective delivery of quality healthcare. The study also revealed that low proportions of clients were told what was wrong with them (43%), or given advice about their illness (46%). About 90% of the respondents were, however, satisfied or very satisfied with the care given during their visit to the health facility.

Silvestro (2005) conducted a comparative study of patient and staff perceptions of quality in UK. It was found that managers, who had least patient contact, were the most out of touch with patient priorities, believing that access was the most important factor for patients, when in fact it was the factor with the lowest rating, and that integrity was the least important of the factors, when in fact it was one of the most important factors to both patient groups. In terms of perceptions, it appeared that all the staff believed patients' perceptions of service to be lower than they actually were. The author concluded that the managers' misconceptions about patient expectations and their perceptions of the actual service delivered, may well have led to inappropriate investment decisions and improvement priorities.

Zhao, Akkadechanunt & Xue (2009) compared nurses and patients perceptions of quality nursing care. They found a statistically significant difference between nurses' and patients' perceptions of quality nursing care, based on staff characteristics, care-related activities and progress of nursing process. The authors concluded that nurses and patients had differing views of quality nursing care, because they may have had different standards and ways in which they viewed these characteristics of care. Nashrath, Akkadechanunt & Chontawan (2011) also found a statistically significant difference between nursing service quality as perceived by nurses and patients, in their study of nursing service quality in a tertiary care hospital in Maldives.

In assessing managers and patients' perceptions of primary healthcare services' quality in Spain, Miranda, Chamorro, Murillo & Vega (2010) found that in general, managers' perception of the services provided in the health centres was quite distant from the views of patients. Most of the gaps between the patients' and the managers' perceptions indicated that the managers were too optimistic about the services that they provided. The differences were particularly important for efficiency attributes; in particular, the ease of making an appointment, waiting times in the health centre before entering the consulting room, and complaints resolution, for which the patients had a lower perception of quality.

Roohi, Asayesh, Abdollahi & Abbasi (2011) evaluated clients' expectations and perception gap regarding the quality of primary healthcare service in healthcare centers of Gorgan. The authors concluded that considering the limitations in resources and equipment, identifying clients' expectations and perceptions would help managers to improve the quality of their services through modification of organizational processes.

3. Methods

3.1. Study Design and Data Collection

This paper is the qualitative aspect of a larger quantitative survey on patients and health provider's perceptions of quality of care in Ghana's hospitals. A total of 17 general hospitals from three regions of Ghana were selected for the study. The data collection was done by research assistants who were trained for three days on data collection methods and other important survey issues. Details of the sample size calculations for the survey are reported in Abuosi (2015). Furthermore, a total of 818 patients and 152 health providers responded to both the quantitative questionnaire and the qualitative questions. The qualitative question was asked last as an open question, to elicit the views of respondents on how quality of care could be improved in hospitals.

We employed convenience sampling to select patients for exit interviews among all the patients seeking general outpatient services from July 22 to August 20, 2013. In each facility, patients on routine visits to the hospital were contacted and those who consented were interviewed. While some patients consented to be interviewed, others declined. Convenience sampling was considered suitable in this study because patients reported and left the health facility at different periods, making it difficult to apply other sampling methods. On average, approximately 7–10 patients were interviewed per day. In-patients were not included in the sample. We collected data by conducting exit interviews with patients, after they had completed their visit and departed from the facility grounds. If a patient was less than 18 years of age, the adult accompanying them participated in the interview. Interviews were conducted by field workers recruited and trained by the researcher. An instrument for assessment of quality health care was adapted from Haddad *et al.* (1998a) (Haddad *et al.*, 1998b). This scale had been successfully used in other developing nations, Burkina Faso, rural Vietnam and India, by other researchers (Baltussen *et al.*, 2002, Van Duong *et al.*, 2004, Narang, 2010, Sharma & Narang, 2011, Robyn *et al.*, 2013). In addition to the quality scale, respondents were asked an open-ended question to elicit their views on how quality of care may be improved.

Purposive sampling was employed to select middle and top healthcare managers of the hospitals for the study. The top management members included medical directors, nurse managers, hospital administrators, pharmacists in-charge and accountants. The middle managers included ward managers, laboratory units heads, medical records unit heads, x-ray unit heads, maternal care unit heads and coordinators of out-patients departments.

3.2. Data Analysis

The qualitative data was entered into SPSS software, version 20, as string variable. The data was then sorted and themes identified and categorized according to various quality dimensions and themes, and subsequently discussed accordingly.

4. Results

For convenience, the results were categorized according to the various dimensions of quality of care[8]. Patients' suggestions were presented separately from those of healthcare providers.

4.1 Patients' Views

Financial Access to Care

The results provided by patients under financial access to care could be categorized into costs of health services, and the effective role of the NHIS. On costs of health services patients were generally concerned about the high costs of medicines and services, especially to uninsured patients. Some of the main concerns raised by patients were as follows:

- Cost of drugs should be reduced.
- Something should be done about the cost of medical care, it is expensive.
- Cost of treatment for uninsured patients should be subsidized.
- People who are uninsured and do not have money to pay for services in the hospital when sick, should be cared for so that they can be given time to pay back later.

Regarding the effective role of the NHIS, patients were generally worried about buying drugs outside the health facility in spite of being members of the NHIS, the sustainability of the NHIS, the cost of premium, delays in issuing NHIS cards to new members, and limited scope of NHIS in respect of medicines and diseases covered. Some of the key suggestions were as follows:

[8] A full description of the dimensions of quality of care within a developing country context as adapted by the author in the study, has been described in Abuosi (2015).

- Doctors should stop writing drugs for patients to buy but rather push the NHIS to buy them for patients.
- We are not on 'cash-and-carry', yet we have to go outside to buy certain drugs.
- NHIS does not cover all the drugs prescribed for patients. Something should be done about it.
- Some exempted diseases like prostate cancer should be involved in the NHIS.
- Efforts must be made to sustain the NHIS, because it is a relief to the poor and vulnerable people.
- Health insurance premium is high, and should be reduced.
- It is difficult getting your NHIS card, even after paying. The waiting time is too long.
- NHIS renewal centre should be provided in hospitals for NHIS members to renew their membership.

Fairness of Care

Under the fairness dimension of quality of care, respondents' suggestions predominantly dwelt on eliminating discrimination between the insured and uninsured, or eliminating preferential treatment in favour of staff relatives, ensuring fairness during the treatment process, and providing special attention to vulnerable patients. The following were some of the suggestions made by respondents:

- Staff should be discouraged from discriminating between insured and uninsured patients.
- When you don't have a relative who is a staff, you always have to suffer; therefore they should desist from this act.
- Patients should be treated on a first-come-first-served basis, because I have observed that staffs allow their friends and family to skip the queue.
- Seriously ill patients should be given separate consulting room.

- Kids and adults should be separated from each other so that the kids could be attended to first.
- Very poor people, whether aged or not should be exempted and treated free of charge.

Adequacy of Resources

Adequacy of resources seemed to be the issue of greatest concern to respondents, because there were so many suggestions under this dimension of quality of care. The most prominent concern of respondents was the need to increase the number of health staff, especially doctors. Another major concern was the need to acquire more equipment, expand the hospital infrastructure, and ensure the availability of medicines always. The following were some of the key suggestions:

- Add doctors to the only one doctor in this big hospital.
- Doctors should be increased, and they should report to work early.
- Employ more doctors, some doctors often vacate their office for a long time.
- Increase the number of medical doctors to reduce the waiting period
- Increase number of doctors and nurses.
- More Lab technicians are needed.
- Staff at dispensary should be increased to shorten waiting period.
- More hospital equipment and supplies must be purchased by the hospital.
- More laboratory equipment must be brought here, so that we don't have to go outside to do lab tests.
- Infrastructure of the hospital need to be improved significantly.
- The hospital should be expanded as a result of increase in the number of patients who come.

- The waiting area of the OPD needs expansion to accommodate all patients.
- An additional dispensary is required in this hospital to ease congestion.
- More chairs should be provided at the OPD waiting area.
- More drugs should be provided to cater for all prescriptions.

Promptness of Services

Closely related to adequacy of resources, respondents expressed concerns about the promptness of services. Most of the suggestions dwelt on reducing delays at various service delivery points, ready availability of drugs, continuous services all the time, and staff reporting early for duties. Some of the prominent suggestions included the following:

- Patients spend too much time before seeing the doctor. This problem must be addressed.
- The records department should help locate patient folders fast to speed treatment.
- Dispensary also delays so we stay in queues for far too long.
- All drugs should be made readily available to patients.
- The hospital authorities should always ensure that all drugs are available, so that patients who come from afar will not have to go home and come back for drugs.
- The doctors should work weekends, because I suffered during weekend when I was brought here.
- Pharmacy should be working in the night.
- Staff should always come to work on time.
- The nurses and doctors should report early to attend to patients.

Effectiveness of Treatment

On the dimension of effectiveness of treatment, respondents were concerned with the need to improve upon the prescription practices of pharmacists, the competence of health personnel, and the quality of medicines for effective treatment and cure. Some of the predominant suggestions were as follows:

- Pharmacists should be careful when issuing medicine. For example, they issue wrong medicine to patients on several occasions.
- More experienced physicians should attend to patients rather than inexperienced ones.
- Qualified doctors and nurses must be brought to work at the hospital.
- Quality drugs must be provided for both insured and uninsured.
- They should take time to diagnose infections presented before prescribing drugs.

Special Care

From suggestions provided by respondents, it emerged that there is the need for special care of certain categories of patients considered vulnerable. These include children, pregnant women and the aged. Some of the key suggestions include the following:

- Seriously ill patients, especially children should be treated first before processing documents.
- More attention should be given to the aged, especially those who are weak and fragile.
- Aged and children should be treated differently from adults and young people.
- Dispensary for pregnant women should be separate from general one.

Technical Aspects of Care

On technical aspects of care, respondents dwelt more on doctors' consultation process and the scientific basis of diagnoses and treatment. These include thorough history taking and diagnostic investigations, and convenient processes of treatment. Some of the suggestions were as follows:

- Doctors should involve patients in decisions concerning tests and treatments.
- Doctors should ask a lot of questions to know what exactly is wrong with patients before medical treatment.
- Feedback about patient's tests and diagnosis should be communicated to patients.
- Treatment must be based on laboratory and diagnostic tests.
- When patients are referred to the lab, X-ray and so on, when they come back, you have to join a queue again; that should be looked at.

Interpersonal Aspects of Care

Under interpersonal aspects of care, respondents emphasized the need for improved interpersonal relationship between healthcare providers and patients. Some of the main suggestions were as follows:

- Human relations between staff and patients should be improved.
- Some of the nurses must be advised on how to deal with patients, especially when pregnant women are in labour.
- The attitude of some nurses is very bad, they shout at patients.
- They should let their relationship with patients be more cordial than it is now, so that patients will feel free to disclose any problem concerning their health to them without fear or shyness.
- Workers of the hospital must be more compassionate and receptive when there are more patients.
- Young nurses should know how to talk to patients, they are disrespectful.

Improving Quality of Care in Ghana's Hospitals: Healthcare Providers' Views

Financial Access

The predominant suggestions made by providers under financial access to health care were on prompt re-imbursement of hospital bills by the NHIS. Other suggestions were for the NHIS to include high quality drugs, and patients should be educated to take receipts for payments made. Some of the key suggestions were as follows:

- Prompt payment of claims to the facility by NHIS could enhance quality of care, and improve access to the needs of the hospital.
- Re-imbursement of claims must be prompt
- NHIS should spread their scheme to cover high quality drugs.
- NHIS should cover important drugs.
- Patients should be educated to take receipt for every payment made.

Adequacy of Resources and Services

Under 'adequacy of resources and services', respondents' views were predominantly on the need to employ more doctors, expand or refurbish the infrastructure, acquire more equipment and supplies, and provide convenient services to patients. Some of the key suggestions include the following:

- More doctors should be employed.
- Posting of more specialist doctors.
- More qualified staff should be posted here by government.
- More consulting rooms should be created.
- Government should assist with infrastructure.
- Total renovation of the hospital infrastructure.

- More space should be created in OPD.
- Better access roads to the hospital are needed.
- Acquisition of modern machines for the lab.
- Ambulance is needed for the hospital.
- Regular supply of drugs and equipment to various units.
- Provide staff accommodation.
- Provide more nurses accommodation.
- Waiting time of patients at the OPD should be improved upon.
- Good and safe environment to patients.
- There should be a proper system for patients/clients complaints.

Staff Training and Motivation

Another area of concern expressed by healthcare providers was staff training and motivation. The major areas they wished could be improved are updating staff knowledge and skills, through organizing more workshops and seminars; training staff on ethics and customer care; providing better remuneration and allowances and special rewards for hard work. The following were some of the key suggestions:

- Organize more workshops and seminars for workers.
- Continuous in-service training for staff.
- Train auxiliary staff on ethics and etiquettes.
- Training on customer care should be organized for staff.
- Better remuneration for staff.
- Best and serious staff members should be motivated.
- More allowances should be provided to improve services.

Management

Management of hospitals was also an area of concern for respondents. Suggestions in this dimension dwelt on the need for supervision by the various levels of management, the need for team work, involving staff in decision-making, a call for change of management, peer-review, and the promotion of staff-community durbars. Some of the suggestions include the following:

- Regular visit or supervision, by the municipal director and the management members of the hospital, is needed.
- Ensure effective supervision at all levels.
- There should be team work to enhance proper patient care.
- Staff should be united and work together as a team.
- Management decision making should involve staff.
- Transfer the management team and bring new ones.
- Peer-review by other hospitals.
- Promote staff-community durbars.

Commitment to Work and Discipline

Another dimension of quality of care the respondents made, as suggestions for improvement was commitment to work and discipline. Suggestions under this dimension included the need for staff to be committed to their work, the need to ensure discipline and sanction staffs who misconducted themselves, the need to report for work early, treat patients promptly, and work efficiently. The following were some of the key suggestions:

- Staff must be committed to work.
- Dedicated staff is what we need.
- Bad staff should be sanctioned.
- High staff discipline and morals should be maintained.
- Some staffs do not report for work on time.
- Prompt treatment should be given to patients.
- Every staff member of the hospital should carry out his/her duties in an efficient and effective manner.

Attitudes Towards Patients

Another concern expressed by respondents was the need to improve attitudes towards patients. Some of the suggestions were as follows:

- Provision of tender love and care to patients.
- There should be proper staff relationship with patients.
- Respect for clients.
- Ensure patients' privacy and confidentiality.
- Staff should be tolerant.

Patient Education

Finally, respondents were also of the view that patient education must form part of a routine health service delivery. Some of the suggestions were as follows:

- There should be morning talk at the OPD about health issues.
- Patients should be educated on their condition and treatment options by all health workers.
- Patients should be educated on the dos and don'ts of the hospital, especially about sanitation.

4.2 Discussion of Findings

Regarding the financial access to health care, whereas patients' main concern was addressing the problem of affordability and the cost of health services and the elimination of out-of-pocket payments, healthcare providers' main concern was the prompt reimbursement for services rendered. The problem of affordability of the cost of health services is consistent with findings of earlier studies in Burkina Faso and Ghana (Baltussen & Ye, 2006b; Baltussen *et al.*, 2002; Turkson, 2009). The concern by healthcare providers regarding delays by the

National Health Insurance Authority to reimburse claims for services provided has been reported as one of the factors affecting quality of care in Ghana (SEND-Ghana, 2010). The exhortation by some providers for patients to ask for receipts after making payments seems to be an acknowledgement that some unofficial fees are being collected from patients in some hospitals. Even though Schieber, Cashin, Saleh & Lavado (2012) report that informal/unofficial payments in Ghana's health facilities are uncommon, anecdotal evidence suggests that informal/unofficial payments exist. It is recommended that a thorough study be done on unofficial payments.

Eliminating discrimination, ensuring fairness to all categories of patients, and giving special attention to vulnerable patients were the main suggestions made by patients in respect of ensuring fairness of care to all categories of patients. Even though these suggestions by patients seem to give credence to empirical evidence of discrimination between insured and uninsured patients (Nguyen, Rajkotia & Wang, 2011, Devadasan, Criel, Van Damme, Lefevre, Manoharan & Van der Stuyft, 2011, Dalinjong & Laar, 2012), results of the quantitative survey found no significant difference in perceptions of fairness of care between the insured and uninsured patients, in all indicators of fairness of care (Abuosi, 2015).

Inadequacy of resources and services was an area of consensus by patients and healthcare providers, as both groups suggested that there was the need for an increase in the numbers of health staff in order to cope with the workload in the hospital. They also expected an improvement in availability of equipment and supplies, especially medicines, and expansion in infrastructure of the hospitals, among others. This concern regarding inadequacy of resources and services is consistent with existing literature (Duong, Binns, Lee & Hipgrave, 2004, Baltussen *et al.*, 2002, Baltussen & Ye, 2006b, Hansen *et al.*, 2008; Mashego & Peltzer, 2005; Juma & Manongi, 2009; Kamuzora & Gilson, 2007; Turkson, 2009).

In line with the literature (Robyn *et al.*, 2013; Juma & Manongi, 2009) effectiveness of treatment is given a favourable response by both patients and healthcare providers. With respect to technical aspects of care, patients emphasized the need to involve patients in their treatment and the need for a thorough medical examination. Generally, much of the literature on technical aspects of care, including patients being physically examined, or being involved in their care, is less favourable (Duong *et al.*, 2004; Baltussen *et al.*, 2002; Baltussen & Ye, 2006b; Turkson, 2009). On the other hand, healthcare providers had no issues with the technical aspects of care. Perhaps, doctors and the other healthcare providers assume that what is important to patients is to get cured of their diseases, and not so much about the processes involved.

Regarding the interpersonal aspects of care, patients called for improvement in interpersonal relationships, especially the need for respect, tolerance and decent speech towards patients by the staff. The literature on interpersonal aspects of care is mixed. Whereas in some studies there are positive reports of interpersonal aspects of care (Duong *et al.*, 2004; Baltussen *et al.*, 2002; Baltussen & Ye, 2006b; Hansen *et al.*, 2008), other reports are negative (Mashego & Peltzer, 2005; Juma & Manongi, 2009; Turkson, 2009). On the other hand, healthcare providers also saw the need to improve on their attitude towards patients, by being more caring, respectful, confidential of treatment and being tolerant to patients were also issues high on the agenda.

There were other areas of concern to patients beyond the quality indicators used in the study. For example, patients expect prompt services at various service delivery points. This suggestion to provide prompt services is supported by an earlier study which found that prompt services were given low ratings in the hospitals studied (Abuosi & Atinga, 2013). Patients were also of the view that special care should be given to the care of various vulnerable groups such as the seriously ill, pregnant women and children and the aged. These were all not identified by healthcare providers as issues deserving attention to improve quality of care. Even though the NHIS makes provision for vulnerable groups such as pregnant women, children and the aged, to be exempted from paying health insurance premium, healthcare providers do not have a policy to give priority of care to these groups. It is therefore recommended that future assessment of quality of care from the patient's perspective may include indicators or dimensions, such as promptness of services, attention to vulnerable patients and 24-hour services throughout the week, in order to inform health policy reforms on quality improvement.

On the other hand, healthcare providers identified the need for staff training and motivation, as well as effective supervision to ensure quality service provision. There was also emphasis on team work, involvement of staff in decision-making, peer-review and the organizing of community durbars, and more seriously, commitment to work and discipline. The suggestion by providers for training and motivation is consistent with a recent study in Ghana on the association between health worker motivation and healthcare quality efforts in Ghana (Alhassan, Spieker, van Ostenberg, Ogink, Nketiah-Amponsah & de Wit, 2013). According to the author, there was a significant positive association between staff satisfaction levels with working conditions and the clinic's effort towards quality improvement. Providers also suggested that patients visiting the hospital need to be educated on various health issues ranging from their personal health needs to issues of sanitation. It is therefore recommended that future assessments of quality of care from the provider's perspective may include such indicators or dimensions as staff motivation, effective supervision, team work, and involvement of staff in decision-making, subjecting the hospital to peer-review, organization of community durbars, discipline and patient education.

This study also lends credence to the general literature, suggesting that perceptions of quality largely differ between patients and healthcare providers (Silvestro, 2005, Zhao *et al.*, 2009, Miranda, Chamorro, Murillo & Vega, 2010, Roohi *et al.*, 2011). Even though patients and healthcare providers agree in a few areas, such as the need for more doctors to be engaged, in general, suggestions by patients for quality improvement differ remarkably from suggestions by health care providers. This implies that efforts to improve upon quality of care in health institutions should not only focus on patients concerns, but also on the views of health care providers.

5. Conclusions

This study reveals that even though patients and health care providers may share similar concerns in some aspects of quality of care, such as in the inadequacy of resources and in interpersonal aspects of care, in many respects, the two groups have different areas of emphasis regarding quality improvement. Whereas patients' major concern relates to lower costs of services, health care providers emphasize timely reimbursements by the NHIS to enable them improve on the quality of services. Efforts must be made to improve financial access to healthcare for the vulnerable, by ensuring their enrolment into the NHIS, and to eliminate unofficial payments to hospitals. The NHIS must take serious measures to ensure prompt reimbursements of health care. Innovative strategies must also be taken to train more clinical staff, involve patients in their care, and improve upon interpersonal relationships.

6. Limitation of the Study

Findings from this study should however be examined cautiously, considering the fact that it is a report on responses to a single open-ended question, as part of a large quantitative close-ended questionnaire survey. There was therefore no in-depth probing into the responses provided. Notwithstanding this limitation, many of the suggestions, especially from patients, were in line with findings from the quantitative survey. However, future studies may require an in-depth interview with patients and providers to validate the dimensions identified in this study. This may even lead to the development of a unique quality of care scale to assess both patients and health care providers.

7. Acknowledgment

This study was conducted with funding support from the University of Ghana-Carnegie Project to support faculty, as well as from the University of Ghana Business School.

References

Abuosi, A. A. (2015). Patients versus healthcare providers' perceptions of quality of care: establishing the gaps for policy action. *Clinical Governance: An International Journal,* 20(4) pp?

Abuosi, A. A. & Atinga, R. A. (2013) Service quality in healthcare institutions: establishing the gaps for policy action. *International journal of health care quality assurance*, *26*(5), 481-492.

Akin, J. S, & Hutchinson, P.. (1999). Health-care facility choice and the phenomenon of bypassing. Health Policy and Planning, 14(2), 135-151.

Alatinga, K. A, & Williams, John J. (2012). Does Membership in Mutual Health Insurance Guarantee Quality Health Care? Some Evidence from Ghana. European Journal of Business and Social Sciences, 1(3), 103-118.

Alhassan, R. K., Spieker, N., van Ostenberg, P., Ogink, A., Nketiah-Amponsah, E., & de Wit, T.

F. R. (2013). Association between health worker motivation and healthcare quality efforts in Ghana. Human Resource for Health, 1(8), 9.pp?

Andaleeb, S. S. (2001). Service quality perceptions and patient satisfaction: a study of hospitals in a developing country. Social Science & Medicine, 52(9), 1359-1370.

Atinga, R. A.. (2012). Healthcare quality under the National Health Insurance Scheme in Ghana: Perspectives from premium holders. International Journal of Quality & Reliability Management, 29(2), 144-161.

Baltussen, RMPM, Bruce, E, Rhodes, G, Narh□ Bana, SA, & Agyepong, I. (2006). Management of mutual health organizations in Ghana. Tropical Medicine & International Health, 11(5), 654-659.

Baltussen, R.M.P.M., Yé, Y., Haddad, S., & Sauerborn, R. S. (2002). Perceived quality of care of primary health care services in Burkina Faso. Health Policy and Planning, 17(1), 42-48.

Baltussen, R., & Ye, Y.. (2006). Quality of care of modern health services as perceived by users and non-users in Burkina Faso. International Journal for Quality in Health Care, 18(1), 30-34.

Brown, S. W., & Swartz, T. A. (1989). A gap analysis of professional service quality. The Journal of Marketing, 53 (2), 92-98.

Dalinjong, P. A., & Laar, A. S. (2012). The national health insurance scheme: perceptions and experiences of health care providers and clients in two districts of Ghana. Health Economics Review, 2(1), 1-13.

De Allegri, M., Sanon, M., & Sauerborn, R.. (2006). "To enrol or not to enrol?": A qualitative investigation of demand for health insurance in rural West Africa. Social Science & Medicine, 62(6), 1520-1527.

Devadasan, N., Criel, B., Van Damme, W., Lefevre, P., Manoharan, S, & Van der Stuyft, P.. (2011). Community health insurance schemes & patient satisfaction-evidence from India. The Indian Journal of Medical Research, 133(1), 40.

Duong, D. V., Binns, C., W., Lee, A. H., & Hipgrave, D. B. (2004). Measuring Client-perceived Quality of Maternity Services in Rural Vietnam. International Journal of Quality Health Care, 6, 447-452.

Franco, L. M., Franco, C., Kumwenda, N., & Nkhoma, W.. (2002). Methods for assessing quality of provider performance in developing countries. International Journal for Quality in Health Care, 14(suppl 1), 17-024.

Ghana Health Service (2007). Quality Assurance Strategic Plan for Ghana Health Service 2007-2011.

Haddad, S , & Fournier, P. (1995). Quality, costs and utilization of health services in developing -countries. A longitudinal study in Zaire. ??Soc... Sci... Med..., 47, 381–394.

Haddad, S., Fournier, P., Machouf, N., & Yatara, F.. (1998). What does quality mean to lay people? Community perceptions of primary health care services in Guinea. Social Science & Medicine, 47(3), 381-394.

Haddad, S., Fournier, P., & Potvin, L.. (1998). Measuring lay people's perceptions of the quality of primary health care services in developing countries. Validation of a 20-item scale. International Journal for Quality in Health Care, 10(2), 93-104.

Haddad, S., Potvin, L., Roberge, D., Pineault, R., & Remondin, M. (2000). Patient perception of quality following a visit to a doctor in a primary care unit. Family practice, 17(1), 21-29.

Hansen, P. M., Peters, D. H., Viswanathan, K., Rao, K. D., Mashkoor, A., & Burnham, G. (2008). Client perceptions of the quality of primary care services in Afghanistan. International Journal for Quality in Health Care, 20(6), 384-391.

Juma, D, & Manongi, R. (2009). Users' perceptions of outpatient quality of care in Kilosa District Hospital in central Tanzania. Tanzania Journal of Health Research, 11(4).

Kamuzora, P. & Gilson, L.. (2007). Factors influencing implementation of the Community Health Fund in Tanzania. Health Policy and Planning, 22(2), 95-102.

Kaseje, D.C., Spencer, H.C., & Sempebwa, E.K. (1987). Usage of community-based chloroquine treatment for malaria in Saradidi, Kenya. Annals of Tropical Medicine and Parasitology, 81, 111-115.

Kogan, J. R, Holmboe, E. S, & Hauer, K. E. (2009). Tools for direct observation and assessment of clinical skills of medical trainees: a systematic review. Jama, 302(12), 1316-1326.

Leonard, K. L, Mliga, G. R. & Mariam, D. H.. (2002). Bypassing health centres in Tanzania: Revealed preferences for quality. Journal of African Economies, 11(4), 441-471.

Mamdani, M., & Bangser, M.. (2004). Poor people's experiences of health services in Tanzania: a literature review. Reproductive Health Matters, 12(24), 138-153.

Maynard-Tucker, Giesele. (1994). Indigenous perceptions and quality of care of family planning services in Haiti. Health policy and planning, 9(3), 306-317.

McCombie, S. C. (1996). Treatment seeking for malaria: a review of recent research. Social Science & Medicine, 43(6), 933-945.

Mashego, T. A., & Peltzer, K. (2005). Community perception of quality of (primary) health care services in a rural area of Limpopo Province, South Africa: a qualitative study. Curationis, 28(2), 13-21.

Miranda, F. J., Chamorro, A., Murillo, L. R., & Vega, J. (2010). An importance-performance analysis of primary health care services: managers vs. patients perceptions. Journal of Service Science and Management, 3(02), 227.

Narang, Ritu. (2010). Measuring perceived quality of health care services in India. International Journal of Health Care Quality Assurance, 23(2), 171-186.

Nashrath, M., Akkadechanunt, T., & Chontawan, R. (2011). Perceived nursing service quality in a tertiary care hospital, Maldives. Nursing & Health Sciences, 13(4), 495-501.

Newman, R.D, Gloyd, S., Nyangezi, J. M, Machobo, F., & Muiser, J.. (1998). Satisfaction with outpatient health care services in Manica Province, Mozambique. Health Policy and Planning, 13(2), 174-180.

Nguyen, HT, Rajkotia, Y., & Wang, H.. (2011). The financial protection effect of Ghana National Health Insurance Scheme: evidence from a study in two rural districts. International Journal of Equity Health, 10(4), 9-10.

Onishi, J, Gupta, S, & Peters, D.H. (2010). Comparative analysis of exit interviews and direct clinical observations in pediatric ambulatory care services in Afghanistan. International Journal for Quality in Health Care, mzq074.

Pretorius, C.F, & Greeff, M. (2004). Health-service utilization by pregnant women in the greater Mafikeng-Mmabatho district. Curationis, 27(1), 72-81.

Reinhardt, U. E, & Cheng, T.. (2000). The world health report 2000-Health systems: improving performance. Bulletin of the World Health Organization, 78(8), 1064-1064.

Robyn, P., Hill, A., Souares, A., Savadogo, G., Sie, A., & Sauerborn, R. (2011). Community-based health insurance and delays to accessing appropriate care: The application of the" Three-Delays" model to childhood illnesses in Burkina Faso. University of Heidelberg, Institute of Public Health.

Robyn, P. J., Sauerborn, R., & Bärnighausen, T.. (2013). Provider payment in community-based health insurance schemes in developing countries: a systematic review. Health Policy and Planning, 28(2), 111-122.

Roohi, G., Asayesh, H., Abdollahi, A. A., & Abbasi, A. (2011). Evaluation of clients' expectations and perception gap regarding the quality of primary healthcare service in healthcare centers of Gorgan. Journal of Jahrom University of Medical Sciences, 9(3), 40.

Schieber, G., Cashin, C., Saleh, K., & Lavado, R. (2012). Health financing in Ghana. World Bank Publications.

SEND-Ghana. (2010). Balancing access with quality of care: An assessment of the NHIS in Ghana Series.

Sharma, J.K. & Narang, R.. (2011). Quality of healthcare services in rural India: the user perspective. Vikalpa, 36(1), 51-60.

Silvestro, R. (2005). Applying gap analysis in the health service to inform the service improvement agenda. International Journal of Quality & Reliability Management, 22(3), 215-233.

Stekelenburg, J., Kyanamina, S., Mukelabai, M., Wolffers, I., & Roosmalen, J. van. (2004). Waiting too long: low use of maternal health services in Kalabo, Zambia. Tropical Medicine & International Health, 9(3), 390-398.

Tipke, M., Diallo, S., Coulibaly, B., Störzinger, D., Hoppe-Tichy, T., Sie, A., & Müller, O.. (2008). Substandard anti-malarial drugs in Burkina Faso. Malar Journal, 7, 95. ?pp

Turkson, P. K. (2009). Perceived quality of healthcare delivery in rural districts of Ghana. Ghana Medical Journal 43(2): 65–70.

Van Duong, D., Binns, C. W., Lee, A. H., & Hipgrave, D. B. (2004). Measuring client-perceived quality of maternity services in rural Vietnam. International Journal for Quality in Health Care, 16(6), 447-452.

Williams, T., Schutt-Aine, J., & Cuca, Y.. (2000). Measuring family planning service quality through client satisfaction exit interviews. International Family Planning Perspectives, 63-71.

World Health Organization. (2006). The world health report 2006: working together for health. Geneva: World Health Organization: WHO Press.

Zhao, S. H., Akkadechanunt, T., & Xue, X. L. (2009). Quality nursing care as perceived by nurses and patients in a Chinese hospital. Journal of Clinical Nursing, 18(12), 1722-1728

PART III

POLICY AND INSTITUTIONAL PERSPECTIVES ON MANAGEMENT DEVELOPMENT IN AFRICA

CHAPTER TWELVE

Issues in the Management of Urban Areas in Africa: Towards a Stewardship, Collaborative and Sustainable Framework

Innocent Chirisa, Liaison Mukarwi and Aaron Maphosa

1. Introduction

Better management of human settlements in the developing nations has become a priority in the aspirations of citizens, of governments and of the concerned international community. Developing countries have remarkable concerns pertaining to urban management that are a consequence of the rate and form of urbanisation and the contemporary economic dynamics (Sirry, 2003). The key issues tasking urban managers include the availability, control, utilisation and access of land for urban development, housing markets, infrastructure financing, in view of high urban poverty, the inadequacy of basic services, transport management and environmental degradation (increasing pollution) and the effects of climate change which induce problems like flooding. These issues are being dealt with in an environment punctuated by effects of patronage and clientilism, global financial crises, diminishing development aid, and increased vandalism of urban assets coupled with increasing mass protestations. Of note is that globalisation has also posed new demands on urban management. Urban management is the effort to co-ordinate and integrate public and private actions to tackle the major problems inhabitants of cities are facing to make a city more competitive, equitable and sustainable (Van Dijk, 2008). In developing countries, issues which include rapid urbanisation and the diseconomies of the absorption of national investments by cities are the chief causes of the serious challenges evident in urban management which are manifesting into environmental degradation, traffic congestion and high urban poverty and decay. Developing countries are experiencing rapid spatial transformations that leave spatial planners and urban mangers with a difficult task in handling the phenomenon. The challenges can therefore be named wicked problems; the challenges are increasingly complex and thus difficult to negotiate because they affect cross-sections and many levels of the society (Suresh, 2003). The rapid growth of urban populations with declining national economies ultimately challenges the future of urban agglomerations as a place to live, work and enjoy leisure (ibid). Thus, this paper seeks to outline and discuss the major issues surrounding the contemporary management of urban areas in Africa. It offers not only a clear description of the issues, but also proposes ways to overcome those problems and challenges in a sustainable way.

2. Research Design and Methods

The study has been achieved mainly through a desktop study involving literature and document reviews. It is qualitative or exploratory in nature aimed to outline and discuss the major contemporary issues surrounding the management of urban areas in developing countries. The literature review is a systematic examination of the knowledge available on the various topics. This includes the use of appropriate peer-reviewed articles to get deep insight into the topic from various experts who had researched and written about it (Ridley, 2008). The literature review enabled us to assess the current state of African cities and the challenges faced by management to achieve sustainable cities. This also assisted us in coming up with recommendation learning from experiences of the developed world.

3. Theoretical Perspectives

Urban Management in Developing Countries

Urban management is defined as a set of instruments, activities, tasks and functions that assures that a city can function, including for example making sure that water gets to every home, there is an efficient transport system for goods and people and that land is provided for various activities essential for its residents (Clarke 2013). It seeks to safeguard public interest against individuals' and firms' interests, making sure that repairs are carried out on infrastructure networks before eventual damage or neglect start affecting people's life (Acioly, 2000). Urban management assures that services are provided for the population and the various private, public and community stakeholders to perform and maximise their intrinsic roles in a harmonic manner. Urban management can husband and efficiently utilise scarce resources, vastly expanding the resource pool available for the needs of urban life (Mattingly 1995). It is the management of the activities of human settlements. Urban management is not separate from planning or from development, but encompasses both of these.

In general, the important tasks of urban management include the provision of water and sanitation, waste management, transportation, health-related facilities, security and safety services, housing and urban land for development. The key processes in urban management are identified as planning, coordinating, resourcing, developing, operating and maintaining (Clarke 2013). Planning orients policies and actions towards management objectives and to the future, so that interrelating policies of the highest priority can be identified and effected / realised / achieved. Coordinating schedules actions and arranges for the various agents involved to act in concert. Providing resources secures the commitment of money, materials, facilities, personnel, institutions, and information for intended actions (ibid). Some of the resources will be used to create the physical facilities, the pools of equipment and the social and administrative organisation which the actions require. Maintenance directs resources to nurture personnel, physical facilities and organisations, so that they can perform continuously. Although development can create systems capable of sustained action, proper resourcing and maintenance are critical to sustain the actions which bring improvement to urban conditions.

In light of the above, the urban manager is there to facilitate the co-ordinated efforts of the various urban players – public sector (local governments, the private sector and the community). The urban managers are supposed to promote efficiency, efficacy and equity in the distribution of public resources and investments generated from within the city and use these resources in further development of the city (Wellman & Spiller, 2012). Urban managers are also responsible for suggesting necessary policy reforms to improve the level of service delivery and to increase the competitiveness of their local economies (Van Dijk, 2008). The idea is that through necessary reforms, the performance of the municipalities will increase by achieving ecological sustainability in cities and thus deal with urban poverty and social exclusion. Improved service delivery requires institutions that are more efficient. Urban management is constantly influenced by or is influencing political decisions, thus national politics and governance are very critical elements in urban management.

4. Urban Management Issues in Developing Countries

To grasp the realities of the challenge of urban management, one may need to know the characteristics of the 'creature' called a city and then link up with the aspects and features of those challenges. Simply defined, cities are concentrations of people, resources, information and activities (Chirisa, Kawadza & Muzenda 2014). The rationale of city growth could be viewed as clever and skilled people in close proximity with each other generate many benefits due to their diverse interactions, and the potential of economies of scale and scope of agglomeration (Wellman & Spiller, 2012). Where this interaction is fluid, dense and diverse, there emerges the potential for innovation and creativity, and this calls for effective urban management. The issues under the urban managers in developing countries are faced with issues that include, but not limited to, land (availability, access, control and utilisation), housing supply and its market, infrastructure and service provision, transport management, environmental protection.

Due to the concentration of various land uses in cities, urban land has become scarce and expensive to acquire. The urban manager has the role to distribute / allocate this resource (land) equitably, among the competing interests. . The increased demand on urban land; its access, acquisition, control and use are surrounded with much controversy. Chaotic land processes are due to unclear policies and institutional bottlenecks. Poor economic performance and the need to promote economic development have also made urban management ineffectual in many developing nations. Tension between an official ideology of socialism as opposed to capitalistic market forces are also observed in many countries, and this creates many loopholes in the system as the capitalistic processes promote skewed access and acquisition of expensive urban land in favour of the elites. Parallel to this process is the informal land acquisition which is usually as a result of peri-urban land invasions and often results in illegal use of that urban land. The onset of informal trading and industry has exacerbated this form of land acquisition. The urban manager has to promote harmony among these uses and there is no way this can be done without employing the heavy hand of the law which always create much acrimony with the urban communities and the representative groups (Human Rights activists, urban residents associations among others).The prohibition orders and the demolition of existing structures to regain official control of the land are always met with hostilities, making it very difficult for those responsible to maintain sanity, order, prosperity and growth in the city. Land distribution is also political, the effects of the political dynamics in Africa has a bearing on access, acquisition and use of land. The centre-local relations become very influential on the availability of land to urban localities as for example in Zimbabwe, where the central government acquired all the farms in the country and it uses its discretion to give this land to local authorities for development. These processes form the complexities in the land issues which always render the urban manager as a developer questionable. The forces of land acquisition prove to be bigger than just a matter of spatial planning, but rather include economic and political dimensions.

The provision of housing is also the responsibility of urban management. The housing market in developing countries has two systems operating parallel to each other. Just like having many issues on land acquisition, the housing market follows the same trajectory. It also has a formal housing delivery system which constitutes the legitimate housing market and also an informal housing delivery system, and this constitutes bogus sellers and land barons meant to extort money from the public. The rapid growth of urban areas has increased the need for housing and other services. Following the conventional and formal way of acquiring land, developing it into residential stands and the construction of houses is very expensive seen against the growing need for houses; this exacerbates the informal housing market (Mendel, 2006). To ensure that the growing populace has access to housing services, the urban mangers have resorted to low income housing delivery initiatives like the incorporation of housing cooperatives in servicing residential stands. The outcome of all these efforts has never proved any good to urban centres in developing countries as the rates of bogus land dealers have rocked many cities in Zimbabwe in the name of cooperatives, leaving the cities in a deplorable state of filthy houses with no services (health, safety, education). The overall result is that, the contemporary urban management in various countries like Zambia, Malawi, Kenya, Ghana, Ethiopia, to name these few, is a failure. The urban management is facing difficulties arbitrating the social, economic and environmental conflicts of the urban areas in the drive for sustainable cities. The economic situations of the developing world has made the provision and access to decent accommodation very expensive and how to balance the informality of random settlements with the needs of environmental protection, urban order and sanity and promotion of a modern urban fabric has become very difficult.

Environmental (ecological) protection is also another crucial role of urban management. The attempt to promote sustainable urban development through the integration of socio-economic and spatial planning and development, as well as preserving the ecosystem, is a very crucial matter which has become a balancing act for urban planners. The sustainable development concept has introduced a paradigm shift to the way spatial planning processes are observed, as they are driven by contradictory economic and social interests and objectives (Yigitcanlar, 2010). A fundamental dimension of sustainable development is sustaining the growth and development of the city, while balancing the benefits with complex ecological systems and the global environment (van Dijk, 2008). The unprecedented growth of the urban populace coupled with industrial and residential development have had significant negative impacts on the natural environment through pollution of the air, of water and land, the loss of land cover and wetland deterioration. This scenario has ushered in a new dispensation to planning and urban management, to promote environmental stewardship. The role of the urban manager becomes that of an ecologist who safeguards the natural environment from human activities. This has called for new urban forms like the compact city, transit oriented development and new urbanism, with the intention to protect the natural environment from jeopardy by human impulses. Tasked with the responsibility of environmental protection, the quality of urban managers in developing nations is always in disrepute, because they seem to ignore environmental dictates due to limited financial resources and the need to promote and attract investment. Environmentalists are blamed of increasing the cost of doing business. Protection of the environment in most instances is named a barrier to development and hence a serious problem to urban managers who are tasked with balancing the two, since economic development has more political power than environmentalism (Mattingly 1995). Financially crippled local authorities cannot invest in sophisticated technology to manage pollution, to manage waste reticulation and disposal, and to undertake research for improvements in the current systems. The result is continued environmental degradation despite the mangers awareness of this important role.

Infrastructure and service provision are responsibilities of the urban managers. The deplorable state of infrastructure and service provision in the developing countries has damaged the reputation of the urban mangers in the developing world. There is a serious need for infrastructure revamping and maintenance for example in Harare, the water drainage is pathetic, the roads are potholed and water and sewer reticulation are in a sorry state. In explanation, the growth of urban population supported by dying industries and collapsing economies has led to the growth of the informal sector to absorb the unemployed urban migrants, and this has serious challenges to urban management since these do not generate revenue for the cities to invest into the dilapidated social and economic infrastructure. The issue of the declining resource base in developing countries has left urban managers as spectators, as the cities they are in charge of are faced with the negative impact of poor service delivery, like cholera outbreaks due to poor waste management and a scanty safe water supply and environmental degradation (waste water or sewage disposal in water sources and land pollution). Harare has lost its Sunshine City status due to deteriorating financial resources, leading to the complete decline of service delivery. Due to high unemployment and social or moral decay, vandalism of city property is on the rise in the cities. This has led to an increase in the cost of service provision with no proved improvement, as most resources are used to replace vandalised property. For example in Harare, the provision of street waste bins is proving useless, as people are either stealing or vandalising them. In states like Egypt where there has been civil unrest, and recently in South Africa due to xenophobia, the urban areas lost money by having to replace vandalised city property.

Taking transport as a substantive area, it can be witnessed that urban managers in developing countries have a lot of issues to deal with, to make this sector sustainable Transport and industrial activities contribute immensely to air pollution, which is considered as one of the causes of climate change. Though Africa has not industrialised like Europe or America, its contribution to air pollution emanates from unsustainable modes of transport and old industrial production methods (Yigitcanlar, 2010). The issue of sprawl development in Africa has led to an automobile dependent community, which has given problems in the provision of sustainable public transport, hence pollution and congestion. Most urban areas in developing countries are using low capacity passenger vehicles which are informal in nature, named Kombis in Zimbabwe, Matatus in Kenya, and Dala Dala in Tanzania. These forms of transport remain informal due to their operation, no fixed timetable, filthy driving behaviour, no fixed fares, no ticketing systems, among other operational traits. In Kenya, these forms of transport have been named 'My Own Way Code' instead of the Highway Code. This mode of transport causes congestion and accidents. The role of the urban manger is to provide a sustainable (in the fight against air pollution) and comfortable, safe, reliable and efficient transport system which can boost the socio-economic activities of a city. Challenges in this sector include the issue of finances (to acquire and maintain formal public transport fleet) and declining economic activities that prevent a reliable and sustained operation in a formal public transport system. High capacity passenger vehicles as economic users of road space, save fuel consumption and hence reduced pollution, but need high patronage hence economic viability support, so that more people will be moving to and from work. Contemporary urban management systems should include the ability to plan and model whole systems that optimise transportation and built environmental, resources including energy, water, and natural systems (Yigitcanlar, 2010).

Taking globalisation as a contemporary issue on the urban manger's desk, it can be noted that there are various benefits from the phenomena, but with the current scenario in developing countries this has posed problems in urban management. Globalisation is a set of economic processes in which production, marketing and investment are integrated across the borders of nations (Suresh, 2003). The liberalization and opening up of markets to the global economy is leading to the emergence of a single market for goods, capital, technology, services, and information, and to some extent labour (ibid).The logic of globalisation is the expansion of trade and investment in search of new markets and competitive production sites. For the development of urban managers, the issue is to address the effects of rapid expansion of corporate interests, for example, to protect ecological stability for local communities against the benefits of the corporate operation. The dilemma here is promoting industrial growth versus environmental and social decay, for in most cases the economic atmosphere forces authorities to go for investment rather than for socio-ecological considerations. Globalisation has generated new challenges in preparing strategies for urban development, as it threatens to exacerbate urban environmental and natural resource degradation. Urban managers have to come up with measures that promote the environmental sustainability as well as keep the city attractive for investment. An issue like city branding to attract investment becomes the important issue, given that the developing world is craving for foreign direct investment. The strategy is to make cities liveable, provide environmental services for the urban population, and protect urban people against environmental hazards (Van Dijk, 2008).

5. Human-Induced Urban Management Issues

Urban environmental problems are threats to people's present or future wellbeing, resulting in human-induced damage to the physical environment in urban areas (Mendel, 2006). The effects of climate change on urban landscapes have also come to the attention of the urban manager. Climate change is a human activity -induced phenomena, which has affected many countries across the globe. The Greenhouse gases (GHG) emitted from industrial and transportation activities, leading to a general increase in global temperatures, have induced the global warming effect. This increase in Africa has affected food production and infrastructure development, as well as industrial activities, due to the frequency and prevalence of droughts, dry spells, floods and cyclones. This has changed the landscape of the African urban centres which the urban mangers have to deal with. . Climate change has made infrastructure deterioration more pronounced due to floods (degradation of roads, collapse of bridges) and reduced agricultural productivity, food shortages, and also has left many agriculture dependent industries scaling down or closing down(ibid). Climate change, projected to exacerbate existing desertification and water stress, constitutes a major threat to Northern Africa's urban populations. The negative effects on agriculture will increase the need for food imports, with adverse effects on the regional balance of payments. Climate change will render most of Northern Africa's cities more vulnerable to disasters associated with extreme weather patterns, especially flooding, while desertification presents a threat to Sudan's rural economy and food production (Saungweme, Matsvai & Sakuhuni 2014). The urban management has to deal with such changing urban landscapes' new demands.

Urban management is also concerned with the issue of governance. The unseen benefit is that the increased pace of urbanisation and its linkages to economic globalisation have reinvigorated interest in good urban governance and management, and its links to economic growth (Suresh, 2003). Despite local diversities in terms of legislation and political structures, there is a global trend towards the transfer of administrative, political and financial responsibilities to local governments in a number of areas of activity (Davy, 2003). This is associated with structural reforms in central governments, and the gradual retreat of the State from productive sectors. The rationale is to bring decision-making and problem solving in the city as close as possible to citizens and their area of residence, redirecting information, public-citizen interface and provision of certain services down to the district and neighbourhood levels. The structure, roles, tasks and functions of local governments, and the way responsibilities are assigned to different agencies and departments directly affect the quality and efficiency of urban management (Van Dijk, 2008). To build friendly and liveable urban communities, cities should promote a harmonious and friendly social environment, and build civil, safe and liveable urban neighbourhoods through rational planning and governance. They should encourage public participation in urban planning and governance, take into consideration the practical and psychological needs of migrants to the cities, and eliminate social barriers and conflicts in its bid to provide high quality public services in employment, healthcare, education, housing, social welfare and other areas. The issue of governance becomes an important pillar in the achievement of sustainable development. To achieve the targets outlined above, urban managers in local governments must possess instruments that allow them to arbitrate development conflicts, mobilise efforts and take advantage from the capacities, potentials and creativity that exist among its constituents, to forge sustainable and equitable local development processes (Newman & Thornley, 2000). Only then will local government be able to assume its leading enabling role in the planning and management of urban growth, establishing strategic public-private-community partnerships, particularly for the tasks for which it does not possess all the means and resources. Most African governance structures are still autocratic, making fluid cooperation and collaboration among urban players very difficult.

6. Challenges in Urban Management in Developing Countries

Rapid urbanisation forms one of the wicked problems that urban managers in developing countries are operating in. This feature in developing countries has made urban planning and management very difficult. According to the ADB (2015), in 2008, more than half of the world human population, 3.3 billion people, lived in urban areas, and the projections are that by 2030 this is expected to balloon to almost 5 billion. This phenomenon has led to the rise of large and growing cities like Cairo (Egypt), Accra (Ghana), Johannesburg-Pretoria (South Africa), Khartoum (Sudan), Kinshasa-Brazzaville (Democratic Republic of the Congo and Republic of the Congo), Lagos (Nigeria), and Nairobi (Kenya). Most urban centres in the developing world are increasing in size. The growth of the urban population has created challenges in the delivery of urban services. The role of urban managers is to mitigate the rate of this growth, to match the growth in population with attendant services like water, housing, employment, health and infrastructure. This is a daunting task, given that the economic performance of many cities is deteriorating thus financing the growth of urban development and infrastructure is stalled in the face of an ever growing population. The rapid growth of the urban population is punctuated by not only unsustainable and deficient service delivery in public sectors like water, sewerage, electricity, solid waste management, telecommunications and health but also in the lack of formal employment (Gutman & Chattopadhyay, 2015). This has resulted in many people being unemployed, contributing to serious urban poverty.

The economic atmosphere in the developing nations is ever worsening (ILO 2002). Poor urban finances have remained the Achilles heel of many towns, impeding both sustainable growth and healthy living environments for an increasing population of urban dwellers across Africa. Urban management, when dealing with urban finances, is supposed to bank roll all the activities that make a city function. In Africa, urban finances are constrained and often abused. The economies are turning informal for several reasons, due to an economic meltdown. Burgeoning city populations, with increasing consumption and production patterns, overtax limited urban resources, and the effects are usually first felt by the ill-equipped urban poor, which urban managers seek to protect (ibid). Urban poverty, in turn, is often accompanied by health and environmental problems related to lack of access to clean water and adequate sanitation. In Africa, cities get its finances from their own activities like the sale of its services (water), fines and fees, rates, central governments through grants, banks (loans and mortgages), global financial institutions and donors (UNHABITAT, 2010). The economic meltdown globally has made these sources dwindle, so most African municipalities are now unable to sustainably fund their activities from internally generated sources and always look up to donor agencies and central governments. Globally, donor aid has reduced, leaving most cities in developing countries wanting. For example, the withdrawal of UNICEF in the purification of Harare water has been felt city wide. Effective urban management instils discipline and accountability in the use and handling of urban finances, and brings innovative funding avenues like the public private partnerships.

Urban management in developing countries face dilapidated infrastructure financing, given that the access to urban services depends very much on the availability and quality of infrastructure. This, in Africa, represents a major challenge given the ballooning demand on the infrastructure, due to rapid urbanisation and globalisation. The demand for transport, energy, water and waste management infrastructure is very high, yet it is in a sorry state in most Africa countries, except in a few like South Africa. The role of the urban manager in the infrastructure development is to strategise on the best and most sustainable ways to finance infrastructure, promoting cooperation and collaboration among constituents in the urban set up (Acioly, 2000). The role of the private sector in infrastructure financing has been widely recognised, thus; through proper urban management and governance, local authorities can take advantage of this source of infrastructure funding. The initiatives of the private sector are affected by policies of the public sector, and the experience in various countries show that the public sector alone is not capable of fulfilling its constituent role.

The issue of politics affects the functioning of the nation at large hence also of the urban areas. Politics is the art and science of 'who gets what' in a society. Due to the significant influence of politics on all matters in developing countries' clientelism, also known as the patron-client model of politics permeates contemporary political systems in the distribution of resources (Goldsmith, 1999a). Clientelism refers to a complex chain of personal bonds between political patrons or bosses and their individual clients or followers (Brinkerhoff & Goldsmith, 2002). These bonds are founded on mutual material advantage; the patron furnishes excludable resources (money, jobs) to dependents and accomplices and, in return, gets their support and cooperation (votes, attendance at rallies). It is customary and expected in most societies for people to help friends and family members, but the same behaviour is improper and, indeed, unlawful when it takes place within a rational-legal civil service organisation where appointments are supposed to be made on merit (McCourt, 2000). In support, Migdal (1988) notes that precarious economic system propels people to focus on immediate consumption and to forsake more long-term and abstract gains. Present-day clientelism thus tends to flourish in insecure political and economic environments like in Africa, both rural and urban, and is an integral part of the 'politics of survival' for both patrons and clients (Saungweme *et al.* 2014). This has promoted corruption and abuse of public resources by public office holders in developing countries. The patron has disproportionate power and thus enjoys wide latitude about how to distribute the assets under his control. In modern politics, most patrons are independent actors, but have links within a larger grid of contacts, usually serving as intermediaries who arrange exchanges between the local level and the national centre (Kettering, 1988).

7. Results and Discussion

The thematic aspects of the study include availability, control, utilisation and access of land for urban development, housing markets, infrastructure financing, and transport management and the supply-side of the urban economics. On the other hand, there are forces putting the urban space into a crucible. These include environmental challenges like increasing pollution, and the effects of climate change which induce challenges like flooding, as well as human-induced challenges like patronage and clientilism, global financial crises and diminishing development aid and increased vandalism of urban assets coupled with increasing mass protestations. These forces exert a lot of pressure on the person of the urban manager. Urban planning efforts in African cities have key challenges in common, which include urban sprawl, a substantial housing backlogs, poverty and inequality, and the proliferation of slums and informal settlements within city centres and in the urban peripheries- all these coupled with inadequate infrastructure, and service provision (Chirisa *et al* 2012). In turn, these have negative consequences for the current urban governance regimes in the African region. These revolve around ensuring democratic participation, alleviating poverty and inequality, improving urban service provision in, for example, transport or housing, mitigating xenophobia and anti-migrant sentiments, coping with local unrest, achieving cohesion between formal and informal systems of trade and improving the fiscal autonomy of local governments (ibid).

Africa is urbanising faster than expected. This urbanisation trajectory has made it very difficult for the African cities to provide services, for example housing, transport, waste (solid and sewage) disposal and infrastructure. In terms of land management (access, acquisition and use), it can be seen that it is a huge paradox. Rapid urbanisation is creating enormous pressure on urban land. The land for urban use is available through formal legal and informal supply mechanisms (Levine 2015). More pronounced is informal access and supply of land. The rapid shift from rural to urban life experienced in developing countries has provoked the cities to convert rural land resources into urban use, without a concomitant growth in the economy. There is no employment or economic opportunities necessary for securing sustainable urban livelihoods in developing nations and hence urban poverty is on the rise. As a result, this forms negative consequences for how people access land and develop/build their homes. The poor, who have limited access to urban land for residential and commercial purposes, feel the impact of this. Space occupied by the poor in the city is often in its sprawling peripheral lands with inadequate access to basic services such as potable water and sanitation. Moreover, few have legal rights and risk evictions from the land they live on.

Informality remains rife in African cities in the housing sector, even though many social housing projects are efforts to reduce the proportion of slum settlements, as for example in Ghana (Accra), Zimbabwe (Harare) and South Africa (Soweto). In part, this reflects a general weakness in formal (and informal) institutions in land management and housing acquisition which is encumbered by bureaucracy, nepotism and inefficiency (Etzold 2009). People also resort to informal practices because the formal public or private land delivery systems provides only a limited supply of plots, which are rarely accessible to poor people (Rakodi, & Leduka 2004). The bureaucratic delays and complexities in obtaining legal tenure make it difficult for low-income households and investors alike to secure land rights. The cost of registering property in Sub-Saharan Africa is the highest globally (IFC, 2009). This not only has a negative effect on investment, but also on the majority of households' ability to afford legal tenure. The lack of access to courts and a general mistrust of the judicial system imply that the poor are unable to defend their rights, and businessmen are unwilling to risk their investment in land (World Bank, 2007). Informal urban land practices are faster, cheaper, less bureaucratic and provide more flexible alternatives to those excluded from the formal systems of land supply (Durand-Lasserve, & Mattingly, 2004). For example in Zimbabwe it costs 7.6% of the total cost of land to register property legally, comparing that with OECD countries where it costs 4.8% of the property value.

The precarious economic growth and poor urban governance have resulted in a lack of investment in land development, infrastructure and housing. With large proportions of the urban population in African cities residing in informal settlements and slums, the ability of local authorities to collect and maintain revenues is low. This renders local authorities unable to provide basic services, address needs of urban citizenry, or plan effectively to accommodate present and future urban growth patterns. Lack of regional and local urban infrastructure hampers sub-regional economic growth and development. Key regional infrastructure deficits in logistics and transport, port infrastructure, information and communications technologies (ICT) and energy, persist to the detriment of efficient storage, transportation of goods and people. The scale of investment required to meet infrastructure deficits, and future needs provides a challenge that demands regional and international cooperation. The same will also be necessary to tackle successfully urban resource pressures and threats like climate change and associated natural disasters. Regional agencies such as the African Development Bank are playing a key role in funding infrastructure development. China is also playing a key role in road, rail and port infrastructure development projects. Infrastructure and technology development plans are needed to cater for context-specific opportunities and requirements, such as the need for low-cost, decentralised solutions that can be deployed and maintained with low levels of skills and training.

Globalisation in Africa has induced many technological advantages but brought with it some serious challenges, which are now crippling growth. In most African cities, there is rampant vandalism of urban infrastructure and assets, emanating from civil unrest and protestation. This is typical of Northern African economies which are failing to recover from the effects of the uprisings, for example, in Egypt, Libya and Tunisia. These countries have experienced continued unrest and this has reduced the chances for resumed economic growth (Smith 2000). The civil unrest in Libya reduced the country's built up areas and current needs are to replace the urban infrastructure, facilities and services.

Changes in the climate and associated environmental changes bring multiple and multifaceted impacts to bear on the developing world, whether predicted or already experienced. It is clear that climate and environment change-related vulnerabilities are on the rise throughout Africa, with higher frequencies and greater severity of catastrophic events (UNHABITAT, 2010; 2012; 2014). Not a single African nation, city or village is exempted from the growing vulnerability associated with climate and environmental change. Because of their intense concentrations of population, assets and functions, urban areas are particularly at risk from calamitous events. The effects of climate change are haunting the urban managers. To the south and south-west of the region, along the coastal belt, the vulnerability of dense urban corridors and agglomerations to climate change-related pressures, such as flooding, storm surges, sea-level rise, saline intrusion and coastal erosion are projected to increase (Armitage, Marschke & Plummer. 2008). A temperature and precipitation change that is seasonal changes, as well as changes in frequency and intensity of precipitation events, is likely to make food insecurity a real threat to the sub-region. Conflict and instability also characterize the region, with climate and environmental pressures often increasing religious and ethnic conflicts in the Sahel, placing additional pressures on cities to absorb conflict refugees and internally displaced persons. Within cities conflicts over belonging, indigenous claims to land ownership, trading rights, as well as religious differences, manifest in contestations that can at times turn violent, and where foreign refugees and economic migrants are targeted. This is a scenario that requires a versatile urban management system to contain such pressures, and be able to arbitrate the conflicts amicably for the public good.

The transport sector is drawing growing attention from the African public authorities, economic analysts and international donors, as an essential vector of growth, poverty reduction and sustainable human development (UNHABITAT, 2014). Public transport operators and private operators are confronted with numerous problems, one of the most crucial being the insufficient and inadequate transport infrastructures. In such a context, to transport operators, the result is a struggle for survival due mainly to the costs to be borne in order to continue the transport activity. The infrastructure decay has led to an increase in accidents aside human error, delays in transport due to congestion and also increased pollution. The African transportation system has come under scrutiny to improve efficiency, environmental friendliness and safety. Public transport is receiving increasing attention in most African cities which suffer from congestion and pollution caused by massive numbers of private motor vehicles, as for example in Lagos, , Johannesburg, and Accra. These cities have successfully embraced a public transportation system. Cost effective and energy efficient mass public transport systems are essential to achieve the internal social synergies, vital to the health of the urban organism.

8. Policy Options and Recommendations

African urban centres have undergone substantial growth and change over the past five or so decades. Most of these urban systems have been neglected, resulting almost everywhere in conditions which are unacceptable by any criteria. This neglect has not only taken the form of meagre resources for essential actions and indifference to the absence of institutions capable of acting, but it has also cultivated a general vagueness about the specific nature of the responsibilities involved and who will bear them. In this section we suggest models and innovations that can be instrumental in transforming African urban centres for the better. One such mode is the Place Stewardship Model.

The Place Stewardship Model has the prospects of changing the fortunes of Africa for effective urban management that speaks to sustainable urban areas. Place-based stewardship and collaborative planning approaches provide the only realistic hope for meeting the complex economic, social, and environmental challenges facing urban areas today (Svendsen & Campbell, 2008). It includes the management of the relationships of the various key actor-organisations, seeing them as resources to be marshalled in the best way for best results, like money or skills. Urban areas are the locale for complex networks of activities essential to basic human functions of living and working. This empowers the place stewards to find practical ways of solving problems by transcending traditional jurisdictions, sectors, and issues, and creating a new framework for collaborative action. It includes collaboration and governance. Collaboration entails cooperation by stakeholders to achieve common goals by working across boundaries through multi-sector and multi-jurisdictional alliances. Governance, on the other hand, entails steering processes to shape private, public, and non-profit sector decisions and actions towards a common end. Donahue (2004) argues that collaborative governance comes in as a new level of social and political engagement between different sectors of society. This constitutes a more effective way to addressing a multiplicity of modern societies.

This model offers many solutions to work in the context of the various challenges African cities are facing, as they benefit from horizontal networks (Svendsen & Campbell 2008) that may facilitate the development and spread of innovative solutions to complex urban management challenges (Bodin & Crona 2009). Given that the problems are arising mainly as a result of rapid urbanisation with deteriorating economic activity constraining public finances to provide and maintain the public spaces, social innovation is required. Civic ecology practices are self-organised, hands-on stewardship efforts that may result in positive outcomes for individuals, communities, and urban ecosystems; they include a variety of activities, such as community gardening, street tree care, volunteer public park maintenance, and watershed restoration, which reduce strain on the urban local authorities on the provision of such. This can be so through the hybrid concept of adaptive co-management which has been used to describe partnerships between communities and government that take an incremental approach to managing natural resources based on insights from continuous environmental monitoring (Armitage *et al.* 2008).

9. Conclusion

Urban areas in Africa are faced with wicked challenges that pose considerable issues for city managements to deal with. . The thematic aspects of the study include availability, control, utilisation and access to land for urban development, housing, markets, infrastructure financing, and transport management and, at least, from the supply-side of the urban economics. On the other hand, a number of forces including environmental challenges (like increasing pollution and the effects of climate change which induce challenges like flooding) as well as human-induced challenges like patronage and clientilism, global financial crises and diminishing development, aid and increased vandalism of urban assets coupled with increasing mass protestations. These forces exert a lot of pressure on the urban manager. The urban manager is there to facilitate and co-ordinate efforts and to resolve conflict of interest among various urban players. Efficiency, efficacy and equity in the distribution of resources and public investments generated from within the city and reverted to its further development, are the basis of urban management. Urban managers are also responsible for the necessary policy reforms to improve the level of service delivery and to increase the competitiveness of their economies. The urban planning efforts in African cities face have key challenges in common which include urban sprawl; substantial housing backlogs; poverty and inequality; segregation; slum and informal settlement proliferation within city centres and on the urban peripheries; as well as inadequate infrastructure and service provision. These have consequences on current urban governance regimes in the African region which revolve around ensuring democratic participation, alleviating poverty and inequality, improving urban service provision, coping with local unrest, achieving cohesion between formal and informal systems of trade and improving the fiscal autonomy of local governments. This therefore implores the need to move towards a Collaborative and Sustainable Framework in managing the African urban areas. The placebased stewardship and collaborative model becomes the way forward for African states and the only realistic hope for meeting the complex economic, social, and environmental challenges facing urban areas today in the region. This empowers the place stewards to find practical ways of solving problems by transcending traditional jurisdictions, sectors, and issues, and creating a new framework for collaborative action.

References

Acioly, C (2000). Note on governance and urban management in Brazil, in A. Hartkoorn (ed.), Cities made by people, Volume II, Tirana, Albania: Copland. (pp. 59-72).

Armitage, D., M. Marschke, and R. Plummer. 2008. Adaptive co-management and the paradox of learning. *Global Environmental Change Vol 8 number 1*:pp.86-98.

Barry, R. Weingast, B. R & Wittman D (2008) *Oxford hand book of political economy.* Oxford, New York: Oxford University Press

Bhowmik, S. K (2005). Street vendors in Asia: A review. *Economic and Political Weekly. 01/2005; 40(22)*:2256-2264

Brinkerhoff, D. W & Goldsmith, A. A (2002) *Clientelism, patrimonialism and democratic governance: An overview and framework for assessment and programming.* Prepared for U.S. Agency for International Development Office of Democracy and Governance. Cambridge: Abt Associates Inc.

Brown, A (2006). *Contested space: Street trading, public space, and livelihoods in developing cities.* London, UK: ITDG Publishing.

Castells, M. & Portes, A. (1989). World underneath: The origins, dynamics, and effects of the informal economy. In A. Portes, M. Castells & Lauren A. Benton, eds. *The informal economy: Studies in advanced and less advanced developed countries.* Baltimore, MD, USA: John Hopkins University Press

Chirisa, I., Kawadza, S T & Muzenda, A (2014). Unexplored elasticity of planning and good governance in Harare,

Zimbabwe. *International review for spatial planning and sustainable development*, vol.2 no.4: pp.19-29.

Davey, J. K (1993). *Elements of urban management: Urban management programme discussion paper* No.11, UNCHS/World Bank, 1993. Washington DC: World Bank

Henton, D., Melville, J. Parr, J. (2006). Regional stewardship & collaborative governance: Implementation that produces results. Monograph Series March 2006, sponsored by the Morgan Family Foundation

Drakakis-Smith, D. (2000). *Third world city*. London: Routledge

Dube, D. & Chirisa, I. (2012). The informal city: Assessing its scope, variants and direction in Harare, Zimbabwe. *Global Advanced Research Journal of Geography and Regional Planning* 1(1): 016-025

Etzold, B. (2009). Street food vending and structural violence in Dhaka. Paper presented at the 7th Open Meeting of IHDP, Bonn. April 27-30, 2009.

Fairclough, N (2003). *Analysing discourse; Textual analysis for social research*. Oxon: Routledge

Figueroa, M. & Sives, A. (2002) Homogenous voting, electoral manipulation and the 'garrison' process in post-independence Jamaica. *Journal of Commonwealth and Comparative Politics*, 40 (1): pp.81-108.

Giles C. (2013). Urban management in developing countries. *Cities*, Volume 8, Issue 2: pp. 93-107.

Goldsmith, A. A. (1999a). Africa's overgrown state revisited: Bureaucracy and economic growth. *World Politics* 51(4): pp.520-46.

Gutman, J., Sy, A & Chattopadhyay, S. (2015). *Financing African infrastructure: Can the world deliver?* Washington DC: Brookings Institute Global Economy and Development

Hartig, P (2008). *Financing urban infrastructure: Innovative financial instruments for cities.* Frankfurt am Main (Germany): KfW Bankengruppe.

Kettering, S (1988). The historical development of political clientelism. *Journal of Interdisciplinary History* 18(3): pp. 419-447.

ILO (2003). *Scope of the employment relationship: Report IV*, International Labour Conference, 91st Session. Geneva: ILO.

International Labour Organisation (2003). *Street traders and their organisations in South Africa.* Switzerland: ILO Publications

Levine. M (2015). *Urban politics: Cities and suburbs in a global age.* New York USA: Routledge.

Mitlin D (2006). The role of collective action and urban social movements in reducing chronic urban poverty. *Institute of Development Policy and Management,* Manchester, UK

McCourt, W (2000). *Public appointments: From patronage to merit.* Institute for Development Policy and Management, Human Resources in Development Working Paper No. 9. Manchester, UK: University of Manchester

Mendel, G (2006). Climate change, urban flooding and the rights of the urban poor in Africa: Key findings from six African cities. *A report by Action Aid October 2006.Lagos: Action Aid International*

Migdal, J. S. (1988*). Strong societies and weak states: State-society relations and state capabilities in the third world.* Princeton, NJ: Princeton University Press.

Newman, P & Thornley, A (2000). Globalisation, world cities and urban planning: Developing a conceptual framework. *Paper delivered at the Planning 2000 Conference* held at the LSE March 27- 29, 2000.

Ridley, D (2008). *The literature review: A step-by-step guide for students.* London: SAGE Publications.

Saungweme, T., Matsvai, S., & Sakuhuni, R., (2014). Economic analysis of unemployment, output and growth of the informal sector in Zimbabwe (1985-2013). ?????

Shanghai Manual (2010) – *A guide for sustainable urban development in the 21st century.* Shanghai: United Nations

Sirry, A (2003). The meaning and scope of urban management: An introductory note. *Urban management practices in secondary cities in Egypt: The case of Belbeis'*, Cairo, Egypt: Elias Modern Publishing House.

Suresh, B. S. (2003). Globalisation and urban environmental issues and challenges. In Martin J.Bunch, V. Madha Suresh & T. Vasantha Kumaran, eds., *Proceedings of the third international conference on environment and health,* Chennai, India, 15-17 December,2003. Chennai: Department of Geography, University of Madras and Faculty of Environmental Studies, York University: pp.557 -561.

Svendsen E. S & Campbell L. K. (2008).Urban ecological stewardship: Understanding the structure, function and network of community-based urban land management. *Cities and the Environment* Vol 1 number 1: pp.1-31.

UNHABITAT (2010*). State of African nations 2010: Governance, inequality and urban land markets.* Nairobi, Kenya: UNHABITAT

UNHABITAT (2012). *Annual Report 2012.* Nairobi, Kenya: UNHABITAT

UNHABITAT (2014). *State of African Nations 2010: Re-imagining sustainable urban transitions.* Nairobi, Kenya: UNHABITAT

Van Dijk, M P (2008). *Urban management and institutional change: An integrated approach to achieving ecological cities.* IHS Working Paper 16: Contribution to an International seminar

Sustainable urbanisation in Libya Tripoli, Hotel Bab Africa, 30 June and July 1, 2007

Wellman, K. & Spiller, M (2012).*Urban infrastructure: Finance and management.* Chicago: John Willey & Sons

Yigitcanlar, T (2010). *Rethinking sustainable development: Urban management, engineering and design.* New York: Idea Group Inc.

CHAPTER THIRTEEN

Challenges Confronting the Efficiency and Effectiveness of the Decentralizaion System in Ghana: The leadership Perspective

Kwasi Dartey-Baah

1. Introduction

Over the course of the past three decades, the world has witnessed a heightened advocacy by both citizens and international organizations (International Monetary Fund (IMF) and the World Bank) for developing countries in particular, to fully embrace a democratic governance system. This fact can be seen in the words of Tulchin and Selee (2004) as they stated that, 'in the past decades, in every part of the world, there has been an unprecedented swing to democratic forms of government'. Indeed, in recent times, citizens of countries such as Egypt and Libya have joined the push for a democratic system of governance in their countries. This current phenomenon could be said to have emerged as a result of the realization by citizens and governments of these countries of the benefits associated with the democratic form of governance, such as the upholding of the principle of rule of law, community participation in the decision making process, freedom of speech, the respect for human rights, accountability and transparency in governance, respect for minority rights, amongst other benefits. Some have also argued that this transformation has come about as a result of the influence of the Western world, whether through direct or indirect means, causing citizens of these countries to revolt against their existing forms of governance. Nevertheless, in both instances, it is realized that the key component is the push for popular or people's participation in governance and in decision making processes.

In view of this desire to increase people's participation in the governance process, some developing countries have adopted the concept of decentralization to achieve this end. According to the UNDP (1999), most developing countries have adopted one form of decentralization or another for this same reason of ensuring popular participation in the governance process. In Crawford's (2004) view, the concept of decentralization has become one of the most opted reforms to the various political and administrative systems in developing countries.

Ghana is currently one of the numerous developing countries worldwide that has adopted this form of governance, due to its strategic importance to development. Ghana, just like most developing countries, adopted this form of governance due to external influences from International organizations such as the International Monetary Fund (IMF) and the World Bank.

The decentralization system in Ghana was adopted in 1988 as part of an administrative reform programme. During this period, the country was divided into districts under the Local Government Law (PNDC Law 207) to serve both political and administrative purposes. However, it is very important to point out that the country at some point in history has experienced one form of decentralization or another. However, the most significant strategy or approach to strengthening this system was the formulation of the Local Government Law (PNDC Law 207) in 1988, under the PNDC regime of Rawlings. This piece of legislation engendered the creation of 110 districts across the length and breadth of the country, with the first non-partisan District Assembly elections held in 1988/1989 (Crawford, 2004).

In furtherance of these, the 1992 constitution of Ghana in Chapter Twenty (20) and the Local Government Act 1993 (Act 462) have brought about an increased appreciation of the concept of decentralization. The country currently has a national or centralized government body, a regional government body (made up of the ten Regional Coordinating Councils – RCC's) and 216 Metropolitan, Municipal and District Assemblies (MMDAs) that have a four-tier and three-tier system of decentralized structure respectively. These MMDAs have been vested with the political (executive and legislative) and administrative authority to manage the local areas, thus creating socio-economic development through the formulation and execution of plans or programmes for the efficient and effective mobilization of local resources. Considering all these efforts by various government regimes to bring governance to the doorstep of Ghanaians, that is, by ensuring popular participation in the governance process, it is no mistake that the country is applauded by international organizations and many developed countries for its tenacity in upholding the various tenets of democracy.

However, the decentralization system in Ghana is confronted with many challenges inhibiting it from being effective and efficient in the performance of its constitutional mandate, or attaining the numerous benefits that the government and advocates of the concept have envisaged. In examining these challenges, various authors on the subject have considered it from three main dimensions or perspectives: political, administrative and fiscal. In view of this, this paper seeks to add to the existing knowledge in this research area by conceptualizing the lack of effective leadership as a challenge that impedes the decentralization system in Ghana, from effectively and efficiently stimulating socio-economic development within the local areas of the country.

Some authors like Crawford (2004) and von Braun and Grote (2000) have raised the issue of certain leadership challenges that surround this discourse, but did not make this the focal point of their discussion. According to Porter (1990), for a nation or an organization to gain a competitive advantage (hence, make it effective and efficient) over others, the contributions made by governments (leadership) in pushing forward or supporting factors of competitiveness such as factor conditions, demand conditions, related and supporting industries, as well as firm strategy, structure and rivalry are very important. Thus, the influence government (leadership) has over the level of development cannot be overlooked. In this respect, this paper is of the view that, in investigating the various challenges confronting the efficiency and effectiveness of the decentralization system in Ghana, the critical role of leadership must be placed in the critical context of local governments.

2. The Concept of Decentralization

The concept of decentralization has been defined in many ways by many scholars, political scientists and even international agencies such as the United Nations Development Programme (UNDP) and the World Bank. Thus, there is no generic definition of what the concept is.

Miller (2002) defines decentralization as, 'the transfer of national responsibilities or functions from central government to sub-national levels of government, or from central agencies/offices to regional bodies or branch offices, or to non-governmental organizations or private concerns'. Also according to the UNDP (1999), decentralizing governance refers 'to the restructuring or reorganization of authority so that there is a system of co-responsibility between institutions of governance at the central, regional and local levels, according to the principle of subsidiarity; thus increasing the overall quality and effectiveness of the system of governance, authority and capacities of sub-national levels'. In the view of von Braun and Grote (2000), 'decentralization is the transfer of authority and responsibility for public functions from a central government to subordinate governments'.

Although the concept has been defined in many ways by different authors, a critical examination of the various definitions bring to the fore the intention to transfer authority from central governments and their administrative machineries to local government authorities and local administrative machineries, respectively; hence making governance (for that matter, the provision of public goods and services) a grass root or a local level activity or affair.

3. Decentralization : The Misconceptions

There is the widespread understanding that the decentralization system is a concept opposed to the centralized system of governance; hence, the perception that the former is a substitute or an alternative to the latter (UNDP, 1999). According to the UNDP (1999), such a belief is false, considering the fact that both concepts (decentralization and centralization) rather complement each other, to ensure that resources are utilized efficiently and effectively at both the national and the local levels. Indeed, authors such as Tanzi (1995) and Prud'homme (1995) have criticized the concept of decentralization for its potential or tendency of engendering corruption at the local levels, creating a disintegrated state due to unhealthy competition and also leading to unequal socio-economic development within states. In view of this, there is therefore the need to ensure that there is a central government body that will seek to promote the welfare of society as a whole, and that will also serve as a check on the power wielded by local government units.

Secondly, the concept of decentralization has been perceived to be the preserve of the public sector alone, hence, out of bounds for the private sector. According to the UNDP (1999), decentralization is rather a reform programme that seeks to bring together various stakeholders (both private and public) in order to pool resources for the engendering of socio-economic development. In view of this, many authors and international agencies such as the UNDP have considered privatization as another form of decentralization.

4. The Decentralization System in Ghana

The decentralization system in Ghana has gone through several reforms targeted at ensuring that the governance process is brought to the doorstep of the ordinary Ghanaian. The motive has also been to ensure that the government function is improved to be more responsive to the needs of the local population. The decentralization system of Ghana can be viewed from three time periods, namely: the colonial period, the post-colonial period (before the advent of the 1992 constitution), and the fourth republican period (advent of the 1992 constitution).

The British authority during the colonial period introduced a system referred to as indirect rule – a semblance of the decentralization system (Ayee, 2000). During this period, the traditional political systems (constituting the traditional chiefs and their council of elders) was involved in the British colonial administration as local authorities with the mandate for mobilizing taxes or levies imposed on the population by the British Authority. This system, as observed by Nkrumah (2000) as cited in Crawford,(2004), promoted accountability to the British authority rather than to the local population because it was adopted to serve the interest of the British colonial administration and not the the interest of the people. In summation, the system during this period exhibited features of an administrative and fiscal form of decentralization, with little or no political authority.

However, after the attainment of independence by the country (but before the advent of the 1992 constitution), major political and administrative reforms were introduced by various government regimes to ensure popular participation. The Acheampong's regime in 1974 made efforts to decentralize the government structure; but this according to Nkrumah (2000, as cited in Crawford, 2004), was in a deconcentrated form (administrative decentralization); thus, making it somehow similar to the system under the British colonial period. The most significant contribution made to the Ghanaian decentralization system was under Rawlings' Provisional National Defense Council (PNDC) (Crawford, 2004). Indeed, Goel (2010) remarked that this period under the PNDC (precisely in 1988) was the starting point for the decentralization system of Ghana. In 1988, a major legislation was passed by the PNDC government known as the Local Government Law (PNDC Law 207). This piece of legislation engendered the creation of 110 districts across the length and breadth of the country, with non-partisan District Assembly elections held in 1988/1989 and subsequently every four years, as purported by Crawford (2004).

Currently, the 1992 constitution of Ghana in article 35 and in Chapter Twenty (20) makes provision for the establishment of the whole decentralization system of Ghana. In article 35(6) of the 1992 constitution, it is captured thus,

> ...the state shall take appropriate measures to – (d) make democracy a reality by decentralizing the administrative and financial machinery of government to the regions and districts, and by affording all possible opportunities to the people to participate in decision-making at every level in national life and in government...(Republic of Ghana, 1993).

This provision, according to the 1992 constitution, is to serve as a mechanism for the achievement of the political objectives stated in article 35. Again, Chapter Twenty (20) of the 1992 constitution captures the entire structure of the decentralization system of Ghana. Furthermore, other statutes such as the Local Government Act 1993 (Act 462), and the District Assembly Common Fund Act 1993 (Act 455), have also been introduced to strengthen the entire decentralization system of Ghana. As a result of these legislations, the country currently has a four-tier metropolitan assembly, a three-tier municipal assembly, and a three-tier district assembly. Figure 13.1 below shows the structure of the decentralization system of Ghana.

Fig13.1. Structure of the Local Government system in Ghana

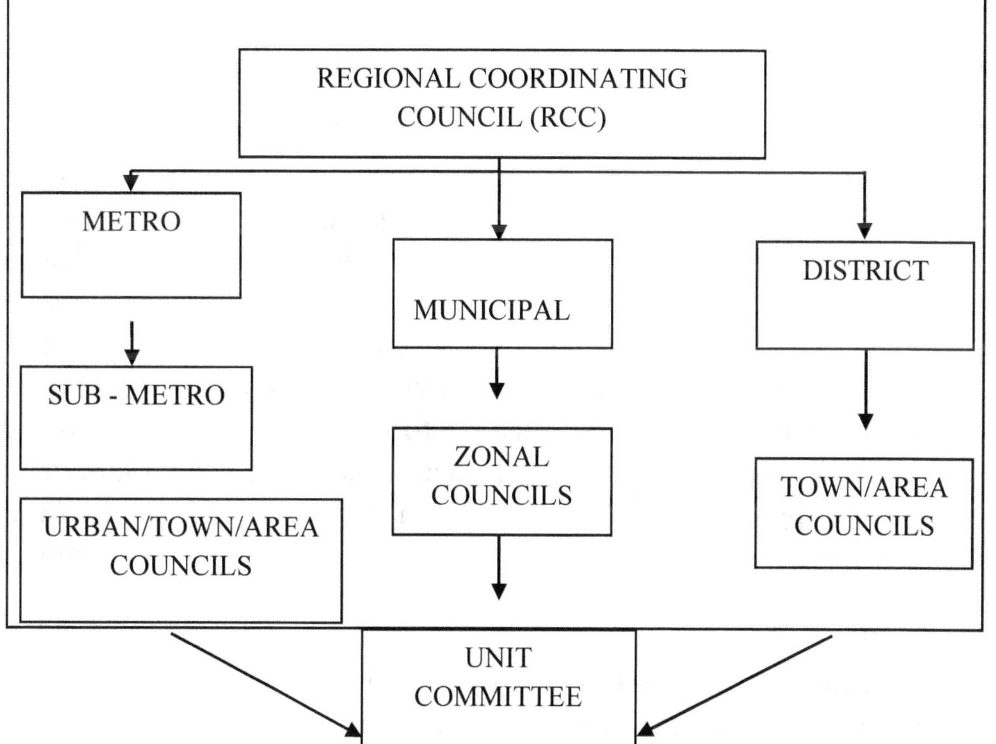

Source: Local Government Act, 1993 (Act 462).

5. Concept of Leadership

The concept of leadership has journeyed through several interpretations over the century. It is therefore futile to propound a universal definition for the concept. Over the years, several schools of thought have tried this and have had their definitions flawed, due to the dynamic or complex nature of societal values and aspirations. In view of this, this section of the paper reviews the various theories propounded by scholars as a means of providing a general idea of what the concept is.

Classical theories on the concept such as the 'Great Man' theories and the 'Trait' theories indicate certain innate qualities or personal traits suitable for leadership roles which all individuals who have successfully reached such heights possess (Bolden, Gosling, Marturano & Dennison, 2003). These theories put emphasis on individual qualities and traits, which in the view of some scholars are deficient, when one considers that those same qualities as posed can be identified in individuals who are not leaders. In view of this, another school of thought has advocated that the focus be shifted from those innate qualities possessed by leaders to a set of behaviours or actions portrayed by them (Bolden, Gosling, Marturano & Dennison, 2003). These views are classified as the Behaviourist theories.

The Behaviourist theories focus on the pattern of behaviours exhibited by leaders and these behavioural patterns are categorised as leadership styles. According to Mullins (1999), the major weakness of style and behavioural theories is that they ignore the important role which situational factors play in determining the effectiveness of individual leaders. It is this limitation that gave rise to the Situational and Contingency theories of leadership (Fiedler, 1967; House, 1971; Vroom & Yetton, 1974) which shifted the emphasis away from 'the one best way to lead' to context-sensitive leadership (Ogbonna & Harris, 2000). Thus, according to these theorists for leadership to be effective one must consider the context within which it is exercised; hence, leadership should conform to the environment within which it finds itself.

However, contemporary theories on the subject such as the Transactional and Transformational (Burns, 1978; Bass, 1985; Judge & Piccolo, 2004) have indicated a network of relationships or exchanges needed to make leadership effective. These theories therefore imply that the relationship between leaders and their followers, and between individual goals and organizational goals are very relevant for leadership to succeed. These more recent theories demand critical consideration.

6. Concept of Efficiency and Effectiveness

According to Moran and Ghoshal (1999), as cited in Mouzas, (2006), historical firm-level theories have focussed the attention on corporate managers more in terms of strategies, and on the concept of efficiency as indicators of a firm's performance on the market; and have placed less importance on the concept of effectiveness. Thus, firms are more interested in minimizing their operational cost, or maximizing their revenues or sales in order to bolster bottom-line growth, rather than managing the existing relationship between themselves and their environment, especially the external environment, in order to be able to create more avenues for growth, expansion and survival. However, the sole reliance on efficiency in the measurement of how competitive a firm is within the market is incomplete, as both (efficiency and effectiveness) concepts, according to Mouzas (2006), are pivotal in assessing and measuring the performance of organizations. According to Mouzas (2006), efficiency is not an indicator of an organization's successfulness in the market, but rather a measure of its operational excellence or productivity. In his view, a firm's successfulness in the market is a measure of its effectiveness. That is, effectiveness is a firm's ability to generate new opportunities or capitalize upon existing opportunities within its environment or surroundings, in order to increase its market share. Thus, efficiency solely measures how profitable a firm's action or production has been; whereas effectiveness reveals the opportunity cost of any business action or decision taken by a firm in order to enable it assess which activity would yield the greatest profit. This therefore means that both concepts are crucial in the assessment of an organization's overall performance.

Fig 13.2. Effect of different levels of Efficiency and Effectiveness

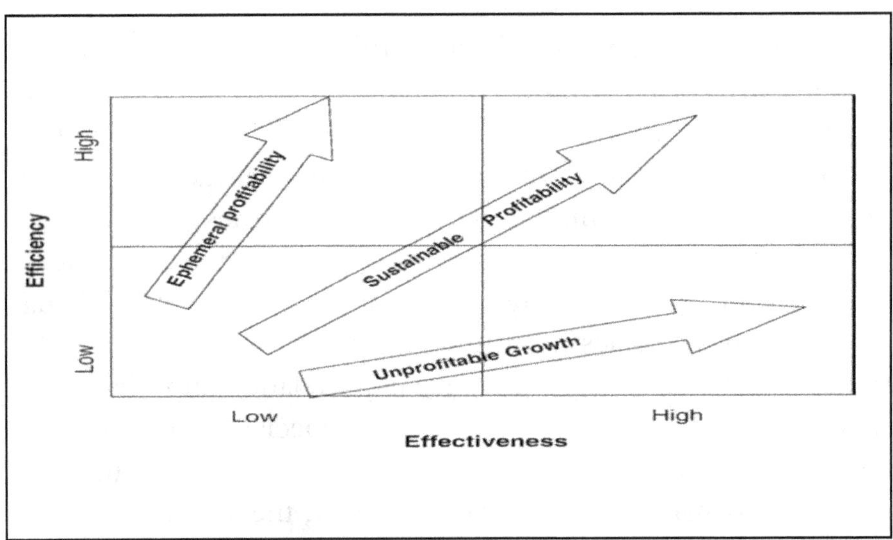

Source: Mouzas (2006)

With reference to figure 13.2 above, Mouzas (2006) explains that by focussing an organization's efforts on efficiency and neglecting effectiveness would only lead to it becoming profitable in the short-term; hence, making it unprofitable or less profitable in the medium to long-term. Inversely, according to him, the focussing of an organization's efforts on effectiveness and neglecting efficiency would result in an unprofitable growth, if the opportunity cost of capital is higher than the resulting profits. In view of these, there is therefore the need to focus organizational activities or strategies on issues regarding efficiency and effectiveness simultaneously, in order to enable a firm maximize its profits in both the short-term and the long-term.

7. Leadership in the Decentralization system of Ghana

The 1992 Constitution of Ghana establishes the country as a democratic state with its own government structure. The government structure of Ghana is made up of three arms, namely the Legislature, Executive and the Judiciary. These organs are charged with the overall running of the state; which is the formulation of laws or policies, the execution or implementation of policies or laws, and the interpretation of laws, respectively. In an examination of the 1992 Constitution of Ghana, the governance structure of Ghana can be said to exist at three levels, namely the national, the regional and the district levels. The country also has a public administration structure which is set up as the machinery for the implementation of government policies and programmes. Furthermore, this administrative machinery is vested with the task of providing goods and services to the Ghanaian public. In Chapter Fourteen (14) of the 1992 Constitution of Ghana, the public administration structure of Ghana can be said to comprise of the Civil Service (Ministries, Departments and Agencies), Public Corporations, Boards / Commissions and Authorities (State-Owned Enterprises, and Educational institutions and Hospitals). The Civil Service Ministries, Departments and Agencies which finds itself directly under the executive arm of government plays a supervisory role over the other areas within the public administration structure. These administrative bodies exist at the national as well as the regional and district levels to ensure the efficient and effective delivery of public services. In view of this, leadership in the public sector of Ghana can be said to include Political leadership and Administrative leadership.

However, the 1992 constitution of Ghana also recognizes the existence of another form of leadership. This form of leadership emanates from the traditional political system – the chieftaincy system. This provision is explicitly captured in Chapter Twenty-two of the 1992 Constitution of Ghana. In recognition of the traditional political system, the constitution mandates the formation of a national house of chiefs and a regional house of chiefs. The constitution in Chapter Twenty (20) also involves the traditional authorities in the appointment of not more than thirty percent of the membership of District Assemblies in Ghana, and also involves some of them as members of the ten regional coordinating councils (RCC).

8. Decentralized Leadership: Effectiveness and Efficiency Nexus

The decentralization concept brings about the transferring or shifting of public service delivery functions from the central government to the local levels to ensure efficiency and effectiveness. Through decentralization, central governments or bodies are able to positively impact the lives of people, since individuals at the local levels are involved in the planning, execution and monitoring of developmental plans or policies. Thus, decentralization brings about economic efficiency in the allocation and distribution of scarce resources, which in turn leads to the central government responding effectively to the needs of the local people (Coulson, 1995).

Thus, a well decentralized system should bring about efficiency and effectiveness in the governmental system, which should lead to development at all levels in the nation. However, the issue of leadership cannot be overlooked, if decentralization is to be well implemented. This is because, the key attribute under decentralization is the movement of power and authority from a higher level (central government) to lower levels (regional, sub-regional bodies, among others). This assertion is reaffirmed by the UNDP's (1999) definition of decentralization as

> …the restructuring or reorganization of authority, so that there is a system of co-responsibility between institutions of governance at the central, regional and local levels, according to the principle of subsidiarity; thus decreasing the overall quality and effectiveness of the system of governance, while increasing the authority and capacities of sub-national levels.

Authority, however, lies in the bosom of leadership. By inference, decentralization is a restructuring of the context of leadership powers, authorities, functions and responsibilities. Therefore, if a nation falls short in terms of good leadership, its decentralization system will be adversely affected. In other words, if there is a leadership challenge in a country, the decentralization system cannot yield the desired efficiency which is a measure of operational excellence or productivity, and effectiveness, which is a measure of an organisation's successfulness in the market or in the environment (Mouzas, 2006) as well as in the governmental system to help that country attain development. Going further, many scholars are of the opinion that effective leadership is seen to have eluded many African countries since the beginning of the post-colonial period, including Ghana. To a large extent, the low level of development in the country can be attributed to this inadequacy in leadership. Thus, the leadership canker in Ghana has in part resulted in the inability of a decentralization system in the country to yield expected efficiency and effectiveness, and subsequent national development. The paper thus proposes a conceptualization of the relationships between and among the concepts of decentralization, leadership, efficiency and effectiveness as well as development. This is depicted in Figure 13.3.

Figure 13.3: Conceptual Framework: Leadership, Efficiency and Effectiveness, and Decentralization (LEED) model

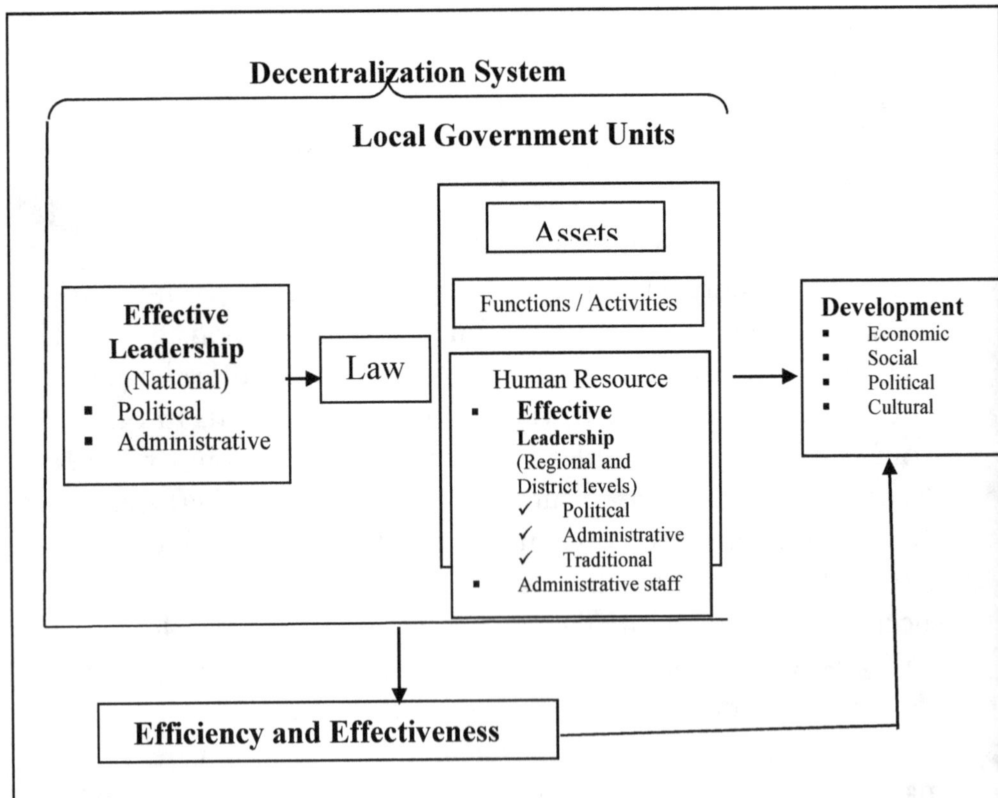

Source: Author (2015)

As seen in Figure 13.3, the decentralization system comprises both the national leadership (political and administrative) as well as the local government units, that is, the assets, functions and leadership at the regional and sub-regional levels. It is also seen that the laws of the country transfer authority and power of leadership, as well as functions, responsibilities and assets, from the national level to the local government levels. Furthermore, efficiency and effectiveness is seen as an outcome variable of the whole decentralization system that results in national development, with regard to four dimensions namely; economic, political, social and cultural. Most importantly, what this conceptual framework depicts is that, for the whole decentralization system to achieve the intended purposes of efficiency, effectiveness and development, leadership, at all levels in the country, must be good and effective. In other words, when leadership at the national, regional and sub-regional levels in the decentralization process are good, effective and purpose-driven, the consequences are efficiency and effectiveness of the system and economic, political and sociocultural development of the nation. Unfortunately, this leadership perspective of the decentralization system remains a formidable challenge for the country, just as the political, administrative and fiscal challenges.

9. Discussion

The overall trend of development in the country could be perceived to be very resilient and strong, in comparison to that of other African countries. However, more could be done through the decentralization system of Ghana to resolve some of the developmental challenges raised in the World Bank report in September 2007, on the development of the country.

As was stated earlier on, development in the country is not a function delegated solely to the central government by the constitution, but rather as a coordinated effort between the central, regional and local government authorities. Through the decentralization system, local support for governmental activities at the rural areas could be mobilized or rallied to ensure efficient and effective implementation. However, the decentralization system of Ghana faces a lot of challenges, rendering it inefficient and ineffective in addressing local level developmental issues, and this in turn has impacted negatively on national development. In a review of Kwamena Ahwoi's book entitled *'Local Government and Decentralization in Ghana'*, Sharma (2010) raises issues such as vague local government laws, insufficient preparatory groundwork for reforms, large – scale transfer of functions, lack of trained and experienced personnel, inadequate financial resources, apathy, bureaucratic obscurantism, corruption and other financial malpractices, as some of the challenges facing the system.

However, these political, administrative and fiscal issues can be addressed when leadership challenges are corrected or resolved. This is due to the fact that all the issues mentioned above revolve around poor leadership and the refusal by the leadership in the decentralization system of Ghana, to effectively and efficiently undertake the functions of decentralization.

One major challenge is national leaders' mistrust of leadership. The 1992 constitution of Ghana seems to imply a partially devolved form of governance. This is due to the fact that, when one considers the membership of the district assemblies in Ghana as captured in article 242 of the constitution, one realizes that about 30 percent of the members are appointed by the President, in consultation with traditional authorities and other interests groups in the district. Also, Metropolitan/ Municipal and District Chief Executives who are the heads of these district assemblies are also appointed by the president; thus obstructing the rights of the local people from electing their leaders under a democratic dispensation. In view of this, the following questions emerge: Do these unelected members represent the local people or the central government? Are they accountable to the local people or to the central government? Do these MCEs and DCEs really carry out the desires and wishes of the local communities, or are they mere puppets of government? Despite all these representation at the local level of the central government, the political leadership at the central level is still reluctant to completely cede its authority to the political leadership (Metropolitan, Municipal and District Chief Executives) at the local levels, to actively promote development within their localities. This fact can be verified by considering the various legislations by the central government, to limit the authority of local government authorities, especially, in financial terms.

Another issue for consideration is the meagre percentage (7.5%) of the total national income allocated to the over 216 MMDAs in the country for purposes of undertaking development at the local levels over a period of one year. Aside these financial matters, there is also the issue of local development plans having to conform with national development plans, even if the national ones do not tackle the peculiar situations or needs confronting a local area. These issues spark notions of mistrust, between the central government and local government authorities, in the mobilization, handling and allocation of resources, especially financial resources, and this suggest a lack of confidence in the capabilities of the leadership at the local level to drive development.

Furthermore, the decentralization system in Ghana faces excessive bureaucratization, and this has, to a large extent, hindered the taking of initiatives at the local level. District assemblies in Ghana, through their political and administrative leaderships, are vested with executive and legislative authorities under the constitution and the local government act, but are still dictated to by leadership at the national level. This has led to district assemblies being unable to efficiently and effectively manage communities under their authority; hence, relying heavily on the central government for direction.

The leadership style adopted by leaders, especially at the national level, in the decentralization system of Ghana is more of the autocratic type, and highly bureaucratic, where leadership at the local levels are to strictly adhere to directives from the central government and are not really involved in the decision-making process at the national level. This type of a top-to-down approach to management does not imbibe a sense of belonging into subordinates, for them to organize goals and objectives, and subordinates are therefore inculcated with little or no motivation to look beyond their parochial interests, and to strive to attain organizationally set goals and objectives. In other words, the decentralization system of Ghana exhibits a master-to-servant form of relationship, where district assemblies and field agencies (servants) of national administrative bodies are to comply strictly to instructions provided to them by the central government and its administrative units (masters). This anachronistic approach to management has hindered the performance of these decentralized bodies, and has also negatively affected employee commitment to the decentralization system.

In addition to the above challenges, leadership's over-reliance on economic indicators of development also hinders the decentralization process. Leadership in the government structure of Ghana has relied so much on economic indicators of development, and has paid less attention to the socio-cultural and political factors. Over the years, issues such as the management of inflation rates, fiscal deficits, per capita income, amongst others, have been the main measurement of performance by central governments, rather than keenly looking at socio-cultural and political issues such as easy accessibility to clean drinking water, food, housing, education, healthcare, and enhancing popular participation (especially the poor) in the governance process at all levels of governance. It is the case, however, that district assemblies are not so keen on these economic indicators in comparison with the central government, but are however indirectly involved through the central government's manipulation of their activities as if rural dwellers do not understand or appreciate these measurements of performance. In view of this, government activities at both the national and local levels have been targeted at ensuring that these economic indicators are improved, in order to serve as the basis for re-elections.

Finally, another set-back in the decentralization system in Ghana is the lack of confidence, or the issue of mistrust, that exists between the rural population and the leadership of regional and local government units. This is as a result of financial misappropriation and embezzlement at the district assemblies. Also, there is usually a sudden status and wealth gap between leaders at the local government level and local residents, though these leaders usually emanate from amongst the local populace, leading to speculations of corrupt practices in the local assemblies. These issues have consequently made it difficult for leadership at these levels to rally support for local government activities from the rural population, through the payment of levies and the volunteering of financial and human support by the people for the undertaking of developmental activities. This situation has given rise to people looking up to the central government for development rather than to the local governments.

10. Implications for Policy

As mentioned earlier, district assemblies in Ghana are confronted with numerous challenges, some of which are caused, by the central government, through the formulation of stringent laws which inhibit the performance of district assemblies in Ghana. It is therefore relevant for the political and administrative leadership at the central level to really appreciate the importance of the concept of decentralization on development, by ensuring that proper laws are put in place to regulate the decentralization process in Ghana. The minimum transfer of 7.5 percent of the total national income to district assemblies, for the purposes of undertaking development, must be reviewed and increased by the central government. This is because in comparing the myriad of responsibilities placed on district assemblies by the constitution, and comparing those with the level of financial support made available to them through the District Assembly Common Fund (DACF), there appears to be a mismatch between the two, resulting in district assemblies being unable to undertake and complete meaningful developmental projects.

In order to maximize the efficiency and effectiveness levels of the decentralization system, there should be a symbiotic relationship between national leadership and the leadership at the regional and local levels. This is because many reforms introduced on paper into the public sector of Ghana have failed as a result of the inability of bureaucrats to understand and appreciate the concept or ideology behind such reforms. Others have also failed as a result of apathy for such programmes by bureaucrats, due to their exclusion in the designing of such programmes. District assemblies in Ghana, through their, leaders should be involved at every stage of national development to create in their minds a sense of ownership of the governance process, as well as the outcomes of such processes. That is, rather than the central government and its administrative units designing and handing over tasks to local governments and their administrative units, they should involve them at all levels of decision making, in order to focus their minds and efforts on the goals and objectives of such tasks. This would go a long way to heighten the participation of the local people in political activities at the local levels; hence, allowing for the will of the local people to prevail in the governance process at the local level.

11. Conclusion

The efficiency and effectiveness of any reform programme, with regards to achieving its set goals and objectives, will, to a large extent, depend on its designers and managers. In view of this, it is very important that the framers of reform programmes really understand and appreciate the impact such initiatives will have on the overall performance of the system. The decentralization system of Ghana was adopted to ensure that popular participation at every stage of the governance process was heightened, and also to afford the local people the opportunity to determine their own future. However, national political leadership (the executive and legislative arms of government) has, through hostile laws and regulations, limited the operations of local governments, and have rather used the system to push forward their own political agendas. Besides, regional and local level political and administrative leaders have also exhibited some level of incompetence with regards to making the system work efficiently and effectively, at the local levels.. To remedy this situation, this paper is of the opinion that leaders at all levels of the decentralization system of Ghana must be involved in restructuring and reorganizing the system to ensure that it functions efficiently and effectively.

In summary, the central government must move away from the political rhetoric of championing the course of decentralization to actually making the required constitutional or legislative amendments needed to make the decentralization functional.

References

Ayee, J. R. A. (2000). Decentralization and good governance in Ghana. *Unpublished paper of May 2000 prepared for the Canadian High Commission,* Accra, Ghana.

Bass, B. M. (1985). *Leadership and performance beyond expectations.* New York, NY: The Free Press.

Bolden, R., Gosling, J., Marturano, A., & Dennison, P. (2003). A review of leadership theory and competency frameworks. *Centre for Leadership Studies – University of Exeter,* 1-44.

Burns, J. M. (1978). *Leadership.* New York: Harper & Row.

Crawford, G. (2004) Democratic decentralization in Ghana: Issues and prospects. *POLIS working paper, 9,* 2-34.

Fiedler, F. E. (1967). *A theory of leadership effectiveness.* New York: McGraw-Hill.

Goel, P. R. (2010). Other country decentralization experiences: *Ghana National Council of Applied Economic Research, 1-7.*

House, R. (1971a). A path-goal theory of leadership. *Journal of Contemporary Business*, 3, 81–97.

House, R. J. (1971b). A path-goal theory of leader effectiveness. *Administrative Science Quarterly*, 16(September), 321–38.

Jugde, A. T., & Piccolo, R. F. (2004). Transformational and transactional leadership: A meta-analytic test of their relative validity. *Journal of Applied Psychology*, 89(5), 755–768.

Miller, K. (2002). *Advantages and disadvantages of local government decentralization.* Caribbean conference on local government & decentralization 25-28 June in Georgetown Guyana. Retrieved from http://www.*citeseerx.ist.psu.edu*

Mouzas, S. (2006). Efficiency and effectiveness in business networks. *Journal of Business Research, 59,* 1124-1132.

Mullins, L. J. (1999). *Management and organizational behaviour.* London: Financial Times.

National Development Planning Commission, (2010). Medium-term national development policy framework: Ghana shared growth and development agenda (2010-2013), Final draft, 1, 1-268. Republic of Ghana

Ogbonna, E., & Harris, L. C. (2000). Leadership style, organisational culture and performance: Evidence from UK companies. *International Journal of Human Resource Management,* 11(4), 766–788.

Porter, M. E. (1990). The competitive advantage of nations. *Harvard Business Review, 73-91.* Retrieved July, 20, 2013, from http://kkozak.wz.cz/Porter.pdf

Prud'homme, R. (1995). The dangers of decentralization. *The World Bank Research Observer, 10(2), 201-220.*

Republic of Ghana (1993). *The 1992 Constitution of the Republic of Ghana.* Ghana Publishing Company Limited, Assembly Press – Accra.

Republic of Ghana (1993). *Local Government Act 1993 (Act 462).* Republic of Ghana

Seers, D. (1969). The meaning of development. *Institute of Development Studies-Communication series no. 44,* 1-26.

Sharma, K.C. (2010). Book review: Local government and decentralization in Ghana. *Commonwealth Journal of Local Governance, (7), 240-245.* Retrieved July, 24, 2013, from http://epress.lib.uts.edu.au/ojs/index.php/cjlg

Tulchin, J. & Selee, A. (2004). Decentralization and democratic governance in Latin America. *Woodrow Wilson Center Report on the Americas, 12,* 1-268.

Tanzi, V. (1995). Fiscal federalism and decentralization: A review of some efficiency and macroeconomic aspects. *Paper prepared for the Annual World Bank Conference on Development Economics,* Washington DC: World Bank.

UNDP (1999). Decentralization: A sampling of definition. *Working paper: Joint UNDP-Government of Germany evaluation of the UNDP role in decentralization and local governance.*

Von Braun, J. & Grote, U. (2000). *Does decentralization serve the poor?* IMF-conference on fiscal decentralization 20-21 November in Washington D.C.

Vroom, V., & Yetton, P. (1974). *Leadership and decision-making.* Pittsburgh, PA: University of Pittsburgh Press.

CHAPTER FOURTEEN

Toll Rates for Highway Construction in Ghana: The Concessionary Projects

Charles Andoh and Daniel Quaye

1. Introduction

Highway construction is a major concern to most governments around the world, as they serve as catalyst to development. Various reasons abound that underpin why highways are necessary in an economy. Proper road networks permit people, goods and services to be transported speedily, facilitating the development of nations. Keane (1996) argues that the employment and industrial base of a locality is linked to its transportation system. Keane (1996) explains that a good highway system allows businesses to receive inputs on production facilities, as well as to transport finished goods to consumers efficiently. Furthermore, a good highway system provides lower transportation costs to businesses, which in turn lowers production costs and improves profits and productivity (Keane, 1996). Holl (2001) adds that highways attract manufacturing firms as opposed to distant communities that lack highways.

The funding of toll roads in many developing nations as a capital expenditure has become a thorny issue. Most of these countries spend a greater part of their budget on recurrent expenditure. The need to develop highways is compounded by other pressing needs such as investment in education, health and food security. This renders the issue of highway construction inconsequential, notwithstanding its importance to the development of these nations (Biau, Dahou and Homma, 2008).

Public-Private Partnership (PPP) has been used in many other sectors in Ghana, but has not been introduced into financing road transport. PPP allows the private sector to either completely finance or join with government in the provision of an essential service to the public. By virtue of inadequate public financing, PPP can be relied upon to provide the funds needed for construction of highways that any country needs.

Efforts by the Government of Ghana, (Ghana Road Fund Secretariat, 2010), have not resulted in achieving a sustained and timely financing for managing the extensive trunk road networks. Four main challenges face the road sector, and these are indeed the direct responsibility of the government of Ghana (Mills, 2010). The challenges are: first, insufficient funds to effectively maintain the wide road network; second, delays in obtaining approval for adjustment of road toll rates and also creation of new toll roads; third, lack of prompt releases of approved budgets; and fourthly, how to disburse funds efficiently and effectively over the network, in view of the high demand. All these factors are major reasons for cost and time overruns often experienced on road projects in Ghana. These challenges explain the inability of the government of Ghana to develop and maintain a greater percentage of the highway network in as good a condition as desired, and also the urgent need for alternative sources of financing.

Andoh, Mills and Quaye (2012) develop a model for determining the optimal profit, optimal number of different vehicle sizes, and the optimal toll rates for a given concessionary period. Their model implicitly assumes that all vehicular types pay an equal amount of the cost of highway construction for every crossing of the toll gate. This would be a reasonable assumption for a new construction, where the history of damage caused by different sized vehicles is unknown. In addition, their model does not discuss the risk exposure of the optimal profit with the different concessionary periods and each vehicular class. An investor would like to know the likelihood that the estimated profit will be realized, before committing a substantial amount of funds, typical of road construction. We introduce a model that incorporates the damage caused, by vehicular class, in the cost of highway construction and its maintenance. We argue that if a vehicular class contributes to a greater deterioration of the highway, correspondingly, it must pay a greater part of its maintenance and construction costs. For a given concessionary period, we decompose operations into the various vehicular usages that expose the riskiest operations for the appropriate toll rate to be charged.

The rest of the study is organized as follows. Section 2 gives a brief review of existing works or materials on PPP arrangements in other countries. In Section 3, we present our model that incorporates the damage caused by a vehicular class in the toll rates. We also derive the conditions under which a PPP arrangement can work for different sized vehicles. Given specified toll rates for different sized vehicles, we derive the number of each sized vehicle that can use the highway. Additionally, given the number of each sized vehicle that uses the highway, we derive the toll rate that should be charged for the PPP arrangement to be sustainable for each vehicular class. Empirical results of analyses, based on data obtained from the Ghana Highway Authority, are presented in Section 4. Section 5 concludes the study.

2. Literature Review

PPP largely describes a government service or private business venture which is funded and operated through a partnership of government and one or more private sector companies. PPP in this sense refers to an arrangement where government states its need for capital-intensive, long-lived infrastructure, and the desired facility is built using a complex combination of government and (mostly) private financing. The built facility is then usually operated by a private entity, under a long-term franchise, contract, or lease (Savas, 2005). The payments are usually spread between 20 to 99 years, incorporating the construction, operation, maintenance, and capital costs. Typical PPP projects are in the form of toll roads, bridges, airports, water systems, pipelines, power plants, prisons, stadiums and schools (Savas 2000). According to Savas (2005), the adoption of market principles in government activities could be considered as PPP.

Sharma (2012), in studying the determinants of PPP in developing countries, argues that large size and relatively higher income markets attract more PPP projects. The empirical evidence also suggests that macroeconomic stability, quality of regulation and governance are important factors in determining PPP usage in infrastructural projects. However, the evidence fails to provide any strong support for the role of political factors and budget constraint in the adoption of PPP. According to Nisar (2007), PPP contracts commonly require the private agent to take responsibilities for the performance of the asset over a long term, at least for a significant part of its useful life, so that efficiencies arising from long term asset management can be obtained. He also proposes that more emphasis needs to be placed on strategies for the transfer of risk, value for money drivers, and project expertise for the successful conclusions of PPP contracts.

In their study of critical government projects that have incorporated PPP in Nigeria, Babatunde, Opawa and Akinsiku (2012) discover that transportation, which includes roads, rails and airports construction, ranks highest, followed by provision of electricity and water; while real estate and educational construction projects rank lowest. On the other hand, Jamali (2007) sought to understand customer satisfaction with PPP schemes and finds a good level of satisfaction with the quality of services received through the PPP in question, but mixed results concerning the impact of consumer characteristics on satisfaction ratings.

Thus Ruster (1997) broadens our understanding of the concept of toll road privatization in his studies on Mexico's private road toll programme. Ruster observes that Mexico's private toll road programme more than doubled the national toll road network—from 4,500 kilometres in 1989 to 9,900 kilometres in 1994. Fifty-three concessions were awarded for the approximately 5,500 kilometres of roads, and by the first quarter of 1995 forty-four were in full or partial operation, representing 5,120 kilometres. The total investment in the programme over the period 1989–94 was US$13 billion. However, gross miscalculation of investment costs and operating income led to an unsustainable set of operating conditions. The financial equilibrium of the sector was further undermined by the Mexican currency crisis of December 1994. The combination of macroeconomic and project-level factors brought new project development to a virtual standstill, despite government estimates that another 6,500 kilometre of roads are needed by 2000. Consequently, restructuring of both project debt and equity investments has been the main focus of recent efforts. According to Ruster (1997) concessionaires and their affiliates were faced with writing off significant portions of their investments. Moreover, the government has been unable to unclog the road construction programme, and has been under severe pressure to inject scarce financial resources into these projects to rescue investors. In the meantime, road users were left with some of the most expensive road tolls in the world. In retrospect, some industry observers have characterized the toll road programme as a rushed and poorly designed effort to develop the infrastructure the country needed to compete effectively in an era of free trade. Others have simply labelled it a mechanism to lift the construction industry out of the economic depression of the 1980s.

Silva (2000) analysed trends in toll roads in developing countries, using figures from the World Bank's Participation in the Infrastructure Project Database. The study concludes that although private activity in toll roads has increased during the 1990s, some projects have had problems. Of the 279 projects awarded during the 1990s, 21 projects, in Hungary, Indonesia, Mexico, and Thailand, accounting for US$9.5 billion in total investment, were taken over by the government. Contract renegotiations have also been common. Among the factors that have contributed to the poor performance of these toll road projects have been overestimation of traffic, inflexible contracts that limit private investors' ability to manage market and construction risks, inadequate strategic network planning, a greater interest by private investors in construction than in operation, and voters' dislike of tolls.

On his part, Young (2012) explores the fixing of the road transport sector infrastructural problems with PPP schemes in Nigeria. He notes that because of the huge capital needed for road development, the government has turned to the private sector to manage road networks. Young (2012) cites the three-year plan for upgrading federal roads as an example. The flagship project of this public-private partnership is the Lekki-Epe expressway which is a 30-year concession between Lagos state and Lekki Concession Company (LCC). The challenge for the Lagos State and the LCC is the need to introduce appropriate methods to manage the project successfully.

The aforementioned suggests that besides the challenges and risks that governments in developing nations face in their bid to implement toll roads, it is also the case that toll roads are largely carried out without any great assessment of the risks involved, and an accompanying effort to disaggregate the categories of vehicles in relation to damage caused to the road vis-à-vis toll pricing. Thus, this study develops a model that incorporates the damage caused by a vehicular class in the maintenance and the construction cost, and estimates the risk exposure for the optimal profit for an agreed concessionary period. We decompose operations into the various vehicular usages that expose the riskiest operations for the appropriate toll rate to be charged. It is worth noting that although this study is on Ghana; its findings are applicable, at least in fundamental aspects, to other developing nations, as Ghana is typical of these nations in that they share similar challenges and risks in their determination to finance highway development.

3. Methodology

Following Andoh *et al.* (2012), we define the following:

t_f: *The total cost (in dollars) of employee wages and the maintenance of E-card centre.*

T_v: *The Total variable cost (dollars) (minor maintenance cost, allowances for staff who man the toll gate,operating expenses such as stationery, printing, electricity, diesel for standby generator,equipment repairs,etc) that varies directly with the number of vehicles that use the road at every crossing.*

s_l: *unit toll charge for light vehicles for using the highway.*

n_{l_i}: The number of light vehicles that cross the toll both in month i,

$i = 1, 2, \ldots, n$ where n is the number of months of concession.

s_m: *unit toll charge for medium vehicles for using the highway.*

n_{m_i}: The number of light vehicles that cross the toll both in month i,

$i = 1, 2, \ldots, n$ where n is the number of months of concession.

s_h: *unit toll charge for heavy vehicles for using the highway.*

n_{h_i}: The number of light vehicles that cross the toll both in month i,

$i = 1, 2, \ldots, n$ where n is the number of months of concession.

s_o: *unit toll charge for "other" vehicles for using the highway.*

n_{o_i}: The number of light vehicles that cross the toll both in month i,

$i = 1, 2, \ldots, n$ where n is the number of months of concession.

AR_c: *Asset replacement cost or capital cost (in dollars). That is the cost of constructing the highway including the construction of bridges, the purchase of toll machines, the cost of engineering studies.*

w_i: The fraction of AR_c that has to be paid off in the ith month, where

$0 < w_i \leq 1, \sum_{i=1}^{n} w_i = 1.$

r: The interest rate in the economy.

Consequently, we modify their profit function for month i,

$$P_{F_i} = n_{l_i}s_l + n_{m_i}s_m + n_{h_i}s_h + n_{o_i}s_o - [T_v + t_f + w_i AR_c(1+r)^i]$$

as

$$P_{F_i} = n_{l_i}s_l + n_{m_i}s_m + n_{h_i}s_h + n_{o_i}s_o - 1 \times T_v - 1 \times t_f - 1 \times w_i AR_c(1+r)^i \quad \ldots . \ (1)$$

and let $1 = w_l + w_m + w_h + w_o$ and $w_l \geq 0,\ w_m \geq 0, w_h \geq, w_o \geq 0.$

The w_l, w_m, w_h and w_o are the weights (that we call damage weights) for light, medium, heavy and 'other' vehicles respectively. This is the classification of vehicles by the Ghana

Highway Authority (the agency charged with the responsibility for the administration, development and maintenance of trunk roads and related facilities, including the management of toll booths). The 'other' category is agricultural tractor and agricultural tractor with trailer vehicles. The criteria for categorization of vehicles into light, medium, heavy and 'other' vehicles can be found in Andoh *et al.* (2012), pp 64. Just as in Andoh *et al.* (2012), we use the average weight of each vehicle class and the frequency of toll booth crossing as proxy for damage weights assignments. The reason is that the heavier the vehicle, the more likely it will cause damage to the highway, and the greater the frequency of usage of the highway, the more likely a vehicle will cause damage to it.
We then consider each vehicular class as independent entities striving for its on sustainability. Consequently, we form the profit functions:

$$P_{Fl_i} = n_{l_i}s_l - w_l[t_f + T_v + w_i AR_c(1+r)^i] \quad . \; . \; . \; . \qquad (2)$$

$$P_{Fm_i} = n_{m_i}s_m - w_m[t_f + T_v + w_i AR_c(1+r)^i] \quad . \; . \; . \; . \qquad (3)$$

$$P_{Fh_i} = n_{h_i}s_h - w_h[t_f + T_v + w_i AR_c(1+r)^i] \quad . \; . \; . \; . \qquad (4)$$

and

$$P_{Fo_i} = n_{o_i}s_o - w_o[t_f + T_v + w_i AR_c(1+r)^i] \quad . \; . \; . \; . \qquad (5)$$

where $P_{Fl_i}, P_{Fm_i}, P_{Fh_i}$ and P_{Fo_i} are the profit associated with light, medium, heavy and "other" vehicles respectively.

Remark 1: Andoh *et al.* (2012) ignores the damage caused by vehicular class to road and the formulation (2), (3), (4) and (5) incorporates the damage caused by a vehicular class (captured by the damage weights w_l, w_m, w_h and w_o) to the road in the cost of construction and the cost of maintaining the road. We argue that if a vehicular class causes greater damage to the road, it must pay a greater portion of the construction and maintenance cost. This is one of the main motivations for this paper.

Hence the profit generated from all four classes of vehicles, P_{F_i}, would simply be

$$P_{F_i} = P_{Fl_i} + P_{Fm_i} + P_{Fh_i} + P_{Fo_i} \tag{6}$$

If we hold light vehicular operations as a business entity on its own, then viability $P_{Fl_i} > 0$. In this case, the number of light vehicles, n_{l_i}, must be such that

$$n_{l_i} > \frac{w_l[t_f + T_v + w_i AR_c(1+r)^i]}{s_l} \quad . \quad . \quad . \quad . \tag{7}$$

Similarly,

$n_{m_i} \in \left[\frac{w_m[t_f+T_v+w_i AR_c(1+r)^i]}{s_m}, \infty\right)$, $n_{h_i} \in \left[\frac{w_h[t_f+T_v+w_i AR_c(1+r)^i]}{s_h}, \infty\right)$ and $n_{o_i} \in \left[\frac{w_o[t_f+T_v+w_i AR_c(1+r)^i]}{s_o}, \infty\right)$ for respective number of medium, heavy and 'other' vehicles respectively.

Remark 2: The splitting of (1) into (2), (3), (4) and (5) permits us to easily verify whether a given toll rate in any month is sufficient to support the traffic volume in any month. In addition, it permits us to determine which vehicular class operations are more risky and, for that matter, may necessitate an adjustment of the toll rate for that vehicular class.

For fixed toll rate s_l, the objective of any concessionaire is to maximize profit. We summarize this in the following optimization problem for light vehicles:

$$\begin{aligned} Maximize\ P_{Fl_i} &= n_{l_i}s_l - w_l[t_f + T_v + w_i AR_c(1+r)^i] \\ subject\ to{:}\ n_{l_i}s_l &> w_l[t_f + T_v + w_i AR_c(1+r)^i] \\ 0 \le n_{l_i} &\le \alpha_i \quad . \ . \ . \ . \end{aligned} \tag{8}$$

where α_i is the maximum number of light vehicles that crosses the toll gate. A similar mathematical programming problem can be formulated for medium, heavy and 'other' vehicles. This problem can be formatted into a spreadsheet and the spreadsheet software can be instructed to compute the solution (see Brandimarte (2002), chapter 3, Bertsimas and Freund (2004), chapter 7 or Winston (2004), pp 204).

3.1 Toll Rate for a Given Number of Light, Medium, Heavy and "Others" Vehicles That Ply the Highway

From equations (2), (3), (4) and (5), if we hold the number of light, medium, heavy and 'other' vehicles fixed and assume that each vehicular class strive for its own sustainability, the viability $P_{Fl_i} > 0, P_{Fm_i} > 0, P_{Fh_i} > 0$ and $P_{Fo_i} > 0$. Thus, the appropriate toll rates for light, medium, heavy and 'other' vehicles are respectively

$$s_l \in \left[\frac{w_l[t_f+T_v+w_iAR_c(1+r)^i]}{n_{l_i}}, \infty\right),\ s_m \in \left[\frac{w_m[t_f+T_v+w_iAR_c(1+r)^i]}{n_{m_i}}, \infty\right),$$

$$s_h \in \left[\frac{w_h[t_f+T_v+w_iAR_c(1+r)^i]}{n_{h_i}}, \infty\right) \text{ and } s_o \in \left[\frac{w_o[t_f+T_v+w_iAR_c(1+r)^i]}{n_{o_i}}, \infty\right).$$

It should be clear from each of these intervals that for highway with high traffic volume, the fair thing to do is to charge low toll rate.

The optimal toll rate s_l, for light vehicles that uses the highway for month i can be determined from the following mathematical programming problem:

$$Maximize\ P_{Fl_i} = n_{l_i}s_l - w_l[t_f + T_v + w_i AR_c(1+r)^i]$$
$$subject\ to: n_{l_i}s_l > w_l[t_f + T_v + w_i AR_c(1+r)^i]$$
$$0 \leq s_l \leq \tilde{\alpha}_i \quad . \quad . \quad . \quad . \qquad (9)$$

where $\tilde{\alpha}_i$ are the maximum permissible charges for month i for light vehicles. We can, in a similar fashion, formulate mathematical programming problem for medium, heavy and 'other' vehicles.

Remark 3: It should be noted that though P_{F_i} may be negative for some month i, $\sum_{i=1}^{n} P_{F_i} > 0$, in which case it will still be prudent for an investor to commit to the arrangement with a public entity. This is because during festive periods like Christmas, Easter and the Muslim pilgrimage to Mecca, the rate of vehicular movement will be high compared to some non-festive periods when rate of vehicular movement may be low. In a similar fashion, positive profit from a vehicular class can make up for losses from another vehicular class or classes.

3.2 Estimating the Risk of the Optimal Profit

Let $P_{Fl_i}^{opt}$, $P_{Fm_i}^{opt}$, $P_{Fh_i}^{opt}$ and $P_{Fo_i}^{opt}$ be the optimal profit for month i, resulting from the usage of a specified number of light, medium, heavy and 'others' vehicles respectively. Because the number of vehicles of each type that crosses the toll gate in a month for a given concessionary period are random, $P_{Fl_i}^{opt}$, $P_{Fm_i}^{opt}$, $P_{Fh_i}^{opt}$ and $P_{Fo_i}^{opt}$ are themselves random variables. Consequently for a given concessionary period of n months, from (6) we can write

$$Var(P_{F_n}^{opt}) = Var(P_{Fl_n}^{opt}) + Var(P_{Fm_n}^{opt}) + Var(P_{Fh_n}^{opt}) + Var(P_{Fo_n}^{opt})$$

as the number of each sized vehicle that crosses the toll gate is independent of each other. We will estimate the risk associated with light vehicular motion. We can then obtain the risk associated with the medium, heavy and 'others' vehicles in a similar fashion.
Note also that from (6), we can also write

$$E(P_{F_n}^{opt}) = E\left(P_{Fl_n}^{opt}\right) + E(P_{Fm_n}^{opt}) + E(P_{Fh_n}^{opt}) + E(P_{Fo_n}^{opt})$$

or

$$\mu^{opt} = \mu_L^{opt} + \mu_M^{opt} + \mu_H^{opt} + \mu_O^{opt}$$

Then for an agreed concessionary period of n months with a public entity,

$$\hat{S}^2_{P_{Fl_n}^{opt}} = \widehat{Var\left(P_{Fl_n}^{opt}\right)} = \frac{1}{n-1}\sum_{i=1}^{n}\left(P_{Fl_i}^{opt} - E(P_{Fl_n}^{opt})\right)^2 \quad . \; . \; . \; . \qquad (10)$$

$\hat{S}_{P_{Fl_n}^{opt}}$ give an estimate of the risk of the optimal profit for concession n for light vehicles. To get an estimate of the true risk, $\hat{\sigma}_{P_{Fl_n}^{opt}}$, for a fixed toll rate of optimal profit for all possible usage of light vehicles during the concessionary period, we solve the optimization problem (8) for all possible number of light vehicles that passes the toll gate within the concessionary period, to obtain the optimal profits
$P_{Fl_n}^{opt(m)}, P_{Fl_n}^{opt(m)}, \; . \; . \; . \; , P_{Fl_n}^{opt(m)}, \; m = 1,2, \; . \; . \; . \; , M \in \mathbb{Z}^+$
and calculate $\widehat{Var\left(P_{Fl_n}^{opt(m)}\right)}$, $m = 1, \; . \; . \; . \; , M$ for each optimal profit. Then the expected average variance for light vehicular profit, $E[Var(P_{Fl_n}^{opt})]$ can be approximated by

$$\frac{1}{M}\sum_{m=1}^{M} Var\left(P_{Fl_n}^{opt(m)}\right) \rightarrow E\left[Var\left(P_{Fl_n}^{opt}\right)\right] \quad . \; . \; . \; . \qquad (11)$$

as $M \to \infty$ and $Var\left(P_{Fl_n}^{opt(m)}\right)$ is the variance of the optimal profit for the path m (compare Andoh (2010), pps 35 & 38). It can be shown that

$$E\left[Var\left(P_{Fl_n}^{opt}\right)\right] = \sigma_{P_{Fl_n}^{opt}}^2 \quad . \quad . \quad . \quad . \quad . \qquad (12)$$

is the true variance in profit (see Berstimas & Freund, 2004, pp 158; Stock & Watson 2007, pp 76).

The expected optimal profit for light vehicular usage, μ_L^{opt}, can be obtained by

$$\frac{1}{M}\sum_{m=1}^{M} P_{Fl_n}^{opt(m)} \to E\left(P_{Fl_n}^{opt}\right) = \mu_L^{opt} \quad . \quad . \quad . \quad . \quad . \qquad (13)$$

as $M \to \infty$. That for medium, heavy and light vehicles can be obtained in a similar fashion.

Now, from the Chebyshev's inequality, for any $\varepsilon > 0$,

$$P\left(\left(E\left(P_{Fl_n}^{opt}\right) - \varepsilon\right) \leq P_{Fl_n}^{opt} \leq \left(E\left(P_{Fl_n}^{opt}\right) + \varepsilon\right)\right) \leq \frac{\sigma_{P_{Fl_n}^{opt}}^2}{\varepsilon^2}$$

(i.e. the smaller the variance of the optimal profit, the more likely that $P_{Fl_n}^{opt}$ will be close to the expected optimal profit, see Promislow (2011) , pp 411).

To compare the riskiness of operations between vehicular classes, we use the coefficient of variation. The optimal coefficient of variation for light vehicular usage that we denote CV_L^{opt} is given by

$$CV_L^{opt} = \frac{\sigma_{P_{Fln}^{opt}}}{\mu_L^{opt}}, \mu_L^{opt} \neq 0$$

We can in a similar fashion deduce the optimal coefficient of variation for medium, heavy and 'others' vehicles. As greater risk imposes greater cost, a concessionaire is interested in comparing the riskiness of the vehicular class usage so as to incorporate this information in the toll rates. We rule out the case where the expected optimal profit for any of the vehicular classes is equal as the variance (or standard deviation) of the optimal profit can be directly compared to select the riskiest operation.

We can also obtain the optimal coefficient of variation for the entire operations via

$$CV^{opt} = \frac{\sigma_{P_F}}{\mu^{opt}}, \mu^{opt} \neq 0$$

This quantity should assist an investor to decide which concession period to opt for. It should, however, be noted that the optimal coefficient of variation of a vehicular class can be compared provided the expected optimal profit is positive.

4. Empirical Results

4.1 Assumptions Underlying The Analysis

Data for the empirical study, analysis, and illustration of our models were obtained from the Ghana Highway Authority. This includes data on the cost of various road construction types and traffic data for trunk roads obtained from 29 toll booths scattered across Ghana for the year 2010. Ghana Highway Authority is charged with the responsibility for the administration, development and maintenance of trunk roads and related facilities in Ghana. This includes the management of all toll booths scattered throughout Ghana.

We assume that the toll booths will be constructed 50km apart, and that higher portion of AR_c will be paid in earlier years than later years. The reason for this latter assumption is the fact that government has come to the realization that mass transportation is the way for the future, and plans are underway to develop the rail sector. If that sector becomes fully operational, it is envisaged that large portions of the population are likely to go by rail. It is also better to pay off higher portions of AR_c in earlier years as a delay will mean higher toll rates in later years by virtue of the interest rate component. The 50km assumption is a government policy for tolling for trunk roads construction, but it can be subject to sensitivity analysis. We also assume that the highway will be constructed single carriageway and the type of construction is reconstruction. Analysis for the other road types, such as dual carriageway and motorway can be accomplished in a similar fashion. Also, we permit all highways for which the average daily vehicular usage exceeds the median number of daily average vehicular usage for 2010 to be potential PPP candidate.

4.2 Data Analysis

Table 14.1 below shows the way in which the damage weights are computed:

Type of vehicle	Average weight of vehicle (kg)	Median number of daily vehicular crossing on toll booth	Total weight on highway (kg)	Damage weight assigned to each vehicular class
Light	2057.97	2798	5758200.05	0.501
Medium	4717.35	367	1731267.45	0.151
Heavy	22185.379	173	3838070.57	0.333
"Others"	12891	13	167583.0	0.015
Totals			11495121.08	1

Table 14.1: Damage weights for different sized vehicles. See Andoh *et al.* (2012), pp 71.

From the table we see that the damage weights are:

$w_l = 0.501,\ w_m = 0.151,\ w_h = 0.333$ and $w_o = 0.015$

Hence from (7), table 1 and substituting values obtained from the Ghana Highway Authority,

$$n_{l_i} > \frac{0.501}{0.49}[57986.06 + 75777003.67 \times 1.0041666^i w_i]$$

where we have chosen 5% interest rate per annum (compare PPIAF-World Bank (2006)). If higher portion of AR_C are paid in earlier years than latter years, then the number of vehicles that must use the highway for the concessionaire to realize profit declines with increasing concessionary period.

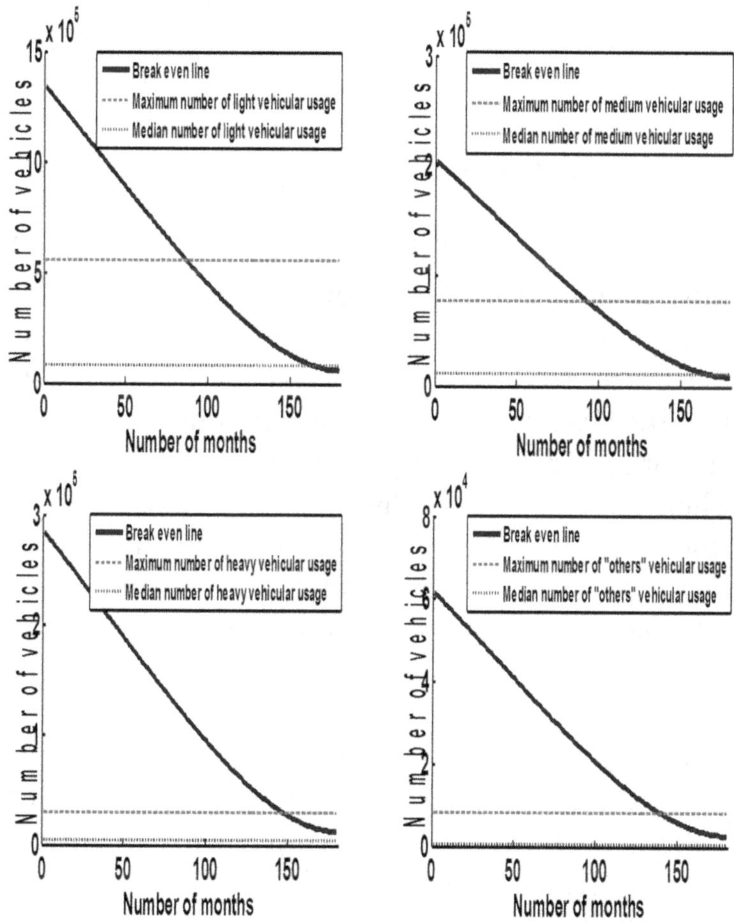

Figure 14.1: Number of vehicles for a 15-year concession for different sized vehicles.

The graph at the upper left of the Figure 14.1 represents the number of light vehicles for a 15 year concessionary period that must pass the toll gate for profitability; the one at the upper right represents the number of medium vehicles for a 15-year concessionary period that must pass toll gate for profitability. That at the lower left represents the number of heavy vehicles for a 15 year concessionary period that must pass the toll gate for profitability, while the one at the lower right represents the number of 'other' vehicles for a 15 year concessionary period that must pass the toll gate for profitability. For example, for profitability of light vehicles operations, the number of light vehicles that must use the toll gate must lie above the break even line (solid line). If we permit all roads for which the medium number of light vehicular usage exceeds the median to be potential candidate for PPP, then we see that the current number of vehicular usage is not sufficient to support profitability for all the years, even when traffic volume is high (dashed line). It can be seen from Figure 1 that between the median number of light vehicular usage (dotted line) and the maximum number of light vehicular usage (dashed line), profitability improves with increasing light vehicular usage above the median vehicular usage. The same observation can be found in the medium, heavy and 'other' vehicles. It should be noted that for heavy and other vehicles, the current medium number of vehicular usage is not sufficient to support profitability during these years of concession. Figure 14.2, Figure 14.3 and Figure 14.4 shows the results of 30, 45 and 60-year concessionary periods.

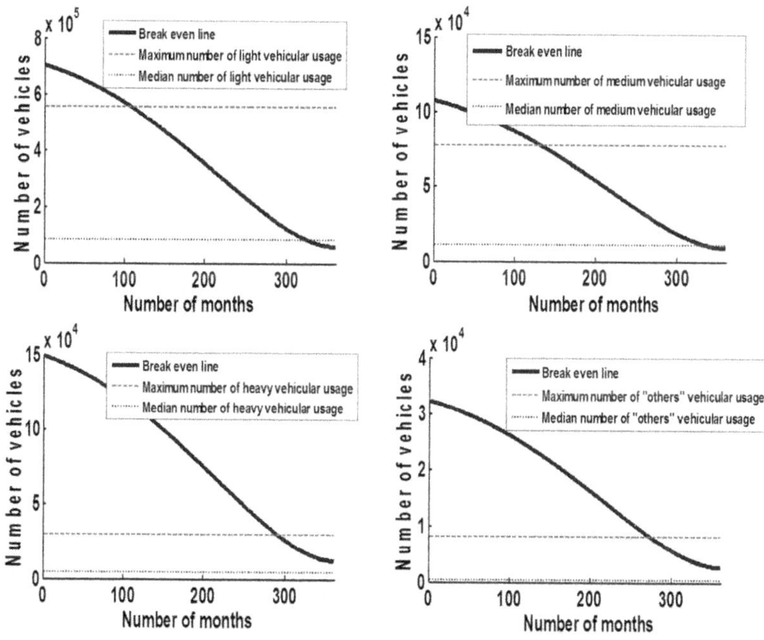

Figure 14.2: Number of vehicles for a 30-year concession for different sized vehicles.

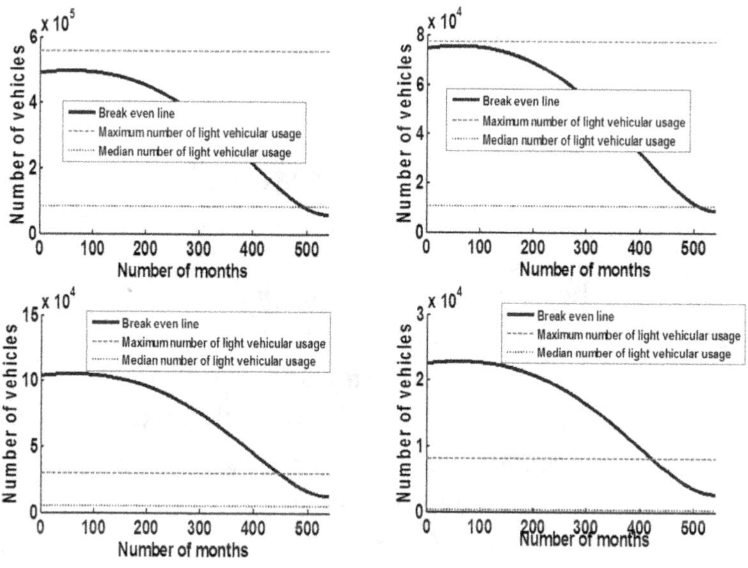

Figure 14.3: Number of vehicles for a 45-year concession for different sized vehicles.

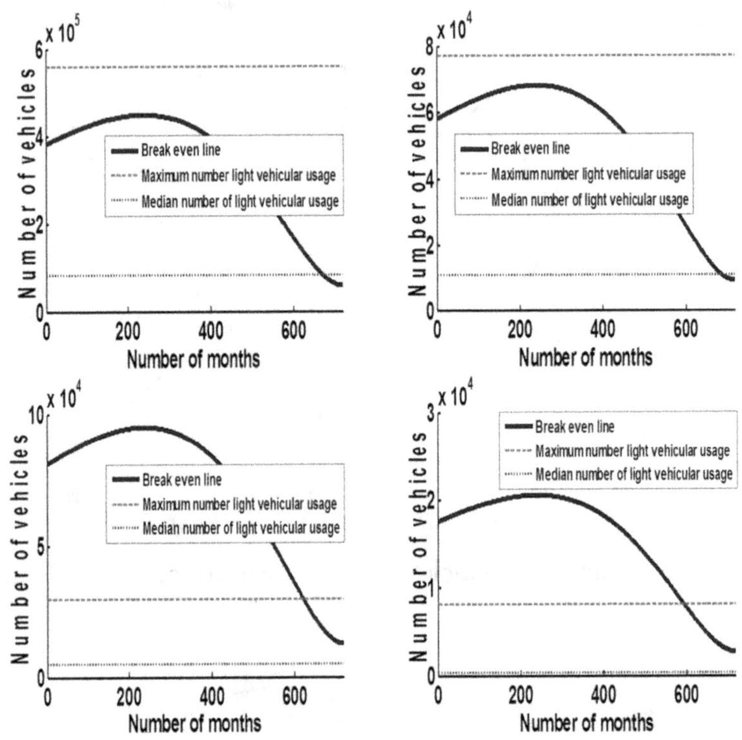

Figure 14.4: Number of vehicles for a 60-year concession for different sized vehicles.

It can also be seen from the upper left plots of Figures 14.1, 14.2, 14.3 and 14.4 that between the median number of light vehicular usage (dotted line) and the maximum number of light vehicular usage (dashed line), the likelihood of the concessionaire making profit is greater with increasing concessionary periods. The same observation can be made in the upper right plots of Figures 14.1, 14.2, 14.3 and 14.4 for medium vehicle. Similar observation can be made for heavy and the 'others' as well. Thus, the concessionaire stands a greater chance of making profit when the number of years of concession is longer.

The toll rate, s_l, for light vehicular movement for month i is

$$s_l \geq \frac{0.501}{n_{l_i}}(57986.06 + 75777003.67 \times 1.0041666^i w_i)$$

For medium, heavy and "others" vehicles, the appropriate toll rates for month i are respectively

$$s_m \geq \frac{0.151}{n_{m_i}}(57986.06 + 75777003.67 \times 1.0041666^i w_i),$$

$$s_h \geq \frac{0.333}{n_{h_i}}(57986.06 + 75777003.67 \times 1.0041666^i w_i)$$

and

$$s_o \geq \frac{0.015}{n_{o_i}}(57986.06 + 75777003.67 \times 1.0041666^i w_i)$$

In 2010, the daily average number of light vehicles that used the highways around the various regions lies in [91, 18616], the highest occurring in the Accra-Kasoa toll booth and the lowest occurring in the Asukawkaw toll booth in the Volta region of Ghana. Consequently, for light vehicles with traffic volume that lies in [2798, 18616] within the concessionary period, the appropriate toll rate for viability for month i lies in

$$\left[0.05 + 67.98 \times 1.0041666^i w_i, 0.35 + 452.28 \times 1.0041666^i w_i\right] \quad . \quad . \quad . \quad . \quad (14)$$

In the similar fashion, the appropriate toll rates for medium, heavy and 'others' vehicles must lie in

$$[0.11 + 147.66 \times 1.0041666^{i} w_i, 0.80 + 1039.27 \times 1.0041666^{i} w_i] \quad . \quad . \quad . \quad . \quad (15),$$

$$[0.65 + 850.48 \times 1.0041666^{i} w_i, 3.72 + 4861.99 \times 1.0041666^{i} w_i] \quad . \quad . \quad . \quad . \quad (16)$$

$$[0.11 + 139.30 \times 1.0041666^{i} w_i, 2.23 + 2914.50 \times 1.0041666^{i} w_i] \quad . \quad . \quad . \quad . \quad (17)$$

for traffic volumes that lie in [367, 2583], [173, 989] and [13, 272] respectively.

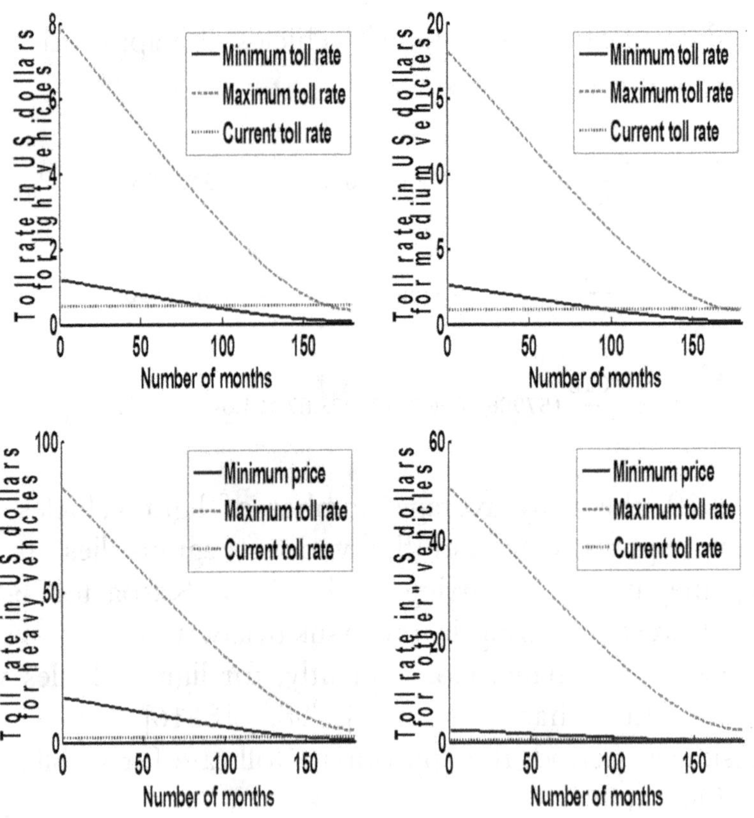

Figure 14.5: Maximum toll rate (dashed line), minimum toll rate (solid line) and current toll rate (dotted line) for 15-year concessionary period.

The graph at the upper left of the Figure 14.5 represents maximum toll rate and minimum toll rate for a 15 year concessionary period for light vehicles; the one at the upper right represents maximum toll rate and minimum toll rate for a 15 year concessionary period for medium vehicles. That at the lower left represents maximum toll rate and minimum toll rate for a 15 year concessionary period for heavy vehicles; while the one at the lower right represents maximum toll rate and minimum toll rate for a 15 year concessionary period for 'others' vehicles.

Figure 14.5 shows the toll rate range based on (14) for the concessionary period 15 years. Clearly, the toll rate to charge for sustainability declines with time. For a fair toll rate for each vehicular class, the toll rate should be set to lie in the solid line and the dashed line of the plot for all vehicular classes. It is cheaper to the user if prices are set close to the minimum price (solid line) which corresponds with greater traffic volume. From Figure 14.5, with 15-years concession, the current toll rate (dotted line) is inadequate for about 10 years. Figures 14.6, 14.7 and 14.8 show the toll rate based on the intervals (15), (16) and (17) for the concessionary periods 30, 45 and 60. Observe from Figures 14.5 to 14.8 that for each vehicular class, the toll rate to charge for sustainability declines with increasing concessionary period. For viability of all concessions periods, the toll rate should be set to lie within the solid line and the dashed line. The greater the number of years of concession, the lower should be the toll rate for the road user.

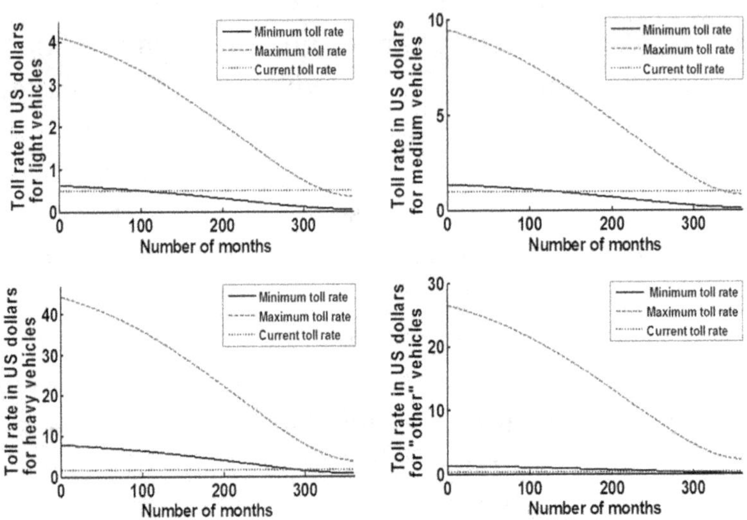

Figure 14.6: Maximum toll rate (dashed line), minimum toll rate (solid line) and current toll rate (dotted line) for 30-year concessionary period.

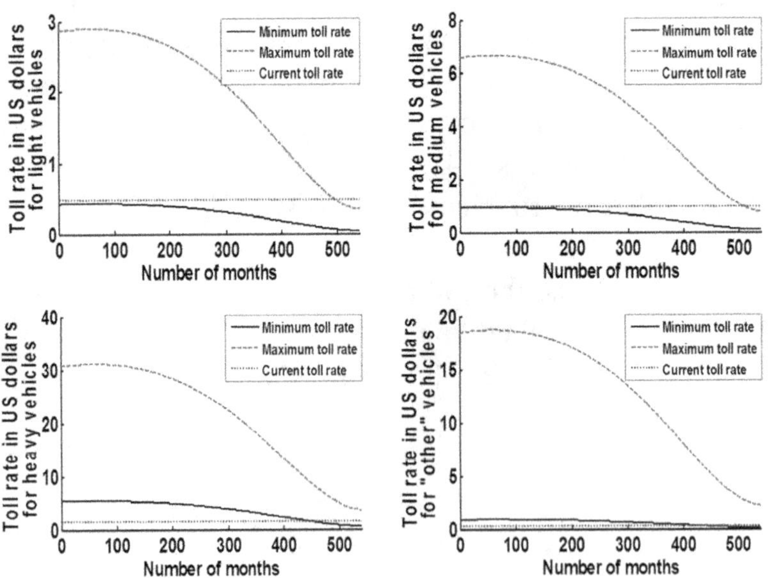

Figure 14.7: Maximum toll rate (dashed line), minimum toll rate (solid line) and current toll rate (dotted line) for 45-year concessionary period.

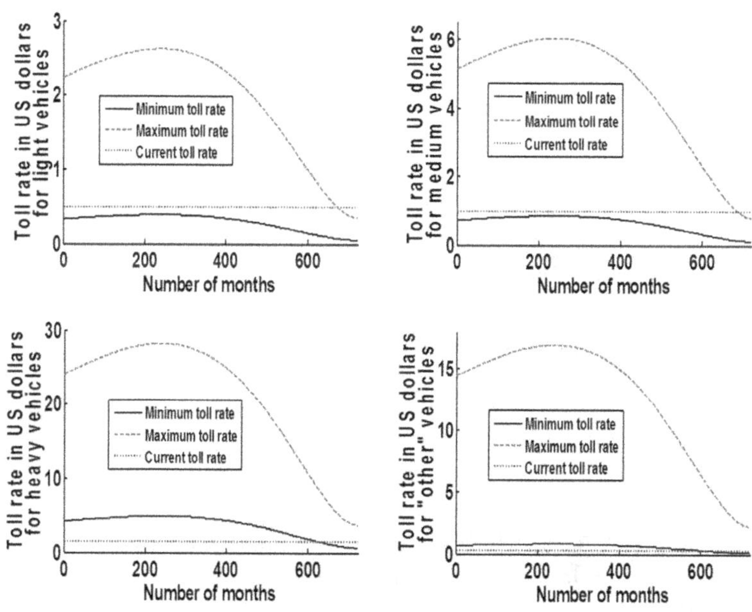

Figure 14.8: Maximum toll rate (dashed line), minimum toll rate (solid line) and current toll rate (dotted line) for 60-year concessionary period.

With a 30-year concession, the current toll rate is inadequate for about 18 years. With 45 and 60 year concessions, the current toll rate is respectively inadequate for about 28 and 41 years. It should be noted that these years correspond to minimum points on the plot when traffic volume is high. If the traffic volume is low, it is clear from the figure that the current toll rate is inadequate most of the years.

Now, we consider light vehicles operations. The objective of a concessionaire is to maximize the profit P_{Fl_i} for month i, as follows:

$$\text{Maximize } P_{Fl_i} = 0.49n_{l_i} - 0.501(57986.06 + 75777003.67 \times 1.0041666^i w_i)$$
$$subject\ to: 0.49n_{l_i} > 0.501(57986.06 + 75777003.67 \times 1.0041666^i w_i)$$
$$0 \le n_{l_i} \le 558480 \quad . \ . \ . \ . \quad (18)$$

For medium, heavy and "others", the corresponding optimization problems for the concessionaire are

Maximize $P_{Fm_i} = 0.97n_{m_i} - 0.151(57986.06 + 75777003.67 \times 1.0041666^{i}w_i)$
subject to: $0.97n_{m_i} > 0.151(57986.06 + 75777003.67 \times 1.0041666^{i}w_i)$
$0 \leq n_{m_i} \leq 77490$,

Maximize $P_{Fh_i} = 1.54n_{h_i} - 0.333(57986.06 + 75777003.67 \times 1.0041666^{i}w_i)$
subject to: $1.54n_{h_i} > 0.333(57986.06 + 75777003.67 \times 1.0041666^{i}w_i)$
$0 \leq n_{h_i} \leq 29670$

and

Maximize $P_{Fo_i} = 0.32n_{o_i} - 0.015(57986.06 + 75777003.67 \times 1.0041666^{i}w_i)$
subject to: $0.32n_{o_i} > 0.015(57986.06 + 75777003.67 \times 1.0041666^{i}w_i)$
$0 \leq n_{o_i} \leq 8160$

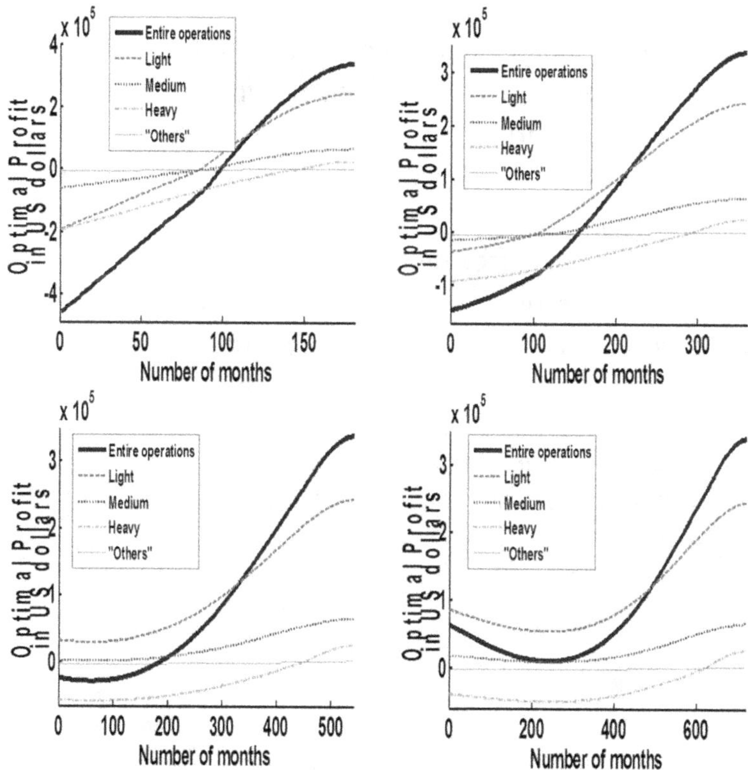

Figure 14.9: Optimal profit for entire operations (solid line) light, medium, heavy and "others" for the concessionary periods 15, 30, 45 and 60 years.

The graph at the upper left of the figure 14.9 represents optimal profit for different sized vehicles for a 15- year concessionary period; the one at the upper right represents optimal profit for different sized vehicles for a 30- year concessionary period for medium vehicles. That at the lower left represents optimal profit for different sized vehicles for a 45- year concessionary period; while the one at the lower right represents optimal profit for different sized vehicles for a 60- year concessionary period. The solid line in each plot represents the optimal profit for the entire operations in each plot. It can be seen from the different concessionary periods that the optimal profit improves with increasing concession for each different-sized vehicle. The potential loss of the entire operational profits and that for the different sized vehicles also declines. Thus, the longer the concession, the less risky are the optimal profits.

A concessionaire often likes to determine the toll rate that will enable him or her to make profit. The following model enables a concessionaire to determine the optimal toll rates that maximize his/her profit for light vehicles.

$$\text{Maximize } P_{F_i} = n_{l_i}s_l - 0.501(57986.06 + 75777003.67 \times 1.0041666^i w_i)$$
$$subject\ to\text{: } 558480s_l > 0.501(57986.06 + 75777003.67 \times 1.0041666^i w_i)$$
$$0 \leq s_l \leq 0.49$$

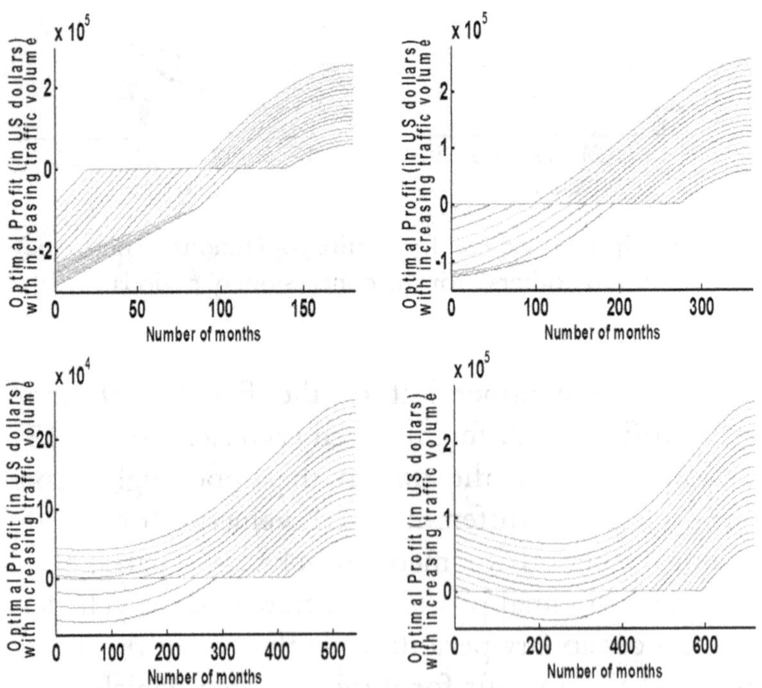

Figure 14.10: Optimal profit for light vehicles with increasing traffic volume for the concessionary periods 15, 30, 45 and 60 years.

We solve the above optimization problem with the toll rate fixed at 0.49, but with increasing traffic volume starting from $n_{l_i} = 181{,}400$, $n_{l_i} = 201{,}334$, . . . to $n_{l_i} = 580{,}068$. We observe that for each concessionary period, as the traffic volume increases, the optimal profit also increases. The corresponding optimal toll rate is depicted in figure 11 below

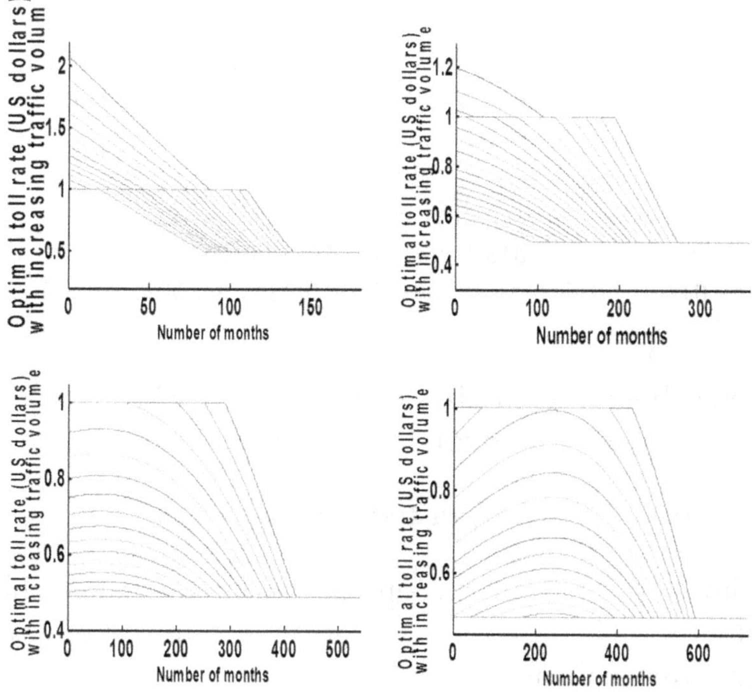

Figure 14.11: Optimal toll rate for light vehicles with increasing traffic volume for the concessionary periods 15, 30, 45 and 60 years.

We observe that as the traffic volume increases, the optimal toll rate reduces until the end point of the decision variable for which it reduces no further. Thus for roads with greater light vehicular traffic volume, the fair thing to do is to charge low rates for light vehicles. The optimal toll rates for 45 and 60 year concessions lie in [0.49, 1]. Also, smaller optimal toll rates

are associated with longer concessions. The fair thing to do is to charge low rate for longer concessionary agreements.
That for medium, heavy and 'others' vehicles are respectively:

$$\text{Maximize } P_{F_i} = 77490s_m - 0.151(57986.06 + 75777003.67 \times 1.0041666^i w_i)$$
$$\textit{subject to}: 77490s_m > 0.151(57986.06 + 75777003.67 \times 1.0041666^i w_i)$$
$$0 \leq s_m \leq 0.97$$

$$\text{Maximize } P_{F_i} = 29670s_h - 0.333(57986.06 + 75777003.67 \times 1.0041666^i w_i)$$
$$\textit{subject to}: 29670s_h > 0.333(57986.06 + 75777003.67 \times 1.0041666^i w_i)$$
$$0 \leq s_h \leq 1.54$$

and

$$\text{Maximize } P_{F_i} = 8160s_o - 0.015(57986.06 + 75777003.67 \times 1.0041666^i w_i)$$
$$\textit{subject to}: 8160s_o > 0.015(57986.06 + 75777003.67 \times 1.0041666^i w_i)$$
$$0 \leq s_o \leq 0.32$$

The upper bound in the last constraint of each optimization problem is the maximum toll charge for each vehicular type.

4.3 *Estimating the Risk of the Optimal Profit*

To estimate the risk of the optimal profit for light vehicles operation for a fixed toll rate, we solve the optimization problem (18) to obtain $P_{Fl_1}^{opt^{(m)}}, P_{Fl_2}^{opt^{(m)}}, \ldots, P_{Fl_n}^{opt^{(m)}}$, $m = 1, \ldots, 1000$ for all possible values of the optimal profit not too far out of the range of light vehicular traffic volume report in November 2010. The average daily traffic volume reported for this period lies [91, 18616] (lies [2730, 558480] in a month). We use the interval steps 600, 1200, 1800, . . . , 600000 to solve model (18) altering the end of the decision variable of this model in each case. An estimate of the risk of the optimal profit for light vehicles can then be obtained by equations (10), (11) and (12).

The results of light vehicles for the different concessionary are shown on table 14.2.

For medium vehicles, we used interval steps 30, 930, 1830, . . . , 89130 as the average daily traffic volume lies in [13, 2583] (i.e. lie in [390, 77490] in a month). For heavy vehicles, we used the interval steps 30, 90, . . , 30000 as the average daily traffic volume lie in [11, 989] (i.e. lie in [330, 29670] in a month). Finally, for 'others', we used the interval steps 1, 91, 181, . . . , 89911 as the average daily traffic volume lie in [0,272] (i.e. lie in [0, 8160] in a month). Just as for light vehicles, we employed equations (10), (11) and (12) to obtain the risk of the optimal profits for medium, heavy and 'other' vehicles and obtained the result shown in table 14.2. The table also gives the overall risk of the optimal profit associated with the different concessionary periods.

Concessionary period (in years)	Risk of optimal profit for different sized vehicles and varying concessionary periods				
	$\hat{\sigma}_{P_{F_l}}$	$\hat{\sigma}_{P_{F_m}}$	$\hat{\sigma}_{P_{F_h}}$	$\hat{\sigma}_{P_{F_o}}$	$\hat{\sigma}_{P_F}$
15	50080.54	15030.33	28083.93	2152.85	77,657.84
30	44420.97	13300.01	21163.81	1724.28	67,610.97
45	42576.49	12764.53	18617.05	1534.38	64,304.30
60	42057.81	12617.19	17984.47	1485.44	63,406.26

Table 14.2: Risk of optimal profit for different sized vehicles for 15, 30, 45 and 60 years concessionary periods.

To obtain the expected optimal profit for light vehicles, we use the optimal profits obtained and apply equation (13). Table 14.3 shows the results for light, medium, and 'other' vehicles. By virtue of the negativity of some of the expected optimal profit shown on table 14.3, we cannot rely on the optimal coefficient of variation to determine the variation in the riskiness of operation across concessionary periods, and across vehicular classes, except for heavy vehicles. There are less variability in optimal profits across concessions for heavy vehicular operations, with 15 year possessing the least variability in expected optimal profit. Hence, we rely on the Chebyshev's inequality to determine variation in the riskiness of operations between the different sized vehicles and across the different concessionary periods. For a 15- year concession, the likelihood that the expected optimal profit will be attained is greatest for 'other' vehicles. This is followed by the medium, heavy and light vehicles, respectively. The same pattern can be observed from the other years of concessions. Consequently, the riskiest operations are the light vehicular usage, followed by the heavy, medium and the 'others'.

Concessionary period (in years)	Expected optimal profit for different sized vehicles and varying concessionary periods				
	$\hat{\mu}_L^{opt}$	$\hat{\mu}_M^{opt}$	$\hat{\mu}_H^{opt}$	$\hat{\mu}_O^{opt}$	$\hat{\mu}^{opt}$
15	53982.70	16766.96	83397.19	−6744	147402.86
30	3114.90	1470.84	51182.20	−9065.79	46702.16
45	−8897.53	−2112.07	43432.53	−9661.60	22761.34
60	−8620.42	−2019.86	42964.09	−9692.47	22631.33

Table 14.3: Expected optimal profit for different sized vehicles for 15, 30, 45 and 60 concessionary periods

Also from the Chebyshev's inequality, the likelihood that expected optimal profit will be realized is greatest for a 60-year concession. Its deviation from the expected optimal profit is $63,406.26. This is followed by 45-year concession, 30-year concession and finally 15-year concession, with deviations from the expected optimal profit $64,304.30, $67,610.97 and $77,657.84, respectively. This confirms the results obtained in Andoh *et al.* (2012) that the shorter the concession, the greatest the risk of attaining the optimal profit.

On the other hand, we observe from table 3 that the expected optimal profit for 'other' vehicles is negative for all concessionary periods. Hence the current level of traffic volume of 'other' vehicles is not sufficient to support operations.

4.4 *How Much Should a Concessionaire Bear to Ensure Optimal Profit?*

We next investigate how much should a concessionaire pay for the PPP to ensure optimal profit for each vehicular class at all times? Our task is to determine the portion of t_f, T_v and AR_c that should be borne by the concessionaire to realize some profit for each vehicular class. To obtain an estimate of this proportion, $\alpha_l \in [0,1]$ for light vehicles, write the P_{Fl_i} as

$$P_{Fl_i} = \tilde{n}_l \tilde{s}_l - \alpha_l w_l [t_f + T_v + w_i AR_c (1+r)^i]$$

where $\tilde{n}_l$ is the number of light vehicles and $\tilde{s}_l$ is the toll rate for light vehicle that passes through a toll gate. For viability, we must have that:

$$\tilde{n}_l > \frac{\alpha_l w_l [T_v + t_f + w_i AR_c (1+r)^i]}{\tilde{s}_l}$$

We verified our estimate of α_l by solving the following optimization problem:

$$\text{Maximize } P_{Fl_i} = 0.49 n_{l_i} - 0.501 \alpha_l (57986.06 + 75777003.67 \times 1.0041666^i w_i)$$
$$\textit{subject to: } 0.49 n_{l_i} > 0.501 \alpha_l (57986.06 + 75777003.67 \times 1.0041666^i w_i)$$
$$0 \le n_{l_i} \le 558480$$

For all appropriately chosen α_l, the optimal profit will lie in the first quadrant of the coordinate axes. We can, in a similar fashion, deduce the portions $\alpha_m \in [0,1], \alpha_h \in [0,1]$ and $\alpha_o \in [0,1]$ for medium, heavy and 'other' vehicles, respectively. Table

14.4 shows the portions of each sized vehicle that the concessionaire can bear for reconstruction. Other road construction types such as upgrading and rehabilitation can be obtained in a similar fashion.

Road type	Concessionary period (in years)	Portion of AR_c that a concessionaire can bear to realize profit for different sized vehicles and varying concessionary periods			
		α_l	α_m	α_h	α_o
Reconstruction	15	0.415	0.378	0.10425	0.1323
	30	0.79224	0.721991	0.199	0.25248
	45	1.0	1.0	0.2826	0.35858
	60	1.0	1.0	0.31225	0.396

Table 14.4: Portion of AR_c that can be borne by a concessionaire to realize profit for different sized vehicles for different concessions.

For all concessions, the greatest portion AR_c for each vehicular class that can be borne by a concessionaire is light vehicles. It is followed by medium, 'other' and heavy vehicles. For a 15-year concession, for example, the concessionaire can bear 41.5% of these costs (i.e. t_f, T_v and AR_c) of light vehicular operations to realize some profit. The greatest portions of the heavy vehicular road construction cost are borne by the public entity that calls for an upward adjustment of the toll charges for heavy vehicles.

Also for all concessions, the greater the number of years of concessions the higher the portions of the vehicular class road construction costs, that can be borne by the concessionaire. Observe that for 45 and 60 year concessions the concessionaire can bear the entire cost of operations and construction costs associated with light and medium operations, and still attain the optimal profit for these vehicular classes.

5. Conclusion

The model we have developed is a (very good) most appropriate model for any businessman interested in partnering with a government in any country for the development and management of highways. The model determines the risk exposure to expected optimal profits, the optimal number of different sized and optimal toll rates incorporating the damage caused by a vehicular class in the toll rates.

On the basis on the analysis done with the model, we conclude that all vehicular classes do not pay a toll rate commensurate with the cost of damage to the highway. The operations of the light and the heavy vehicles are the riskiest among the four vehicular classes. The greatest expected optimal profit is associated with the shortest concession and the shorter the concession, the riskier the PPP arrangement. For the arrangement to be viable for the concessionaire, the government must bear a greater part of the construction cost of heavy and 'other' vehicles.

As the number of vehicles in a particular class can fall or rise with a given period, proper records of the type of vehicle and the number of vehicles that go through the toll gate has to be kept. This will allow for an update of the damage weights cause on a regular basis, for proper toll rate assignment.

References

Andoh, C., Mills. E. A., & Quaye, D. (2012). Public private partnerships as an alternative source of financing highway(s) in Ghana. *Annals of Management Science*, Vol. 1, number 1, 61-82.

Andoh, C. (2010). GARCH family models under varying innovations. *Decisions*, Vol. 37, Number 1, 35 & 38.

Babatunde, S., Opawole, A., & Akinsiku, O. (2012). Critical success factors in public-private partnership on infrastructure delivery in Nigeria. *Journal of Facilities Management,* Vol. 10 Iss: 3, 212 – 225.

Bertsimas, D., & Freund, R. M. (2004). *Data, Models, and Decisions: The Fundamentals of Management Science.* Dynamic Ideas, chapter 7, 347-345.

Biau, C., Dahou, K., & Homma, T. (2008). How to increase sound private investment in Africa's road infrastructure: Building on country successes and OECD policy tools. Expert Roundtable on 11 December 2008, OECD/NEPAD, pp 6.

Brandimorte, P. (2002). *Numerical Methods in Finance. A Matlab-Based Introduction.* Wiley series in Probability and Statistics. Chapter 3, pp 128-132, 179 – 180.

Ghana Road Fund Secretariat (2010). Annual Report of the Ghana Road Fund

Secretariat, pgs 1-5. Available at the Ghana Road Fund Secretariat.

Holl A. (2001). *Manufacturing locations and impacts of road transport infrastructure. The case of Spain.* Nectar Conference No. 6. European Strategies in the Globalisation Markets; Transport Innovations, Competitiveness and Sustainability in the Information Age

Jamali, D. (2007). A study of customer satisfaction in the context of a public private partnership. *International Journal of Quality & Reliability Management*, Vol. 24 Iss: 4, 370 – 385.

Keane, T. F. (1996), The economic importance of the national highway system, *Public Roads*, Vol. 59, Spring, pp 1.

Mills, E. A (2010). *Public private partnership as an alternative source of financing highway in Ghana: Prospects and challenges.* Unpublished thesis submitted to Kwame Nkrumah University of Science and Technology, CEMBA.

Nisav, T. M. (2007). Value for money drivers in public private partnership scheme. *International Journal of Public Sector Management*, Vol. 20 Issue 2, 147-156.

Promislow, S. D. (2011). *Fundamentals of actuarial mathematics* (second edition). John Wiley and Sons Limited, (pp 411).

PPIAF-World Bank (2006). Toolkit for PPP in Highways. [Online] available at (http://www.ppiaf.org. Accessed November 13, 2012).

Ruster, J. (1997). A retrospective on the Mexican toll road program (1989–94). Public Policy for Private Sector, Note No. 125, pp 1-2.

Sharma, C. (2012). Determinants of PPP in infrastructure in developing economies. *Transforming Government: People, Process and Policy*, Vol. 6 Iss: 2, pp.149 – 166.

Savas, E. (2005). *Privatisation and public-private partnerships.* New York, USA: Chatham House Publications.

Savas, E. (2000). *Privatisation in the city: Successes, failures, lessons.* Washington DC: CQ Press, pp 4.

Silva, G. F. (2000). Toll roads: Recent trends in private participation. *Public Policy for Private Sector*, number 224, pp 4

Stock, J. H., & Watson, M. W. (2007). *Introduction to econometrics (second edition).* Pearson Addison Wesley, (pp 76).

Young, J. (2012). A fresh start: fixing the transportation sector in Nigeria Accessed 14 December 2012 from INTERACTIVE BUSINESS NETWORK RESOURCE LIBRARY, pp 4.

Winston, W. L. (2004). *Operations research: Applications and algorithm (*fourth edition). Thomson. Brooks/Cole. Chapter 4, pp 202-210.

CHAPTER FIFTEEN

Tax Planning Practices of Small and Medium Enterprises in Ghana

Cyprian Amankwah, Mohammed Amidu and S.N.Y. Simpson

1. Introduction

Taxes represent a significant cost to businesses; thus, many businesses anticipate circumstances and identify opportunities to proactively minimize their tax in their bid to reduce cost, increase after-tax revenue and achieve a competitive advantage in the marketplace. Levenson (1999, p. 16) notes: *'(Certain) strategies … can help companies reduce their effective tax rates from the typical 40 to 35 percent to as low as 10 percent. This reduction translates to higher earnings per share and ultimately places companies in a more favorable light with analysts when compared to competitors'.* The adoption of innovative strategies to minimize, postpone or altogether eliminate tax liabilities has been referred to as tax planning or aggressiveness (Prichard & Bentum, 2009; Richardson, Lanis & Taylor, 2013).

According to Richardson *et al.* (2013, p.29) tax aggressiveness (tax planning) 'is *the downward management of taxable income through tax-planning activities. It thus encompasses tax-planning activities that are legal or that may fall into the gray area, as well as activities that are illegal. Hence, tax aggressiveness can range along a continuum with many cases falling in the disputed gray zone on that continuum'.* This practice is said to bring with it significant benefits for management and shareholders, and society as a whole (Richardson *et al.*, 2013, p.1). Inger (2012, p.1) adds that;

'the benefits of tax planning are a function of the implementation costs and these costs vary with the complexity of the tax planning strategy'.

However, from extant literature, tax planning seems to be the preserve of big business firms; hence, evidence of many studies which have examined tax planning of big corporations (Francisco, Elena & Antonio, 2012; Nurshamimi & Rohaya, 2012; Zaimah, 2012; Rohaya, Nursyazwani & Nor'Azam, 2010; Adhikari, Derashid, & Zhang, 2006; Harris & Feeny, 2000; Gupta and Newberry, 1997). These studies argue that big companies are able to organize their activities to reduce the amount of tax that will be payable given their scale and capacity, resources and expertise, among others, which give them advantages for tax planning.

The foregoing suggests that small and medium enterprises (SMEs) by their nature do not enjoy the size, scale and scope of advantages that big firms have, and that give them advantages in tax planning. That notwithstanding, both SMEs and big corporations are exposed to similar economic conditions which may instigate the need to adopt innovative strategies to minimize, postpone or altogether eliminate tax liabilities. To this end, this study posits that SMEs ought to engage in tax planning to reduce their tax burden. In fact, tax planning by SMEs has the potential to make significant cost savings and ultimately improve their bottom line, given the role SMEs play in many countries of the world. Moreover, SMEs are said to face numerous challenges including relatively high effective taxes which make them fail to realize their full potential (Abor & Quartey, 2010; OECD, 2009), hence, tax planning may provide some relief so that they can remain engines for economic growth (Daniels, 2004).

Like many other countries, SMEs in Ghana are crucial in the socio-economic development of the country. They are a significant part of the private sector, and account for the majority of enterprises and a substantial proportion of employment (Kwabena, 2000). For instance, the Ghana Statistical Service (GSS, 2012) indicates that about 90% of businesses in Ghana fall within the SME category. SMEs have the potential of helping generate greater sustainable economic and social benefits through employment creation, equitable distribution of income, inter-industry linkages, and they can help people expand their asset base, build wealth, and exit poverty.

This paper argues that the potential of SMEs will be enhanced if most SMEs were able to reduce their tax liabilities and the regulatory burden imposed by tax legislation. By so doing, they will significantly reduce the cost of doing business, and will begin to make progress in realizing their full potential. Empirically, while it is believed that big firms are engaged in exploiting the legislative loopholes to plan their tax payments, it is not yet known how SMEs are taking advantage of these opportunities to plan their taxes. Also, in Ghana, like in many other countries in the developing world, empirical studies have yet to be done on the tax planning activities of SMEs, particularly due to the difficulty in tracking their tax activities.

In view of the above, this study sought to examine the nature of the tax planning activities of SMEs in various sectors of Ghana to, among other things, ascertain the SME sectors with low effective tax rate and higher tax savings. Specifically, answers to the following research questions were sought: (i) What is the nature of SMEs' tax planning in Ghana; (ii) In which sector do SMEs experience low effective tax rates? And (iii) in which sector do SMEs in Ghana have higher tax savings? This study will contribute to the discussion and to a large extent, facilitate a deeper and better understanding of tax issues of small businesses, and will drive and deepen the understanding of the principles and practices of tax planning of SMEs in Ghana. It will also extend the knowledge and understanding of this area and the existing tax literature.

2. Literature Review

2.1 Theories of Corporate Tax Planning

Theories are conceptual frameworks for organizing knowledge and provide a blue print for action (Griffin, 2004). They are a coherent set of assumptions put forth to explain the relationship between two or more observable facts and to provide a basis for predicting future events (Stoner, Freeman & Gilbert Jr, 1995). Theories that explain corporate tax planning are examined below.

2.1.1 Agency Theory

The agency theory derives from the agency problem that mostly exists between managers and shareholders. According to Richardson at el (2013, p. 1), the theory 'is appropriate in the corporate environment due to the principal-agent relationship between shareholders and management'. This problem arises because managers (agents) who are entrusted with the responsibility of running, or managing the business on behalf of shareholders (principals) sometimes engage in activities, including tax planning, which can lead to a divergence in between the interests of managers and that of shareholders'. If such divergence is allowed to develop and persist, then managers will have an opportunity to expropriate the wealth of shareholders for themselves (Jensen & Meckling, 1976: Fama & Jensen, 1983).

In the context of tax planning, the problem occurs when management uses the discretion available to them within the boundaries of the law to manipulate tax liability for their own or their shareholders' benefit. Evidence that this occurs has been documented in numerous empirical studies including Desai and Dharmapala (2006), Frank, Lynch & Rego (2009), Dyreng, Hanlon, & Maydew (2008) and Rego and Wilson (2009), among others. Although it is generally thought that top management use tax planning as an opportunity to hide their activities and shield their managerial opportunism (Desai & Dharmapala, 2006), it is not in all cases that managers undertake tax planning activities to benefit themselves only.

In some instances, corporate tax planning may come about by shareholders' preference for tax avoidance (Chen, Chen, Cheng, & Shevlin, 2010), especially when the benefits to be received are perceived to offset the hidden costs arising from management who mask their rent extraction activities. Thus, shareholders will encourage tax planning in instances in which managers act in the interest of the shareholders in a way that brings tax savings to the organization, and the likelihood that lower effective tax rate will lead to shareholder wealth maximization. The agency theory of tax planning is not just a well known theory but, also has great empirical research to support it.

2.1.2 Political Cost Theory

The political theory stipulates that large firms are subject to greater public scrutiny due to their larger size and higher visibility and thus become victims of greater regulatory actions by government. They, as a result, incur a 'political cost' and taxes are a part of the total political costs borne by firms. The theory claims that larger firms have higher Effective Tax Rate (ETR) than small firms, because of the political cost of greater government and public scrutiny, as governments and regulatory authorities find ways to effectively restrict and reduce their tax avoidance efforts. As a result, large firms are less likely to circumvent their tax responsibilities by choosing tax reducing accounting methods (Watts & Zimmerman, 1978).

Although the political cost hypothesis has been difficult to prove or test empirically, there has been considerable public opinion and academic research on it. Deegan and Unerman (2011) argue that large firms come under scrutiny by various groups, including government, employee groups, consumer groups, environmental lobby groups and so on. The size of a firm is often used as an indication of market power, and this in itself can attract the attention of regulatory bodies. They further argue that government and interest groups may publicly promote the view that a large organization is generating excessive profits, and not paying its 'fair share' back to society.

2.1.3 Political Citizen Theory

The political citizen theory stipulates that large firms in fact pay less tax because they can devote more resources to tax planning and political lobbying, which may result in 'political benefit'. In addition, political connections and ties with the government can help firms gain comparative advantages, including favourable tax treatment (Adhikari Derashid, & Zhang, 006; Faccio, 2006). Salaman and Siegfried (1977) argue that larger firms possess superior economic and political power, relative to smaller firms, and are therefore able to avoid tax burdens. Also Watts and Zimmerman (1978) argue that large firms which are politically sensitive and vulnerable to wealth, extracting political transfers in the form of legislation or regulation, can reduce the possibility of adverse political attention and the associated costs. They increase taxes, by adopting a number of strategies, including government lobbing and a selection of accounting procedures that lead to a reduction in reported profits, thereby reducing their expected costs.

Cahan (1992) adds that the political-cost hypothesis predicts that managers confronted with the possibility of politically- imposed- wealth transfers will choose accounting strategies that reduce the size of the transfer pricing. For example Porcano (1986), in a study analysing ETR of U.S. corporations during 1982 and 1983, finds evidence of a negative association between firm size and ETR. Thus Porcano (1986) argues that using greater resources available to them, larger firms may influence the tax they pay: '… a larger volume of assets, sales and/or net income might be better able to utilize various tax precisions which reduce the firm's overall tax rate' (p.22).

2.1.4 Adopted Theories

The theories that were adopted in this study are the political cost and political citizen theories; two sides of the same coin that try to explain tax planning. Political Cost and Political Citizen theories try to explain tax planning with divergent points of view relating to the issue of firm size. Political Cost sees large firms size as disincentive in tax planning, as large firms are subject to greater public scrutiny due to their larger size and higher visibility and thus become victims of greater regulatory actions by government. This means that relatively large SMEs, no matter the sector of the economy they can be found in, may have higher ETRs than large firms because of the political cost of greater government and public scrutiny, as governments and regulatory authorities find ways to effectively restrict and reduce their tax avoidance. On the other side of the coin, it is thought that large firms in fact pay less tax because they can devote more resources to tax planning and political lobbying, which may result in 'political benefit'. Political connections and ties with the government can help firms gain favour, including favourable tax treatment (Adhikari *et al.*, 2006; Faccio, 2006). Large SMEs may therefore be able to avoid tax or reduce tax burdens and may thus have lower ETRs.

The Political Cost and Political Citizen theories were more useful in explaining SME tax planning than the Agency theory because they deal with size of firms which can be measured and data can be collected on. The Agency theory is about the separation of ownership from management which, with regard to most SMEs in Ghana, does not apply, as most managers of SMEs are the owners themselves. As a result, most owners of SMEs have the greater say in the management of SMEs including on tax issues. Moreso, data could not be collected on this variable; thus the estimated model did not capture firm ownership, as this study sought not to study this issue.

2.2 Empirical Literature Review

Many empirical studies have been done on corporate tax planning. As far back as the 1980s, using cross sectional data, Stickney and McGeel (1982), who were among pioneer empirical researchers of tax planning, examined the effect of size, capital intensity, leverage and involvement of natural resources, among other factors on the effective corporate tax rate of firms. Their findings showed no significant relationship between average ETR and firm size. However, capital intensity, leverage and involvement in natural resources resulted in lower ETR. In a similar vein, the following year, Zimmerman (1983), a noted empirical tax researcher, found a positive, though not strictly monotonic, relationship between average ETR and firm size.

In the 1990s, many studies examined the relationship between ETR and firm specific attributes such as size, return on assets, leverage, capital intensity and inventory intensity. Wang (1991), for example, examined the relationship between firm size and effective tax rates as a test of a firm's political success. Data for six year period 1978–1983 were collected for the sampled firms. Using a path analysis to isolate the effect of firm size and effective tax rates that were attributable to Net Operating Losses (NOLs), the study found an indirect relationship through Net Operating Losses (NOLs). The path analysis results indicated that the indirect effects of NOLS have a statistically significant impact on the overall relationship between firm size and effective tax rates. This indicates that NOLs constitute an important omitted variable in prior firm - size -oriented studies.

Moving into the 2000s, many works were done on corporate tax planning around the world. For example, Guha (2007) examined company size and effective corporate tax rates in Indian private manufacturing companies, using panel data for 1992-2001. With a mul-tivariate framework, it was found that the size of the companies influences their effective tax rate, and that the larger the company, the lower is the effective tax rate. He did not find very clear cut reasons behind a negative relationship due to lack of transparency on the part of the tax department in revealing information regarding the tax returns of the companies. But there may be an unknown factor built into the political administrative system of Indian, through which larger companies are able to reduce their effective tax rate.

Arrifin (2012) examined whether industry affiliations affect corporate- tax avoidance in Malaysia. The study tested the relationship by using a cross sectional time series valuation, and panel data analyses involving Tobit estimations. The results showed that companies across different industries do have significantly different characteristics and levels of tax avoiding activity. The results also confirm the importance of industry differences in explaining the tax burden. The evidence showed that companies across different industries do have significantly different characteristics and levels of tax avoiding activity.

A study in Ghana on a similar topic is that of Nguyen–Tanh and Stupert (2012). They sought to answer the question: *Is the burden too small?,* using an extended Devereux Griffith methodology and data from 2008-2012, and found that the wide range of tax incentives leads to a high variation of effective average tax rates in Ghana. They found that the tax holidays and the preferential income tax rates reduce the effective tax burden significantly, and encourage tax avoidance strategies.

3. Methodology

3.1 Study sample

The empirical data for the study was obtained from the database of the National Board for Small Scale Industries (NBSSI). On the NBSSI database, there are 1223 SMEs grouped into two business categories or sectors of the economy: manufacturing and services sectors. Of the total, 571 were manufacturing, while the remaining 652 fell into the services sector. In selecting the sample from the population, the 10% condition for the Central Limit Theorem was used, which states that: 'When the sample is drawn without replacement (as is usually the case), the sample size, n, should be no more than 10% of the population' (Berry and Lindgren, 1990: p.?). Ten percent (10%) of each category of the target population of 1223 SMEs was drawn to reflect the two sectors of the economy. The sample period spans from fiscal year 2010 through 2012, resulting in 366 total observations. However non-existing SMEs, or existing SMEs on the NBSSI database, that had relevant information for the study missing in the financial statements, were deleted. Hence the final sample was 122; resulting in 357 SME-year observations.

3.2 Model Specification

To examine the relationship between ETR and SMEs' firm characteristics, the study follows a regression model that is widely used in tax planning studies. The model is specified below:

$$ETR_t = \beta 0_i + \beta 1SIZE_{it} + \beta 2ROA_{it} + \beta 3LEV_{it} + \beta 4CAPINT_{it} + \beta 5INVINT_{it} + \beta 6SECTORDUMMY_{it} + \varepsilon_{it}$$

In the OLS regression model above, the effective tax rate (ETR) is expressed as a linear function of many exogenous, explanatory or independent variables, including size, return on equity, capital intensity, inventory intensity and sector dummy.

3.3 The dependent Variable

The ETR in this study was calculated as: current-based ETR, which is current income tax expense (income tax expense minus deferred tax expense) divided by pretax income for a given SME i in year t multiplied by 100 percent.

3.4 Independent Variables

SIZE represents the SME size, measured as the natural logarithm of the total assets or sales since the model is a liner function. *ROA,* which represents the return on assets and denotes a firm's profitability, was calculated as the pretax income divided by the total asset. *LEV* is SMEs' capital structure or leverage, measured as total debts or total liabilities divided by total assets. To control for factors that are expected to influence SMEs' asset, the researchers included *CAPINT,* and *INVINT. CAPINT* is the capital intensity, measured as fixed assets divided by total assets. *INVTNT* is inventory intensity, measured as inventory divided by total assets. *Sector dummy* is the sector dummy. It controls for potential sector effects in the estimation.

3.5 Panel Data Methodology

The success of an regression analysis depends on the availability of the appropriate data. The data that was available for the empirical analysis in this study was panel data. The general form of the panel data regression model can be specified as:

$$y_{it} = \alpha + \beta' X_{it} + u_{it}$$

Where the subscript *i* denotes the cross-sectional dimension (equal to 1……122), and *t* represents the time-series dimension (1 to 3 years). This means that the same tax information on an SME is surveyed over time. *Yit* represents the dependent variable in the model, which is ETR. *X* contains the set of explanatory variables in the estimation model. *a* is the constant and *ß* represents the coefficients. $u_{it} = \mu_i + \lambda_t + v_{it}$ where μ_i is an unobserved individual specific effect, λ_t is an unobserved time specific effect and v_{it} is a zero mean random disturbance with a variance of σ_v^2. According to Baltagai (2001: p.?), the panel data regression gives 'more informative data, more variability, less collinearity among variables, more degrees of freedom and more efficiency'. However, since two techniques: fixed effects and random effects could be used, the researcher ran a Hausman test to decide between the models. The *random effects* model was found to be appropriate in this study.

4. Discussion of Empirical Results

4.1. Descriptive Statistics

The descriptive statistics of the sample calculated in this study include the mean, median, standard deviation and skewness. Table 15.1 gives the descriptive statistics used in the study.

Table 15.1: Descriptive Statistics

Variable	N	Minimum	Maximum	Mean	Std. Deviation	Skewness
ETR	357	-3.68	1.01	0.1781	0.27241	-7.479
SIZE	359	3.60	8.16	5.8095	0.77285	.388
ROA	358	-0.48	3.82	0.1343	0.28777	7.406
LEV	358	0.00	11.29	0.5136	0.76213	8.790
INVINT	305	0.00	2.68	0.2906	0.32009	2.777
CAPINT	305	0.00	41.17	0.8341	3.71596	8.776

Variable definitions: ETR = income tax expense (income tax expense minus deferred tax expense) divided by pretax income for a given SME i in year t multiplied by 100 percent; SIZE = the natural logarithm of total sales; ROA= firm's profitability, calculated as the pretax income divided by the total asset; LEV = SMEs' capital structure or leverage, measured as total debts or total liabilities divided by total assets; INVINT= inventory intensity, measured as inventory divided by total assets; and CAPINT = the capital intensity, measured as fixed assets divided by total assets.

Table 15.1 reports the descriptive statistics of all the variables in the regression model. *SIZE* (log of total sales) has a mean of 5.8095. *ROA* (return of assets) has a mean of 0.1343. *LEV* (leverage) has a mean of 0.5136. *INVINT* (inventory intensity) has a mean of 0.2906 and *CAPINT* (capital intensity) has a mean (median) of 0.8341. Overall, with a range of 0-1, it is clear that the means of all the variables, except *SIZE* (log of total sales), are within reasonable limits. It is also observed that there is a reasonable level of consistency between the means, reflecting normality of distributions. In addition, an acceptable range of variation is observed for all of the estimated variables in the model. To see the variation of ETR within and across sectors over time, an analysis of the sectors: manufacturing and services, through three years, 2010, 2011 and 2012, were done as shown in Table 15.2.

Table 15.2: Variations of Effective Tax Rate of SMEs across Sectors and Years

Year	Sector		Overall
	Manufacturing	Service	
2010	0.2	0.15	0.17
2011	0.19	0.13	0.16
2012	0.19	0.21	0.2

From the results it is clear that sector results of ETRs of sampled SMEs show variations across the three years. In the manufacturing sector, for example, the ETR for 2010 is 0.2 while the ETRs for both 2011 and 2012 are 0.19. This shows variation. In the services sector, ETR was 0.15 in 2010, 0.13 in 2011 and 0.21 in 2012. There is also variation. Within-sector ETR variations are indicative of individual differences among SMEs in their tax planning effort confirming the argument of

Ali-Nakyea (2007), Murphy (2004), Prichard and Bentum (2009) that not all companies have the same level of inclination to tax planning. Across sectors, results, as reported in Table 15.3, show that SMEs in the manufacturing sector have, on average, higher ETRs than SMEs in the services sector. Differences in sector ETRs are indicative of sector-specific factors that account for tax planning activities of SMEs in that sector, which may offer advantages or disadvantages to SMEs in that sector in their tax planning.

The investigation of the association between tax planning and tax savings of taxed SMEs was done in this study. SMEs' tax savings could be explained by any unexplained excess of statutory tax rates (STR) over ETR, which can be the result of tax planning. All things being equal, the wider the gap between the STR and ETR (i.e. STR>ETR) the higher the tax planning intensity. The overall effective tax rates of the sampled SMEs for the study period are compared with the applicable STR of 25%, and the difference is the tax savings. These relationships are illustrated in figure 15.1.

Figure 15.1: Statutory Tax Rate, Effective Tax Rate and Tax Savings

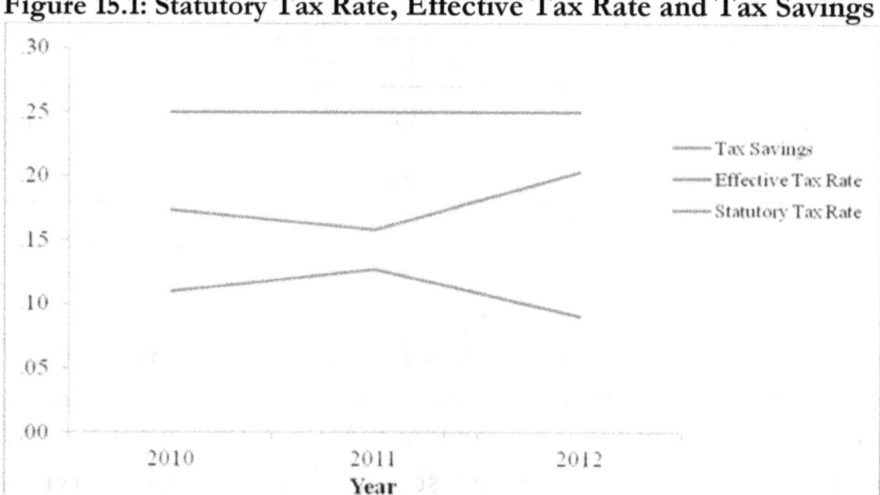

Figure 15.1 shows the statutory tax rate, the effective tax rate and the tax savings of SMEs over the three-year- period the study considered. The graph shows that the statutory tax rate, which is fixed, is higher over 2010-2012 year period at 0.25 (that is 25 percent) than the effective tax rate, which on average, hovers around 0.18, 18% over the same period. The results show that the effective tax rate of SMEs is approximately 7% lower than the statutory tax rate. That means SMEs' tax savings, which is the unexplained difference between the statutory tax rate and the effective tax rate, is arrived at after adjusting for reliefs and rebates. The economic significance of the result is great. The magnitude of the tax savings is very large compared to what pertains in the literature. The results also contradict what is in principle common in most countries (Chen & Mintz, 2011).

On the nature of the SME tax savings, whether it is conservative, moderate or aggressive, Table 15.3 reports results of the analysis of the nature of the tax savings.

Table 15.3: Nature of Tax Savings of SMEs

Sector	Conservative		Moderate		Aggressive		Total	
	Frequency	%	Frequency	%	Frequency	%	Frequency	%
Manufacturing	36	60	4	6.67	20	33.33	60	100
Service	39	50.65	2	2.6	36	46.75	77	100
Total	75	54.74	6	4.38	56	40.88	137	100

From the results of the analysis reported in Table 15.3, it is seen that on the whole, SMEs in the manufacturing sector have higher figures for conservative (60%) and moderate (6.67%) tax savings compared to SMEs (50.65% and 2.6% respectively), in the services sector. SMEs in the services sector have a higher figure for tax aggressiveness, 46.75%

compared to 33.33% of manufacturing SMEs. These results imply SMEs in the manufacturing sector have lower tax savings and confirm the higher ETRs obtained for SMEs in the manufacturing sector. However, SMEs in the services sector are more tax aggressive, and have more tax savings, which confirm the lower ETRs firms in this sector are found to have. The results on the nature of tax savings further confirm that sampled SMEs in the services sector have on average lower ETRs, and this means that they have effectively planned their tax burdens for the period of the study better than those in manufacturing. It can be argued from the results that SMEs in the services sector probably invest more in tax planning than their counterparts in the manufacturing sector, and this may be what allows them to achieve greater tax savings relative to those in the manufacturing sector.

4.2 Correlation Results

Before presenting and discussing the regression results, the results of the correlation analysis showing the association between variables, are first presented and discussed. This is necessary since regression only deals with the dependence of one variable on other variables, and does not necessarily imply causation. In the words of Kendall and Stuart (1961:p) 'a statistical relationship, however strong and however suggestive, can never establish causal connection; our ideas of causation must come from outside statistics, ultimately from some theory or other'. Thus, the correlation results showed association of ETR with the independent variables, and this helped unravel the causation between the variables. Results of Pearson's pairwise correlation which measures correlation of various variables in the sample are presented Table 15.4.

Table 15.4: Pearson Pairwise Correlation Results

Variable	Effective Tax Rate	Log of Total Sales	Return of Assets	Leverage	Capital Intensity	Inventory Intensity
Effective Tax Rate	1					
Log of Total Sales	-0.024*	1				
	(.650)					
Return of Assets	-0.124**	-0.046	1			
	(.020)	(.386)				
Leverage	-0.148**	0.186	0.164	1		
	(.005)	(.000)	(.002)			
Capital Intensity	-0.360**	-0.066	0.830	0.176	1	
	(.000)	(.249)	(.000)	(.002)		
Inventory Intensity	0.080**	0.046	0.119	0.254	0.028	1
	(.163)	(.425)	(.038)	(.000)	(.624)	

N = 122 for all variables.
The probability value, p-values are two-tailed tests.
* Significance at the .10 level.
** Significance at the .05 level.
*** Significance at the .01 level.

From Table 15.5, the correlations show the *strength* or *degree* of *linear association* between the variables in the regression model. In the Pearson correlation results above, coefficients that are significant (p-value < 0.05) have the double asterisk. From the results, the correlations show that ETR, the dependent variable, is found to be negatively linearly associated with: log of total assets, return of assets, leverage and capital intensity at 5% level of significance. However ETR is positively associated with inventory intensity. These imply that the higher the levels of log of total assets, return of assets, leverage and capital intensity, the lower will be the level of SME ETR. It also implies that the higher the inventory intensity, the higher the SMEs' ETR.

Multi-collinearity

The researchers feared that from the correlation results reported in Table 15.4 above there may be the problem of correlations between the independent variables; the situation where there is either an exact or approximately exact linear relationship among the independent variables (Gujarati, 2004). In testing for multicollinearity, a suggested rule of thumb is that the benchmark correlation matrix should be 0.50. Any correlation matrix above 0.50 is considered high, and is indicative of the presence of multicollinearity. Although from observing the estimated pair correlation, it must be admitted that the magnitudes of the estimated coefficients on some of the variables were found to be somewhat low, the researchers had to prove the relationships by calculating the variance inflation factors (VIFs), to determine how much the variance of an estimated regression coefficient is increased due to collinearity. Thus, the study tested for signs of multi-collinearity among the explanatory variables by calculating the VIFs. Table 5.5 reports the correlations between the explanatory variables and the variance inflation factors (VIFs) resulting from them.

Table 15.5: Correlations between the Explanatory Variables and Variance Inflation Factors

Model	T	Sig.	Correlations			Collinearity Statistics	
			Zero-order	Partial	Part	Tolerance	VIF
(Constant)	1.974	.049					
Log of Total Sales	-.715	.475	-.018	-.041	-.037	.961	1.040
Return of Assets	4.652	.000	-.170	.261	.240	.291	3.436
Leverage	-2.340	.020	-.138	-.135	-.121	.870	1.150
Capital Intensity	-7.536	.000	-.360	-.401	-.389	.292	3.422
Inventory Intensity	1.572	.117	.080	.091	.081	.917	1.091
Sector	1.236	.217	-.021	.072	.064	.960	1.042

Table 15.5 shows that only moderate levels of collinearity exist between most of the explanatory variables in the model. Where significant multi-collinearity exists in some variables, as in the case of correlation of return on assets and capital intensity, (Pearson correlation = 0.830), they may not be as problematic as is anticipated, since the results of tests for multi-collinearity confirm that no VIFs exceed five (5) for any of the explanatory variables. This means that multi-collinearity is not problematic in the regression model, and the explanatory are not highly collinear to the point that they can disturb the relationships and the findings of the study.

4.3 Discussion of Regression Results

The OLS regression was estimated using panel data from SMEs sampled from data from the NBSSI database. The Hausman tests confirmed the use of the *random effects* model. Results of random-effects panel regression are shown in Table 15.6.

Table 15.6: Random-Effects Panel Regression Model Analysis for Effective Tax Rate

Variables	Random-Effects Model	Fixed Effect Model
Constant	0.224**	0.232**
	(0.114)	(0.115)
Log of Total Sales	-0.014	-0.015
	(0.019)	(0.019)
Return of Assets	0.426***	0.422***
	(0.091)	(0.092)
Leverage	-0.046**	-0.046**
	(0.020)	(0.020)
Capital Intensity	-0.055***	-0.055***
	(0.007)	(0.007)
Inventory Intensity	0.075	0.077
	(0.0048)	(0.048)
Sector	0.037	0.037
	(0.030)	(0.030)
R-Squared	0.6719	0.6782
Wald chi2(6)	77.70	
Prob> chi2	0.0000	0.0000
Corr (u_i, *b)		0.0397
F(6, 295)		12.74

* Significance at the .10 level.
** Significance at the .05 level.
*** Significance at the .01 level.
Standard Error in Parenthesis

With regard to the regression results, the R-square statistic (the R^2 value of 0.67) means that about 67% of the variation in the effective tax rate is explained by: size (log of total sales), return on assets, leverage, capital intensity and inventory intensity. Since R^2 lies between 0 and 1 and at most can be 1, the R^2 value of 67% suggests that the estimated regression line quite fits the data well. It means that the tax variables provide the largest parts of the explanation of the dispersion in ETR. The R^2 is typical in cross sectional studies as one obtains low R^2 values, probably because of the diversity of the units in the sample (Gujarati, 2004). Since the data for analysis was panel (which includes cross-section data), the R^2 value of 67% was acceptable. Also since the model was not meant to be used for prediction but for explanation, the R^2 was acceptable.

6. Conclusions

The study found that effective tax rates give a clearer picture of the true tax burden faced by SMEs than statutory tax rates. The higher statutory tax rate and lower ETRs of SMEs mean that ETR is more indicative of the true tax costs SMEs in Ghana face. The study reveals that there is a difference in ETRs of SMEs in the manufacturing and services sector and among the three financial years investigated. The study finds that SMEs in the manufacturing sector have the highest effective tax rates, compared to those in the service sector. The researchers conclude that manufacturing SMEs are not very successful in managing their tax burdens, compared with their services sector counterparts and, thus, they have lower tax savings. A policy implication is that if these SMEs compete with each other in the marketplace, the substantial differences in ETRs can give advantages to SMEs with lower ETRs and higher tax savings, and large disadvantages to those with higher ETRs and lower tax savings. The study will be useful to academics, practitioners and policy makers. However it is not without limitations. The study sample was drawn from the NBSSI database. Because of the high mortality of SMEs in Ghana, the existence of SMEs which are on the NBSSI database could not be established. It was difficult to determine the exact sample, as the SME population always changes with updates. In addition to this, some of the sampled SMEs did not have some of the information required for the study. This may have affected the quality of the results obtained. The ETR was calculated based on financial statement data obtained from the NBSSI database, since tax return data on SMEs are private and publicly unavailable. Plesko (2003), among other researchers, questions the veracity of financial-statement-based tax aggressiveness measures. Future studies can address the limitations of this study.

References

Abor, J. & Quartey, P., (2010). Issues in SME development in Ghana and South Africa. *International Research Journal of Finance and Economics, 39*(6), pp.215-228.

Abakah, R. E (2010). *A strategic approach to taxation.* Cape Coast: Cape Coast University Press

Adhikari, A., Derashid, C., & Zhang, H. (2006). Public policy, political connections, and effective tax rates: Longitudinal evidence from Malaysia. *Journal of Accounting and Public Policy,* 25, 574-595.

Adom, D. (2010). Successfully handling tax investigations. The tax practitioner: *Journal for Chartered Institute of Taxation,* 2. 15-17

Ali-Nakyea, A. (2007). *Taxation in Ghana: Principles, practice and planning (2nd ed).* Accra: Black Mask Ltd.

Ariffin, Z.Z (2012). Do industry affiliations affecting corporate tax avoidance in Malaysia. Paper presented at International Conference on Management, Economics and Finance.

Baltagai, B. H., (2001). *Econometric Analysis of Panel Data.* ??: John Wiley and Sons Ltd.

Berry,? & Lindgren,? (1990) *Statistics: Theory and Methods.* Pacific Grove, Calif.: Brooks/Cole Publishing Co.,

Cahan, S.F. (1992). The effect of antitrust investigations and discretionary accruals: A refined test of the political-cost hypothesis. *The Accounting Review, 67,* 1 (January). 77-95

Chen, D. & Mintz, J. (2011). New estimates of effective corporate tax rates on business investment.*Tax and Budget Bulletin No. 64 Cato Institute.*

Chen, S., Chen, X., Cheng, Q., & Shevlin, T. (2010). Are family firms more tax aggressive than non-family firms? *Journal of Financial Economics* 95, 41–61.

Deegan, C., & Unerman, J. (2011). *Financial accounting theory*, ??: McGraw-Hill.

Desai, M.A., & Dharmapala, D. (2006). Corporate tax avoidance and high-powered incentives. *Journal of Financial Economics* 79, 145-179.

Dyreng, S., Hanlon, M., & Maydew, E. (2008). Long-run corporate tax avoidance. *The Accounting Review*. 83: 61-82.

Faccio, M. (2006). Politically connected firms. *The American Economic Review*. Vol. 96, No.1 (Mar., 2006), pp. 369-386

Fama, E.F., & Jensen, M.C. (1983). Agency problems and residual claims. *The Journal of Law and Economics*, 26 (2), 288-307

Francisco, J., D., Elena, F., & Antonio, M., A. (2012). Size and other determinants of corporate effective tax rate in US. Listed companies. *International Research Journal of Finance and Economics*. ??? p.?

Frank, M., Lynch, L., & Rego. S. (2009). Are financial and tax reporting aggressiveness reflective of broader corporate policies? *The Accounting Review*, 84 (2), 467-498. Ghana Statistical Service Quarterly Report. (2012)

Griffin, E. (2006). *A first look at communication theory (6th Ed.)* New York: McGraw-Hill

Guha A. (2007) Company size and effective corporate tax rate. Study on Indian private manufacturing companies. *Economic and Political weekly May 19. Pp?*

Gujarati (2004): *Basic Econometrics*, Fourth Edition, New York: McGraw−Hill

Gupta, S., & Newberry, K. (1997). Determinants of the variability in corporate effective tax rates: evidence from longitudinal data. *Journal of Accounting and Public Policy*, 16 34. ?pp

Harris, M. N. & Feeny, S. (2000). *Habit persistence in effective tax rates: Evidence using Australian tax entities.* Working Paper, University of Melbourne.

Inger, K. K. (2012). *Relative valuation of alternative methods of tax avoidance.* Dissertation submitted to the faculty of the Virginia Polytechnic Institute and State University in partial fulfilment of the requirements for the degree of Doctor of Philosophy in Accounting and Information Sciences.

Jensen, M.C., & Meckling, W.H. (1976). Theory of the firm: Managerial behavior, agency costs and ownership structure. *Journal of Financial Economics* 3, 305-360.

Kendall M. G. and Stuart A. (1961). *The advanced theory of statistics.* New York: Charles Griffin Publishers, ,

Kwabena, L. (2000). *Rural Finance Review Study.* Report Prepared for Ministry of Finance, World Bank, NBFI Project. PP 32.

Levenson, A. (1999). Worldly planning for global firms. *Electronic News* 7/5/99, 16.

Murphy, K. (2004). Aggressive tax planning: Differentiating those playing the game from those who don't. *Journal of Economic Psychology,* 25, 307-329.

Nguyen – Than, D., & Strapat C. (2012). Is the burden too small? Effective tax rate in Ghana *Ruhr Economic Papers No. 389*, http://dx.doi.org/10.4419/86788444

Nurshamimi, S., & Rohaya, M., N. (2012). *Tax planning and corporate governance.* Paper presented at the International conference on management economics and finance.

Organization for Economic Co-operation and Development (2009). Taxation of SMEs: Key ` Issues and Policy Considerations. *OECD, Paris*

Porcano, T.M. (1986). Corporate tax rates: progressive, proportional, or regressive. *Journal of the American Taxation Association* 7, 17–31.

Plesko, G.A., 2003. An evaluation of alternative measures of corporate tax rates. *Journal of Accounting and Economics* 35 (2), 201–226.

Prichard, W & Bentum, I. (2009). Taxation and development in Ghana: *Finance Equity and ??? ?Details*

Rego, S., Wilson, R. (2009). *Executive compensation, tax reporting aggressiveness, and future firm performance.* Working paper, University of Iowa.

Richardson, G., &Lanis, R. (2007). Determinants of the variability in corporate effective tax rates and tax reform: Evidence from Australia. *Journal of Accounting and Public Policy* 26, 689-704.

Richardson, G., Lanis, R. & Taylor G. (2013). The impact of board of director oversight characteristics on corporate tax aggressive: an empirical analysis. *Journal of Accounting and Public Policy*. 32 (3): 68-88

Rohaya, M. N., NurSyazwani M. F. & Nor' Azam, M. (2010). Tax planning: A study on corporate effective tax rates Malaysian listed companies. *International Journal of Trade, Economics and Finance*, 1, (2), 1-5.

Salaman, L. M., & Siegfried, J. J. (1977). Economic power and political influence: The impact of industry structure on public policy. *The American Political Science Review*, *71*, 1026–1043.

Stickney, C. P., & McGee, V. E. (1982). Effective corporate tax rates: The effect of size, capitalintensity, leverage and other factors. *Journal of Accounting and Public Policy*, *2*, 125-152.

Stoner, J. A. F., Freeman E. A., & Gilbert Jr. D. A. (1995). *Management* 6th ed. EnglewoodCliffs, NJ: Prentice-Hall.

Wang, S.W. (1991). The relationship between firm size and effective tax rates: a test of firm's political success. *The Accounting Review*, Vol. 66. No. 1 pp. 158 – 169

Watts, R. L. & Zimmerman, J. L. (1978). Positive accounting theory of the determination of accounting standards. *Accounting Review* 53, 112-134.

Zaimah, Z. A. (2012). *Do industry affiliations affecting corporate tax avoidance in Malaysia?* Paper presented at the International conference on management economics and finance.

Zimmerman, J. L. (1983). Taxes and firm size. *Journal of Accounting and Economics*, *5*,

CHAPTER SIXTEEN

Audit Expectation Gap in the Public Sector of Ghana

Ibrahim Bedi, Joseph Onumah and Emelia B. Derkyi

1. Introduction

Audit expectations gap (AEG) is a topical issue due to the damage it could bring to the very core of the auditing profession, which enunciates trust. The concept is an issue for auditors as a greater 'expectation gap' will lead to low credibility, low fee income and low prestige associated with their work. It is also an issue for the financial statement users, particularly investors, since wealth-creation and political stability in a capitalist economy depend significantly on confidence and accountability. AEG is an emerging issue in the public sector, especially in developing countries, where much research has centred on the private sector. Many studies have been conducted on this subject in the developed countries, mainly due to the high profile financial scandals within those economies. Auditing literature has accepted the existence of AEG, and has called for action to reduce the gap and/or its effect on auditors (Porter, 1991; Canadian Institute of Chartered Accountants, 1988). The concept was defined by Liggio (1974) as the 'difference between the level of expected performance as envisioned by the independent accountant, and by the user of financial statements'. Porter (1991) gave a more succinct definition as 'the gap between the public's expectation of auditors and auditors' perceived performance'. Porter (1993) further analysed the total gap into three separate components, namely substandard performance, deficient standards and unreasonable expectations.

The study of AEG in the context of performance audits has largely been conducted in developed countries. However, these studies are applicable to developing countries as well, considering the perception that fraud, corruption and economic mismanagement are high in the public sector of most developing countries (Kaufmann, 1997; Gray & Kaufmann, 1998; Sandholtz & Koetzle, 2000). Humphrey (1992) posits that the importance of the expectations issue derives from public accountability and stewardship and that those who exercise power should be accountable for that power. In this vein, public sector organisations are responsible for many critical services, and since they are predominantly funded by taxes, their performance is of great importance to the public. Public sector performance is therefore receiving increasing attention, and a greater demand is placed on the reporting agencies by various stakeholders.

According to Humphrey, Moizer & Turley (1993), issues associated with AEG have remained similar for a substantial period of time, and now as wide as ever. However, such studies have concentrated on the private sector. A study in this regard provides an opportunity to promote the public sector audit quality needed to reduce the economic sabotage facing most developing countries. Again, it contributes to the literature by bringing AEG from the public sector and the African perspective into the literature. Studies have been done on this subject in Africa, but with reference to AEG in the private sector (Gloeck & De Jager, 1993; Onumah, Simpson & Babonyire, 2009; Tanko, 2011; Okoye & Okaro, 2011). Therefore, this study adds to the global empirical literature on

AEG from the public sector perspective, and broadens the application of AEG framework from the African perspective. The main objective of this study was to examine AEG in public sector audit of Ghana. Specifically, the study's objectives were to:

i. Examine the components of AEG with regard to Choudhury's (1996) framework
ii. Identify the factors that contribute to the AEG
iii. Examine the public perceptions of AEG
iv. Identify ways to reduce AEG

2. Literature Review

Though the concept of AEG is as old as modern day auditing (Humphrey *et al.*, 1993), Liggio (1974) is believed to be the first to have formally used the term to describe the differences that exist between the perceptions of auditors and those of financial statements users on the work of auditors. Since this formal application of the term, several attempts have been made by both academic and professional accountants to investigate the concept from diverse perspectives. Most of the pioneering work on the concept examined the existence, components, causes, problems and ways of addressing its persistence or escalation. However, a large number of recent studies tended to focus on the characteristics of the gap relative to diverse circumstances, to users and to reporting implications. Comparative studies have even been conducted so that evidence from different business environments are assessed. Interestingly, however, most of these studies indicate that there is little consensus on the definition or meaning of the concept. For instance, Guy and Sullivan (1988), one of the early studies following the work of Liggio (1974), define the concept as referring to the differences between what the public believes to be within the responsibilities of the auditors, and what auditors themselves believe to be within their responsibilities. Similarly, the AICPA (1992) defines the concept as: '…the difference between what the public and financial statement users believe auditors are responsible for, and what auditors themselves believe their responsibilities are'. Monroe and Woodliff (1993) on their part define the AEG as the difference in beliefs between auditors and the public about the duties and responsibilities assumed by auditors, and the messages conveyed by audit reports. Again, McEnroe and Martens (2001) used the expectation gap to refer to the differences between what financial statement users recognise as being part of the auditors' responsibilities, and what the auditors consider their responsibilities involve.

Academics and professional accountants share a common view on the fundamental role of the external auditing, which is the provision of assurance on the credibility of financial statements. To the contrary, the same cannot be said of the users of audited financial statements (Gay, Schelluch, & Baines, 1998). Therefore, this has resulted in significant differences in perceptions between financial statements users and auditors about what the users expect from the audit function, and what the auditors themselves perceive as their role in the assurance process. In particular, following the widely publicised cases of the Enron and WorldCom phenomena, several attempts have been made with the view to modifying the duties, roles and responsibilities of auditors as one of the ways of addressing the issue of the expectation gap. Despite these attempts at simplifying and/or clarifying the responsibilities of auditors, several of the Post-Enron expectation gap studies still reveal persistence and, in some cases, an escalation of the level of the expectation gap (Sidani, 2007).

Research evidence has examined and confirmed the gap in specific areas such as the nature of the audit function, the perceived performance level of auditors, auditors' duties and responsibilities, the independence of auditors and non-audit services and the business environments of different economies. Humphrey *et al.*'s (1993) study reveals a significant difference between the views of the auditors and the respondents on the nature of auditing. The research specifically confirmed the existence of gap in areas such as the nature of the audit function and the perceived performance of auditors. The study by Sidani (2007) confirms the existence of gap between what auditors actually do or perceive themselves to be doing, when compared to the perceptions of financial statement users. In particular, there was a significant difference on the perception of the role of the auditor pertaining to fraud detection.

The work of Chowdhury (1996) identifies the following six components of AEG in public sector audits:

i. **audit independence**

Auditor independence is a '*freedom from those pressures and other factors that compromise or can reasonably expect to compromise an auditor's ability to realize unbiased audit decisions*' (Independence Standards Board of the American Institute of Certified Public Accountants, 1997).

ii. **audit competence**

Hassal, Dunlop & Lewis (1996) define competence as '*The ability to perform to recognised standard. A person described as competent in an occupation or profession is considered to have a repertoire of skills, knowledge and understanding which he or she can apply in a range of contexts and organisations'*.

iii. **audit scope**

This refers to the responsibilities of the auditor. In the case of the public sector, the auditor's scope of work is stipulated in the Country's Constitution and in the various financial administration laws and regulations of the country. Other aspects of the scope of the audit works are found in the respective statutes and laws governing the various MDAs.

iv. **audit ethics**

Audit ethics has been defined as *'the systematic study of behaviour based on moral principles, philosophical choices and values of right and wrong conduct'* (Shaikh & Talha, 2003).

v. **audit reporting**

This is the formal communication of the opinion of the auditor on the financial statement. The reporting adds value to the financial statement and increases its credibility.

vi. **audit standard**

Auditing must be based on standards. These standards include international auditing standards, the Constitution, audit laws and the statutes establishing the auditee's institution. The audit standard can be referred to as audit performance (Porter, 1993).

Education has been cited as a major strategy to reduce AEG. According to Darnill (1991), an unreasonable expectation among auditees and beneficiaries can be reduced by creating awareness through mass communication about the nature and function of an audit. The findings of Siddiqui, Nasreen, & Choudhury-Lema (2009) confirm (the fact) that audit education helps in reducing AEG. Chowdhury *et al.*

(2005) also recommend training of the staff of the Controller and Accountant General and PAC as a means of reducing AEG in the public sector. Strengthening the monitoring of auditors' performance and improving the quality control in audit firms could be implemented to ensure quality performance of the auditors, which in turn reduces the gap (Porter & Gowthorpe, 2001).

3. Public Sector Audit Environment of Ghana

The public sector of Ghana is audited by the Auditor General who is the administrative head of the Audit Service of Ghana. The Ministries, Departments and Agencies (MDAs) of Ghana have legislative instruments that establish them. The Auditor General, in addition to generally accepted auditing principles, is required to audit them in-line with the law(s) establishing them. The Auditor-General is mandated by the 1992 Constitution and the Audit Service Act, 2000 (Act 584) to audit all public institutions and any other institution that subsists or is funded from the Public Funds of Ghana. All Heads of MDAs and the Controller and Accountant General are to submit the annual accounts and the annual public accounts, respectively, within three months after the end of the financial year, to the Auditor–General. The Auditor–General is required to express an opinion on an Audit Report to Parliament not later than six months after the end of the financial year.

The Auditor-General has the following responsibilities towards public institutions, as identified in Section 11 of the Audit Service Act 2000, Act 584:

i. Auditing and reporting on the public accounts of the central and local governments, the courts, the universities, other public corporations and institutions of government that are established by Act of Parliament.

ii. Having access to the books of accounts and financial records of all the public institutions that are to be audited as listed above.
iii. Approving the financial and accounting systems and any other forms which the institutions should follow in keeping their books of accounts and financial records.
iv. Approving any changes to the established financial and accounting systems before the implementation of such changes,
v. Charging any heads of public institutions who fail to inform the Auditor-General of any of such changes for his approval.
vi. Receiving the final audit reports or any other internal audit reports on internal audit activities from the internal audit units/departments of any of the public institutions.

4. Research Method

In this study, the mixed data collection method was used to gather data. This approached was employed to establish people's views of what they think, believe, value or feel, in order to discover those views for their own sake, or to support an argument a researcher is presenting, sampling a population of potential respondents in order to generalize conclusions more widely. For the primary data, a combination of a questionnaire, face-to-face and telephone interviews were used.

Using Chowdhury's (1996) accountability-based framework in the six audit concepts of auditor independence, auditor competence, audit scope, auditor ethics, audit reporting and performance auditing, the test of statistical differences was based on a 95% confidence level. The Likert scale was used, with 1 being the least, representing 'strongly disagree' and 5 being the highest, representing 'strongly agree'.

The study administered questionnaires to selected members of the general public who were purposively selected based on their knowledge in the subject area. Data was gathered on sampled MDAs selected based on convenience sampling. Members of the Public Accounts Committee of the Parliament of Ghana and Ghana Audit Service were interviewed. The sample size used was 115, broken down as:

i. General Public (GP) - 63
ii. Ministries, Departments and Agencies (MDAs) - 50
iii. Public Accounts Committee (PAC) - 1
iv. Audit Service (AS) - 1

5. Results and Discussions

Demographic Statistics

The study used four groups of respondents as indicated in Table 16.1 below. The majority of the respondents among the general public were male. Gender was important to the study to determine if there are statistical differences among gender on AEG. A higher proportion of the respondents had obtained a Degree/Higher National Diploma. The study obtained this data to test for statistical differences on how education could influence perception about AEG. The percentage of the respondents that works in the private sector was greater than those in the public sector. Again, this statistic was important to test for statistical differences on how the nature of occupation could influence perception on AEG.

Table 16.1: Type of Respondents

Type	Frequency	Percent
General Public	63	55
MDA	43	43
PAC	1	1
Audit Service	1	1
Total	**115**	**100**

Source: Research Survey, 2012

The general public refers to ordinary people with an appreciable level of experience with public sector audit in Ghana. The MDAs are responses from audited governmental or quasi-governmental agencies, not those of an individual as in the case of the general public.

Table 16.2: Sex of General Public Respondents

Sex	Frequency	Percent
Male	38	60.3
Female	25	39.7
Total	**63**	**100**

Source: Research Survey, 2012

There is dearth of empirical literature to show how the level of education can influence AEG. Therefore, the study obtained data in this regard to test for such statistical differences.

Table 16.3: Highest Level of Education of General Public Respondents

Education Level	Frequency	Percent
No Degree/HND	30	47.6
Hold Degree/HND	33	52.4
Total	**63**	**100**

Source: Research Survey, 2012

Literature has not established if working in a particular sector could influence perception of AEG. It is expected that persons will understand and appreciate auditing wherever they work, hence, this data on the occupation was gathered to test for statistical differences in AEG.

Table 16.4: Occupation of General Public Respondents

Occupation	Frequency	Percent
Public Worker	29	46
Private Worker	34	54
Total	**63**	**100**

Source: Research Survey, 2012

Determination of AEG

This section examines the components of AEG in Ghana's public sector based on the framework of Chowdhury (1996).

Perception on Audit Independence

The study used six elements to test for AEG attributable to audit independence. The elements are the nature of appointment, professionalism, intimidation, familiarity, resources and financial influence. Financial influence tops the factors perceived to influence audit independence. The PAC and AS indicate that the public perceives public sector auditors as lacking independence due to financial influence, even though not proven (the case). The lack of resources to undertake public audit is next, and the last being the professional behaviour of staff. The PAC and AS agree that lack of resources and skilled manpower is a major challenge to public sector auditing in Ghana. The political appointment to the position of the office of the Auditor General was cited by PAC and AS, to be a contributory factor to the perception by the public that audit independence is impaired in Ghana. Though this may be the case in some instances, the PAC and AS asserted that, it is not true in all cases, particularly in the public sector audit of quasi-governmental bodies and MDAs with less political influences.

Table 16.5 AEG based on Independence

Type of Respondent		Independence-Appointment	Independence-Professional	Independence-Intimidation	Independence-Familiar	Independence-Resources	Independen Financial Influence
General Public	Mean	4.1587	2.0317	2.8889	3.4603	3.6667	3.9524
	N	63	63	63	63	63	63
MDA	Mean	2.6600	2.6000	3.0200	3.9400	3.9000	3.7600
	N	50	50	50	50	50	50
Total	Mean	3.4956	2.2832	2.9469	3.6726	3.7699	3.8673
	N	113	113	113	113	113	113

Source: Research Survey, 2012

Note: The mean is based on the Likert scale of 1 meaning Strongly Disagree; 2-Agree; 3-Moderate; 4-Agree and 5-Strongly Agree for this and all subsequent tables and means.

There were two statistical differences between the types of respondents on AEG based on independence, namely professional behaviour of staff of the AS and familiarity with significance values of 0.15 and 0.36 at a 95% confidence level, respectively. Therefore, the study shows that the general public and the MDAs do not share a similar perception on how the professional behaviour of staff of the Audit Service and familiarity affect audit independence. However, the study shows that both respondents agree, with an average mean of 3.7194, that audit independence is a component of AEG.

There were no statistical differences on audit independence based on level of education and occupation. However, there are statistical differences among the sexes on intimidation and resources, and how they affect audit independence.

AEG based on Competence

The study used five (5) variables to test for audit competence. These are professionalism of the Auditor General, staff competence, skills of staff, resources constraints and loss of focus. The public perception of the professionalism of the Auditor General is not in doubt. However, the public views the staff of the AS to have moderate skills and competencies needed for public sector audit. This view was rebutted by the AS and the PAC when they indicated that the staff of AS are well and continuously trained for the task. Additionally, the study shows that the public view the staff of the AS to lack adequate resources for the execution of their responsibilities. The public views the AS to lack focus on their core mandate of auditing using all the current generally accepted auditing principles. The PAC and the AS also rebutted this allegation, asserting that the Service carries its mandate to the best of its abilities, and within the available resources.

Table 16.6: AEG based on Competence

Type of Respondent		Competence-Professional	Competence-Staff Incompetence	Competence-Skill Incompetence	Competence-Resource Constraints	Competence-Focus Lost
General Public	Mean	4.2381	2.4286	2.8571	3.0794	2.0952
	N	63	63	63	63	63
MDA	Mean	4.0800	1.9000	2.0400	3.6600	2.4400
	N	50	50	50	50	50
Total	Mean	4.1681	2.1947	2.4956	3.3363	2.2478
	N	113	113	113	113	113

Source: Research Survey, 2012

There were statistical differences between the general public and the MDAs in the areas of staff competence, skills and resource constraints. The general public has a lower view, that the staffs of the Service have the competencies and skills required for public sector audit. On the other hand, the general public has a higher view that the Service is not well-resourced. There were no statistical differences in competence between the general public respondents based on sex, level of education or occupation. Hence, the general public has a similar view on audit competence as the MDAs.

Table 16.6.1: Test for Statistical Differences for Audit Competence

		Sum of Squares	Df	Mean Square	F	Sig.
Competence-Professional * Type of Respondent	Between Groups (Combined)	.697	1	.697	2.486	.118
	Within Groups	31.109	111	.280		
	Total	31.805	112			
Competence-Staff Incompetence * Type of Respondent	Between Groups (Combined)	7.788	1	7.788	6.976	.009
	Within Groups	123.929	111	1.116		
	Total	131.717	112			
Competence-Skill Incompetence * Type of Respondent	Between Groups (Combined)	18.614	1	18.614	12.943	.000
	Within Groups	159.634	111	1.438		
	Total	178.248	112			
Competence-Resource Constraints * Type of Respondent	Between Groups (Combined)	9.398	1	9.398	5.496	.021
	Within Groups	189.823	111	1.710		
	Total	199.221	112			
Competence-Focus Lost * Type of Respondent	Between Groups (Combined)	3.313	1	3.313	2.246	.137
	Within Groups	163.749	111	1.475		
	Total	167.062	112			

Source: Research Survey, 2012

The study reveals an average mean score of 3.2404 for audit competence. Hence, audit competence is agreed by the public to be part of AEG.

AEG based on Audit Scope

The study used the variables of size, manual accounting system, quality of service, access to evidence and legal backing to test for audit scope. The public perceived the use of the manual accounting system as the major challenge which affects the scope of public sector audits. This was collaborated by the PAC and AS.

Table 16.7: AEG based on Audit Scope

Type of Respondent		Scope-Large size	Scope-Manual Accounting	Scope-Quality Defect	Scope-Access to Evidence	Scope-Legal Backing
General Public	Mean	3.5873	3.9683	3.3333	3.1429	4.0952
	N	63	63	63	63	63
	Std. Deviation	1.01019	.78223	1.44802	1.46856	.89288
MDA	Mean	3.4000	4.1000	2.6400	4.0600	3.7600
	N	50	50	50	50	50
	Std. Deviation	1.08797	.83910	1.41075	.81841	1.23817
Total	Mean	3.5044	4.0265	3.0265	3.5487	3.9469
	N	113	113	113	113	113
	Std. Deviation	1.04475	.80689	1.46665	1.30241	1.06771

Source: Research Survey, 2012

There were statistical differences between the general public and the MDAs on their views on quality of audit and access to evidence, with significance values of 0.012 and 0.000 respectively at a 95% confidence level. The general public has

a lower view about the quality of audit, and a higher view that the Service has access to audit evidence. The PAC and AS stated that the Service ensure quality public audits. Legally, they stated the Service has unimpeded access to any evidence except in cases of loss and hiding / suppression of evidence.
There was no statistical difference based on level of education or occupation. However, there was a statistical difference among the sexes on the quality of audit and on access to evidence. More females view the AS higher in the quality of audit service offered and more males have a higher view that the Service has access to audit evidence.

The study showed an average mean score of 3.8421 for audit scope as a component of AEG. Hence, the public agree that audit scope is a challenge in the public sector audit in Ghana. However, the Service asserted that it is able to carry-out its mandate, though with challenges.

AEG based on Audit Ethics

The study used independence, objectivity, due care, corruption and professionalism to test for audit ethics. The public views the AS as performing averagely on the variables, except for due care, which scores a higher mean.

Table 16.8: AEG based on Audit Ethics

Type of Respondent		Ethics-Independence	Ethics-Objectivity	Ethics-Due Care	Ethics-Not Corrupt	Ethics-Professionalism
General Public	Mean	2.6032	2.4444	4.0952	2.3016	2.6032
	N	63	63	63	63	63
	Std. Dev	1.22527	1.01247	5.23547	1.32756	1.23836
MDA	Mean	2.5800	3.3400	3.7800	1.8200	2.5800
	N	50	50	50	50	50
	Std. Dev	1.17959	1.50658	1.03589	.96235	1.27919
Total	Mean	2.5929	2.8407	3.9558	2.0885	2.5929
	N	113	113	113	113	113
	Std. Dev	1.19998	1.32669	3.95824	1.19939	1.25098

Source: Research Survey, 2012

There were statistical differences between the general public and the MDAs on objectivity and corruption. MDAs rank objectivity higher in public sector audit compared to the general public. The general public perceives corruption higher in the public sector audit compared to the MDAs. The PAC and the AS indicated on this public perception that there is corruption in the public sector audit, as arising from the general perception on corruption in the public sector. The public assume everyone working in the public sector is corrupt, said the PAC and the AS.

There was statistical difference between the sexes on the level of corruption of the staff of the AS. There were no statistical differences based on the level of education and occupation on audit ethics. Hence, level of education and occupation do not influence a person's perception of the adherence to ethical principles. The study reveals an average score of 3.1785 for audit ethics as a component of AEG.

AEG based on Audit Reporting

The study used timeliness, quality, basis of opinion, reporting guidelines and report informativeness to test for audit reporting. The untimely release of the public sector audit report was cited as the poorest aspect of audit reporting in Ghana. However, the PAC and AS argued that the Service release the report on time. Rather, the MDAs are those that delay the audit process, which affect the time of releasing the reports.

Table 16.9: AEG based on Audit Reporting

Type of Respondent		Reporting-Timely	Reporting-High Quality	Reporting-Basis of Opinion	Reporting-Guidelines	Reporting-Informative
General Public	Mean	1.5714	4.0952	3.5714	3.7937	3.9048
	N	63	63	63	63	63
	Std. Deviation	.61472	.64042	1.20100	1.24640	1.11752
MDA	Mean	2.0200	4.0200	2.9800	3.5600	3.2000
	N	50	50	50	50	50
	Std. Deviation	1.18649	1.02000	1.40683	1.24802	1.53862
Total	Mean	1.7699	4.0619	3.3097	3.6903	3.5929
	N	113	113	113	113	113
	Std. Deviation	.93550	.82682	1.32341	1.24699	1.36039

Source: Research Survey, 2012

There were statistical differences between the general public and the MDAs on the timeliness, basis of opinion, and the informativeness of the reports. The general public has a higher view on informativeness and basis of opinion, and a lower view on timeliness than the MDAs.

There were statistical differences based on sex on audit reporting. There was no difference based on level of education and occupation. Males view adherence to audit guidelines higher than female. The PAC and the AS asserted that at all times; public sector audit reports are always prepared in compliance with the reporting guidelines. The study scored audit reporting 3.5708 as a component of AEG.

AEG based on Audit Performance

The study used five variables to test for AEG on audit performance. The variables are organisation, planning, evidence gathering, assignment of tasks and supervision. The public perceive audit planning in the public sector to be good. On the whole, the public audit performance is seen to be satisfactory. Contrary, the PAC and the AS stated that the standard of audit performance is high. This explains why most of the anomalies in public sector financial management are identified and reported.

Table 16.10: AEG based on Audit Performance

Type of Respondent		Performance-Organised	Performance-Planned	Performance-Sufficient Evidence	Performance-Proper Staff Assignment	Performance-Supervision
General Public	Mean	3.0635	3.5238	3.0159	2.6190	2.0635
	N	63	63	63	63	63
	Std. Dev	1.21646	1.28084	1.38532	1.32505	1.10531
MDA	Mean	3.7600	3.9800	3.4400	4.9200	2.6400
	N	50	50	50	50	50
	Std. Dev	1.31801	2.91716	1.16339	8.18121	1.33646
Total	Mean	3.3717	3.7257	3.2035	3.6372	2.3186
	N	113	113	113	113	113
	Std. Dev	1.30380	2.16402	1.30356	5.61894	1.24115

Source: Research Survey, 2012

There were statistical differences between the general public and the MDAs on organisation, assignment of tasks and supervision. The MDAs perceived a higher planning, proper assignment of tasks and supervision in the conduct of the public sector audit compared to the general public. The MDAs are the direct beneficiaries of public sector audits, hence, they have a first-hand appreciation of how the audit works. The public's lack of appreciation of public sector auditing is what informs their perception on these areas of audit performance. There were no statistical differences on audit performance based on level of education and occupation. However, there were differences among the sexes on audit performance in the areas of evidence gathering and supervision. Females perceive a higher level of sufficient evidence gathering and supervision in public sector audit than males. The study obtained a score of 3.4978 for audit reporting as a component of AEG.

Components of AEG in Public Sector Audit in Ghana

The study ranks the components of audit scope highest among the AEG in Ghana. The study finds the lowest scoring component to be audit ethics. The PAC and the AS indicated that the public sector audit is comprehensive and covers all aspects.

Table 16.11: Components of AEG in Ghana's Public Sector

Component	**Mean Score**
Scope	3.8422
Independence	3.7194
Reporting	3.5708
Performance	3.4978
Competence	3.2404
Ethics	3.1785

Source: Research Survey, 2012

The AEG, due to the audit scope emerges from the common sense approach used by citizens. A number of issues are publicly discussed and debated in the media based on little knowledge. This has fed into the AEG of public sector audits, where the respondents' view of the scope of audit is totally different from the requirements of the Constitution or the legislation. The AEG, due to audit independence, stems from the appointment of the Auditor General. The only political appointment to a public sector audit in Ghana is the appointment of the Auditor General. However, the majority of people perceive the Audit Service as not independent despite the level of professionalism and calibre of staff of the Service. The inability of the Audit Service to issue audit reports on a timely basis explains this variable of AEG. However, the study traces this delay to the inability of the MDAs to prepare timely financial statements, and to respond to audit queries. This difficulty is not recognised by the general public, and the Audit Service is seen as being inefficient. The public accord a broad and wider audit performance requirement for public sector audit, which is totally different from what the laws require of those auditors. The majority of citizens do not know the standards of performance for public sector audit, and this has fed into this AEG component.

The calibre of staff of the Audit Service is not in the public domain. However, the public assume the staff of the Service to be incompetent, mainly, due to the delays in the release of statutory audit report. The study found that the Service has highly qualified staff for statutory audit. Nevertheless, the labour force is low and there is the need to increase the size. Ethical issues in the public sector as a whole are a topical issue in Ghana and in Africa as whole. The general perception of the public sector is that of corruption and fraud. This perception is pervasive to the extent that the public hardly believe there are honest people in the public sector. This perception has affected public sector audits, where the public perceive the Audit Service not to be ethical. The other perception facing the Service is the extent to which the Service is seen as concealing instances of fraud and corruption, by taking bribes or protecting the image and members of the ruling government. Though some aspects of this perception may be valid, in the majority of cases, instances of fraud and corruptions are unearthed, reported and persecuted, or the monies are recovered and the perpetrators are dismissed.

Reduction of AEG

The respondents had a consensus that education is key to reducing the AEG. The three major aspects of education advocated by the respondents were the use of the media, public forums and accurate media reportage on public sector auditing. The PAC and the AS also support these media and indicate the need for funding such activities.

Table 16.12 Reduction of AEG

Type of Respondent		AEG Reduction-Media	AEG Reduction-Public Forum	AEG Reduction-Media Reportage
General Public	Mean	4.0794	2.6349	3.8413
	N	63	63	63
	Std. Dev	1.00485	1.41765	1.20759
MDA	Mean	3.9600	3.5800	3.9000
	N	50	50	50
	Std. Dev	1.10583	1.38638	1.11117
Total	Mean	4.0265	3.0531	3.8673
	N	113	113	113
	Std. Dev	1.04762	1.47503	1.16116

Source: Research Survey, 2012

The study found no statistical differences between the general public and the MDAs on the use of the media and proper media reportage. However, there was a statistical difference on the use of public forums. The MDAs have a higher support to that approach than the general public.

Table 16.12.1: Test of Statistical Differences for AEG Reduction

		Sum of Squares	df	Mean Square	F	Sig.
AEG Reduction-Media* Type of Respondent	Between Groups (Combined)	.397	1	.397	.360	.550
	Within Groups	122.523	111	1.104		
	Total	122.920	112			
AEG Reduction-Public Forum* Type of Respondent	Between Groups (Combined)	24.898	1	24.898	12.632	.001
	Within Groups	218.783	111	1.971		
	Total	243.681	112			
AEG Reduction-Media Reportage* Type of Respondent	Between Groups (Combined)	.096	1	.096	.071	.791
	Within Groups	150.913	111	1.360		
	Total	151.009	112			

Source: Research Survey, 2012

The study found no statistical differences based on sex, level of education and occupation on the educative approach to reduce AEG.

The study obtained a consensus among respondents that education was needed to reduce AEG. Education remains the major approach to reducing AEG in the literature. Three main education approaches were identified, made up of the use of media education, public forums and promoting accurate media reportage of public sector audits. The finding of this research confirms the study by Darnill (1991) that education via the mass media can reduce AEG.

Again, the findings of the study confirm the study of Chowdhury *et al.* (2005) and that of Siddiqui (2009) that training and education can be used to reduce AEG in the public sector. Chowdhury *et al.* (2005) advocate for better training programmes to educate the public and the staff of the AS, as a means to reducing AEG. Similarly, Siddiqui (2009) echoes the need to use education to promote appreciation, and to bridge AEG. What this study had done differently, is the identification of the specific education or training approach to use as mentioned above.

6. Conclusion

The study identified six (6) components of AEG made up of audit independence, competence, audit scope, audit ethics, audit reporting and audit performance. The results of this study confirm the work of Chowdhury (1996) and Porter (1993) who identify those six broad components for public sector audits. The study concludes that AEG exists in the public sector just as in the private sector, but is more pronounced in the public sector than in the private sector audits. The study confirms mass education to be the most appropriate approach to reduce AEG and use of public forums for education of MDAs.

The study reveals that AEG is densely and more pronounced in the public sector than in the private sector, due to feeling of national ownership and politics; and the causes of this AEG can be attributed to a general time lag, as advocated by Tricker (1982). The time it takes for the statutory audit report to be issued takes sometimes 5 years. This delay certainly contributes to AEG. Another reason is political theory. The continuous power struggle and public demands for accountability also contributes to AEG in the public sector, as argued by Gaa (1991). As it was noted earlier, Ghanaians feel that the AS is not living up to its responsibilities and has been compromised. This perception certainly adds to the AEG in statutory audits.

Corporate failure is not an issue in Ghana. However, corporate failures elsewhere and the associated news fuel AEG as asserted by Gay *et al.* (1998). Quite a number of state-owned institutions have collapsed and all this makes the citizens uncomfortable. This leads to a higher demand on or expectation from statutory auditors.

Further Studies

The components and ranking of AEG revealed by this study set the tone for further global studies on the components of AEG in the public sector and the private sector audits of Africa.

References

Canadian Institute of Chartered Accountants (CICA). (1988). *Report of the commission to study the public's expectation of audits,* Canada: Canadian Institute of Chartered Accountants

Chowdhury, R. R. (1996). *Audit expectation gap in the public sector of Bangladesh.* Unpublished PhD thesis, Department of Accountancy and Business Finance, University of Dundee.

Chowdhury, R. R., Innes, J., & Kouhy, R. (2005). The public sector audit expectations gap in Bangladesh. *Managerial Auditing Journal, Vol. 20* Iss: 8, 893 – 908.

Darnill, A. (1991). The profession and the public. *Accountancy,* May, 72-73.

Epstein, M. J., & Geiger, M. A. (1994). Investor views of audit assurance: recent evidence of the expectation gap. *Journal of Accountancy*, *Vol. 177* No. 1, 60-64.

Gaa, J. C. (1991). The expectations game: Regulation of auditors by government and the profession. *Critical Perspective of Accounting*, *Vol. 2,* 83-107.

Gay, G., Schelluch, P., & Baines, A. (1998). Perceptions of messages conveyed by review and audit reports. *Accounting, Auditing & Accountability Journal*, *Vol. 11*, No. 4, 472-494.

Gloeck, J. D., & De Jager, H. (1993). The focus point of the audit expectation gap in the Republic of South Africa. *Meditari,* 1-42.

Gray, C. W., & Kaufmann, D. (1998). Corruption and development. *Finance and Development*, March, 7 – 10.

Guy, D., & Sullivan, J. (1988). The expectations gap auditing standards. *Journal of Accounting*, *Vol. 165*, No. 4, 36-46.

Humphrey, C., Moizer, P., & Turley, S. (1993). The AEG in Britain: An empirical investigation. *Accounting and Business Research*, *Vol. 23,* No.91A, 395-411.

Hassal, T., Dunlop, A., & Lewis, S. (1996). Internal audit education: Exploring professional competence. *Managerial Auditing Journal*, *Vol. 11*(5), 28-36.

Independence Standards Board (1997). *Serving the public interest: A new conceptual framework for auditor independence.* New York: American Institute of Certified Public Accountants.

Kaufmann, D. (1997). Corruption: The facts. *Foreign Policy,* 107, 114-131.

Liggio, C. D. (1974). The expectation gap: The accountant's legal Waterloo? *Journal of Contemporary Business*, *Vol. 3*, 27-44.

Monroe, G. S. & Woodliff, D. R. (1993). The effect of education on the audit expectation gap. *Accounting and Finance, Vol. 33*, 61-78.

Ojo, M. (2006). Eliminating the AEG: Myth or Reality? *http: / / mpra.ub.uni-muenchen.de / 232/* MPRA Paper No. 232.

Okoye, E. Ik. & Okaro, S. C. (2011). *Forensic accounting and audit expectation gap – The perception of accounting academics.* [Online] available at http://ssrn.com/abstract=1920865 accessed on 18/6/2012

Onumah, J. M., Simpson, S. N. Y., & Babonyire, A. (2009). The audit expectation gap concept: Examining views on auditors' reports from Ghana. In M. Tsamenyi & S. Uddin (Eds), *Research in accounting in emerging economies, Vol. 9*, pp.321-343

Porter, B. A. (1991). The audit expectations-performance gap-A contemporary approach. Pacific *Accounting Review Vol. 3*(1), 1-36.

Porter, B. (1993). An empirical study of the audit expectations-performance gap. *Accounting and Business Research, Vol. 24*, Winter, 49-68.

Porter, B., & Gowthorpe, C. (2004). Audit expectations-performance gap in the UK in1999 and comparison with the gap in New Zealand in 1989 and in 1999, Edinburgh: The Institute of Chartered Accountants of Scotland.

Power, M. (1994). *The audit explosion*, London: Demos.

Power, M. (2000). The audit explosion: Second thoughts. *International Journal of Auditing, Vol. 4*(1), 111-119.

Sandholtz, W., & Koetzle, W. (2000). Accounting for corruption: economy structure, democracy and trade, *International Quality, Vol. 44*(1), 31-50.

Schelluch, P. (1996). Long-form audit report messages: Further implication for audit expectation gap. *Accounting Research Journal,* Vol. 9, 48-55.

Shaikh, J., & Talha, M. (2003). Credibility and expectation gap in reporting on uncertainties. *Managerial Auditing Journal, Vol. 18*(6/7), 517-29.

Sidani, Y. M. (2007). The AEG: evidence from Lebanon. *Managerial Journal ofAuditing, Vol. 22* No. 3, 288-302.

Siddiqui, J., Nasreen, T., & Choudhury-Lema, A. (2009). The audit expectations gap and the role of audit education: The case of an emerging economy. *Managerial Auditing Journal, Vol. 24,* Iss: 6, 564 – 583.

Sikka, P., Puxty, A., Willmott, H., & Cooper, C. (1998). The impossibility of eliminating the expectation gap: some theory and evidence. *Critical Perspectives on Accounting, Vol. 9,* No. 3, 14-24.

Tanko, M. (2011). Audit expectation gap: The trend to close the gap in the 21st Century. [Online] available at http://ssrn.com/abstract=195759 accessed on 20/6/2012.

Tricker, R. I. (1982). Corporate accountability and the role of the audit function. In A. G. M.Hopwood, Broomwich & J.Shaw. (Eds). *Auditing Research: Issues and Opportunities,* London: Pitman.

INDEX

A

B

C

D

E

G

H

I

J

K

L

M

N

O

P

Q

R

S

T

U

V

W

Y

Z

www.ingramcontent.com/pod-product-compliance
Lightning Source LLC
Chambersburg PA
CBHW060126280326
41932CB00012B/1434